This b
iatel'

D1612954

OXFORD HISTORICAL MONOGRAPHS

PROPAGANDA AND THE ROLE OF THE STATE IN INTER-WAR BRITAIN

Mariel Grant

CLARENDON PRESS · OXFORD
1994

Oxford University Press, Walton Street, Oxford OX2 6DP
Oxford New York
Athens Auckland Bangkok Bombay
Calcutta Cape Town Dar es Salaam Delhi
Florence Hong Kong Istanbul Karachi
Kuala Lumpur Madras Madrid Melbourne
Mexico City Nairobi Paris Singapore
Taipei Tokyo Toronto
and associated companies in
Berlin Ibadan

Oxford is a trade mark of Oxford University Press

Published in the United States
by Oxford University Press Inc., New York

British Library Cataloguing in Publication Data
Data available

Library of Congress Cataloging in Publication Data
Grant, Mariel.
Propaganda and the role of the state in inter-war Britain / Mariel
Grant.
p. cm. — (Oxford historical monographs)
Includes bibliographical references.
1. Government publicity—Great Britain—History—20th century.
2. Great Britain—Politics and government—1910–1936. 3. Great
Britain—Politics and government—1936–1945. I. Title.
II. Series.
JN329.P8G725 1994
303.3'75'09410904—dc20 94–15546
ISBN 0–19–820444–2

1 3 5 7 9 10 8 6 4 2

Typeset by Graphicraft Typesetters Ltd., Hong Kong
Printed in Great Britain
on acid-free paper by
Bookcraft Ltd.
Midsomer Norton, Avon

Acknowledgements

I WOULD like to thank my doctoral supervisor, Asa Briggs, for his support and encouragement of this research. I am also indebted to Ross McKibbin, Colin Matthew, and Stuart Robson for their constructive criticism and advice.

The research behind this book could not have been undertaken without the assistance of the staffs of the Public Record Office at Kew in London, the British Library, the Post Office Archive, and the Bodleian Library, Oxford.

I also gratefully acknowledge the financial support of the British Council, and the Social Sciences and Humanities Research Council of Canada.

This book is dedicated to my mother, Margaret, and the memory of my father, Robert.

Special thanks to my husband, Stuart.

M.G.

Victoria, BC, Canada

Contents

List of Illustrations

Acknowledgements

The following illustrations are Crown Copyright and are reproduced by permission of HM
Stationery Office:

'Get Fit—Keep Fit'
'In Work or Play Fitness Wins'
'Use Your Health Services'
'Infant Diets Display at British Empire Exhibition, Wembley 1924'
'Milk Bars'

The following illustrations are reproduced by permission of the Bodleian Library, University of Oxford, from T. Crew, *Health Propaganda (Ways and Means): Covering the Propaganda Services of the National Health Associations and Others, Organisation of Health Exhibitions and Health Week Campaigns* (Leicester, 1935), Bodleian Library reference 1672.e.697, pp. 43, 62, 103–4, 201:

'How to *clean* the Teeth', 'How Decay Spreads in a Tooth'
'Rat Week'
'Childlessness is Frequently Caused by Neglected Syphilis or Gonorrhoea'
'The engine driver', 'Who will tell them?'

Abbreviations

ACGA	Advisory Committee on Government Advertising
ADM	Admiralty
AIR	Air Ministry
AWWW	*Author's and Writer's Who's Who*
BIF	British Industries Fair
BMA	British Medical Association
BSHC	British Social Hygiene Council
BT	Board of Trade
CAB	Cabinet Papers
CCHA	Cabinet Committee on Home Affairs
CCHE	Central Council for Health Education
CCRPT	Central Council for Recreative Physical Training
CID	Committee of Imperial Defence
CO	Colonial Office
COI	Central Office of Information
DOT	Department of Overseas Trade
ED	Board of Education
EMB	Empire Marketing Board
FO	Foreign Office
GC	Grants Committee (National Fitness)
GPC	General Purposes Committee
GPO	General Post Office
HLG	Housing and Local Government Board
HMSO	Stationery Office
HO	Home Office
ICCGP	Inter-Departmental Coordinating Committee on Government Publicity
ICPE	Inter-Departmental Committee on Publicity Expenditure
INF	Information Papers
LPTB	London Passenger Transport Board
MAF	Ministry of Agriculture and Fisheries
MH	Ministry of Health
ML	Ministry of Labour
MMB	Milk Marketing Board

MOI	Ministry of Information
MRC	Medical Research Council
MT	Ministry of Transport
NAC	National Advisory Committee on Physical Fitness
NCMS	National Clean Milk Society
NFC	National Fitness Council
NFDA	National Federation of Dairymen's Associations
NFU	National Farmers' Union
NMPC	National Milk Publicity Council
NPA	Newspaper Proprietors' Association
NPHCC	National Public Health Campaign Committee
NSC	National Savings Committee
NSCVD	National Society for the Combating of Venereal Diseases
PAC	Publicity Advisory Committee
PEP	Political and Economic Planning Group
PLH	People's League of Health
PMG	Postmaster-General
POM	*Post Office Magazine*
Post	Post Office Papers
PRO	Public Record Office
SMOH	Society of Medical Officers of Health
STAT	Stationery Office Papers
T	Treasury Papers
TDA	Telephone Development Association
TPC	Telephone Publicity Advisory Committee
TSB	*Telephone Sales Bulletin*
WO	War Office

1

Introduction

1 October 1939: The Ministry of Information comes off worst with
everybody. The man in the street feels, rather naturally, that he is
paying plenty for this war . . . [and] that he is entitled to know what
is happening. He feels that something is rotten in a system which
recently went through the most complicated acrobatics of releasing,
suppressing, and releasing again even such a harmless piece of news
as Her Majesty's return to London from a visit to the Princesses at
Balmoral.

(Mollie Panter-Downes, *London War Notes 1939–1945*)

[W]hat propaganda efforts are being made by the government
. . . are so hopelessly amateurish that they have succeeded in achieving only one effect, that, fortunately, not quite useless, to convince
people that their case must be better than it appears. There is,
in fact, not only no plan and no policy, but appalling technique.
Worst of all, there is very little realization officially that a good job
is not being done.

(Peter Cromwell, 'The Propaganda Problem', 1941)

A quiet day at the Ministry of Information. The more energetic
neutral correspondents had mostly left the country by now, finding
Axis sources a happier hunting-ground for front-page news. The
Ministry could get on with its work undisturbed. That afternoon a
film was showing in the Ministry theatre; it dealt with otter-hunting
and was designed to impress neutral countries with the pastoral
beauty of English life. . . . [T]he room [was] empty.

(Evelyn Waugh, *Put Out More Flags*, 1942)

DURING the early stages of the Second World War there was some
debate as to whether security considerations would permit publication of
the exact location of the Ministry of Information (MOI). One journalist
echoed public sentiment in commenting: 'God knows why! Hitler'd never
bomb this place. It's the only victory he's won so far!'[1] From the

---

[1] Norman Riley, *999 and All That* (1940), 42. Throughout, unless otherwise stated, place
of publication of all books cited is London.

contemporary perspective the bureau required protection from the British public, not the Germans. Prone to embarrassing errors which made it appear hopelessly inept, the MOI was an object of widespread criticism and mimicry for at least the initial half of the war.[2] 'Public Failure Number One' and the 'Ministry of Aggravation' were popular sobriquets.[3] Even its own staff could find little positive to say about a publicity bureau which refused to divulge the contents of the propaganda leaflets it was dropping over Germany lest the information reach the enemy.[4]

Contemporaries were almost unanimous in their condemnation of the bureau. Not until 1941–2, when Brendan Bracken's appointment as minister led to significant operational changes and gave it a firmer Parliamentary base, did the department's public image begin to improve. Even so, the MOI has yet to discard its reputation for failure. Memoirs and biographies published since the war have confirmed and reinforced the picture of an inept and ineffective organization.[5] General studies dealing with the home front in the Second World War make only passing reference to the ministry, little of which is favourable.[6] Another indication of the disdain in which it has been held is the lack of an official history of the department in the New Whitehall Series.

During the war the ministry's obvious shortcomings were attributed to

[2] House of Commons Debates (hereafter Hansard), 21 Sept. 1939, vol. 351, cols. 1059–61; 9 Oct. 1939, vol. 352, cols. 15–16. Cecil H. King, 'We Could Build a Team to beat Goebbels', *World's Press News*, 26 Oct. 1939. 'Propaganda', *Evening Standard*, 13 Dec. 1939. *The Times*, 27 Dec. 1939. Beverley Baxter, *Men, Martyrs and Mountebanks* (1940), 179–85. John Hargrave, *Propaganda* (1940), 5–30. Mass-Observation, *War Begins at Home*, ed. Tom Harrisson and Charles Madge (1940). Mass-Observation, *Home Propaganda* (1941). Ivor Thomas, *Warfare by Words* (1942), 9. Peter Cromwell, 'The Propaganda Problem', *Horizon*, 3/13 (1941), 17–32.

[3] *The Times*, 27 Dec. 1939. The 'Ministry of Aggravation' originated on the BBC's 'It's That Man Again'; Asa Briggs, *The History of Broadcasting in the United Kingdom*, iii. *The War of Words* (1970), 564.

[4] Harold Nicolson, *Diaries and Letters 1939–1945*, ed. Nigel Nicolson (1967), ii. 32. Also noted in Susan Briggs, *Keep Smiling Through* (1975), 107. On the poor morale of staff see Ian McLaine, *Ministry of Morale* (1979).

[5] Regarding the period before 1942 see Kenneth Clark, *The Other Half* (1977), 9–22. Alfred Duff Cooper, *Old Men Forget* (1953), 280–8. Lord Macmillan, *A Man of Law's Tale* (1952), 166. Sir Robert Marett, *Through the Back Door* (1968), 5–7. Charles Stuart (ed.), *The Reith Diaries* (1975), 234–53. Nicolson, pp. 94–7, 104–5. Lord Birkenhead, *Walter Monckton* (1969). Andrew Boyle, *Only the Wind Will Listen* (1972), 304–19. Regarding Bracken's tenure, Ernest Thurtle, *Time's Winged Chariot* (1945), 173–5. Andrew Boyle, *Poor, Dear Brendan* (1974), 264–89, 305–6.

[6] Angus Calder, *The People's War* (1969), 66, 136–7, 241. Arthur Marwick, *The Home Front* (1976), 105–9. E. S. Turner, *The Phoney War on the Home Front* (1961), 199–200, 276, 294–5. Leonard Mosley, *Backs to the Wall* (1971), 134. Marion Yass, *The Home Front* (1973), 38. Tom Harrisson, *Living through the Blitz* (1976), 285.

misguided planning and staffing. Critics charged that the department had been assembled too quickly and without adequate thought. Devoid of clearly defined guiding principles, it was 'rather like a child's home-made scooter, nailed together from bits of an old packing-case . . . the wheels tied on with string'.[7] Said to consist mainly of retired admirals, museum curators, and assorted civil servants, the staff was deemed unqualified and incompetent. A perceived dearth of journalists and advertising experts within the organization provoked quips that 'complete unsuitability' had been the main criterion for employment.[8] Taken together, these factors were interpreted at the time as an indication of governmental reluctance to engage in propaganda.[9]

Those few historians who have investigated the roots of the MOI's early difficulties have reached similar conclusions.[10] Stressing the deficiency of pre-war preparations and criticizing both planners and staff, Ian McLaine claims that 'the cult of the amateur reached its apogee' in the recruiting process: 'While it was difficult to find at short notice experts in such nebulous fields as morale and propaganda, the possession of experience in, say, psychology and journalism seems almost to have been a positive disqualification for employment.'[11] McLaine argues that the staff also lacked an understanding of and respect for the general public. Biased in class and attitude, MOI personnel adopted a condescending and didactic approach which doomed the ministry's efforts to failure.[12]

Philip Taylor also regards the attitude of the propagandists as the major factor which impeded success, but focuses greater attention on the manner in which propaganda itself was approached. In a study of developments in government publicity abroad in the 1930s, Taylor shows that although propaganda was eventually employed as a tool of diplomacy and 'national projection', it was adopted reluctantly, almost as a last resort. He claims that, even with the onset of war, many officials were unwilling to accept the need for a centralized information bureau, and argues that the failure of the MOI was not a product of insufficient planning, but

[7] Hargrave, p. 57.   [8] Baxter, pp. 183–4. Riley, pp. 19, 61–4. Cromwell, p. 31.
[9] Hargrave, pp. 5–30, 72. Cromwell, pp. 18–19, 27–31. Thomas, pp. 9, 29. Riley, pp. 12–26, 35–9, 61–4. Baxter, pp. 179–85.
[10] McLaine, *Ministry*. Philip M. Taylor, 'Techniques of Persuasion: Basic Ground Rules of British Propaganda during the Second World War', *Historical Journal of Film, Radio and Television*, 1/1 (1980), 57–67. Philip M. Taylor, *The Projection of Britain* (Cambridge, 1981), 260–93. Temple Willcox, 'Towards a Ministry of Information', *History*, 69/227 (1984), 398–414. Temple Willcox, 'Projection or Publicity: Rival Concepts of the Pre-War Planning of the Ministry of Information', *Journal of Contemporary History*, 18 (1983), 97–116.
[11] McLaine, p. 6.   [12] Ibid. 10–11.

reflected the shortage of individuals within Whitehall who recognized the value of propaganda and were prepared to exploit it. Those responsible for creating the ministry not only lacked experience, they 'represented a generation of British public servants which could not reconcile itself to accepting such work as a legitimate peacetime activity of British government. "Propaganda" remained a dirty word which left an unpleasant taste in the mouths of English gentlemen.'[13]

Given the predominance of the staffing issue in these theories, surprisingly little inquiry has been undertaken into the qualifications of those recruited. No attempt has yet been made to gauge what proportion of MOI employees had previous experience in journalism or publicity work, nor to ascertain where any such individuals were deployed within the organization. Also, the degree to which the planners sought out, or were hindered in obtaining, qualified personnel has not been examined. Moreover, due consideration has not been accorded to the fact that the people employed must have been judged competent or they would never have been recruited. Rather than searching for faults in the staffing procedure, one should raise questions regarding the concept of expertise which governed the choices made.

Similarly, the role of pre-existing government publicity machinery in shaping the MOI has never been adequately assessed. While several recent publications dealing with the growth of official publicity abroad in the inter-war years have traced the impact exerted on pre-war planning by organizations such as the Foreign Office (FO) News Department and the British Council, the influence of concurrent developments in the domestic sphere has not been thoroughly explored.[14] Analysts of the MOI, such as McLaine and Michael Balfour, have shown that a large portion of the MOI's early problems were also attributable to the fact that, though held responsible in the public mind for the distribution of all government news and publicity, the department was not the only official body disseminating information, and, until Bracken's arrival, encountered difficulties in exercising control over the activities of other departments.[15]

---

[13] Taylor, *Projection*, 291–2.

[14] Both Taylor and Willcox have focused on the role of the Foreign Office News Department and the British Council in the pre-war planning process. The former claims that the early problems of the MOI stemmed from the fact that the FO was thwarted in its attempts, first to control the ministry, and later to influence its development. Willcox also claims that the FO was thwarted in developing the MOI along its own lines; a claim challenged below (see p. 242). Taylor, *Projection*, 264–87. Willcox, 'Towards a Ministry', 412–14.

[15] McLaine, pp. 6–7, 34–8. Michael Balfour, *Propaganda in War, 1939–1945* (1979), 57–70.

However, sufficient attention has not been focused on the reasons why these other ministries were allowed to maintain their own publicity bureaux. While Balfour has noted departmental opposition to centralization during the planning process,[16] he has not adequately investigated the arguments on which departments based their objections, nor recognized that the roots of the problem dated back much further than the pre-war period.

During the First World War, a number of government departments established publicity branches and/or distributed their own information alongside that issued by the central propaganda bureaux.[17] Most of this machinery was dismantled when hostilities ceased, the remainder falling prey to the post-war financial crisis and economy drive (the so-called Geddes Axe).[18] In November 1923 only six departments employed staff specifically for publicity purposes, with expenditure totalling under £5,000 per year.[19] However, by 1937 seventeen departments maintained permanent public relations and/or press divisions at an annual cost in salaries alone of £137,607.[20] In themselves, these figures are not an adequate measure of the extent of government activity, but they do indicate that during the inter-war years the use of publicity at home underwent considerable expansion. The concept of official propaganda may not have been universally accepted by 1939, but it is clear that, even before the onset of the Second World War, publicity had been recognized as a legitimate function of government departments. There were officials within Whitehall who were experienced in publicity and willing to employ it.

By virtue of their timing alone, these developments merit close attention. Given circumstances in other countries, and the ongoing debate about propaganda over the entire period, it is essential to consider how, why, and to what degree publicity came to be accepted as a necessary and justifiable task of a democratic government. The emphasis placed on the MOI's problems on the home front, and the explanations that have been advanced regarding official attitudes towards propaganda, render it doubly necessary to investigate the nature and extent of the State's experience in dealing with its own citizenry in the years before the Second World War. Indeed, the planning and staffing of the MOI must be re-examined

---

[16] Balfour, pp. 54–6.   [17] See below, Ch. 2 n. 102.

[18] Sir Eric Geddes chaired a Committee on National Expenditure appointed in 1921 to effect economies in government spending.

[19] Hansard, 15 Nov. 1923, vol. 168, cols. 458–9.

[20] *Report from the Select Committee on Estimates*, Cmd. 158 (July 1938), appendix 3, table 1.

in light of these developments. Finally, such an inquiry is of vital importance given the further insight it provides into the changing nature and role of the State in Britain in the twentieth century.

To date, peacetime publicity in the domestic sphere has been virtually ignored by historians. Although the use of propaganda in and by Britain in the twentieth century has been the subject of extensive research in recent years, most modern scholarship has focused on the concept of propaganda, the emergence of its pejorative connotations in the aftermath of the First World War, and its role as a weapon of war.[21] Historians who have touched on the inter-war decades have concentrated on the development of government publicity overseas, or, where domestic matters have been discussed, on the use of propaganda in and by certain organizations, and in specific cases. The tendency has been to examine particular issues, such as: the marketing of the Empire; the establishment of publicity organizations in political parties; the use of propaganda as a temporary and secretive measure to forestall and combat industrial unrest; or the formation of what was to become the government film unit.[22]

Such studies are not intended, nor do they attempt, to provide an overview of and explanation for the growth of government publicity at

[21] Terence Hall Qualter, 'The Nature of Propaganda and its Function in Democratic Government: An Examination of the Principal Theories of Propaganda since 1880', Ph.D. dissertation, London, 1956. Oliver Thomson, *Mass Persuasion in History* (Edinburgh, 1977). Lindley Fraser, *Propaganda* (1957). M. L. Sanders and Philip M. Taylor, *British Propaganda during the First World War, 1914–1918* (1982). M. L. Sanders, 'Wellington House and British Propaganda during the First World War', *Historical Journal*, 18/1 (1975), 119–46. Trevor Wilson, 'Lord Bryce's Investigations into Alleged German Atrocities in Belgium, 1914–1915', *Journal of Contemporary History*, 14/3 (1979), 369–85. Alice Goldfarb Marquis, 'Words as Weapons: Propaganda in Britain and Germany during the First World War', *Journal of Contemporary History*, 13 (1978), 467–99. Cate Haste, *Keep the Home Fires Burning* (1977). Philip Knightley, *The First Casualty* (1975). Charles Roetter, *Psychological Warfare* (1974). Charles Cruickshank, *The Fourth Arm* (1981). George Begley, *Keep Mum!* (1975).

[22] Timothy John Hollins, 'The Presentation of Politics: The Place of Party Publicity, Broadcasting and Film in British Politics 1918–1939', D.Phil. dissertation, Leeds, 1981. Judith Freeman, 'The Publicity of the Empire Marketing Board 1926–1933', *Journal of Advertising History*, 1 (1977), 12–14. John M. Mackenzie, *Propaganda and Empire* (Manchester, 1984). Regarding the use of publicity to combat industrial unrest see Keith Middlemas, *Politics in Industrial Society* (1979), 131–2, 150–8, 351–4. Julian Symons, *The General Strike* (1957). G. A. Phillips, *The General Strike* (1976), 167–88. Patrick Renshaw, *The General Strike* (1975), 190–8. The development of a government film unit is discussed in Paul Swann, *The British Documentary Film Movement, 1926–1946* (Cambridge, 1989). Paul Swann, 'John Grierson and the G.P.O. Film Unit 1933–1939', *Historical Journal of Film, Radio and Television*, 3/1 (1983), 19–34. Paul Rotha, *Documentary Diary* (1973). Elizabeth Sussex, *The Rise and Fall of British Documentary* (1975). Forsyth Hardy, *John Grierson* (1979). Jack C. Ellis, *A History of Film* (Englewood Cliffs, NJ, 1979), 223–35. Margaret Dickinson and Sarah Street, *Cinema and the State* (1985).

home. Yet even general publications overlook the subject of the normal activities of government as opposed to the aberrant or secretive. In the only official history of the information services, Sir Fife Clark devotes a mere seven pages to the years before 1939, three of which cover the First World War. When the inter-war period is considered, the reader is provided with little more than a list of dates indicating when each department acquired its publicity branch.[23] Marjorie Ogilvy-Webb and John Black go further, dealing in greater depth with the establishment of organizations such as the Empire Marketing Board and the Post Office public relations division, but neither investigates the broader motivations behind these bodies, nor considers their relationship to similar developments elsewhere in Whitehall.[24]

The official histories of each department are equally unenlightening. Sir Frank Newsam's reference to the Home Office public relations division provides a characteristic example of the manner in which the subject has been treated in the New Whitehall Series:

> It was started in 1936, partly to relieve busy officials of the duty of replying to enquiries from journalists and others about their work, and partly to provide a better source of news and information to the press and the B.B.C. The duties of the Branch soon widened, and they now cover the whole range of the Department's publicity.[25]

The absence of a comprehensive inquiry into domestic publicity arrangements is not entirely surprising. Because a central organization responsible for the co-ordination and/or distribution of all government information was not created in the period, it is difficult to speak in general terms and draw broadly based conclusions. Developments were sporadic and links between them often indiscernible. A notable dearth of controversy, and hence public debate on the subject, further complicates matters, as little pressure was exerted on Whitehall to impose universal guidelines governing departmental behaviour. This in turn makes it difficult to conduct a specific and comparative analysis; for example, how does one assess the relative functions of one ministry's press bureau, another's information branch, and a third's public relations division? Even providing comparative statistics on expenditure levels is problematical, as

[23] *The Central Office of Information* (1970), 22–8.
[24] Marjorie Ogilvy-Webb, *The Government Explains* (1965), 51–6. John B. Black, *Organising the Propaganda Instrument* (The Hague, 1975), 1–8.
[25] *The Home Office* (1954), 209. Also see Sir Gilmour Jenkins, *The Ministry of Transport and Civil Aviation* (1958), 203. Lord Bridges, *The Treasury* (1962), 156–7.

departments used their own criteria to determine what they deemed to be their publicity costs.[26]

On the other hand, the general approach adopted by the government can only be elucidated through a comparative examination of specific developments. Merely providing lists indicating when publicity bureaux were formed tells us little about why they were established and how they functioned. Similarly, detailing the amount of money spent on advertising reveals nothing of the actual nature of campaigns, the motivations behind them, and the degree of success attained.

In a study of this length, it would be impossible to undertake an examination of the use of publicity in and by every government department. Therefore, the next chapter will provide an overview of developments during the inter-war years, discussing their relationship to the general debate surrounding both propaganda and its role in a democracy; in subsequent chapters the examination will focus on developments in the Stationery Office (HMSO), the Post Office (GPO), and the Ministry of Health (MH).

As the state publishing house, the HMSO was nominally responsible for the preparation and distribution of all official documents. Thus an examination of its activities provides an excellent point of departure for an analysis of government information services. The Post Office and Ministry of Health, on the other hand, are perfect foils. The former was the first department in Whitehall to establish a large-scale publicity organization, which apparently served as the model for, and impetus behind, the creation of similar machinery elsewhere. A commercial undertaking with commodities to sell, the GPO could and did explain its adoption of publicity on business grounds. As a service department, the Ministry of Health was slower to employ publicity and cited public service responsibilities as its justification for creating a publicity bureau. Representative of two different types of department, the GPO and MH can be usefully contrasted and compared.

While it is essential to examine the evolution of publicity organizations, it is equally important to consider how this machinery functioned. Analysing particular campaigns provides insight into the way in which theory worked in practice, revealing the manner in which departments developed and approached publicity. Hence three specific appeals will

---

[26] In 1938, when the Select Committee on Estimates investigated government advertising, the Treasury asked departments to supply comprehensive figures on their expenditure. In tabulating their spending, ministries used radically different criteria to define their publicity activities; see p. 226 below.

also be discussed. Telephone publicity and the national health campaign are obvious choices, as they involved the GPO and the MH. They also provide a useful basis for comparison, as one entailed the sale of a product, the other of an idea. Similarly, milk publicity will be examined because the campaign spanned the entire inter-war period and was handled by a number of different departments.

By analysing specific developments, one can draw general conclusions regarding the course of government propaganda during this period. Indeed, despite the lack of a central directing organization, a domestic publicity policy did evolve over the inter-war years. The intellectual climate of the period, the pervasive influence of the Treasury, and the fact that a surprisingly small group of individuals were involved in the process of advising ministries on their publicity arrangements were all contributing factors. Although the motivations behind them were not always the same, departmental efforts were guided by similar principles. By 1939, virtually every ministry in Whitehall had some experience in publicity work, and was confident of its ability to supervise its dealings with the public. As we shall see, this exerted an enormous influence on the pre-war planning of the Ministry of Information and on all other attempts to centralize government publicity arrangements both before and after the Second World War.

2

Perceptions of Propaganda in Inter-War Britain: An Overview

Partisan appeal by means of misinformation, emotional pleading and the short-circuiting of thought is no new thing. . . . But the power of modern publicity is that it is directed by individuals who have greater understanding of the effective manipulation of motives, impulses, and attitudes. Hence with all its limitations, the effectiveness of modern publicity is unprecedented in history.

(William Albig, *Public Opinion*, 1939)

The ordinary man, not yet armored against propaganda, succumbs like an Eskimo to measles. . . . [P]sychologically assaulted and ravaged with impunity . . . he will be found enthusiastically supporting campaigns aimed at his own subversion. . . . He thinks, when he thinks, on the ideas and facts presented. The control of his thought materials, through selection and interpretation, is accordingly a most effective control over his convictions and conduct. Suffering from the effects of propaganda the sufferer is the last to admit that he is sick. . . . The sensations that the propaganda germ set up have the seeming authenticity of normalcy.

(Arland D. Weeks, *The Control of the Social Mind*, 1923)

A scientific Government would understand that no great social change can be made without friction, unless the mind of the nation is clarified and focused *first of all*. Now by this I do not mean that it should be doped with secretive, backstairs 'propaganda'. Propaganda does not always mean publicity. The publicity I mean is frank advertisement of facts.

(Charles Frederick Higham, *Looking Forward*, 1920)

The chief problem of propaganda in a democracy does not lie . . . in proving its necessity, but rather in developing its wise and democratic use along the path of education.

(John Grierson, *Grierson on Documentary*, 1946)

T H E context in which language is used in a society can yield penetrating insights into common beliefs and attitudes, particularly when the definition of a specific term alters over a precise period of time. Developments in social nomenclature reflect changes in the community and/or people's perceptions of it, and colour the interpretation of associated terms and events.[1] Hence the emergence in the early years of the twentieth century of the modern definition of propaganda as a powerful manipulative force merits consideration. The word first appeared in the seventeenth century, when it referred to a committee of cardinals in the Roman Catholic Church responsible for the care of foreign missions, the Congregation of the Propaganda. Until the nineteenth century, when it acquired political connotations, propaganda was a descriptive and non-controversial term. In 1909, the *Oxford English Dictionary* defined it as 'any association, systematic scheme or concerted movement for the propagation of a particular doctrine or practice'.[2] Although some of its new applications were negative, the word had yet to be applied solely with a pejorative connotation. Indeed, both contemporaries and historians have agreed that the decidedly negative definition of propaganda as a means of 'tampering with the human will',[3] as an evil 'narcotic',[4] and a 'poison',[5] emerged in response to the success of British propaganda in the First World War,[6] and post-war revelations that a

---

[1] Peter L. Berger and Thomas Luckmann, *The Social Construction of Reality* (1967), 52–5. Asa Briggs, 'The Language of "Mass" and "Masses" in Nineteenth-Century England', in David E. Martin and David Rubinstein (eds.), *Ideology and the Labour Movement* (1979), 64. Raymond Williams, *Keywords* (1977).

[2] *Oxford English Dictionary* (Oxford, 1933; in the earlier serial publication of the *Dictionary*, the fascicle containing *propaganda* appeared in 1909).

[3] Alice Goldfarb Marquis, 'Words as Weapons: Propaganda in Britain during the First World War', *Journal of Contemporary History*, 13 (1978), 467–8.

[4] Arland D. Weeks, *The Control of the Social Mind* (1923), 73.

[5] Serge Chakotin, *The Rape of the Masses*, trans. E. W. Dickes (1940), 126–7. George Sylvester Viereck, *Spreading Germs of Hate* (1931), 266.

[6] On the success of British propaganda see H. C. Peterson, *Propaganda for War* (Norman, Okla., 1939), 326; James Duane Squires, *British Propaganda at Home and in the United States from 1914 to 1917* (Cambridge, Mass., 1935). Lord Northcliffe, the press baron who from 1918 directed propaganda to enemy countries, was widely credited with having won the war and/or advanced its completion. Norman Angell, *The Public Mind* (1926), pp. iii, 148–71. Sir Campbell Stuart, *Secrets of Crewe House* (1920). General von Ludendorff alleged in his memoirs that Germany had only been defeated because its population, demoralized by British propaganda and the Allied blockade, had 'stabbed the army in the back'. The theory that propaganda had 'won' was given credence on both sides: *Advertising World*, 48/2 (1925), 125. George G. Bruntz, *Allied Propaganda and the Collapse of the German Empire in 1918* (Stanford, Calif., 1938), 220. Chakotin, p. 154. H. C. Engelbright, 'How War Propaganda Won', *The World Tomorrow* (Apr. 1927), 159. Adolf Hitler, *Mein Kampf*, trans. Ralph Manheim (1969), 161, 167–70. Richard S. Lambert, *Propaganda* (1938), 30. Sidney Rogerson, *Propaganda in the Next War*, ed. Captain Liddell Hart (1938), 2. Henry Wickham Steed, *Through Thirty Years 1892–1922*, 2 vols. (1924), ii. 185–92, 227. *The Times History and Encyclopedia of the War: British Propaganda in Enemy Countries*, xxi (1919), pt. 270, ch. 314: 329–42, 350–5.

considerable portion of the information that had been disseminated had been based on falsehood and fabrication.[7] Memoirs and exposés published in Britain, Germany, and the United States in the early 1920s conveyed the impression that the citizens of each nation had been unwittingly duped and manipulated by propaganda.[8] The apparent ease with which this had been accomplished, coupled with the perceived effectiveness of what was thought to be mainly fraudulent commercial advertising, reinforced existing theories and anxieties regarding the irrationality and malleability of man in the mass and/or mass man, at a time when near universal suffrage, improvements in literacy, and the growth and development of new means of communication were increasing the power and importance of the average citizen in a democracy.[9]

Correspondingly, the success of propaganda and advertising confirmed

[7] William Albig, *Public Opinion* (1939), 284. Edward L. Bernays, *Propaganda* (1928), 21–7. Bruntz, p. v. John Grierson, *Grierson on Documentary*, ed. Forsyth Hardy (1946), 280. Hitler, p. 161. Lambert, p. 22. Harold D. Lasswell, Ralph D. Casey, and Bruce Lannes Smith, *Propaganda and Promotional Activities* (Minneapolis, 1935), 3. Frederick E. Lumley, *The Propaganda Menace* (1933), 43–5. Rogerson, pp. 8–9, 20, 30–1. Ivor Thomas, *Warfare by Words* (1942), 63. Timothy John Hollins, 'The Presentation of Politics: The Place of Party Publicity, Broadcasting and Film in British Politics 1918–1939', D.Phil. dissertation, Leeds, 1981, 4–5. Terence Hall Qualter, 'The Nature of Propaganda and its Function in Democratic Government: An Examination of Principal Theories of Propaganda since 1880', Ph.D. dissertation, London, 1956, 21–2, 132–4. Marquis, pp. 467–8. M. L. Sanders and Philip M. Taylor, *British Propaganda during the First World War, 1914–1918* (1982), 1. Philip M. Taylor, *The Projection of Britain* (Cambridge, 1981), 1–2.

[8] e.g. Philip Gibbs, *Now It Can Be Told* (Garden City, NY, 1920), 12, 68; Arthur Ponsonby, *Falsehood in Wartime* (New York, 1928). Post-war writers focused on the many fabricated atrocity stories. See Albig, pp. 283, 314. Angell, pp. 31, 40–1. Lumley, pp. 229–32. Viereck, pp. 146–53, 250. Robert Graves and Alan Hodge, *The Long Weekend* (New York, 1940), 14–16. Walter Lippmann, *Public Opinion* (New York, 1922), 10. Actual atrocities had been committed, but this was overlooked; once any such stories came into question, all became suspect. See Angell, p. 74. James Morgan Read, *Atrocity Propaganda 1914–1919* (New Haven, Conn., 1941), 82–3. Trevor Wilson, 'Lord Bryce's Investigations into Alleged German Atrocities in Belgium, 1914–1915', *Journal of Contemporary History*, 14/3 (1979), 381–2.

[9] Concern about the 'tyranny of the majority' and gullibility of the masses was hardly novel; see J. S. Mill, *'On Liberty'*, ed. R. B. McCallum (Oxford, 1946), 3–4; L. T. Hobhouse, *Liberalism* (1911), 230. Yet the growing socio-political importance of the majority, coupled with the rise of mass communications and the development of more sophisticated techniques of persuasion, gave a new urgency to élitist anxieties. See José Ortega y Gasset, *The Revolt of the Masses* (New York, 1930), 7–12; and Everett Dean Martin, *The Conflict of the Individual and the Mass in the Modern World* (New York, 1932), 29–37, 143–8. Angell, *The Public Mind*, pp. ii, 12–26, 185–6. Also note Stanley Baldwin's references to the dangers of the 'mass mind', *Service of our Lives* (1937), 100–2, 116. Hubert Henderson, the editor of the *Nation*, stressed the difficulties of publishing intelligent books in a society increasingly dominated by mass culture, H. Henderson *et al.*, *Books and the Public* (1927), 13–14. On the whole issue also see D. L. LeMahieu, *A Culture for Democracy* (Oxford, 1988), 107–8.

and gave further impetus to the emergent hypotheses of the new social sciences that individuals were guided by 'herd instincts', and thus were susceptible to exploitation by those with a knowledge of 'human suggestibility'.[10] Social psychology, in turn, legitimated and seemingly verified existing theories about the masses giving the latter an alleged scientific base they had hitherto lacked.[11] The fact that much of this theory has since been refuted[12] is of secondary importance, as it was influential at the time. The process was circular and self-perpetuating, for if the perceived effectiveness of propaganda provided evidence in support of prevailing theories about the masses, the latter in turn lent credence to the belief that propaganda was indeed 'one of the most powerful instrumentalities in the modern world'.[13] It, too, achieved scientific status:

the public mind to the trained propagandist is a pool into which phrases and thoughts are dropped like acids, with a foreknowledge of the reactions that will take place, just as [a biologist] . . . can make a thousand crustaceans stop swimming aimlessly about in the bowl and rush with one headlong impulse to the side where the light comes from, merely by introducing into the water a little drop of a chemical.[14]

[10] The success of advertising and propaganda was often cited as supposedly factual evidence in support of pre-existing theories on human susceptibilities; William MacPherson, *The Psychology of Persuasion* (1920), 69–74. Bertrand Russell, *Free Thought and Official Propaganda* (1922), 32. Weeks, pp. 72–4. Chakotin, p. 12. Thomas, pp. 10–11.

[11] Not all social scientists believed the masses were completely malleable: see Abbott Lawrence Lowell, *Public Opinion in War and Peace* (1923), 124. Helge Lundholm, 'Mark Antony's Speech and the Psychology of Persuasion', *Character and Personality*, 6 (1937–8), 293–305. Some argued that the stupidity of the masses limited the potential for manipulation: Lumley, pp. 394–5. Rogerson, pp. 26–7. On the other hand, most highlighted 'suggestibility' and stressed the power of group influence: Gustave Le Bon, *The Crowd* (1896), pp. xv–xxiii, 11–12. W. Trotter, *Instincts of the Herd in Peace and War* (1920), 13–27, 113–15. William McDougall, *The Group Mind* (Cambridge, 1920), 12–13. Everett Dean Martin, *The Behavior of Crowds* (New York, 1920). Robert H. Thouless, *Straight and Crooked Thinking* (1930), 87–9. Paul R. Farnsworth and Alice Behner, 'A Note on the Attitude of Social Conformity', *Journal of Social Psychology*, 2 (1931), 126–8. Robert H. Thouless, *Social Psychology* (1935), 244–59. Martin L. Reymert and Harold A. Kohn, 'An Objective Investigation of Suggestibility', *Character and Personality* (Durham, NC), 9 (1940–1), 44–8. Angell, *Public Mind*, 139. Hargrave, pp. 47–8, 181–5. Chakotin, pp. 12–18, 118–19. Weeks, pp. 216–17.

[12] R. N. Soffer, 'New Elitism: Social Psychology in Prewar England', *Journal of British Studies*, 8/2 (1969), 111–40. Briggs, 'Language of "Mass" '. Some still adhere to these theories: Michael D. Biddiss, *The Age of the Masses* (Hassocks, Sussex, 1977), 16–17, 194, 311.

[13] Bruntz, p. 221.

[14] *New York Tribune*, 12 July 1918, quoted in Harold Lasswell, *Propaganda Technique in the World War* (1927), 209. Also see Hillel Bernstein, *Choose a Bright Morning* (1936), 70–1; Sir Charles Higham, *Advertising* (1925), 12–15.

Inclined to accept such claims at face value, most contemporaries investigating the subject assumed that propaganda was almost limitless in its
capabilities.[15]

Studies on propaganda published since the Second World War have
tended to address the validity of these claims, rather than examine the
influence which they exerted at the time.[16] Concern over the need to
verify the facts about propaganda and reveal its limitations has meant that
the ongoing debate in the inter-war period, which dealt not with the
power of propaganda but with how best to harness such a potent tool, has
been overlooked. Indeed, although the First World War and its aftermath
debased the term, its connotations were still not entirely pejorative. In the
Supplement to the *Oxford English Dictionary* compiled in 1933, the 1909
entry was left unaltered. Not until a further *Supplement* appeared in 1982
did one find reference to the 'systematic propagation of information or
ideas by an interested party, especially in a tendentious way in order to
encourage or instil a particular attitude or response'.[17]

The ambiguity surrounding propaganda in the inter-war years was
reflected in the varied applications of the term. In March 1929, for
example, an editorial in *The Times* stressed the importance of giving
greater 'publicity' to the minorities question in order to counteract the
effects of 'propaganda' against the League of Nations. A day later, the
same newspaper published a letter from the Council for the Preservation
of Rural England advocating the use of 'propaganda' to warn the public
of the menace caused by 'advertising'.[18] The fact that the words publicity,
advertising, propaganda, and sometimes education were used inter-
changeably makes it difficult to provide adequate definitions which properly convey the meaning of these terms during this period.[19] The paradox

---

[15] Some queried whether propaganda was an absolute science: Lumley, pp. 411–12. Yet,
relatively few challenged these assumptions; see Peter H. Odegard's criticisms in 'Review of
Books', *Public Opinion Quarterly*, 1/4 (1937), 144–6.

[16] Most of these studies stress the iimited powers of propaganda: Lindley Fraser,
Propaganda (1957), 191, 209. Qualter, pp. 1–4. Charles Roetter, *Psychological Warfare*
(1974), 188. Oliver Thomson, *Mass Persuasion in History* (Edinburgh, 1977), 7–9. Taylor,
Projection, 1–2. Taylor and Sanders, pp. vii–xi, 1. Daniel Lerner, 'Introduction: Some
Problems of Policy and Propaganda', in Daniel Lerner (ed.), *Propaganda in War and Crisis*
(New York, 1951), pp. xi–xvi, 1–2. Hans Speier, 'Morale and Propaganda', in Lerner, p. 10.
None the less, several analysts have affirmed inter-war theories: E. K. Bramsted, *Goebbels
and National Socialist Propaganda 1925–1945* (Detroit, 1965), 455. Blanche B. Elliott, *A
History of English Advertising* (1962), pp. xv, 214–15. James Playsted Wood, *The Story of
Advertising* (New York, 1958), p. vi. Philip Knightley, *The First Casualty* (1975), 80–1. Cate
Haste, *Keep the Home Fires Burning* (1977), 1–4.

[17] *A Supplement to the Oxford English Dictionary*, iii (Oxford, 1982), 837.

[18] *The Times*, 1, 2 Mar. 1929.   [19] Qualter makes this point, pp. 4–5.

was not lost on contemporaries; Harold Lasswell, the first academic seriously to consider the subject, observed that 'propaganda against propaganda is just another propaganda'.[20] The problem stemmed from the fact that, while propaganda generally connoted some form of manipulation of public opinion,[21] this was not necessarily perceived to be pernicious.

True, most of the numerous studies published on the subject in the inter-war years stressed the pejorative nature of the tool. Working from the *a priori* assumption that propaganda was extremely powerful, the majority of contemporary theorists sought remedies and antidotes to undermine its influence. Battle and disease imagery were rife in the texts of the period, with analysts stressing the need to immunize the public and increase its psychic defences.[22] Many believed the solution rested in education, in teaching people to think, and encouraging the development of individualism, so as to generate an enlightened public opinion.[23] Once the latter was in place, it was argued, propaganda would cease to have any role or influence in society:

Impartiality is recognized as the highest intellectual virtue, education is an impartial process of giving information; and even propagandists find it wisest to claim the virtue of impartiality. . . . There would be no propaganda needed in a country with strong individualist traditions and a first-rate university educational system; for the latter would produce citizens capable of thinking and acting upon the merits of the facts in each problem that came before them.[24]

On the other hand, it was recognized that widespread education was part of the problem. As Bertrand Russell observed, the growth of literacy had made it much easier to spread misinformation.[25] The breakdown of older methods of social control, coupled with the emergence of new means of large-scale communication, further increased the potential for mass manipulation. Current educational arrangements were not thought to provide an adequate bulwark, critics charging that the system distributed information without imparting intelligence, and thus did not

[20] Quoted in Albig, p. 282.
[21] Advertising was also defined in this manner: 'Originally the term signified communication or the conveying of information, but advertising is now most commonly thought of as involving persuasion of some sort as well as information' (Leverett S. Lyon, 'Advertising', in *Encyclopedia of the Social Sciences*, ed. Edwin R. A. Seligman, i (1930), 469). Also see Lambert, p. 20.   [22] Lumley, pp. 414–31. Weeks, pp. 72–3. Viereck, pp. 11–12.
[23] Lumley, pp. 424–31. Viereck, pp. 264–7. Russell, pp. 43–4. Lambert, p. 159. Weeks, pp. 81–2. Note the creation of organizations such as the Association for Education in Citizenship: Ernest Simon and Eva M. Hubback, *Training for Citizenship* (1935), 45.
[24] Lambert, p. 18.   [25] Russell, p. 42. Also Lambert, pp. 157–8.

properly equip the average individual to exercise fully his/her proper role in a democratic society.[26]

Yet, if only an enlightened public opinion could withstand the on-slaught of propaganda, leading democratic theorists had begun to contend that it was an 'intolerable and unworkable fiction' to assume that every individual in society could possibly acquire a competent knowledge of all matters relating to public affairs.[27] The American political scientist Walter Lippmann argued in 1922 that representative government could only work successfully if an independent expert organization made the necessary facts intelligible to those who had to make the decisions. Noting that most liberals believed the press should fulfil this function, Lippmann observed that as presently constituted it did not serve as a panacea for the defects of the system.[28] Many British intellectuals, including Graham Wallas, the first professor of political science at the London School of Economics, and the writer Norman Angell, shared this disillusionment with the ability of a mass commercial press to cultivate an intelligent public opinion; several contemporaries concluded that the salvation of democracy lay in limiting the political power of the average citizen.[29] Others believed that the natural leaders of society could only retain their authority by harnessing the new tools of mass manipulation. Conspiracy theory was rife:

The steam engine, the multiple press, and . . . [growing literacy] . . . have taken the power away from kings and given it to the people. . . . Universal suffrage and universal schooling reinforced this tendency, and at last even the bourgeoisie stood in fear of the common people. For the masses promised to become king. To-day, however, a reaction has set in. The minority has discovered a powerful help in influencing majorities. It has been found possible so to mould the mind of the masses that they will throw their newly gained strength in the desired direction. . . . Whatever of social importance is done to-day . . . must be done

---

[26] Martin, *Conflict*, 30–3. Russell, pp. 24–9. Angell, *Public Mind*, 26, 45. Viereck, pp. 264–7. Lumley, pp. 308–20.

[27] Lippmann, pp. 18–20. Graham Wallas, quoted in Russell, pp. 5–13.

[28] Lippmann, pp. 19–20. Lippmann's first major work, *Public Opinion*, published in 1922, was reviewed in *The Times*, 20 June, and *Times Literary Supplement*, 31 Aug. Although the book does not appear to have been widely reviewed in Britain, Lippmann's theories were known in Whitehall; see F. R. Cowell, 'The Uses and Dangers of Publicity in the Work of Government', *Public Administration*, 13/3 (1935), 290–3. Indeed, Lippmann had a formative influence on John Grierson; see below.

[29] Wallas, quoted by Russell, pp. 5–13. Norman Angell, *The Press and the Organization of Society* (Cambridge, 1933), 6–10, 21–7. Angell, *Public Mind*, 135–8, 185–6. Ortega y Gasset, pp. 12–15, 83–5. Martin, *Conflict*, 35–7.

with the help of propaganda. Propaganda is the executive arm of the invisible government.[30]

Yet inherent in such statements was the assumption that there was nothing wrong with propaganda *per se*; its evil or goodness was dependent on who controlled it and their motives.

A number of analysts advanced this theory,[31] albeit with the opposite intention, heralding propaganda as the best means of counteracting mass manipulation, and as a force for social good.[32] In many important circles propaganda came to be regarded as an essential adjunct to the democratic process and a chief means of counteracting propaganda of a questionable nature. Indeed, in direct response to Lippmann's pronouncements on the failure of the liberal concept of education to meet the needs of a demo-cratic society, John Grierson, a Scottish social scientist undertaking re-search at the University of Chicago between 1924 and 1927, began to explore the possibility of employing the cinema as a means of ' "bridg[ing] the gap" between the citizen and his community'.[33] Impressed by the development of films such as *Nanook of the North*, which conveyed a 'creative treatment of actuality', Grierson became convinced of the potential of employing the 'documentary' (a term he coined) to impart necessary information to the electorate. He endeavoured to design a new

---

[30] Bernays, pp. 119–20. Also see Arthur Calder-Marshall, *The Changing Scene* (1937), 28–9.

[31] See Lowell, pp. 105–6. MacPherson, p. 75. John Hargrave, *Propaganda* (1940), 34. Odegard, p. 145.

[32] e.g. Sidney Webb's Introduction to G. W. Goodall, *Advertising* (1914), pp. xiv–xv. Sir Arthur Lowes-Dickinson, 'Publicity in Industrial Accounts with a Comparison of English and American Methods', *Journal of the Royal Statistical Society*, 87/3 (1924), 412. George E. Gordon Catlin, 'Propaganda as a Function of Democratic Government', in Harwood Lawrence Childs (ed.), *Propaganda and Dictatorship* (Princeton, NJ, 1936), 125–45. Amber Blanco White, *The New Propaganda* (1939). 'In the Propaganda Arena', *Public Opinion Quarterly*, 2/3 (1938), 495–6. Chakotin, pp. 126, 284.

[33] Grierson often cited Lippmann's theories as an explanation for his development of the documentary film. On Grierson's philosophy see John Grierson, 'Films in the Public Service', *Public Administration*, 14 (1936), 366–72; 'Perspectives of Salesmanship', in *The Post Office: Telephone Sales Bulletin*, 2/4 (1936), 57–8; 'Propaganda for Democracy', *The Spectator*, 11 Nov. 1938; *Grierson*. Paul Rotha, *Documentary Diary* (1973), 16–37. Also see Ian Aitken, 'John Grierson, Idealism and the Inter-War Period', *Historical Journal of Film, Radio and Television*, 9/3 (1989), 247–58; Nicholas Pronay, 'John Grierson and the Documentary—60 years on', *Historical Journal of Film, Radio and Television*, 9/3 (1989), 228–30. Although relying mainly on advertising agencies for their revenues, both the Gallup polls and Mass-Observation were founded out of a similar concern with the need to find new means of bridging the gap between government and governed in a complex democracy: George Gallup, *Public Opinion in a Democracy* (Princeton, NJ, 1939), 5–14. Mass-Observation, *The Pub and the People* (1943), 7–14.

model of education, arguing that the system 'must inevitably reach further in the use of the dramatic media if it is to secure for the citizenry a true sense of their living relationship to events'.[34] Current educational arrangements were flawed because they taught people the 'three "R's" ' without instilling the fourth, 'Rooted Belief'. Propaganda was 'the part of democratic education which the educators forgot':[35]

If we are to persuade, we have to reveal; and we have to reveal in terms of reality. Recognizing this responsibility to the local and particular, recognizing the deeper levels of understanding and exposition into which information in a democracy must inevitably reach, it is possible to appreciate that even the once-haunted concept of propaganda may have a democratic interpretation, and that its democratic interpretation makes propaganda and education one.[36]

On his return to England in 1927 Grierson approached Stephen Tallents, the secretary of the Empire Marketing Board (EMB), with proposals for developing the cinema into an educational force. After being commissioned to study the use of instructional films abroad, Grierson was hired in 1928 to produce the board's first film, which dealt with the herring industry. Cognizant that the Treasury would probably oppose the production, Tallents had chosen this subject deliberately, in the full knowledge that the current Financial Secretary to the Treasury, Arthur Samuel, was the author of *The Herring: Its Effect on the History of Britain*. *Drifters* won critical acclaim and, as a result, the EMB was able to form its own film unit in 1930 under Grierson's direction.[37]

As has been well documented, the film unit was not established or maintained without serious opposition from both outside and within Whitehall.[38] Grierson later linked the hostility which the Treasury manifested towards the entire EMB publicity organization to the fact that the business of running a creative concern within and by the Civil Service, of

[34] Grierson, *Grierson*, 292. Also, Grierson, 'Films in the Public Service', 371.

[35] Grierson, *Grierson*, 246. Also see Grierson's Preface to Paul Rotha, *Documentary Film* (1936), 7–12.

[36] Grierson, *Grierson*, 294.

[37] Rotha, *Documentary Diary*, 16–65. Paul Swann, *The British Documentary Film Movement, 1926–1946* (Cambridge, 1989), 19–34.

[38] The film trade objected to the competition; Conservatives believed the unit had a left-wing bias; socialists accused Grierson of reinforcing the status quo instead of addressing real issues; and the Treasury was openly hostile to the arrangements in general. Swann, pp. 22–4. Rotha, *Documentary Diary*, 36–142. Hollins, p. 65. Max Beloff, 'The Whitehall Factor: The Role of the Higher Civil Service 1919–1939', in Gillian Peele and Chris Cook (eds.), *The Politics of Reappraisal 1918–1939* (1975), 221–3.

having officials actively involved in interpreting policy to the public, was a relatively new concept. He observed that attitudes altered only slowly over the inter-war decades, as 'two or three of us came into Whitehall with very different ideas'.[39]

It is indisputable that certain key individuals, such as Grierson and Tallents, were instrumental in introducing and legitimating the concept of government publicity during these years. However, the obvious influence exerted by the few should not blind us to the fact that, by the middle of the inter-war period, a growing number of civil servants and their political masters had begun to recognize and consider the importance of avowedly non-partisan public relations to the functioning of the modern democratic state. As we shall see below, public relations became an important topic of discussion amongst those directly concerned with the development of new techniques of public administration, so that, concurrent with the creation of information and publicity bureaux in government departments during the inter-war era, there developed a conceptual framework regarding the legitimacy of official activities in this sphere. That this could occur was a by-product of several interrelated developments which had their roots in the nineteenth century, most notably a profound transformation in the character of the State and, emergent from this, changing perceptions regarding public service and the functions appropriate to government officials, especially with regard to subjects such as the distribution of information.

Clearly, the direct involvement of the State bureaucracy in both intelligence work and activities designed to influence or shape public opinion was hardly novel to the early twentieth century. Political leaders, whether on the throne or in parliament, had been active propagandists for centuries, readily employing the official channels at their disposal. The Tudor monarchs, for example, made extensive use of pageantry as a form of political propaganda intended to cement the dynasty and advance specific domestic and international policies.[40] Under Henry VII the scope of extra-parliamentary government administration was extended and with it the ability of the Crown both to garner information and to make known the royal will.[41] It was during the Tudor period, for example, that it became the prerogative of the Post Office to open suspect correspondence and transmit intelligence to the secretaries of state, a practice which

---

[39] Quoted in Rotha, *Documentary Diary*, 36–7.
[40] See Sydney Anglo, *Spectacle, Pageantry, and Early Tudor Policy* (Oxford, 1969).
[41] Kenneth O. Morgan, *The Oxford History of Britain* (Oxford, 1988), 268–73. Lacey Baldwin Smith, *This Realm of England 1399–1688* (Toronto, 1988), 92–8.

continued well into the eighteenth century.[42] After the Reformation, the Church came under the closer control of the Crown, further extending the instruments of influence available to government. By the reign of Elizabeth I, agents of the Crown were active in sounding out and endeavouring to shape popular sentiment through measures as broad-ranging as the employment of spies and the distribution of pamphlets.[43] As well, the circulation of printed materials 'likely to threaten the throne' was strictly controlled.[44] The passage of Licensing Acts restricting the publication of news and comments ensured that monarchs retained a monopoly over propaganda well into the Stuart era.[45]

The apparatus of both Church and State continued to be put to similar purpose as political authority shifted from Crown to parliament. Although the bureaucracy remained small by modern standards,[46] throughout the seventeenth and eighteenth centuries various tools were available through which government leaders could collect intelligence and direct opinion. Days appointed by authority of the State for church services of humiliation or thanksgiving were common, and were frequently used as 'political weapons of party'.[47] The fifth of November, the anniversary of the Gunpowder Plot, provided a specific opportunity for political preaching and gave rise to a whole literature of special sermons.[48] Generally speaking, church sermons were an important element in public life and in the formation of public opinion.[49] So too were 'addresses'; to demonstrate the support which they commanded in the country, politicians used official channels to issue proclamations adjuring public declarations of loyalty to the monarch or Parliament.[50] As one historian has noted, such addresses not only reflected public opinion, but could also help to create it.[51] Given the scope of its organization, and strict limitations on the franking of printed papers, the Post Office provided a valuable means for circulating official publications and newspapers.[52] In the early 1700s it was the only

---

[42] Kenneth Ellis, *The Post Office in the Eighteenth Century* (1958), 66. Clive Emsley, 'The Home Office and its Sources of Information and Investigation 1791–1801', *English Historical Review*, 94 (1979), 538.   [43] Smith, p. 171.

[44] Brian Lake, *British Newspapers* (1984), 21.

[45] Jeremy Greenwood, *Newspapers and the Post Office 1635–1834* (1971), 1.

[46] During the mid-17th c., e.g., the number of paid officials numbered under 2,000: Morgan, *Oxford History*, 345. By 1902 the figure was over 100,000; see below.

[47] Charles J. Abbey and John H. Overton, *The English Church in the Eighteenth Century*, ii (1878), 454–5.   [48] Ibid. 456.

[49] S. C. Carpenter, *Eighteenth-Century Church and People* (1959), 25.

[50] Robert R. Dozier, *For King, Constitution, and Country: The English Loyalists and the French Revolution* (Lexington, Ky., 1983), 2.

[51] James E. Bradley, *Popular Politics and the American Revolution in England* (Macon, Ga., 1986), 92.   [52] Ellis, *Post Office*, 47–8.

agency of distribution to the provinces, and by custom allowed ministerial pamphlets to be sent into the country post-free.[53] The lapse of the Licensing Acts after 1695 spurred the growth of an independent newspaper press, but, beginning in 1712, the government enacted a series of stamp duties designed to curb circulations.[54] Moreover, the secretary of the Treasury supervised the many newspapers receiving official subsidies.[55] In his last decade in power Robert Walpole spent an average of £5,000 annually from the secret service budget on influencing writers and editors.[56] The press was also controlled by other means; for example, government advertisements, a lucrative form of revenue, were placed only in friendly papers.[57] As well, at its own expense the government purchased and circulated newspapers favourable to its point of view and made unauthorized disclosures to such journals.[58]

These types of activities tended to accelerate during times of crisis, such as the American Revolution and the French Revolution. During both of these periods the State bureaucracy was used to gather intelligence regarding the extent of pro-revolutionary sentiment and operations in Britain.[59] The government also engaged in anti-revolutionary propaganda, encouraging the formation of loyalist societies,[60] raising stamp taxes and censoring newspapers,[61] mobilizing the government press and the Church,[62] and publishing and distributing pamphlets, tracts, and sermons through official and quasi-official channels.[63]

These few examples highlight certain characteristics regarding the nature of government efforts in this sphere. In the first place, such activities were often secretly organized and financed. The secret service budget, from which subsidies to the press and similar expenditures were drawn, was not under direct parliamentary control.[64] Revelations regarding Walpole's largesse ensured that his successors had to exercise greater caution in their use of such moneys.[65] It is hardly surprising that on

---

[53] A. Aspinall, *Politics and the Press c.1780–1850* (1949), 177.

[54] Greenwood, pp. 6–8. Lake, pp. 33–5, 50–7.

[55] On the expansion of the government press, see Aspinall, pp. v, 66–9, 372.

[56] Alexander Andrews, *The History of British Journalism*, i (1968), 138.

[57] Aspinall, p. 126, claims this became common only in the 1820s; Greenwood, p. 31, suggests the policy dated from 1798.   [58] Aspinall, pp. 148–62, 183–97.

[59] Dozier, pp. 33–7. Emsley, pp. 536–9.

[60] Dozier, pp. 48–52. H. T. Dickinson, *British Radicalism and the French Revolution 1789–1815* (Oxford, 1985), 32–3.

[61] Dickinson, pp. 39–41. Aspinall, pp. 1–2, 179. Lake, pp. 63–5.

[62] Dickinson, pp. 29–32. Lake, p. 63. Bradley, pp. 92–4, 213. E. R. Norman, *Church and Society in England 1770–1970* (Oxford, 1976), 20–1, 30.

[63] Aspinall, pp. 152–3. Dickinson, pp. 26–31. Norman, p. 30.

[64] Aspinall, pp. 66–9. Emsley, p. 539.   [65] Ellis, *Post Office*, 48.

recommending the creation of a government information bureau in 1829 to deal with newspapers, a prominent civil servant emphasized that this 'ought to be done in the most profound secrecy'.[66] Secondly, the information imparted was openly partisan; it was designed to shore up existing power relationships. Finally, a sporadic rather than a consistent policy was pursued. Government interest in propaganda tended to vary with the strength and vitality of the opposition. Thus the relative tranquillity of the latter years of the reign of George II ensured that the period saw a considerable reduction in the scope of the government press.[67] In short, the propaganda activities of the unreformed State cannot be classified as examples of open or professedly impartial attempts to influence public opinion.

By the early nineteenth century the ability of political leaders to engage in partisan propaganda through the medium of the State bureaucracy was diminishing. A number of elements were at work. First, the period witnessed a relative decline in the size and influence of the State itself.[68] Growing adherence to liberalism and the doctrines of classical political economy served as 'an important conditioning factor which tended to check . . . expansion'.[69] Indeed, although the classical economists were not committed to complete non-interference by the State, 'during the heyday of its influence, the markedly individualistic tenor of utilitarian and economic theory, when translated into the sphere of practical politics, interposed a steady check upon governmental action'.[70] Secondly, the political influence of the established Church was waning and hence its effectiveness as a channel for propaganda. Although active in matters of direct import to the Church, the Anglican clergy effectively banned itself from all but limited participation in politics.[71] Tellingly, the period saw the end of many traditional religious propaganda activities, such as 5 November sermons. Thirdly, it is apparent that many of the sources of information and influence open to governments in power had begun to evaporate or be supplanted. Increasing advertising revenues, coupled with the decline of official subsidies and stamp taxes, ensured that over the course of the century the press proliferated[72] and was rendered more financially independent of the government.[73] Newspapers became less

---

[66] Quoted in Aspinall, pp. 232–5.   [67] See Ellis, *Post Office*, 48–9.

[68] Moses Abramovitz and Vera F. Eliasberg, *The Growth of Public Employment in Great Britain* (Princeton, NJ, 1957), 8.   [69] Ibid. 19–20.

[70] Ibid. 21. Also see Harold Perkin, *Origins of Modern English Society* (1969), 221–30, 308–19.   [71] Norman, pp. 72–6.

[72] Glyn Williams and John Ramsden, *Ruling Britannia* (1990), 276–7.

[73] Subsidies began to dwindle in the 1830s but remained an issue until into the 1850s, by which point stamp duties were being rescinded: Aspinall, pp. 373–4, 379.

reliant upon and even hostile to information supplied by the bureaucracy; in some circles official intelligence was viewed as being tainted given its source.[74] Changes in the socio-political environment, in particular growing democratization, also contributed to the change. The large expansion of the electorate in 1867 necessitated the development of new forms of party organization and the adoption of novel techniques of mass electioneering, in turn made possible by technological innovations in communications.[75] The concurrent reform of the Civil Service ensured that the political influencing of the masses came to be regarded as the purview of the political parties, not the State bureaucracy. The end of government subsidies to newspapers was symptomatic of the trend.

The reform of the Civil Service was indeed a crucial element in the equation. During the late eighteenth century abuse of franking procedures and the growth of opposition newspapers ensured that the Post Office was rendered more impartial.[76] From 1796 onward it was obligated to extend its facilities to the opposition press and freely circulate all stamped papers.[77] Hence its role as a medium of propaganda for the government in power began to decline.[78] Of equal importance, during the late eighteenth century concern over levels of government expenditure led to the creation of several commissions of inquiry into the administration of public business.[79] Down to 1828 numerous reforms were introduced which were designed to give parliament greater control over the appointment and remuneration of public officials and do away with offices from which the public derived little benefit. By taking charge of pay arrangements, parliament in effect converted those employed in government departments from being servants of their respective ministers into servants of the Crown.[80] In keeping with the ideological tenor of the times, the period 1828–48 was characterized by the introduction of changes intended to streamline the Civil Service in order to cut all forms of public expenditure.[81] In the latter part of the century, however, the focus of concern changed. From 1848 to 1890, the main aim of reformers was to make the service more efficient by improving the quality of its personnel and developing a canon of appropriate behaviour in the conduct of public business. Hence the period saw an end to patronage appointments

---

[74] Ibid. 373, 379–80.
[75] H. C. G. Matthew, 'Rhetoric and Politics in Great Britain, 1860–1950', in P. J. Waller (ed.), *Politics and Social Change in Modern Britain* (Brighton, 1987), 36–7. Williams and Ramsden, pp. 258–9.   [76] Greenwood, pp. 42–4.
[77] Aspinall, p. 177.   [78] Ellis, *Post Office*, 59.
[79] Emmeline W. Cohen, *The Growth of the British Civil Service 1780–1939* (Hamden, Conn., 1965), 20.   [80] Ibid. 20–1, 69–70.
[81] Ibid. 69–70.

and the sale of offices, as well as the formulation of a strict code of discipline, with limitations being placed, for example, on the political involvement of public servants.[82] At the same time the administration began slowly to expand. Levels of government expenditure rose steadily,[83] as did the number of public employees. Whereas there were 16,000 'persons in public offices' in 1797, by 1902 the State employed 107,782 officials.[84] This growth accelerated in the early twentieth century. Between 1890 and 1950 government employment, excluding nationalized industries, increased by 450–500 per cent; in 1891 only 3.5 per cent of the labour force were public employees as compared to 5.8 per cent in 1901 and 14.1 per cent in 1950.[85] Over virtually the same period government expenditure rose forty-seven times in money terms and ten times in real terms.[86] What this indicates, of course, is the resurgence of the State. Several factors, not least among them liberal doctrine itself with its insistence on rational and efficient government, ensured that during the latter half of the nineteenth century the State came increasingly to be regarded as an impartial body capable of standing outside and above politics. Out of Benthamite thinking there emerged a new concept of the State as a positive force distinct from parliament and the Crown. This facilitated the evolution of a new and broader definition of what constituted official responsibilities and, in light of the social and economic pressures associated with industrialization, led to the acceleration of government forays into new policy areas.[87] A significant result of this change was a transformation in the very character of the public service. Although it happened quite gradually, by the early twentieth century a higher percentage of civil servants was employed in the social services than engaged in the defence and security functions which had dominated the Victorian State.[88] Whereas in 1851 social service agencies employed a mere 313 persons, by 1914 31,000 were involved. The figure rose to nearly a quarter million after the First World War.[89]

As the nature of government altered, so too did standards of public administration. With the State assuming greater influence over the daily life of its citizens by expanding the range of services which it provided,

---

[82] Ibid. 19–21.

[83] See Abramovitz and Eliasberg, pp. 16–17. Perkin, *Origins*, 123–4.

[84] The latter figure excludes industrial grades; Harold Perkin, *The Rise of Professional Society: England since 1880* (1990), 18–21.

[85] Abramovitz and Eliasberg, pp. 8, 25–6.

[86] Alan T. Peacock and Jack Wiseman, *The Growth of Public Expenditure in the United Kingdom* (Princeton, NJ, 1961), p. xxi.

[87] Abramovitz and Eliasberg, pp. 21–2, 27–30. Perkin, *Rise*, 13.

[88] Abramovitz and Eliasberg, pp. 16–18.   [89] Ibid. 62–6.

it became less credible to conceive of government activities as either entirely regulatory or businesslike. At the same time, government was rendered more complex and impersonal. Economy, efficiency, and equity demanded the development of uniform services as well as the uniform implementation of policy. This necessitated greater centralization in the administration of services and increased the role and importance of the bureaucracy, while at the same time necessitating its political neutrality.

It cannot be overemphasized that this was a slow evolutionary development. Not until into the twentieth century did the science of public administration come under scrutiny.[90] Nor was the bureaucracy suddenly rendered completely impartial; for example, despite the end of newspaper subsidies, as late as the 1880s official advertisements were still being placed only in papers which supported the party in office.[91] Clearly, while the foundations were laid in the nineteenth century, the modern bureaucratic State did not come into being until the twentieth century. But by the time of the period covered by this study, a profound distinction was being drawn between the political and administrative arms of government: one concerned primarily with the retention of power, the other with the use of it. The differentiation was never rigid; political and administrative functions could easily overlap, as for example when public servants prepared political statements for ministers.[92] Neither is the use of such a definition meant to imply that the ideal was always upheld, nor that the bureaucracy did not develop an ideological framework of its own. Quite the contrary. As will be suggested below, a canon clearly emerged regarding the use of publicity by public servants; at its core was a commitment to non-partisanship, and an emphasis on the idea that government and party political information were distinct from each other. Whereas the propaganda activities of the unreformed State were consciously and often recognizably designed to further the aims and aspirations of those holding power, the propaganda of the modern State, while hardly devoid of the potential for bolstering the political status quo, laid claim to impartiality, at least in principle. In order to trace this important development, it is necessary to examine the evolution of the modern information services in Britain.

During the latter half of the nineteenth century some departments in Whitehall did become involved in the dissemination of avowedly non-partisan publicity. Following Rowland Hill's reforms, the Post Office began in 1854 to publish an annual report in order to correct misapprehensions

---

[90] See below.   [91] Aspinall, pp. 382–3.
[92] This practice became common during the 20th c.; see Matthew, p. 54.

arising because information about the department was inaccessible.[93] As well, before the turn of the century several departments began to publish their own journals.[94] After its approval by Parliament, David Lloyd George initiated an official lecture campaign in 1912 in support of the National Insurance scheme.[95] Some government departments even created information divisions. The Office of Special Inquiries and Reports at the Board of Education, for example, dated from 1895. However, it had numerous and varied responsibilities and maintained little direct contact with the public, only supplying 'information to individuals so far as this . . . [was] consistent with other calls upon its time'.[96] Until the First World War the government had only limited experience in the large-scale dissemination of non-partisan information, which the development of new mass media and the growth of literacy had recently made possible. Any official publicity emanating from Whitehall was the responsibility of permanent officials as part of their regular duties, and expenditure was reportedly negligible.[97]

Expanding government activities and the consequent increase in the volume of data flowing into and out of Whitehall did ensure, however, that the subject of government information was given serious consideration in the Edwardian period. A standing House of Commons Select Committee on Official Publications, created in 1906 to oversee and effect economies in the preparation of parliamentary reports, was highly critical of the disjointed manner in which papers were distributed and advertised. It wanted the entire process removed from the control of commercial agents and centralized in the HMSO. As existing contracts could not be terminated until 1915, there was little scope for improvement in this area, nor could much be done to centralize government press advertising in general.[98]

Before the First World War the Stationery Office also lacked authority to compel other departments to use it as a channel for the insertion of press advertisements. As a result, many ministries entered into

[93] Raymond Nottage, 'The Post Office: A Pioneer of Big Business', *Public Administration*, 37 (1959), 57–9.

[94] A Board of Trade *Journal* was created in 1886, the Ministry of Labour *Gazette* in 1893.

[95] Marjorie Ogilvy-Webb, *The Government Explains* (1965), 48.

[96] 'Memorandum upon the Office of Special Inquiries and Reports', Oct. 1908, Public Record Office (hereafter PRO), Board of Education Papers, ED 23/588.

[97] Hansard, 24 May 1921, vol. 142, col. 36. W. R. Codling, the controller of the Stationery Office, noted in 1921 that it was impossible to provide accurate statistics on pre-war advertising expenditure; *Report from the Select Committee on Publications and Debates Reports* (11 Aug. 1921), Proceedings, 17 Mar. 1921, mins. 140–1.   [98] See below, p. 57.

independent agreements with commercial firms.[99] Incensed by the varying levels of rates charged under these arrangements, the Treasury began
to lobby in 1913 for greater centralization of control in the HMSO.
Stressing the benefits of a more streamlined approach, first on grounds of
economy and efficiency, and later by emphasizing the value of having an
expert department oversee the work, the Exchequer persuaded the Cabinet
to adopt the policy. However, as this decision was taken in August 1914,
and met with departmental opposition, it proved difficult to enforce.
Treasury pressure continued into 1915, but to no avail.[100]

Censorship and the distribution of information to the press were centralized during the First World War, but not in the HMSO. The Foreign
Office News Department, Home Office Press Bureau, and Neutral Press
Committee were created in the early months of the conflict to handle
these duties. A secret propaganda bureau stationed at Wellington House,
the home of the National Insurance Commission, was responsible for
influencing foreign opinion. Headed by the chairman of the commission,
the Liberal politician C. F. G. Masterman, it was staffed mainly by
prominent intellectuals, historians, and writers who concentrated their
efforts on reaching educated audiences through what purported to be
unofficial channels. Initially confident of public support, the government
did not establish specific machinery to disseminate propaganda on the
home front. Responsibility for maintaining domestic morale fell to voluntary organizations, of which there were many.[101] Several ministries did have
publicity bureaux, and/or distributed information independently.[102] Where
civil servants did not control the process, there was a tendency to employ
individuals with experience in journalism. George (later Lord) Riddell,
the chairman of the Newspaper Proprietors' Association (NPA), served
as an adviser to the government from the outset of the war, in 1915

[99] Letter to Controller, 9 Oct. 1913, PRO, Stationery Office Papers, STAT 14/18.
[100] Ibid. Treasury letter, 14 Aug. 1914; Controller's letter, 11 Sept. 1915, STAT 14/18.
'Government Advertising', Memorandum from the Treasury, G.T.8334, 15 Oct. 1919,
PRO, Cabinet Papers, CAB 24/90.
[101] Regarding these arrangements and the approach adopted by Wellington House see
Sanders and Taylor, pp. 15–54. Marquis, pp. 467–99. Haste, pp. 30–40. Squires, pp. 25–
34, 48–60. M. L. Sanders, 'Wellington House and British Propaganda during the First
World War', *Historical Journal*, 18/1 (1975), 119–46.
[102] The Admiralty, Air Ministry, Boards of Agriculture and Trade, Home Office, Na-
tional War Savings Committee, ministries of Food, Labour, Munitions, Reconstruction,
and Transport, and the War Office: H. V. Rhodes, 'Publicity Division: Preliminary Note on
Machinery', 3 Sept. 1938, Appendix G, PRO, Ministry of Information Papers, INF 1/709.
H. J. Creedy to H. Parker, 11 July 1923; 'Ministry of Pensions', 1923, PRO, Treasury
Papers, T 162/42/2862.

becoming the official press representative at the War Office and Admiralty.[103] The ministries of Munitions and Pensions also appointed journalists to their staffs.[104] Although prominent advertising executives, such as (Sir) Charles Higham,[105] were asked to assist in recruiting and war bonds propaganda and many departments employed agencies, it is noteworthy that professional agents did not serve in departments during the war.[106] This reflected the superior reputation of the press compared to advertising in these years.[107]

Mounting criticism in 1916 induced the Cabinet to reconsider the current propaganda arrangements. In January 1917 Lloyd George, by now Prime Minister and infamous for his close ties with the press, commissioned Robert Donald, editor of the *Daily Chronicle*, to investigate. He filed a damning report recommending greater centralization and the adoption of a more aggressive publicity policy. As a result, a Department of Information was established in February 1917. Although it absorbed Wellington House and the existing press bureaux, the division encountered difficulties with the news department of the Foreign Office, as well as its own advisory committee composed of journalists, including Donald. In October the latter prepared yet another report which led to

[103] Chairman of the *News of the World* from 1903, Riddell helped settle the coal strike of 1912 and was close to Lloyd George. He was the British delegation's press liaison officer at the Paris Peace Conference of 1919 and the Washington Naval Conference of 1921. From 1919 to 1926 he chaired the Advisory Committee on Government Advertising. Riddell was President of the Advertising Association 1928–30. *Lord Riddell's War Diary 1914–1918* (1933). *Advertising World*, 58/6 (1930), 453–5. Marquis, pp. 472–3. Sanders and Taylor, p. 31.

[104] 'Ministry of Pensions', 1923, T 162/42/2862; Rhodes, 'Publicity Division', 3 Sept. 1938, INF 1/709.

[105] Director of his own firm, Higham was one of the best-known agents of the day and the first to become an MP; *Advertising World*, 47/5 (1925); 57/4 (1930), 300–2; 58/1 (1930), 42; 59/3 (1931), 240–5. *The Times*, 27 Dec. 1938. He participated in wartime campaigns, joined the secret government subcommittee established to deal with publicity during the railway strike of 1919, and assisted during other industrial crises: Supply and Transport Committee, Minutes, TC(30), 12 Apr. 1921, min. 308, CAB 27/73. Higham's agency was employed by several departments during the inter-war period; see W. Vaughan to K. Clark, 17 Jan. 1941, INF 1/341 and p. 33. He had close ties with the Conservative Party's publicity organization (see Hollins, p. 37) and was a leading advocate of government publicity. Charles Frederick Higham, *Looking Forward* (1920), and *Advertising*, 220–1. *Advertising World*, 51/3 (1927), 370–6; 70/11 (1938), 7. *The Times*, 25 Apr. 1933.

[106] T. B. Lawrence (ed.), *What I Know about Advertising* (1921), p. vii. Frank Presbrey, *The History and Development of Advertising* (New York, 1929), 107. National Savings Committee (NSC) to Treasury, 19 Nov. 1920, T 162/42/2862. T. R. Nevett claims that the 'most notable feature' of advertising in the First World War was the 'extent to which its men were used by the government in the national interest': *Advertising in Britain* (1982), 141–2. The very fact that agents remained outside Whitehall would seem to suggest the opposite.

[107] See below, pp. 31–2.

the formation of a Ministry of Information in 1918 under Lord Beaver-brook. Northcliffe, the other great press lord, took charge of a new Department of Enemy Propaganda at Crewe House.[108]

The recruitment of the press barons and the successful approach to propaganda which they supposedly introduced have been highlighted and overrated ever since. Credited with securing the Allied victory, Beaver-brook and Northcliffe were elevated to the status of great propagandists, creating, or perhaps reinforcing the view of the newspaper proprietor as publicity expert.[109] In fact, the appointments and the new administrative structure introduced had a relatively limited impact. Journalists had long been assisting in official propaganda and the ministry did not develop an approach significantly different from that pursued to date.[110] Moreover, the dissemination of information to the home front remained outside its domain. A purportedly non-official body, the National War Aims Com-mittee, was established by the government in August 1917 to co-ordinate voluntary efforts, and counteract war-weariness and the burgeoning peace movement.[111] Departments which already had publicity machinery retained it, a number creating bureaux during the final stages of the war.[112]

Of far greater significance, in the long term, was the fact that in 1917 the Government succumbed to pressure from the newspaper trade, which was complaining of political favouritism and inequities in the distribution of departmental notices, and agreed to implement the Cabinet decision of 1914 and concentrate control over government advertising in the Station-ery Office.[113] In June, the HMSO appointed James Willing Limited as the government agent.[114] That autumn, an Advisory Committee on Gov-ernment Advertising (ACGA), representative of outside experts, was estab-lished to assist the Stationery Office in supervising these arrangements.

The ACGA was apparently the brainchild of the Advertising Manager of W. H. Smith's.[115] Although consultation with outside experts was

---

[108] Sanders and Taylor, pp. 56–65, 70–89.

[109] See below, pp. 31–2, and Reginald Pound and Geoffrey Harmsworth, *Northcliffe* (1959), 612–69; A. J. P. Taylor, *Beaverbrook* (1972), 138–56.

[110] Sanders and Taylor have shown the continuity of approach between Wellington House and later organizations. Also see Sanders, pp. 119–46.

[111] Sanders and Taylor, pp. 65–70.

[112] e.g. the Air Ministry and the Ministry of Pensions.

[113] Circular letter, 19 Jan. 1917; Minute, 15 June 1917; letter from Baldwin, 26 June 1917, STAT 14/18. Treasury Memorandum, G.T.8334, CAB 24/90.

[114] *Report from the Select Committee on Publications and Debates Reports* (11 Aug. 1921), Proceedings, 17 Mar. 1921, mins. 144–8. Scorgie, 'Press Advertising: Brief Summary of the History of Stationery Office Contracts', 15 Dec. 1938, Appendix 1, T 162/530/40020/1.

[115] A. L. Screech to Controller, 29 Jan. 1917, STAT 14/18.

hardly a novel prospect,[116] the concept of employing an advisory body composed of non-government officials was a relatively new idea, but one which was gaining support within Whitehall. The Machinery of Government Committee established under Lord Haldane in July 1917, to investigate the length and limits of ministerial responsibilities, delineated ten areas into which the business of government should fall. Alongside basic functions, such as external affairs and finance, the State was expected to engage in 'research and information'. In its modern commercial context, research is generally coupled with development, and refers to gathering information in order to provide a proper basis for formulating future policy. Although the wording seems redundant, this was what the Haldane committee had in mind. Clarification is crucial, for if 'research and information' connoted research and development, it did not mean the acquisition of material for dissemination to the public. Rather, the committee believed that government officials should endeavour to acquire a greater knowledge of policy requirements, and thus attached 'special importance' to 'cooperation with advisory bodies in matters which bring departments into contact with the public'.[117]

Special expert committees were very popular in the inter-war decades. The Ministry of Health, created in 1919, had appointed over one hundred of them by 1939.[118] In 1940, the Oxford University Politics Research Committee attributed the general proliferation of advisory bodies over the period to a corresponding expansion in government services, which, by providing civil servants with novel tasks and responsibilities, while at the same time necessitating alterations in techniques of administration, had increased the need for external advice.[119] Given the dearth of above-board machinery by which government could gauge public opinion,[120] the consultative process so institutionalized provided officials with a valuable means of obtaining information and expertise. Harold Laski believed no better formula existed for the 'reciprocal training of civil servants and the

---

[116] Samuel H. Beer, *Modern British Politics* (1965), 7. J. D. Stewart, *British Pressure Groups* (Oxford, 1958), 6–8.

[117] Ministry of Reconstruction, *Report of the Machinery of Government Committee*, Cmd. 9230 (1918), 22–35.

[118] R. V. Vernon and N. Mansbergh (eds.), *Advisory Bodies* (1940), 53. They were believed to be essential: Hansard, 26 Feb. 1919, vol. 112, cols. 1836–7.

[119] Vernon and Mansbergh, pp. 19–21.

[120] George Gallup developed his opinion polls in the mid-1930s, but they were not introduced into Britain until 1937. Mass-Observation, which endeavoured to survey society through less direct means, was founded in the same year.

public'.[121] External assistance was particularly necessary in areas such as publicity where officials lacked training, experience, and precedents to cite for guidance. As the HMSO did not intend to enlist special staff to handle government advertising contracts, it is not surprising that an advisory committee was created.

All of the appointments to the ACGA were of a personal nature as opposed to being representative of particular interests. Yet its members were drawn almost entirely from the newspaper trade. Riddell served as chairman and was assisted by Ernest Benn of the Periodical Trade Press and Weekly Newspaper Proprietors' Association, Frank Bird of the Newspaper Society, John Mudie of the Scottish and Irish press, and two MPs, John Boyton and J. S. Higham. Although its membership changed slightly, the ACGA retained the same type of composition over its ten-year existence, the HMSO refusing to appoint delegates from specific organizations.[122] In practice, however, the committee was representative; when Bird resigned in 1922, for example, the Newspaper Society was invited to choose a new member.[123]

The ACGA was responsible for counselling the controller of the HMSO 'as to the newspapers in which Government advertisements . . . should be inserted with a view to securing the necessary publicity for each particular class of advertisement with due regard to economy and to avoiding any selection of papers for merely political or personal reasons'.[124] That newspapermen were recruited for this task might seem somewhat illogical. They could hardly be termed impartial on the subject of press advertising. On the other hand, the impetus behind centralization had come from the NPA. By giving journalists a degree of control over the procedure the Government may have been attempting to distance itself from any future controversy. Accusations of conflict of interest could also

---

[121] Quoted in Sir Harold Bellman, 'The Traditions of the Public Services: Can They be Extended to Business?', *Public Administration*, 14 (1936), 130–1.

[122] After Boyton and Higham were not re-elected, the Select Committee on Publications suggested that MPs should sit on the committee as public representatives rather than as individuals: *Report from the Select Committee on Publications and Debates Reports* (11 Aug. 1921), para. 7; Proceedings, 17 Mar. 1921, mins. 230–2. The HMSO disagreed: Scorgie to Treasury, 24 Sept. 1921, STAT 14/24. None the less, in 1922 Charles Barrie and Vernon Hartshorn were appointed 'as MPs': A. W. Hurst to Codling, 19 Oct. 1921; Treasury Minute, 8 Apr. 1922, STAT 14/24. Offering to resign, Higham was informed that his appointment had been 'personal': Higham to Screech, 8, 15 Dec. 1922; reply, 13 Dec. 1922, STAT 14/24.

[123] Codling to F. Phillips, 30 Jan. 1922; Treasury Minute, 27 May 1922, STAT 14/24.

[124] Treasury Minute, 19 Oct. 1917, STAT 14/24.

be countered by the argument that the trade possessed the greatest expertise in this area. Newspaper advertising was the chief form of publicity of the day, other mass media having yet to be developed to a sufficient extent or to make considerable headway in the market-place.[125]

The members were deemed so sufficiently qualified that it was not considered necessary to include members of the advertising profession on the committee. The Incorporated Society of British Advertisers requested permission to nominate delegates, arguing that the committee could only be properly balanced if it were representative of both 'buyers' and 'sellers'. Apprehensive that other groups would advance similar claims, the Treasury refused to concede this point.[126] More tellingly, Riddell found the suggestion incomprehensible. He could not fathom 'what advertisers have to do with the work of this Committee'! Responding to the society's assertion that it had 'many experienced publicity buyers among its membership', Riddell retorted that this was no measure of expertise:

The mere fact that a man is an advertiser does not imply that he has special qualifications as a watchdog, charged with the duty of seeing that public departments do not place their advertising with a view to personal or political advantage. Nor does this fact imply that he is an authority on advertising. Unfortunately there are many foolish advertisers.[127]

Riddell's comments are indicative of the poor reputation of advertising and advertising agents in the period. If the First World War gave propaganda a bad name, advertising already had one. Long regarded as the purview of quacks and swindlers, it was becoming respectable only slowly, as the industry's attempts to curb abuses, set standards, and organize itself into a profession began to take effect.[128] That Riddell did not regard commercial agents as experts in advertising also reflected the fact that the profession was still in its infancy. While firms laid claim to being staffed by experts,[129] the qualifications required of a good agent were not clear. It

---

[125] David S. Dunbar estimates that in 1912 advertising expenditure in Britain totalled £15 million; £13 million of this was directed toward press advertisements, the balance going to posters and transport. By 1920, £28 million out of £31 million was spent on press advertising: 'Estimates of Total Advertising Expenditures in the U.K. before 1949', *Journal of Advertising History*, 1 (1977), 9–11.

[126] H. T. Humphries to the Treasury, 26 Sept. 1921; Hurst to Codling, 19 Oct. 1921; Codling to Riddell, 20 Jan. 1922, STAT 14/24.

[127] Riddell to Codling, 25 Jan. 1922, STAT 14/24.

[128] E. S. Turner, *The Shocking History of Advertising* (1952), 100–12, 118–20, 149. Elliott, pp. 196–8. Nevett, pp. 110–37. LeMahieu, pp. 155–7.

[129] Charles Higham, 'The Advertising Agent: His Value and Functions', in Lawrence, p. 45.

seemed, so the how-to books of the day implied, that anyone with a
measure of common sense and intelligence could be successful in the
profession.[130] Dorothy L. Sayers, of the S. H. Benson agency, certainly
conveyed this impression in her 1933 novel, *Murder Must Advertise*, when
she had her popular fictional detective Lord Peter Wimsey masquerade as
an agency copy-writer. Within a month of joining a firm, the Balliol-
educated sportsman, who had taken on the job because he thought 'advertising might be good fun', had developed the most effective publicity
scheme his agency had ever prosecuted.[131] The most influential practitioners of the day lacked training and/or experience in the field. The
'advertising giants' Charles Higham and William Crawford provide a case
in point.[132] Successful directors of their own agencies, both were highly
respected in the profession and served as advisers to a number of government departments over the period, yet neither had received a university
education, nor had any background in journalism or the arts.[133] Frank Pick,
the director and later vice-chairman of the London Passenger Transport
Board (LPTB), who was responsible for the development of its innovative and influential publicity during the inter-war decades, was a solicitor
and statistician. He had been placed in charge of Underground publicity
in 1907, only because he had complained about its quality![134] Similarly,
Stephen Tallents, a career civil servant without practical experience in advertising, was one of the most important figures in government publicity

---

[130] See Sir William Crawford, *How to Succeed in Advertising* (1931), 6–9.

[131] Dorothy L. Sayers, *Murder Must Advertise* (1933), 227–31. She was not alone in assuming that the 'university man' would have little trouble mastering the profession. Herbert
Morgan (see below, p. 126) believed the 'best way to secure efficient leadership in advertising' was to recruit more personnel from the universities: *Advertising World*, 47/6 (1925),
474–5.   [132] *Advertising World*, 66/2 (1934), 11.

[133] They appeared so often in *Advertising World* that a reader requested that they be
omitted from at least one issue: 59/5 (1931), 340. On Higham, see above, n. 105. Crawford
founded an agency in 1914, which by 1950 had thirty-seven offices world-wide. He held
several posts in advertising associations and published studies, including *How to Succeed in
Advertising*, and, with Charles Higham, *Advertising and the Man in the Street* (Leeds, 1929).
He was credited with improving the reputation of advertising by raising creative standards:
Judith Freeman, 'The Publicity of the Empire Marketing Board 1926–1933', *Journal of
Advertising History*, 1 (1977), 14. In the early 1920s, Crawford advised the MH (see below,
p. 127). He was vice-chairman of the EMB publicity committee, established close ties with
Tallents, and was credited with the success of EMB campaigns: *Advertising World*, 53/3 (1928),
274–6. He was deputy chairman of the Post Office publicity committee from 1931, and
official publicity adviser to the Ministry of Agriculture 1929–50: G. H. Saxon Mills, *There
is a Tide . . .* (1954). *Advertising World*, 60/1 (1931), 70.

[134] On Pick's influence see below, pp. 52–3, and Christian Barman, *The Man Who Built
London Transport* (1979), 25–41, 202–12. T. C. Barker and Michael Robbins, *A History of
London Transport*, ii. *The Twentieth Century* (1974), 140–8, 250, 285. Freeman, pp. 12–14.

in the inter-war years. He was secretary to the Cabinet committee dealing with the General Strike of 1926 and, as secretary to the EMB from 1926 to 1933, supervised its publicity arrangements. In 1933, Tallents became the first public relations officer of the Post Office, concurrently acting as chief publicity assistant to the Supply and Transport Committee of the Cabinet, a secret organization responsible for handling domestic crises. In 1935, Tallents established the public relations division at the BBC, and was involved in the creation of the BBC Foreign Service. As Director-General Designate of the MOI from 1936 to 1938, he was responsible for the planning of the wartime publicity organization. In 1932, he published *The Projection of England*, which advocated the pursuit of 'dignified' British publicity abroad.[135] As this discussion should indicate, the leading advertising practitioners of the period were not professionals.

Agents may also have been excluded from the committee because, on paper at least, the ACGA had little to do with government publicity arrangements *per se*. It had not been established to counsel individual ministries on their requirements—on whether they should place advertisements or conduct campaigns—but rather to assist the HMSO in securing a favourable contract for the insertion of official notices in the press. On the other hand, Riddell believed the ACGA had executive functions; it had been 'set up to control, not to obey orders', or merely provide advice.[136] Elaborate plans for the centralization of all departmental advertising were drafted by the committee and submitted for Treasury approval in the autumn of 1917. Although fully in agreement with the proposals, the Treasury lacked authority to compel departments to consult with the ACGA, and/or employ the government advertising agent.[137] This rendered the committee virtually powerless. The problem was not rectified until after the war, when the question of centralization came before the Cabinet in its consideration of the future of the wartime propaganda machinery.

In October 1918 Beaverbrook suggested to the Cabinet that the Ministry of Information should be retained in the post-war period as a domestic propaganda organization.[138] Although some of its functions were transferred to the news department of the Foreign Office, the ministry

---

[135] See Taylor, *Projection*, 105–13; Ian McLaine, *Ministry of Morale* (1979), 13–18; Freeman, pp. 12–14.

[136] Riddell to George Barstow, 2 Mar. 1926, T 161/140/12336.

[137] Treasury letter, 8 Jan. 1918; Codling to ACGA, 12 Jan. 1918; Treasury to Riddell, 14 Feb. 1918, STAT 14/18.

[138] 'Functions of the Ministry of Information on the cessation of hostilities', G.T.6007, CAB 24/67.

was closed soon after the cessation of hostilities. Crewe House and the National War Aims Committee were also dissolved.[139] Several historians have argued that these decisions reflected the Government's distaste for its success at propaganda during the war.[140] There are strong grounds for this claim; yet, in focusing on the disbandment of these bodies, analysts have overlooked the fact that the Cabinet decision did not affect the departmental publicity organizations established between 1914 and 1918. The immediate post-war period actually saw an expansion in this area, with the appointment of full-time intelligence and/or press officers in a number of ministries.[141] As well, on a number of occasions in 1918–19 the Cabinet gave consideration to the formation of information machinery to serve Whitehall as a whole.

Concerned by the supposed spread of Bolshevism and the apparently related problem of increasing industrial unrest in the months following the Armistice,[142] the Cabinet resolved in February 1919 to retain the Home Office Press Bureau temporarily to censor cables for subversive propaganda.[143] It was also decided to create a secret committee to 'take in hand not only the preparations and organization necessary to meet a strike but also publicity and propaganda'.[144] The activities of the Supply and Transport Committee and its propaganda branch during the railway strike of 1919, the coal strikes of 1920–1, and the General Strike of 1926 have been documented adequately elsewhere.[145] While the creation of this machinery is relevant to this study, in the sense that it provides an early example of government using publicity as a policy alternative (in this case in place of legislation or coercion), the Supply and Transport organization constitutes an aberration rather than the norm. Although it existed

---

[139] Cabinet Minutes, WC501(11), 13 Nov. 1918, CAB 23/8. Hansard, 24 Feb. 1919, vol. 112, cols. 1365–7. [140] Sanders and Taylor, pp. 248–9.

[141] Examples include the ministries of Labour (1918) and Health (1919); War Office (1919); and Board of Trade (1920). A salaried press secretary was appointed to Buckingham Palace in 1918: Kenneth Rose, *King George V* (1984), 227. By 1920 at least 47 staff in 11 departments were engaged in unspecified publicity work, at an annual cost in salaries of £21,000; see replies to a Treasury inquiry of Nov. 1920, T 162/42/2862. Departmental expenditure on press advertising in 1920 was approximately £750,000: 'Summary of Returns', Mar. 1920, T 161/3/213.

[142] Reports reaching the Cabinet indicated the problems were closely linked; see 'Bolshevik Propaganda', G.T.5986, 12 Oct. 1918, CAB 24/66; 'The Progress of Bolshevism in Europe', G.T.6857, 28 Jan. 1919, CAB 24/75. Sir Basil Thomson, *The Scene Changes* (1939), 376–87.

[143] 'Proposed Closing of the Press Bureau', G.T.6742, 3 Feb. 1919, CAB 24/74. Cabinet Minutes, WC531, 12 Feb. 1919, CAB 23/9.

[144] Cabinet Minutes, WC521, 28 Jan. 1919; WC525, 4 Feb. 1919, CAB 23/9.

[145] See Keith Middlemas, *Politics in Industrial Society* (1979), 130–2, 153–8, 352–4.

on a semi-permanent basis over the entire inter-war period, the propaganda committee only functioned during crises, that is, in what might be termed war-like situations. Its creation did not represent the adoption of a consistent or long-term domestic publicity policy. Moreover, despite the fact that it was concerned mainly with influencing the British public, the organization was secret. Unlike the departmental publicity organizations which came to exist alongside it, the Supply and Transport organization was not an exercise in above-board public relations.

Similarly, attempts made to censor the media during periods of industrial unrest or otherwise do not fall into the category of information which government openly disseminated or, more to the point, wanted to be seen distributing. This is not to overlook the fact that the withholding of information is a form of public relations. Government departments could and did exercise self-censorship, choosing not to provide data or reveal information for political reasons and/or to protect their public image. However, the absence of both general debate on the matter within Whitehall and the formulation of guidelines governing departmental publicity activities is indicative of the fact that such situations were confronted as they arose, generally behind the scenes.

During the post-war period the Cabinet also considered the possibility of forming more conventional types of information machinery. As noted, the Haldane report of 1918 advised all government departments to engage in research. In January 1919, H. A. L. Fisher, the President of the Board of Education, submitted a memorandum to the Cabinet advocating the creation of a new department to act as a 'central organ for scientific discovery and information . . . unburdened by the routine of current administration'.[146] When the issue was raised again in February, by the Under-Secretary for Air,[147] the Prime Minister appointed Auckland Geddes to investigate the advisability of adopting the proposal. Apparently overlooking the inference in Fisher's report to the need for greater co-ordination in government information services, Geddes noted that, as research work already fell within the purview of the Ministry of Reconstruction and the Privy Council, a new department was not required. He also rejected a further suggestion for the establishment of an 'unbiased authority' to which the public could turn with complaints against specific

---

[146] 'A Ministry of Research', Memorandum by the President of the Board of Education, 29 Jan. 1919, CAB 24/5.
[147] 'A Ministry of Research', Memorandum by the Under-Secretary of State for Air, G.T.6753, 4 Feb. 1919, CAB 24/74. Also see 'A Ministry of Research', Memorandum by the Secretary for Scotland, G.T.6863, 20 Feb. 1919, CAB 24/75.

ministries, observing that, if the Cabinet decided such an agency was needed, it should be attached to the Prime Minister's office.[148] No action was taken.

One month later, the directors of the Press Bureau, Sir Frank Swettenham and Sir Edward Cook, advised the Home Secretary, Edward Shortt, that as press censorship was soon to be abandoned the division should be closed.[149] When the matter came before the Cabinet, a number of ministers requested that the bureau be retained as a channel of information between government departments and the newspapers.[150] Shortt opposed this, claiming that an official organization could never be as effective as a press agency in distributing peacetime communiqués.[151] A Cabinet committee under his chairmanship decided to disband the press bureau at the end of April.[152] At this point, the Minister of Labour, R. S. Horne, suggested attaching a section of the organization to the publicity branch of his own ministry, where it would serve as a 'common mouthpiece' for Whitehall, by handling press relations, organizing advertising campaigns, and acting as a central distributing agency for all government information.[153] Asserting that the task was inappropriate to the Ministry of Labour, Shortt rejected the idea, observing that the press agencies would be hostile to the competition.[154] Other ministers also opposed the proposal, stressing that they preferred to control their own dealings with the public. Accordingly, the Cabinet decided that government publicity arrangements should not be centralized,[155] and, in so doing, set what was to become an important precedent.

Although hostile to the idea of the State maintaining a press bureau, the newspaper trade was at this time lobbying for greater centralization in the allocation of official press advertisements. Expenditure in this area totalled just under £750,000 in 1919, a mere £150,000 of which was placed through the HMSO-appointed agents.[156] After the NPA sent

---

[148] 'Research and Information', Memorandum by A. C. Geddes, G.T.6756, 6 Feb. 1919, CAB 24/74.
[149] 'Proposed Closing of Press Bureau', Memorandum by the Home Secretary, G.T.6960, 10 Mar. 1919, CAB 24/76.
[150] Ibid. Cabinet Minutes, WC544, 13 Mar. 1919, CAB 23/9.
[151] Memorandum, 10 Mar. 1919, CAB 24/76.
[152] 'Closing of the Press Bureau', G.T.7062, 1 Apr. 1919, CAB 24/77.
[153] 'Central Agency for the Issue of Official Communiqués by Government Departments', Memorandum by the Minister of Labour, G.T.7154, 28 Apr. 1919, CAB 24/78.
[154] 'Central Agency for the Issue of Official Communiqués by Government Departments', Memorandum by the Home Secretary, G.T.7160, 30 Apr. 1919, CAB 24/78.
[155] Cabinet Minutes, WC561, 1 May 1919, CAB 23/10.
[156] 'Summary of Returns', c.Sept. 1920, T 161/3/213.

delegations to Downing Street in the autumn of 1919, the Prime Minister referred the question of government advertising to the Cabinet Committee on Home Affairs (CCHA).[157]

In a memorandum submitted to the CCHA, the Treasury acknowledged that to date departments had shown legitimate grounds for refusing to use the government advertising agents, as the contractors had been 'unable to furnish expert advice'. However, as this problem was now being rectified by the inclusion of an expertise clause in the new contracts, there was no further 'justification for not employing [the appointed agents] . . . on all Government advertising and publicity work'.[158] Departmental representatives present when the committee considered this paper were willing to concede the point with regard to advertising, which they defined as the insertion of notices and advertisements in the press, but raised the 'strongest possible objection' to any attempt to centralize the control of publicity, that is, the distribution of news and information. The Minister of Agriculture, Lord Lee, accused the Treasury of having confused the two functions: 'the advertising and news departments of a newspaper are entirely separate and distinct and it would be fatal to employ an advertisement agent to place news material.' Christopher Addison stated that 'he could not agree to the publicity work of the Ministry of Health being controlled by any other Department. Each Department must reply to criticisms . . . in its own way.' Indeed, it was claimed, editorial advertising had to be supervised from within the ministry concerned, as only the latter could possibly understand and interpret its own requirements. Because the HMSO could raise no suitable objection, the CCHA directed that, while 'advertising' should be centralized, responsibility for 'publicity' could remain in departmental hands.[159]

The concentration of control over advertising in the HMSO/ACGA did not result in any immediate economies, mainly because of the large expenditure of the Disposal Board in selling off war materials. Once this work had ceased in 1922, the volume of government press advertising did begin to decline, falling from approximately £390,000 in 1920 to £32,000

[157] ACGA to Treasury, 23 Sept. 1919, STAT 14/18.
[158] 'Government Advertising', Memorandum from the Treasury, G.T.8334, 15 Oct. 1919, CAB 24/90.
[159] CCHA, Minutes, HAC(43), 24 Oct. 1919, CAB 26/2. The ministries of Health and Munitions, the boards of Agriculture and Education, the War and Scottish Offices, the Treasury, the Admiralty, and the HMSO were represented. 'Government Advertising', Memorandum by the President of the Board of Agriculture and Fisheries, G.T.8390, 23 Oct. 1919, CAB 24/90.

by 1924.[160] There was a decrease in real volume as well, as the expertise clause had steadily increased the cost of the contract.[161]

A similar pattern emerged in the sphere of government publicity, as departments came under pressure from both the Treasury and parliament to abolish their wartime information divisions. In June 1921, ten ministries maintained press or publicity branches or employed staff in this area, spending £20,000 annually on salaries alone.[162] This machinery was a prime target for criticism in the post-war climate of austerity. From both ends of the political spectrum publicity bureaux were attacked as an extravagant waste of public money.[163] Aside from the rather different case of the administration's anti-strike propaganda, the legitimacy of government information services was not debated as a party or political issue. Public discussion did not centre on the question of whether departments should disseminate information, but rather on why special staff and/or machinery was needed for the task when neither had been common in Whitehall before the war. Members of Parliament were apparently more concerned by the fact that few ex-servicemen were recruited to these divisions than with whether departments were justified in engaging in any form of publicity at all.[164]

Accusations of political puffery did arise; there were a number of scandals concerning official publicity, and/or government information officers during the early 1920s. Aside from obvious political controversies, such as that surrounding the Foreign Office's publication of the Zinoviev letter in 1924 (which, in any case, was not a situation in which the publicity division of the department involved was accused of engaging in political propaganda), the infractions tended to be relatively minor and innocuous; the press officer at the Post Office, for example, excited considerable comment in July 1923 when, hoping to attract attention to

[160] 'Government Advertising', 18 Feb. 1926, T 161/140/12336. Figures submitted in 1938 differ slightly but show the same degree of decline: N. G. Scorgie, 'Press Advertising', 15 Dec. 1938, Appendix 2, T 162/530/40020/1.
[161] Memorandum by H. E. Daney, 27 Sept. 1920, STAT 14/18.
[162] Hansard, 7 June 1921, vol. 142, cols. 1689–90.
[163] Hansard, 10 Nov. 1920, vol. 134, cols. 1208–9; 29 Nov. 1920, vol. 135, col. 949; 13 June 1921, vol. 143, cols. 8–11, 53; 14 June 1921, vol. 143, cols. 197–9; 30 July 1923; vol. 167, cols. 1028–9. *Third Report from the Select Committee on Estimates* (12 July 1922), Proceedings, 22 May 1922, mins. 104–14, 279–83. Even before the Geddes inquiry, the Cabinet 'laid down quite specifically' that a chief economy would be the disbandment of this machinery: Minute, 21 July 1920, PRO, Ministry of Health Papers, MH 55/27. Treasury to A. T. Davies, 10 Dec. 1920, T 162/42/2862.
[164] Hansard, 21 Mar. 1922, vol. 152, col. 272; 19 June 1922, vol. 155, col. 842; 27 July 1922, vol. 157, vol. 704.

the department, he issued a laudatory statement about the Postmaster-General to coincide with the latter's estimates address in Parliament.[165] Similarly, in March 1924, the intelligence officer of the Admiralty created a scandal after holding a press conference on Eastern trade routes, which was interpreted as propaganda for the Government's controversial policy on the Singapore naval base.[166] Crises of this nature were not common, however, as few departments were pursuing an active publicity policy.[167] This, coupled with the fact that puffery was condemned on all sides of the House of Commons,[168] may explain why the subject was never the centre of a general debate in Parliament. Similarly, as the Cabinet and the departments concerned treated such scandals on an individual basis, regarding them as mistakes, or aberrations from the norm, no guidelines were laid down governing the distribution of information by departments.

The Cabinet appears to have been more concerned with ensuring that government ministers were not seen to be active in this area. Wishing to distance itself from the practices of Lloyd George's tainted administration, Bonar Law's Cabinet passed a resolution in 1923 banning its members from submitting to the press signed articles on current topics. Stanley Baldwin endorsed this principle when he became Prime Minister that year.[169] By the late 1920s, ministers were questioning this limit on their powers of expression. Noting that leading members of the opposition were willing and able to use newspaper articles to condemn government actions and present alternative policies, several ministers argued that it was essential to the proper execution of their duties that they be allowed to present their views on matters 'on which it was desirable to enlighten the public'.[170] The Cabinet resolved in 1928 that, provided he/she dealt only with departmental issues, a minister could publish articles to 'supplement means already used' for informing the public of government policies.[171] None the less, and chiefly for political reasons, the privilege

---

[165] See below, p. 86.

[166] Cabinet Minutes, C(18)24, 5 Mar. 1924; C(19)24, 12 Mar. 1924, CAB 23/47. 'Communication of Information to the Press', Note by the First Lord of the Admiralty, C.P.162(24), 7 Mar. 1924, CAB 24/165. *The Times*, 4 Mar. 1924. Hansard, 5 Mar. 1924, vol. 170, cols. 1395, 1557–62.

[167] By 1923 only 6 departments employed any form of publicity staff: Hansard, 15 Nov. 1923, vol. 168, cols. 458–9.   [168] See e.g. below, pp. 86–7.

[169] Cabinet Minutes, C3(23), 26 Jan. 1923, CAB 23/45. 'Cabinet Ministers and the Press', Note by the Lord Privy Seal, 24 Apr. 1924, C.P.265(24), CAB 24/166. Cabinet Minutes, C28(24), 29 Apr. 1924, CAB 23/48. The post-war period also witnessed the stricter imposition of Cabinet secrecy and tighter controls over disclosure: Middlemas, p. 363. Yet limiting a Cabinet minister's ability to comment on the activities of his/her department was hardly the same thing.

[170] Cabinet Minutes, C52(28), 21 Nov. 1928, CAB 23/59.   [171] Ibid.

was not extended to other media, such as broadcasting. In 1929, for example, the Controversy Committee of the BBC decided that ministerial broadcasts should always be given by civil servants, with ministers only participating in discussions or speaking on subjects which were not of a party political nature.[172]

Lack of public controversy in the 1920s reflected the dearth of organized government publicity in the domestic sphere. Many departments were engaged in promoting and encouraging the publicity activities of local authorities and voluntary organizations;[173] however, large-scale official campaigns were confined to specific causes, such as the marketing of Empire produce and the promotion of British industries. Ironically, it was the specialist nature of these schemes which undermined the authority exercised by the ACGA over all official press advertising, and thus resulted in an even greater decentralization in government publicity arrangements by mid-decade than had prevailed earlier.

In 1921, the Department of Overseas Trade (DOT) was accorded responsibility for publicizing the British Industries Fair, receiving its first grant for this purpose in 1925–6.[174] On the recommendation of an advisory committee dominated by businessmen, the department made independent arrangements for Charles Higham to conduct its £25,000 campaign, which he decided should consist mainly of display advertisements in the press.[175] The DOT made these plans without consulting the ACGA. This was the Stationery Office's fault; Codling had forgotten to inform the DOT of the existence of the committee. Faced with a *fait accompli*, the Treasury at first tried to ignore complaints from the ACGA and, when this proved impossible, defended the actions of the DOT, noting the special nature of the campaign and the fact that most of the advertising was to be conducted abroad.[176] Riddell reacted angrily, asserting that it was ridiculous for the government to maintain an advisory committee which could be ignored every time a department planned an extraordinary campaign.[177] Just as the ACGA had counselled against allowing only one agency to hold the government advertising contract,

---

[172] Hollins, pp. 335, 343.   [173] e.g. MAF and MH; see below, pp. 126, 201.

[174] 'British Industries Fair: Publicity for: Expenditure on', Memorandum by the President of the Board of Trade, C.P.14(28), 24 Jan. 1928, CAB 24/192. W. M. Hill to J. Cairncross, 2 Feb. 1939, T 162/530/40020/2.

[175] Codling to the Treasury, 9 Nov. 1925; T 161/140/12336. *Advertising World*, 51/3 (1927), 370–6.

[176] J. R. Chambers to A. E. Banham, 1 Jan., 10 Nov. 1926; Banham to A. W. Hurst, 8 Jan. 1926, T 161/140/12336.

[177] Riddell to Warren Fisher, 24 Feb. 1926, T 161/140/12336.

lest it acquire enough financial influence over the press to turn an administration out of office,[178] Riddell warned the Treasury of the 'abuses' likely
to 'creep in' were departments permitted to spend large sums on newspaper advertising without the supervision of 'some independent body'.
The ACGA had been established, he claimed, because 'it was thought
necessary in the public interest to make . . . restrictions'. Contending that
a serious principle was at stake, he requested that the matter be referred
to the Cabinet.[179] Having been appeased by assurances from the Treasury
that all future DOT activities would be subject to its approval,[180] the
committee resigned *en masse* in December 1926 when the newly created
Empire Marketing Board, 'having regard to its novel functions and special needs', was given permission by a 'higher authority' to assume control over its own publicity arrangements.[181]

Riddell claimed that government departments had resented the inter-
ference of his committee.[182] Yet it does not appear that the EMB, which
had been established to encourage the sale of Commonwealth produce in
Britain as compensation for the government's failure to implement a
promised preferential tariff,[183] was permitted to follow an independent
course because of dissatisfaction with the ACGA. Although some Treasury officials believed the committee had been inactive and biased, others
praised its efforts and expressed apprehension over its demise lest the
Government had alienated influential members of the press.[184] As well,
neither the Treasury nor the HMSO had abandoned its support for
centralization. Indeed, continued Stationery Office control over press

[178] Memorandum by Daney, 27 Sept. 1920, STAT 14/18.

[179] Riddell to Fisher, 24 Feb. 1926; Riddell to Barstow, 2, 6 Mar. 1926, T 161/140/
12336.

[180] The Treasury provided no guarantee, but smoothed the waters, while at the same
time informing Riddell that the committee lacked executive authority: Banham to Hurst, 8
Jan. 1926; Barstow to Riddell, 1, 5 Mar. 1926, T 161/140/12336. The DOT was persuaded
to consult with the ACGA in 1926: Banham to Evans, 20 Mar. 1926; C. L. Stocks to
William Clark, 30 Mar. 1926; Stocks to Barstow, 19 Apr. 1926; Riddell to Barstow, 16 Apr.
1926, T 161/140/12336.

[181] The EMB was supposed to entrust the technical aspects of its campaigns to the
ACGA: Barstow to R. McNeill, 20 Apr. 1926, T 161/140/12336. However, after arguing
that it alone understood what was required, the board was permitted to handle its own
arrangements; Memorandum, *c.*July 1926, PRO, Colonial Office Papers, CO 758/101/5.
L. S. Amery to Riddell, 12 Nov. 1926, T 161/140/12336. The ACGA resigned on 31 Dec.
1926; Riddell to the Prime Minister, STAT 14/24.

[182] Riddell to Barstow, 6 Mar. 1926, T 161/140/12336.

[183] Promotion of Empire goods in Britain was supposed to place Commonwealth countries in a better economic position to purchase English products; *Advertising World*, 51/3
(1927), 397–9. John M. Mackenzie, *Propaganda and Empire* (Manchester, 1984), 107–9.

[184] Stocks to Hurst, 28 July 1926; reply, 29 July 1926, T 161/479/29573/02.

advertising was viewed as being essential from an economic perspective. Departments acting on their own behalf incurred much higher costs on press advertising than the HMSO; they were charged commercial rates set under a 1921 price-fixing agreement between newspaper owners and advertising agencies, whereas the HMSO, which had entered into contracts before price-fixing had come into effect, was exempt from it. Advertisements placed through the HMSO-appointed agents were handled at a commission ranging from 2.5 to 5 per cent, whereas the commercial rate averaged 10 per cent.[185]

In fact, relatively few departments ceased to employ the government agents to place their press advertisements.[186] Still, an important precedent had been set. Departments such as the EMB were eliminating the barrier constructed between advertising and publicity. Once display advertisements were being used for the distribution of official information, the distinction drawn by the CCHA was superfluous. Departments began to argue that their advertising requirements could not be met under a centrally controlled contract secured by tender. Agents had to be assessed in terms of the publicity to be conducted, with quality not cost determining choice. Official advertising had become 'a question of exercising a judgment and discrimination born of experience in the public reaction to this or that type of appeal, of drawing, [and] of copy'.[187] It followed logically from such arguments that the procedure for choosing agents had to be placed in the hands of experts. Not surprisingly the DOT, which had not recruited specially qualified staff to handle its publicity arrangements, quickly formed an advisory committee to supervise its campaign. The EMB did employ journalists and publicists within its organization,[188] but also established a similar body. These committees served a less explicitly critical function than the ACGA; rather than exercising control over expenditure, they counselled their respective departments on how to employ publicity.

Commenting years later on the demise of Riddell's committee, N. G. Scorgie, the deputy controller of the HMSO, observed: 'the history of the break away of departments . . . from . . . centralisation is mainly the

---

[185] See Scorgie, 'Note on the Trade Agreement', and 'Press Advertising', 15 Dec. 1938, T 162/530/40020/1.

[186] By 1937, only five departments had entered into independent contracts; see below, p. 230.

[187] See arguments advanced by journalist Francis Meynell in 'On the Organization of Official Advertising', Mar. 1934, T 162/978/30201.

[188] e.g. A. P. Ryan of the *Daily Telegraph* and J. D. Woodruff of *The Times* were recruited on an unestablished basis to assist in press publicity.

history of the growth of the influence of individual publicists, external or internal, in the councils of the departments concerned.'[189] As this statement implies, the publicity advisory committees established in the DOT and EMB (and subsequently in several other departments in Whitehall) also differed in composition from the ACGA. Yet Scorgie's remarks are misleading, for none of the panels created in the inter-war years were dominated by publicists, that is, advertising agents. The DOT's committee was composed primarily of businessmen.[190] Aside from William Crawford, who served as its vice-chairman, the advisory body formed by the EMB was made up of executives of large companies which engaged in advertising (for example, Sir Woodman Burbidge, the Chairman of Harrods, and Frank Pick of London Transport), as well as representatives of organizations directly involved in colonial affairs. Thus other members included Viscount Burnham of the Empire Press Union, Sir William Perring of the Chamber of Trade, and Sir William Furse of the Imperial Institute.[191] Publicity buyers, rather than advertising practitioners, were the type of experts recruited to these and similar committees established elsewhere in Whitehall.[192] This mirrored the composition of other official advisory bodies in the period,[193] and reflected the type of advice that departments were thought to require. Technical information could be obtained from any advertising agency; what officials needed was access to individuals with a knowledge of the market-place and experience in dealing with the agencies available; in other words, their commercial counterparts, not their prospective employees. Where 'publicists' were included on committees, they were generally agency proprietors, Crawford being the prime example. In response to criticism, and conflict of interest queries, the Treasury reported honestly in 1934 that there was 'no evidence' that advertising agents served on these bodies 'to an undesirable extent'.[194]

Following the resignation of the ACGA in 1926, no further attempts were made to centralize domestic publicity arrangements until well into the 1930s. The idea that control over the distribution of information had to rest with the departments concerned had been accepted by the mid-1920s, even in the Exchequer. In 1924, the Treasury had appointed

---

[189] 'Press Advertising', Scorgie to J. Cairncross, 15 Dec. 1938, T 162/530/40020/1.

[190] The members were executives of large companies, such as Dunlop Rubber and Imperial Chemical: DOT to Treasury, 26 Mar. 1934, T 162/978/30201. Hill to Cairncross, 2 Feb. 1939, T 162/530/40020/2.

[191] EMB, *A Second Year's Progress: May 1927 to May 1928* (1928), 48.

[192] See below, p. 232.   [193] Vernon and Mansbergh, pp. 19–20.

[194] 'Government Publicity', Apr. 1934, T 162/978/30201.

a cinematograph adviser to the HMSO to act as a technical consultant on the production of all government films.[195] It had been intended originally that his section 'should serve as a centre of information for the Public Service generally and that the Stationery Office should be employed as the agent of Departments in the making of contracts in order to secure co-ordination'.[196] However, by 1927, the Treasury had altered the division's mandate so that any element of 'centralised *control* as distinct from centralised *advice* . . . disappeared'.[197] As departments were permitted to supervise their own arrangements, they developed the use of film independently from the HMSO. The EMB formed its own production unit in 1930, which, when transferred to the Post Office in 1933–4, became a centre of creative advice.[198] Paul Rotha, who served in the film unit, later observed that the government cinematograph adviser had 'mainly swept up the dust in official film vaults'.[199]

Departmental spending on press advertising did not undergo a substantial increase as a result of these decisions.[200] The extent to which other forms of publicity were employed and the total volume of government expenditure in this area are difficult to gauge, for aside from the DOT and EMB allocations, moneys designated for publicity purposes (if any) are not readily discernible in the estimates tabled by each department. On the rare occasions when questions were raised publicly regarding expenditure levels, the Treasury provided figures relating only to press advertising and/or staff costs.[201] Similarly, although reports indicate that, by 1930–1, twelve departments (not including the EMB) were employing at least part of the time of forty-four personnel on publicity or press work,[202] it is almost impossible to identify more than a handful of the officers concerned, or to ascertain where they were deployed in their

---

[195] Hansard, 15 Dec. 1925, vol. 189, col. 1172. 'The Government Cinematograph Adviser', 30 Jan. 1939, T 162/530/40020/2.

[196] *Report from the Select Committee on Estimates* (2 July 1934), Proceedings, 16 Apr. 1934, mins. 1043–50.   [197] Ibid., min. 1044.

[198] Ibid., mins. 1049–55. Also see Proceedings, 16 Apr. 1934, min. 759. The GPO unit also made films for other departments, thereby exciting the hostility of the trade; Swann, 'Grierson', p. 22.   [199] Rotha, *Documentary Diary*, 268.

[200] Most departments continued to employ the HMSO agents. Annual expenditure on press advertising averaged £85,000 from 1926 to 1930; Scorgie to Cairncross, 15 Dec. 1938, 'Press Advertisements', T 162/530/40020/1.

[201] See Hansard, 30 July 1925, vol. 187, cols. 609–10; and below, pp. 225–6.

[202] Replies to a Treasury inquiry in 1937 indicated that the number of civil servants deployed on publicity work in 1930–1 was: ADM (2), MAF (3), AIR (5), CO/DO (2), Board of Education (5), FO (7), MH (6), India Office (6), NSC (5), GPO (1), MT (1), WO (2); T 162/971/12190/01.

respective ministries and the nature of their duties.[203] In the Civil Service
lists of 1930–1, it appears that only five ministries had staff qualifying
under this heading.[204] Not until after 1933 is it possible to speak compre-
hensively and in comparative terms about the personnel employed.[205]
This is because the establishment of a public relations division in the Post
Office in 1933 spawned the creation of similar bureaux throughout
Whitehall, so that by 1939 virtually every department possessed some
form of established information or publicity machinery.

The timing of these last developments begs the question of their relationship to the emergence of organized government propaganda in other
countries, such as New Deal publicity in the United States, or the creation
of a domestic propaganda bureau in Nazi Germany. Philip Taylor has
shown that the use of propaganda by the fascist regimes in Europe did
influence the manner in which Britain developed publicity abroad in this
period.[206] Certainly, the 'Continental flight from democracy' 'set people
"thinking furiously" not only about the uses of government but the uses
and status of public officials in democratic communities'.[207] It is also
evident that the approach which government departments adopted
towards the British public reflected a reaction against the type of propaganda believed to be practised elsewhere. On the other hand, there
is little evidence to suggest that domestic publicity arrangements were
developed in direct response to the use of propaganda within other
countries.[208] Rather than reflecting a reactive new departure, the establishment of permanent public relations machinery in Whitehall represented
the culmination and continuation of a long process whereby officials and
politicians came to regard publicity as a necessary function of the government departments of a democratic State. Clearly, the growth of a
mass advertising industry in this period influenced this development. A
committee appointed by the Treasury in 1949 to examine domestic

---

[203] A perfect example is the MH. Although the department did not maintain a publicity
division in 1930, the two officers who handled press relations (see below, pp. 138–9) appear
in the Civil Service lists as an assistant principal and a higher clerical officer: *British Imperial
Calendar* (1930–1).
[204] Officers readily identifiable as publicity staff were: the Director of Naval Recruiting,
ADM; a press officer, AIR; publicity and intelligence officers, CO/DO; information officers,
India Office; and the publicity officer, NSC: ibid.   [205] See below, p. 225.
[206] Taylor, *Projection*, 123–6, 162–4, 182–5.
[207] Arthur L. Dakyns, 'Democracy and the Public Service', *Public Administration*, 13 (1935),
339.
[208] Tallents thought that the publicity methods of foreign governments should be criti-
cally assessed; see his *Post Office Publicity* (1935), 3–4; and *The Projection of England* (1932),
29–32. There is little evidence this was done.

information services accounted for the growth of government public relations divisions in the 1930s by citing the 'remarkable expansion' in the use of publicity in the commercial sphere. Yet the emergence of government information services also reflected the expanding size of the electorate, the development of new media, and above all the changing nature of the State; indeed, the committee noted that, faced with 'practical reasons' for keeping the public informed on an increasing variety of subjects, departments had 'turned, *naturally and inevitably*, to advertising and other forms of publicity [my italics]'.[209]

Tracing administrative attitudes with regard to the development of these publicity services is problematical. Departments formulated their arrangements independently of each other and public relations was not a general or official topic of discussion within Whitehall. Officials usually expressed opinions on the subject only in relation to specific matters as they arose within their own ministries. Thus the way in which publicity was perceived within government is most clearly manifested by the manner in which it was employed. Hence the necessity of examining actual developments within departments. On the other hand, the Civil Service in this period formed a relatively homogeneous group, similar in social and educational background and general outlook.[210] Changes in recruiting procedure and the unification of the Civil Service under Treasury control in 1919 resulted in the evolution of more uniform techniques of public administration and ensured that the transfer of officials between government departments became more common than had hitherto been the case.[211] Although the impact is difficult to measure, the erosion of rigid departmentalism obviously facilitated both a greater flow of information within Whitehall on all aspects of government service and the emergence of a new ethos of public administration.

Of equal importance is the fact that many civil servants did express their views on the subject of public relations through the medium of the Institute of Public Administration. Established in 1922 by a group of higher government officials,[212] this organization endeavoured to promote the acceptance and growth of public service as a profession, counteract ill-informed criticism of the Civil Service, and provide a forum for the

---

[209] *Report of the Committee on the Cost of Home Information Services*, Cmd. 7836 (1949), para. 4.

[210] Beloff, pp. 210–11. R. K. Kelsall, *Higher Civil Servants in Britain* (1955), 147–56. Perkin, *Rise*, 91.   [211] Beloff, pp. 210–11.

[212] The President was Sir John Anderson, under-secretary, HO. Vice-Presidents included Sir Horace Wilson, under-secretary, ML, and Sir Henry Bunbury, accountant-general, GPO.

general discussion of relevant issues, including the development of the science of public administration and the proper role of the civil servant in a democratic state.[213] The very creation of the institute reflected a recognition on the part of civil servants both of the growing importance of the bureaucracy, due to the relatively recent expansion in government activities noted earlier,[214] and the fact that they shared interests above and beyond common pecuniary considerations.[215] The institute was very active. It held conferences and issued an annual journal, *Public Administration*, which published articles by government servants and other interested parties. A broad range of topics was addressed, including, for example, the relationship between business and government administration,[216] and the role of the universities in the education of civil servants and the study of bureaucratic techniques.[217] Publicity and public relations received much attention, both in their own right,[218] and as issues cited in articles covering many other diverse subjects. In the absence of a general debate within Whitehall itself, the journal provides an important means to gain insight into how officials perceived their role and responsibilities with regard to the dissemination of information.

As they became increasingly active in the application of government policies, civil servants recognized that they were becoming policy-makers in their own right.[219] While this engendered some concern, as it was feared

[213] See H. G. Corner, 'The Aims of the Institute of Public Administration', *Public Administration*, 1 (1923), 49–55. Viscount Haldane, 'An Organized Civil Service', *Public Administration*, 1 (1923), 7. Viscount Milner, 'The Aims of the Institute of Public Administration', *Public Administration*, 1 (1923), 85–91.

[214] See E. J. Foley, 'Officials and the Public', *Public Administration*, 9 (1931), 17–18. Sir Adair Hore, 'Officials and Policy', *Public Administration*, 5 (1927), 463–5. Bellman, p. 119. Stephen Tallents, 'Salesmanship in the Public Service: Scope and Technique', *Public Administration*, 11 (1933), 259.

[215] Numerous Civil Service groups existed before the institute came into being, but their main concerns were of a financial or social nature: Cohen, p. 140.

[216] See e.g. Sir Josiah C. Stamp, 'The Contrast between the Administration of Business and Public Affairs', *Public Administration*, 1 (1923), 158–71; John Lee, 'The Parallels between Industrial Administration and Public Administration', *Public Administration*, 4 (1926), 216–22; Sir Geoffrey Clarke, 'Business Management of the Public Services', *Public Administration*, 8 (1930), 10–15.

[217] See e.g. W. G. S. Adams, 'University Education in Public Administration', *Public Administration*, 4 (1926), 431–3; C. Grant Robertson, 'University Education in Public Administration: The Universities and Administrative Science', *Public Administration*, 4 (1926), 438–42; T. J. Mackie, 'The Relationship of the Universities to Public Affairs', *Public Administration*, 8 (1930), 180–91.

[218] Between 1923 and 1942 seventeen articles were published dealing specifically with publicity and propaganda, and another twenty-three addressed 'general relations with the public'; see *Journal of Public Administration: Index 1923–42* (1942), 28–30.

[219] G. D. H. Cole, 'The Method of Social Legislation', *Public Administration*, 9 (1931), 4–7. H. H. Ellis, 'The Relations between State Departments and the Nation', *Public*

that the bureaucracy was usurping legislative authority and entering into
the 'debatable ground on which administration comes into touch with
politics',[220] it also resulted in greater attention being focused on the need
for new techniques of administration. Officials began to emphasize the
importance of breaking down the old traditions of Civil Service reticence,
and 'humanizing' government, so as to foster the public co-operation
needed to ensure that services were properly and effectively utilized.[221]
Correspondingly, further expansion and greater efficiency of service was
thought to be dependent on government obtaining a better picture of
public needs and desires.[222] It was also deemed essential that the public
should 'know itself to be well served', so that civil servants would receive
the type of constructive criticism and positive feedback that would give
them a sense of satisfaction in their work, thereby spurring them to
greater effort.[223] Finally, officials stressed that, given the expansion of
both the State and the electorate, government departments had nothing
less than an obligation to make policy accessible to the public.[224] As Lord
Haldane put it in 1923, only thus could democracy flourish:

> As the result of a continuously developing method public opinion has to-day a
> vastly increased efficacy. . . . I do not think that it has attained . . . the possible
> high-water mark in its power. Questions of the franchise are . . . substantially
> disposed of. . . . It is no longer the means that can be said to remain inchoate. It
> is the condition of public opinion itself. Until we have a democracy keen, in the
> only way in which it can be made keen, through a higher degree of enlightenment

Administration, 4 (1926), 97. Herman Finer, 'Officials and the Public', *Public Administration*, 9 (1931), 25–6. Harold J. Laski, 'The Growth of Administrative Discretion', *Public Administration*, 1 (1923), 92–3.

[220] Milner, p. 88. Also see Bellman, p. 127.

[221] Bellman, pp. 124, 132. T. S. Simey, 'A Public Relations Policy for Local Authorities', *Public Administration*, 13 (1935), 246. Harold Whitehead, 'Salesmanship in the Public Service: Scope and Technique', *Public Administration*, 11 (1933), 269. I. G. Gibbon, 'The Appellate Jurisdiction of Government Departments', *Public Administration*, 7 (1929), 275. Higham, *Looking Forward*, 55–6, 92–3.

[222] Cowell, pp. 290–2. H. F. Carlill, 'Administrative Habits of Mind', *Public Administration*, 8 (1930), 123–4. This argument was also being advanced outside Whitehall: see Gallup, *Public Opinion. Planning*, 1/9 (1933), 15; 1/23 (1934), 4–5.

[223] Sir Henry N. Bunbury, 'The Management of Public Utility Undertakings', *Public Administration*, 7 (1929), 111–19. J. H. Broadley, 'The Management of Public Utility Undertakings', *Public Administration*, 7 (1929), 125. Ernest Bevin, 'The Management of Public Utility Undertakings', *Public Administration*, 7 (1929), 132. P. C. Lyel, 'Some Psychological Factors in Public Administration', *Public Administration*, 8 (1930), 132. H. Townshend, ' "Practical Psychology" in Departmental Organisation', *Public Administration*, 12 (1934), 66. Carlill, p. 130. Ellis, 'Relations', 99–103.

[224] Laski, pp. 99–100. Also see J.J.T., 'The Message of the Institute of Public Administration', *Public Administration*, 8 (1930), 238–9; S. P. Vivian, 'Statistics in Administration', *Public Administration*, 1 (1923), 110–11.

resulting from the better education of its grown-up members, the democracy will continue to be relatively inert and sluggish.[225]

With the State becoming more democratic and orientated to public service, it was recognized that it needed to adopt commercial methods of administration such as publicity.

Civil servants were not oblivious to the difficulties involved in determining both the extent to which State publicity was permissible in a democracy and the proper role of the administrator in this sphere. Stephen Tallents addressed these issues at a conference of the Institute of Public Administration in 1933 devoted to the subject of government publicity.[226] Noting that the growing complexity of the State rendered public relations a necessary task of every department, he asserted that official publicity had a number of legitimate applications: interesting the public in government activities and thereby fostering intelligent criticism; explaining complex policies; encouraging the use of public services; publicizing the results of research; aiding in the administration of other policies; and creating an *esprit de corps* within Whitehall. F. R. Cowell, of the Stationery Office publications department, advanced similar arguments in a paper submitted to *Public Administration* in 1935, observing that though the development of public relations presented dangers, 'the provision of information' and ' "promotion" ' which was not 'veiled' were essential to the functioning of a democracy.[227] As noted, he was far from being alone in advancing such arguments, or in assuming that the government would not engage in 'power propaganda'. Indeed, Tallents asserted that departments would not be justified in 'go[ing] all out with methods of high-power salesmanship'.[228] In his influential book *The Projection of England*, published in 1932, Tallents stressed that publicity of a dignified type, 'honest self-expression' as distinct from 'self-advertisement', should be employed to promote government interests both at home and abroad.[229]

Tallents put these views into practice while serving as secretary of the EMB from 1926 to 1933. As noted, the marketing board had been established to encourage the sale of Empire produce in Britain. By its very existence, the EMB represented the use of publicity as a policy alternative. However, most of its £1 million budget was directed into agricultural research projects. Advertising was regarded as a secondary task, 'the last

[225] Haldane, p. 7.   [226] 'Salesmanship', pp. 259–66.   [227] Cowell, pp. 290–3.
[228] Tallents, *Post Office Publicity*, 3; Tallents, in *Advertising World*, 67/5 (1935), 14.
[229] The book dealt primarily with the need for 'national projection' abroad, but Tallents also believed publicity should be developed in the domestic sphere. He adhered to the same principles in either case: Tallents, *Projection*, 40–4.

stage in the process'.[230] Here the chief objective was to publicize the 'idea' of Empire as opposed to specific products, in other words, to create a positive background for the commodity advertising of the countries concerned.[231] Like any commercial firm, the board employed posters, press advertisements, leaflets, shop cards, and exhibitions. Yet, having 'essayed a very novel task—the task of advertising . . . an idea, a conception',[232] which 'presented problems of special difficulty',[233] the board adopted what it considered to be a novel approach to publicity. EMB advertising was of what came to be seen as a prestige rather than a popular nature, that is, artistic, aesthetic, and educational. Attempting to promote the sale of products such as pineapples, for example, the board exhibited posters illustrating their cultivation or showing the wildlife of the countries in which they were grown, instead of advertisements exhorting people to buy tropical fruit. Prominent artists, such as McKnight Kauffer, were commissioned to design advertisements to 'bring alive' the Empire in the same way that Grierson employed documentary films.[234]

Although it was widely praised for raising advertising standards,[235] the EMB was criticized for employing an approach which was not perceived to be commercially viable.[236] One MP observed that a poster he had seen 'looked as if . . . [it] had come out of the Encyclopedia Britannica', and remarked,

I should like to see the efforts of the Empire Marketing Board produce the maximum possible result, and when I look at these advertisements, charming and beautiful as no doubt many of them are, I doubt whether the modern advertising

[230] While figures quoted in Parliament and EMB reports vary, it appears that from 1926 to 1929 under £250,000 was spent on publicity: Hansard, 27 June 1928, vol. 219, col. 524; EMB, *Note on the Work of the Board . . . from July 1926 to 31 March 1929*, Cmd. 3372 (1929), Appendix 2, p. 30. By 1932 expenditure averaged £60,000 per year: *First Report from the Select Committee on Estimates* (1934), Proceedings, 17 Feb. 1932, min. 35. Regarding the secondary role attached to publicity see *Note on the Work of the Board . . . from July 1926 to May 1927*, Cmd. 2898 (1927), 9–10; and *A Second Year's Progress*, 5.

[231] EMB, *A Second Year's Progress*, 35.   [232] Ibid. 39.

[233] Hansard, 18 Apr. 1929, vol. 227, col. 490. EMB, *Empire Marketing Board: May 1928 to May 1929* (1929), 22–3. The advertising of ideas was perceived to necessitate the use of different techniques; see Tallents, 'Salesmanship', 259. Also see below, p. 163.

[234] In 1916, Kauffer, an American Modernist, was recruited by Frank Pick to design posters for the London Underground: Barman, pp. 40–1. His work was widely praised and he was said to be one of the greatest poster artists of the day: Graves and Hodge, p. 194. Shell-Mex and BP Limited, *Art in Advertising*. Also see LeMahieu, pp. 208–9.

[235] For praise of the EMB's methods and materials see *The Times*, 2 May 1927; 9 Oct. 1933. *Advertising World*, 53/3 (1928), 274; 60/3 (1931), 228; 71/5 (1939), 7. Simey, p. 247. *Planning*, 1/5 (1933), 14. 'Government Public Relations', *Planning*, 1/13 (1933), 12.

[236] Commercial advertisers questioned the value of this type of approach: *Advertising World*, 57/4 (1930), 314; 58/1 (1930), 42.

genius . . . would be proud of some of [them]. . . . The advertising genius, which is utilised to so much effect overseas, might very well be applied to that task here, if only as a supplementary to the more artistic methods already utilised.[237]

The board had difficulty in justifying its methods on financial grounds, as it was difficult to measure the results of this type of publicity. However, it cited 'substantial evidence from the Press, the public and trade interests' that its advertisements were 'an advantageous instrument . . . [in] creating a background of interest in the subject of Empire buying'.[238] William Crawford defended the board's policy, noting that while the appeal was of a type that 'many advertising men would have condemned as being too highbrow', such publicity fostered the public goodwill which was prerequisite to increased sales.[239]

Ironically, in adopting this type of publicity, the EMB was emulating a noted commercial firm, the London Passenger Transport Board. Under the direction of Frank Pick, the company had introduced innovative advertising techniques before the war, endeavouring to persuade the public to use its services by marketing the city of London; it employed artistic posters illustrating where people could go and what they could do if they took the Underground. When critics charged that the advertisements were beyond the grasp of the average individual, Pick countered:

those who decry posters which require some pains and thought for their understanding underrate the urge to stretch the mind a bit more than usual, underrate indeed the intellectual level of an urban population. It is foolish to descend to an elementary treatment of a subject on the ground that there should be nothing above the heads of the public. The public like something above their heads, if only it is attainable.[240]

These arguments made little headway in commercial circles,[241] though several firms, including the Gas Light and Coke company and Shell-Mex, did begin to copy the example of London Transport and the EMB,[242] a number recruiting former EMB employees to their staffs.[243] Not surprisingly, Tallents continued to employ prestige advertising when he

---

[237] Hansard, 12 Nov. 1928, vol. 222, cols. 626–9. Also see Hansard, 21 Mar. 1927, vol. 204, cols. 21–2; 13 Nov. 1929, vol. 231, cols. 2020–1.

[238] Ibid. 12 Feb. 1930, vol. 235, cols. 385–6.

[239] 'Creating the Empire Mind', in Crawford and Higham, pp. 8–9.

[240] Barman, p. 212.

[241] Some advertisers agreed with Pick, but most queried the commercial value of this type of approach; see *Advertising World*, 65/6 (1934), 287; 70/1 (1938), 27.

[242] See LeMahieu, pp. 266–7.

[243] e.g. A. P. Ryan joined the gas company, and Gervas Huxley the Ceylon Tea Propaganda Board.

assumed control over publicity arrangements in the Post Office in 1933. He also advised other government departments to use the LPTB as a model for their publicity.[244] As we shall see below, such advice was hardly necessary; the assumption that government had to approach the public in a dignified, non-commercial, manner was already well established in Whitehall by the time permanent public relations machinery became common.

[244] Tallents, 'Salesmanship', 259–66. Tallents, in *Advertising World*, 67/5 (1935), 13–14.

3

The Stationery Office and Government Information

It is no very recondite deduction from the principles of democracy to argue that the political responsibilities of the masses demand that they should be in possession of adequate information upon the acts and intentions of their Governments.

(F. R. Cowell (HMSO Publications Division), 'The Uses and Dangers of Publicity', 1935)

[W]e know that the masses get their 'information' so compounded with 'news' and camouflaged by party feeling that it is sheer luck if their sound native intelligence is not destroyed. We all know this; and we live in an age when sane public opinion is more vitally important than at any other period in our history. Yet its nourishment is left to chance. The distribution of ideas remains haphazard, while the distribution of soap and cars is organised.

(Charles Higham, *Looking Forward*, 1920)

[I]nformation of vital importance to the future of the United Kingdom, obtained by a large outlay of public money, has been left pigeon-holed for years.... We cannot be satisfied so long as the obtaining of information of ... immense importance is considered worth the expenditure of public money while its turning to practical account is left to chance.

(*Planning*, 3/71 (1936))

AFTER the demise of the Advisory Committee on Government Advertising in 1926 the Stationery Office relinquished even the small degree of control it had exercised over departmental publicity arrangements. The Stationery Office continued to act as a channel for general press advertising, but had no authority over official campaigns. Yet it did retain responsibility for government information *per se*, in its capacity as a publisher. Departments prepared official documents, but the HMSO handled their distribution and publicizing.

The Stationery Office had been established in the late eighteenth century to print government papers for the benefit of officials and MPs. As early as 1835, parliament had affirmed the public's right of access to these materials, directing the HMSO to prepare extra copies of all reports for universal distribution. Yet this ruling did not obligate the department to disseminate information as widely as possible, for these publications were meant to be sold, albeit 'at the lowest price they . . . [could] be furnished', rather than provided freely to the public at large. The HMSO was expected to turn a profit on the enterprise.[1] This policy came under attack during the early years of the twentieth century, as increasing attention was focused on the importance of a well-informed public opinion to the proper functioning of a democracy. In the years before the Second World War, the HMSO had to reconcile the Treasury's insistence that it operate at a profit with growing pressure from within and outside Whitehall to fulfil its responsibilities as a department of State by maximizing the distribution of official papers regardless of cost. While conflicting, these two objectives were not mutually exclusive, for in the long run it was only by raising public consciousness about the availability of government information that the HMSO could hope to increase sales. However, the department did encounter difficulty in convincing the Treasury on this point; by 1939, the obligation of government to disseminate information had been accepted within Whitehall, but up to the outbreak of war financial considerations, rather than public service objectives, continued to govern the approach adopted towards the distribution of all official publications.

The first Stationery Office vote in 1824 totalled £59,760. By 1900–1, annual expenditure was £370,000, with the estimates reaching the £1 million mark just before the First World War. In 1913, printing for all other departments accounted for £360,000 of the total spent; by 1919, that portion of the budget alone was £1,215,000.[2] The rising cost of paper during the war accounted for part of the increase, but it also reflected the expansion of government activities in these years. Inroads into novel policy areas and the consequent creation of new departments greatly increased the volume of data pouring into and out of Whitehall, as did

---

[1] *The Times*, 4 Mar. 1924. Hansard, 11 July 1922, vol. 156, col. 1168; 23 Jan. 1930, vol. 234, col. 338.

[2] *Report from the Select Committee on Official Publications and Debates Reports* (23 July 1906), appendix A. (Hereafter all references to this committee will be to 'Publications Committee' followed by the year. In first references the exact date of the report will be given.) *The Times*, 10 Apr. 1920, 8 Apr. 1924. Hansard, 11 July 1922, vol. 156, cols. 1163–5; 8 Apr. 1930, vol. 237, cols. 1951–2.

growing recognition of the importance of information to the governing process.[3]

Alarm at the rising rate of expenditure in this area was voiced as early as 1906. At the insistence of several back-bench members, the House of Commons appointed a standing Select Committee on Official Publications and Debates to review government publishing.[4] As originally constituted, the committee was responsible for overseeing parliamentary reports, that is, command papers which had to be printed regardless of demand. It was charged with reducing their number, either by dropping 'unnecessary' documents or by reclassifying certain reports as Stationery Office publications. Although the latter, and materials prepared for departmental use, were not included in its mandate, the committee soon assumed control over these papers, as they accounted for considerable expenditure,[5] especially after 1921 when a large proportion of command papers were reclassified as HMSO publications.[6] In 1909, the committee was also accorded responsibility for Hansard, the printed debates of parliament.[7]

In its first report, issued in 1906, the publications committee termed official publishing 'excessive' and wasteful.[8] The statistics available bore out the criticism. In 1905 the HMSO issued 2,670,000 parliamentary papers: 750,000 were sold; 1,460,000 were allocated to MPs and departments; and 460,000 were held in reserve. Sales revenue amounted to approximately £14,000 in 1904–5.[9] Noting that, in 'practice', each department orders what 'printing it chooses, gives away gratuitously as many copies of each of its own publications as it cares to do and charges the whole cost upon the Estimates of the Stationery Office',[10] the committee stressed the need for greater control to be exercised over the preparation and distribution of all publications. Yet, because they lacked 'absolute power to forbid an expenditure which another Department consider[ed] necessary', neither the Treasury nor the HMSO could

[3] *The Times*, 10 Apr. 1920. Hansard, 15 Feb. 1926, vol. 191, cols. 1585–6. G. D. H. Cole, 'The Method of Social Legislation', *Public Administration*, 9 (1931), 4.

[4] Hansard, 12 Mar. 1906, vol. 153, col. 934; 20 Mar. 1906, vol. 154, col. 341.

[5] Publications Committee (1906), *Report*, p. iii.

[6] G. L. Barstow to all departments, 6 Sept. 1921, PRO, Home Office Papers, HO 45/17926. Hansard, 13 Dec. 1920, vol. 136, col. 57; 16 May 1922, vol. 154, cols. 235–7.

[7] Publications Committee (1909), *Report and Special Report* (23 Sept. 1909).

[8] Publications Committee (1906), *Report*, p. vii.

[9] Publications Committee (1906), Proceedings, 9 Apr. 1906, mins. 110–11. The extent of gratuitous distribution is unclear; see below, p. 59.

[10] Publications Committee (1906), *Report*, p. viii. Also see Proceedings, 25 June 1906, mins. 2206–8.

undertake such supervision.[11] Indeed, although nominally responsible for meeting government printing requirements, the Stationery Office had little input into the process. At this time it did not even have its own presses.[12] A publications branch was established in 1907 to provide technical advice to departments,[13] but, despite several attempts by the publications committee to secure the establishment of an official printing works, printing was tendered to contractors until well into the First World War.[14] During the war the HMSO and several other departments did acquire their own presses, but had to overcome opposition from the trade in order to retain them.[15] While in principle all government printing was centralized in the HMSO in 1919,[16] by 1923 the department was compelled to bow to external pressure and contract out at least two-thirds of it to commercial firms.[17]

The distribution of official documents was also controlled by commercial agents. In 1874, the Select Committee on Public Departments had recommended to no avail the establishment of a sales office in the HMSO. Until 1887, when a contract was tendered, any firm of standing could sell official publications.[18] In January 1905, Wyman and Sons was contracted to handle the arrangements for the next ten years, receiving one-third of the cover price of each document.[19] Confined to a secondary role, the HMSO had little access to information regarding the relative costs of publications or the return they secured.[20] Not even the company kept detailed statistics on the volume of sales or wasted publications.[21] Unable to provide departments with accurate figures, the HMSO could hardly accuse them of filing excessive or unrealistic printing orders. The

[11] Publications Committee (1906), *Report*, p. viii.

[12] Publications Committee (1906), Proceedings, 9 Apr. 1906, min. 45.

[13] Publications Committee, *Report* (26 July 1907), Proceedings, 31 May 1907, min. 17.

[14] Publications Committee (1906), *Report*, p. xi. Publications Committee (1920), *Third Report* (22 Dec. 1920). Hansard, 30 Oct. 1906, vol. 61, cols. 1140–86. Publications Committee (1913), *Report* (23 July 1913), para. 2.

[15] Hansard, 11 July 1922, vol. 156, cols. 1166, 1174; 11 June 1923, vol. 165, cols. 46–7. They were also branded an extravagance: *The Times*, 10 Apr. 1920.

[16] Although departments retained the right to commission their printing elsewhere, the HMSO could refuse to pay for it; Publications Committee (1919), *Report* (22 Dec. 1919), Proceedings, 22 Dec. 1919, mins. 1067–9.

[17] Hansard, 11 June 1923, vol. 165, cols. 46–7. *The Times*, 30 Jan., 28 July 1922, 1, 2 Apr. 1927.   [18] Publications Committee (1915), *Report* (27 July 1915), pp. x–xvii.

[19] Publications Committee (1906), Proceedings, 9 Apr. 1906, mins. 97, 106. Publications Committee (1911), *Report* (9 Aug. 1911), Proceedings, 24 May 1911, mins. 20, 68–9.

[20] Publications Committee (1915), Proceedings, 13 May 1915, mins. 293–9.

[21] Publications Committee (1906), Proceedings, 9 Apr. 1906, mins. 109–10; 28 May 1906, min. 1519; 25 June 1906, mins. 2204, 2220. Publications Committee (1915), Proceedings, 13 May 1915, mins. 275, 293–300.

Stationery Office also lacked incentive to try and stimulate demand for official publications, as a large portion of any profits secured would accrue to the contractor, not the government.[22] Unlike commercial publishers, then, the department did not engage in consistent or concerted advertising. In its first report, the publications committee attempted to alter the situation, recommending that the HMSO should assume control over the distribution process and endeavour to bring official papers to public notice.[23] However, despite repeated pressure from the committee, the contract with Wymans was not terminated.

Although officials later claimed that Wymans had never engaged in advertising,[24] the company was quick to defend its record, particularly when the contract was reviewed in 1915. The chairman, Henry Burt, informed the publications committee that his firm was 'more interested in pushing the sale of Government publications than anyone', as it was losing money under the current arrangements.[25] Because it was not legally bound to advertise, Wymans determined the extent and nature of any publicity undertaken. Commercial considerations alone determined policy. Publications were not issued through booksellers, for example, because this would have reduced the company's profits.[26] Advertising was confined to sending circulars, catalogues, and lists of publications to the press, libraries, and regular subscribers, as well as displaying notices in some seventy post offices.[27] When criticized for not employing more popular methods, such as press advertising, Burt countered that experiments in this area had been unsuccessful:

I made special efforts . . . to push the sales, and I began to advertise military publications in military papers, agricultural publications in agricultural papers, and general publications in the 'Times' and other newspapers, but I found that I wasted my money . . . special advertising . . . did not assist the sale of Government publications.[28]

[22] Publications Committee (1906), Proceedings, 27 June 1906, min. 2452.

[23] Publications Committee (1906), *Report*, p. x.

[24] Publications Committee (1918), *Report* (30 Jan. 1918), 11–12. Publications Committee (1919), Proceedings, 26 Mar. 1919, mins. 54–5.

[25] Publications Committee (1906), Proceedings, 25 June 1906, mins. 2194–2200, 2212–13. Publications Committee (1915), Proceedings, 1 July 1915, mins. 774–5, 880.

[26] Publications Committee (1915), Proceedings, 13 May 1915, min. 271.

[27] Publications Committee (1906), Proceedings, 25 June 1906, mins. 2194–2200, 2238–42; 27 June 1906, min. 2453. Publications Committee (1915), Proceedings, 5 May 1915, mins. 235, 241; 1 July 1915, mins. 775–7.

[28] Publications Committee (1915), Proceedings 1 July 1915, mins. 755–80. Also, Publications Committee (1906), Proceedings, 25 June 1906, mins. 2203, 2245.

Government departments had long been critical of the arrangements because of this emphasis on financial gain. Maintaining that documents were only advertised when the company anticipated a profit, officials noted that many important papers did not receive the attention which they merited.[29] When it was suggested to Burt in 1915 that the government might wish to advance the sale of certain publications, 'whereas Messrs. Wyman do not', he replied '[w]e push everything we can see money in.' The chairman of the publications committee, Sir George Toulmin, observed that this was a 'very fair and proper commercial remark', but added,

suppose that a Department wishes to push something for educational reasons, apart from profit . . . It is done now in a three-legged way: the Department has not the information which the Stationery Office has, and the Stationery Office has not quite the information that you have, and it does seem as if the propagandist part might be more concentrated than it is? [my italics]

More to the point, another member interjected, '[y]ou would never deal with the questions from the non-commercial point of view, would you? The Government wish to push certain publications because of the matter that they contain.'[30]

Similarly, Wymans was criticized because it had not cultivated editorial attention by issuing review copies of government publications to the press. Efforts in this area were limited because the Treasury refused to allow free copies to be allocated for this purpose.[31] Gratuitous distribution had met with opposition from the Treasury since the 1850s; the department constantly attempted to curb the practice.[32] Although lacking evidence, Treasury officials claimed that the value of free copies distributed ran 'into thousands of pounds annually'.[33] In the years before the First World War, the Treasury cited the publications committee's emphasis on the need for economy as a justification for laying down strict guidelines in this area.[34] By 1913, government ministries were allowed without prior sanction to distribute only one hundred free copies of any

---

[29] Publications Committee (1906), Proceedings, 9 Apr. 1906, mins. 1517–22; 25 June 1906, min. 2218. Publications Committee (1915), Proceedings, 7 July 1915, mins. 972–80.

[30] Publications Committee (1915), Proceedings, 1 July 1915, mins. 875–8.

[31] Ibid., Proceedings, 13 May 1915, min. 238.

[32] See Treasury minutes dating from 10 Mar. 1848 to 17 July 1876, STAT 14/23.

[33] Publications Committee (1911), Proceedings, 31 May 1911, mins. 246–8.

[34] See Publications Committee (1912–13), *Report* (30 July 1912), Proceedings, 7 Mar. 1912, mins. 30–5.

parliamentary paper. No uniform rule applied to Stationery Office publications.[35] After the reclassification of command papers in 1921, however,
a mere twenty-five copies of any publication could be given away unless
special permission was obtained.[36] By 1924 free distribution was only
permitted where an exchange of equal value was given, or, in certain
cases, for book reviews.[37]

Gratuitous distribution was opposed on the grounds that it impeded
sales.[38] Several departments countered that this was of secondary importance as they had a responsibility to disseminate information as widely
as possible. Addressing the publications committee in 1907, an official
representing the Local Government Board noted that the latter made a
practice of providing free copies, even of documents which might otherwise have sold. Asked to explain the rationale behind this policy, Mr
Lithiby replied:

> The view taken by the Board is that the services which the Board render to
> local authorities should be given as far as possible free of cost. . . . There is no
> doubt whatever that local authorities would be perfectly willing to pay the
> cost . . . and yet we issue [reports] . . . and no charge is made. . . .
> MR CLELAND. You said that local authorities attached considerable value to your
> Reports? . . . The price is 4*s*. 7*d*. Is any local authority that attaches value to
> them going to make the 4*s*. 7*d*. a bar to whether it will have a copy or not?
> MR LITHIBY. We do not consider that at all. We distribute it simply on the
> principle that they ought to have it, and it is our practice to supply the
> information we collect to local authorities free of cost.[39]

These arguments held little sway with the Treasury or Wymans.[40]
Although the HMSO supported the practice of issuing review copies,
noting that other publishers used this means of publicity to generate
sales, it too had misgivings about gratuitous distribution.[41] None the less,

---

[35] Publications Committee (1914), *Report* (29 July 1914), Proceedings, 22 Apr. 1914,
min. 448. Publications Committee (1915), Proceedings, 7 July 1915, mins. 952–68.

[36] Barstow, 'Form and Distribution', HO 45/17926.

[37] HMSO to all departments, 28 July 1924, HO 45/11908.

[38] Meiklejohn to Home Office, 7 Sept. 1923, HO 45/11908.

[39] Publications Committee (1907), Proceedings, 21 June 1907, mins. 553–64. Publications Committee (1906), Proceedings, 28 May 1906, min. 1341.

[40] Wymans had been complaining about the practice since 1906: Publications Committee
(1906), Proceedings, 25 June 1906, mins. 2206–8, 2218, 2243, 2252, 2256.

[41] Publications Committee (1906), Proceedings, 27 June 1906, mins. 2452–3. In 1915,
Atterbury used commercial arguments to criticize the Treasury's attitude towards review
copies: Publications Committee (1915), Proceedings, 13 May 1915, min. 238. However, the
HMSO continued to oppose gratuitous distribution: W. R. Codling to Treasury, 14 June
1921, STAT 14/23.

in his testimony before the publications committee in 1915, Frederick Atterbury, the controller of the HMSO, endeavoured to convey the impression that, if placed in control, the Stationery Office would handle the entire distribution process differently from Wymans, paying greater heed to public service considerations.[42] Noting the success of experiments in direct selling conducted by the department, the controller stressed the likely economic benefits of terminating the contract, but used the department's other responsibilities as the basis of his argument:

If, as I believe, the sale[s] . . . could be increased, there would naturally be additional profit. But the great thing, I think, would be that much more use would be made of the Government publications than is at present made; they would be very much more widely circulated, and, in as much as they concern the welfare of the country, the probability is that other advantages than mere monetary ones would arise.[43]

Toulmin responded that, while it was essential to try 'to sell State publications', success was dependent on making them more attractive. He advised Atterbury that if the HMSO could bring in 'some man who knows the public taste, and who would serve out the publications in a form which the public like, you would increase your sales very largely'.[44] As this indicates, official publications were assumed to be unmarketable in their present form. The implication, of course, was that more than mere surface advertising would be required to improve demand. This point was apparently lost on Atterbury, who replied that determining the content and presentation of materials went 'beyond the scope of the work of the Stationery Office'.[45] Indeed, although his primary goal was to modernize the HMSO and turn it into an up-to-date publishing house, the controller made no attempt to secure editorial control over State publications.[46] As well, it is clear that despite his testimony Atterbury had no intention of engaging in anything more than surface advertising. His plans for a publicity campaign, when and if the contract with Wymans was terminated, followed closely the company's example. Advertising was to be as selective as ever, appeals being directed towards those

---

[42] Toulmin drew this inference from Atterbury's testimony: Publications Committee (1915), Proceedings, 24 June 1915, min. 732.

[43] Publications Committee (1915), *Report*, paragraph 15; Appendix 4; Proceedings, 13 May 1915, mins. 345–7. The same points had been raised in 1911; Proceedings, 24 May 1911, min. 22.

[44] Publications Committee (1915), Proceedings, 13 May 1915, min. 353.

[45] Publications Committee (1915), *Report*, para. 23.

[46] Ibid., Proceedings, 13 May 1915, mins. 307–11; 7 July 1915, mins. 984–96.

already predisposed to show interest in particular documents: 'I should propose to make lists—sorts of generic lists—of the various bodies all over the country who are interested in certain sections of Government publications, and to send out lists or circulars very widely in connection with many of the publications that were put out.'[47] General publicity was ruled out on economic grounds:

> To cover the cost of an advertisement in a paper like the 'Times' you have to sell a very large number of copies, and it seems to me that it is extremely unlikely that the sale of a Government publication will, as the result of any advertisement of the kind mentioned, reach a number of copies sufficient to pay.[48]

A number of reforms introduced by Atterbury at this time indicate that under his tenure financial considerations took precedence in determining Stationery Office policy. A perfect illustration is found in his decision to alter the pricing scale for publications so as to equate the costs of production and purchase. Under arrangements fixed in 1889, documents were priced at 3*d.* per thirty-two pages.[49] Citing lower printing costs, the publications committee of 1913 considered a reduction in charges, but Atterbury blocked the proposal by noting that new and potentially more expensive contracts would soon be tendered.[50] The controller himself increased prices in 1915, arguing that, as wastage was inevitable, some means had to be found of compensating for losses. A new scale was introduced under which publications were priced in terms of production costs and likely sales.[51] As this led to huge increases in the prices of most documents, the policy was not popular. The matter was raised during the debate on the estimates in 1922, when several Liberal and Labour MPs accused the HMSO of trying to subvert the public's access to information.[52] Lower rates were also advocated on commercial grounds; politicians on all sides of the Commons claimed that higher charges impeded demand. Controversy raged for years, but the HMSO refused to relent.[53] Costing by weight was reintroduced in 1930, with charges calculated at a

[47] Publications Committee (1915), Proceedings, 13 May 1915, min. 326.

[48] Ibid. 5 May 1915, min. 235.

[49] Publications Committee (1906), Proceedings, 9 Apr. 1906, min. 106.

[50] Publications Committee (1913), Proceedings, 25 June 1913, mins. 756–9.

[51] Publications Committee (1915), Proceedings, 13 May 1915, mins. 306–8, 331; 1 July 1915, min. 780. Also see Hansard, 4 July 1921, vol. 144, cols. 23–4. *The Times*, 11 Nov. 1921.

[52] Hansard, 11 July 1922, vol. 156, cols. 1166–72, 1176–9, 1183. Also see 16 May 1922, vol. 154, cols. 235–7. *The Times*, 24, 25, 28 July 1922.

[53] *The Times*, 4 Mar., 8 Aug. 1924. Hansard, 4 Mar. 1925, vol. 181, cols. 475–6; 29 Apr. 1926, vol. 194, cols. 2194–5; 23 Jan. 1930, vol. 234, col. 338.

rate of one penny per six pages. As this did not result in significant price reductions, critics remained unappeased.[54]

Another important change which took place during the war was the termination of the contract with Wymans. In 1915, the publications committee concluded that the distribution process would be managed more effectively by the HMSO. Commenting on the publicity arrangements hitherto in place, it observed that internal expertise was as important to successful advertising as technical knowledge:

> the prime necessity of success appears . . . to be that the agent of publicity shall be in close connection with the author. At present the chain is broken at more than one point. . . . When the issue passes to the sale agent it is already three removes from the author. Here the whole of the experience as to public demand, the specialties of various wholesale firms . . ., the advisability of early reprints— in fact the whole intelligence of the publishers' craft is beyond the ken of the Stationery Office. The information and experience which should be part of the office knowledge, directly at the disposal of any department desiring publicity for work upon which skilled and highly-paid officials may have spent much time and labour, is dissipated between two sections of the Government organization and the private firm, whose object is, frankly, commercial gain.[55]

In making this statement, the committee affirmed the need for the systematic advertising of all official documents, and designated the HMSO as a sort of research and information service for other departments. Clearly, the latter was expected to function along the lines which Toulmin had suggested, exerting influence over the preparation and presentation of government publications as though it were a commercial publisher.

Yet the HMSO could not function like a regular publishing house. Despite complaints that it lacked the necessary expertise, the Treasury, rather than the Stationery Office, was the final arbiter in determining the volume of departmental printing.[56] After 1915 the HMSO did become the sole agent responsible for the distribution of government publications, and endeavoured to centralize control over the process,[57] but it lacked

---

[54] Publications Committee (1930–1), *Report* (6 Oct. 1931), Proceedings, 30 Sept. 1931, mins. 17–30. For complaints see Publications Committee (1936–7), *Second Report* (27 July 1937), para. 7; Proceedings, 15 June 1937, mins. 321–6. Hansard, 10 May 1938, vol. 335, cols. 1414–15.

[55] Publications Committee (1915), *Report*, para. 26; Proceedings, 13 May 1915, mins. 314–15.

[56] Publications Committee (1916), *Report* (2 Aug. 1916), para. 7. Publications Committee (1918), *Report*, para. 3. Publications Committee (1923), *Special Report* (28 Mar. 1923), Proceedings, 23 Mar. 1922, min. 128.

[57] Codling to departments, 22 Aug. 1921; Codling to Hurst, 20 Apr. 1927, STAT 14/23.

the power to compel other ministries to yield to its authority. By 1930 the majority of official documents were issued through the Office, but the latter was unable 'to decide the importance of publications emanating from other Departments'.[58] This meant that the government publisher could neither co-ordinate the distribution of papers, nor ensure that a large number of significant materials were not issued simultaneously. Simultaneous publication was virtually unavoidable, as the HMSO brought out an average of thirty to forty documents a day and could not legally delay the publication of Acts of parliament.[59] Yet, whenever faced with having to review several important papers on the same day, the press accused the HMSO of engaging in '[u]nbusinesslike [p]ublicity'.[60] By 1934, such criticism had resulted in the establishment of procedures governing the distribution of advance copies to the press, but control over the process was centred not in the Office but in the Treasury's press office.[61] The HMSO did not begin to experiment in the large-scale advertising of government publications until 1917, when circulars were sent to targeted potential customers. Owing to wartime paper shortages the scheme had to be curtailed; lack of paper actually necessitated that the department endeavour to reduce sales. Advertising was subsequently confined to documents dealing with issues of national importance only, such as health care.[62]

The first publications committee to sit after the war devoted considerable attention to the question of publicity, which was not surprising given that the advertising executive, Charles Higham, became a member in 1919. Observing that it was pointless to publish valuable information without ensuring that it reached a receptive audience, Higham stressed the importance of both improving the presentation of documents and engaging in widespread advertising campaigns. Conscious of the committee's mandate, he justified these suggestions on economic grounds:

There is a certain stereotyped style of Stationery Office printing which has what is called the 'Government look' about it. It is uninterestingly presented and therefore ineffective. One does not want any more money spent, and if possible to print less, but let that less be used. . . . Printers complain that the Stationery Office invariably ask for the lowest price, and therefore no consideration can be given to the quality of the work. . . . [I]t is not worthwhile printing a thing if

[58] Publications Committee (1929–30), *Report* (23 July 1930), Proceedings, 18 Dec. 1929, mins. 144–6. Minute, 1 Apr. 1927, STAT 14/23.   [59] Ibid., STAT 14/23.
[60] See e.g. *The Times*, 1, 2 Apr. 1927. Hansard, 7 Apr. 1927, vol. 204, col. 2266.
[61] J. A. Barlow to all departments, 7 July 1934; Treasury notice, 25 July 1934, T 162/337/30623.   [62] Publications Committee (1917–18), *Report* (7 Jan. 1918), 11–12.

people do not read it, and a tremendous amount of money is wasted by the Government in printing thousands of copies which nobody buys.[63]

W. R. Codling, the new controller of the HMSO, concurred,[64] and the department began to give consideration to approaching the Treasury with proposals for the adoption of a broadly based advertising policy.[65] Codling also sought further commercial advice.

In April 1920, R. McKean Cant, the manager of an Edinburgh advertising agency, was asked to submit a report detailing how an agent would market government publications.[66] Approaching the subject as though it were a scientific problem, Cant outlined everything from the 'Substance of the Commodity', to the 'Field of Appeal' (an approximate list of the persons he considered likely to be interested in the papers of any individual department). Stressing the importance of brand identification, Cant observed that it was necessary to convince the public of the general quality of the official publication:

Government publicity if it is COMPETENTLY DONE WILL PLANT IN THE MINDS OF [*sic*] *Britain's millions certain information and desires which will pre-dispose them favourably towards the literature which the Government are publishing.* If this fact is rightly handled by the Government Authorities and put before the booksellers in a convincing way, it would enable them to mature the big number of undeveloped sales that would be lying idle in the nation's mind.

Rather than attempting to increase the sale of specific documents, Cant wanted to create a situation in which any publication bearing the government seal would be saleable whatever its content. He framed his proposals with long-term goals in mind, but noted that, initially at least, general aims might be facilitated through specific campaigns: 'If . . . a special objective is set for each year the whole field would be gradually fertilised.'

Cant's championing of the application of social psychology to advertising, and some of his proposed descriptive slogans, such as 'full of meat' (termed 'undignified' and 'not suitable to Government publications'), prejudiced the reception of his report. Yet the proposals were rejected mainly because the long-term objectives he espoused were not those of the department. Commenting on the report, H. G. Pearce of the Stationery Office observed:

In this rather grandiose scheme the emphasis is throughout laid on Publicity. The question of gain or loss is not treated as a vital factor. By Mr. Cant's methods we

[63] Publications Committee (1919), Proceedings, 26 Mar. 1919, mins. 49–52.
[64] Ibid., min. 64.   [65] Minute, 28 Apr. 1919, STAT 14/23.
[66] 'ANALYSIS OF THE SITUATION', Cant to Controller, 8 Apr. 1921, STAT 14/23.

shall undoubtedly obtain publicity; but the cost could greatly outweigh any profits. If it were the function of this Department to increase public interest in education, agriculture, science, etc., even at a loss (and probably at a great loss) the scheme might be considered. But if publicity be regarded as secondary to profits in regard to our publications . . . then it seems to me that Mr. Cants [*sic*] specimen scheme 'o'er leaps itself'. It is a riot of advertisement.[67]

As his use of the terms 'publicity' and 'profit' indicate, Pearce recognized that advertising could fulfil more than one function, though in his view the two were mutually exclusive. It followed that the type of advertising policy pursued was dependent upon the priority attached to each objective. Attention to profit motives pervaded Pearce's counter-proposals. He suggested that Treasury sanction be obtained for circularizing, press advertising, and, 'in any case where our experience indicates that their cost would at least be recovered through increased sale profits', the distribution of review copies to the press. Discussing the prospect of increasing sales through advertising, he noted that, if the department created 'a public demand by means of any appeal the Trade . . . [would get] a large share of the resulting orders (upon which we barely get any profits)'. Thus he argued that HMSO advertisements should only give the addresses of official sales offices and not include the information that publications were available in bookshops: '*Wholesale Trade should be regarded as being in the interests of Publicity: Retail Sale Offices as our chief source of profit.*'

Pearce's proposals formed the basis of a publicity scheme presented to the Treasury in June 1921. Referring to the Treasury's recent decision to allow the Ministry of Agriculture to publicize its *Journal*, Codling assumed that, as the Exchequer was apparently 'no longer opposed to the policy of advertising official publications', it was 'presumably necessary . . . only to justify the amount of the expenditure now proposed'. An annual budget of £2,000 was requested to cover HMSO advertising. This was to be directed towards the regular insertion of one-quarter or one-half column publication announcements in major London, and selected regional, newspapers on the day of the week on which book reviews most frequently appeared. Noting that sales returns averaged £130,000 annually, Codling claimed that this expenditure would be recouped were a mere 8 per cent of sales transferred from wholesale to retail trade.[68] Codling also requested sanction to issue to the press review copies of selected documents. Noting the existence of an anomaly whereby museums were allowed to

[67] Pearce to Hill, 28 Apr. 1921, STAT 14/23.
[68] Codling to Treasury, 14 June 1921, STAT 14/23.

send out their catalogues, while permission was 'denied to the Department whose business it is to sell the publications', he again used economic arguments:

The discriminate issue of review copies is in any case a cheap and effective method of securing publicity; and as the cost of such copies could be taken into account in fixing the price of the book, the expense to the State would be virtually nothing, while at the same time benefit would undoubtedly be derived from increased sales.

The Treasury agreed to these proposals on a trial basis, but asked the Advisory Committee on Government Advertising for its opinion on the merits and probable results of the advertising scheme. While expressing confidence in the idea, the ACGA was unwilling to commit itself on the likelihood of success and withheld comment.[69]

Press advertising began in December 1921 and lasted for eleven weeks. A year later, Pearce prepared a progress report.[70] Assessment was difficult, not least because the department had been slow to recognize the importance of the 'little job' of tabulating results.[71] The only cases in which success could be statistically measured were those in which advertising had been undertaken in support of works published for some time. Here, Pearce had to concede defeat, for the figures were not encouraging.[72] He blamed the medium. Constrained by its budget, the HMSO had been forced to tie itself to specific journals in order to obtain block discounts. Daily newspapers had not been used, both because of the cost involved, and because, as a government department, the HMSO would have had to employ a wide range of journals reflecting every shade of political opinion. On these grounds Pearce concluded that advertising government publications in the press would never be profitable:

repetition . . . is essential in newspaper advertising, and if there is to be any relation between possible recovery by sales of the cost of advertising, repetition in the daily press is out of the question. If, however, the grant had been increased to cover adequate advertising in the newspapers, an enormous and almost impossible increase in the sales would have been required to cover the sum laid out.

Noting a rise in trade sales over the past year, he argued, none the less, that it was 'fair to attribute part of these increases to advertising'. Indeed,

[69] Meiklejohn to Codling, 22 June 1921; Scorgie to Treasury, 17 Sept. 1921, STAT 14/23. [70] 'Advertising of S.O. Publications in the Press', 18 Nov. 1922, STAT 14/23.
[71] Pearce to Hill, 26 Aug. 1921, STAT 14/23.
[72] Subsequent references are to 'Advertising of S.O. Publications in the Press', 18 Nov. 1922, STAT 14/23.

the experiment had been productive because 'the majority of the people now know of the Stationery Office and the nature of some of its publications'. Having earlier rejected Cant's general emphasis, Pearce justified a continuation of the scheme on the very same grounds, and echoed Cant's other proposals:

Most of our works are specialised and as we have been precluded . . . from using the daily press we have been restricted—and in my opinion to our financial advantage—to appealing to the various classes making up the community through the advertisement pages of their specialised journals. We certainly make sure of reaching the specialist there. . . . Every chemist, I should imagine, reads 'The Journal of the Society of the Chemical Industry', but he might be Tory, Liberal or Labour, or even a reader of his provincial paper only.

Informing the Treasury that 'contrary to expectations' official publications were not suited to ordinary press avertising, Codling suggested that the annual budget be reduced to £1,000, adding that future campaigns would be of a selective nature.[73] Similarly, review copies were now to be distributed only in cases where increased sales seemed a likely result. Given the economic climate, the Treasury was not averse to these proposals. Indeed, with the Geddes Axe looming, the emphasis had shifted away from encouraging the sale of documents to eliminating the 'thousands' of unsold copies published. It is worth noting, however, that the HMSO was not singled out for criticism in the Geddes reports. Indeed, the Committee on National Expenditure expressed itself 'satisfied' that necessary steps were taken by the Stationery Office to restrict the quantity and cost of government publishing, and placed the onus on other departments to reduce their printing requirements.[74] Thus, despite cut-backs,

[73] Codling to Treasury, 31 Mar. 1923; reply, 15 Aug. 1923, STAT 14/23.
[74] *Third Report of the Committee on National Expenditure*, Cmd. 1589 (1922), 110–16. From 1911 onward all government expenditure on stationery and printing was carried on the HMSO Vote. Departments forecast their annual needs, the HMSO budget being derived from these figures. These estimates tended to be inaccurate, and departments were criticized for their consistent overspending: Publications Committee (1920), *Second Report* (27 July 1920), Appendix 2. Publications Committee (1925), *Report* (15 Dec. 1925), Appendix 2. Yet the Stationery Office was equally culpable; pleading volume of work, it repeatedly refused to provide departments with details regarding the costs of printing specific papers: Publications Committee (1911), Proceedings, 31 May 1911, mins. 251–9. Publications Committee (1914), Proceedings, 13 May 1914, mins. 527–8. Publications Committee (1919), Proceedings, 26 Mar. 1919, mins. 102–10. Publications Committee (1920), *Second Report*, para. 6. Publications Committee (1921), *Report* (11 Aug. 1921), paras. 3, 5. Publications Committee (1923), *Special Report*, Proceedings, 23 Mar. 1923, mins. 128–55. Publications Committee (1925), *Special Report* (19 Mar. 1925), para. 5; Appendix 3; Proceedings, 17 June 1924, min. 1568.

press advertising of official publications continued over the next three years, along similar lines to what had been done before. Sales increases were recorded and, although direct links with these campaigns were difficult to prove, advertising was accorded some of the credit.[75]

Stationery Office publicity was formulated with four aims in mind: giving a good send-off to a work on its publication; maintaining the demand after the first orders probably would have subsided; reviving demand; and increasing the sale of periodicals. Advertisements were presented in a dignified form rather than a popular manner. Instead of using slogans or catchy phrases, the HMSO adopted a formal approach believed to be more in keeping with its official status. In 1924, for example, it was decided to add the Royal Arms to all notices as it was 'thought that the advertisements . . . [were] rendered at once somewhat more dignified and attractive by its use'.[76]

In 1925, as a substitute for press advertising, half the funds available were earmarked for literary journals having a 'large circulation amongst an intelligent reading class'. The balance of the budget was apportioned equally between technical papers, the journals of learned societies, and special schemes. No appeals were directed towards the public at large.[77] The 1925 campaign to publicize the Ministry of Labour *Gazette* typifies the manner in which individual publications were advertised. Using the Census of Production as a reference point, the HMSO forwarded 1,060 specimen copies of the journal to targeted potential subscribers, and issued 400,000 leaflets to selected groups and individuals. Although there was no indication that the former had met with more success than the latter, and overall results were disappointing (only 650 orders were obtained), the HMSO continued to champion selective advertising, claiming that it was making headway with the general public as well.[78]

To coincide with its participation in the British Empire Exhibition at Wembley in 1924, the HMSO published a 'Brief Guide to Government Publications', which summarized its activities. A tone of self-congratulation pervaded this brochure. Taking it at face value, one reviewer gushed,

---

[75] 'Report on Advertising in the Press during the year ended Oct. 31, 1924', undated; 'Report on the Advertisement of Government Publications in the Press 1 Nov. 1925–31 Oct. 1926', 1 Dec. 1926, STAT 14/23.

[76] 'Report . . . year ended Oct. 31, 1924', STAT 14/23.

[77] 'Report on advertising in the Press during the year ending 31 Oct. 1925', undated, STAT 14/23.

[78] Publications Committee (1926), *Second Report* (14 Dec. 1926), Proceedings, 7 Dec. 1926, mins. 640–3.

This is a more interesting pamphlet than its title indicates, and it reveals the Stationery Office as publisher and seller of literature which, in variety and scope, in authority, and in cheapness, is unsurpassed. The pamphlet observes that the phrase 'as dull as a blue-book' which 20 or 30 years ago was one of the cruellest things that could be said of any book, is today heard less often, and the blue-book is becoming, if not a 'best-seller', at least an understood and recognized part of the publishing activities of the country. Whether this can be attributed to the improvement in the blue-book itself or to the wider horizons of the book buying public is a matter for dispute. What is certain is that the publications of H.M. Stationery Office are steadily growing in public favour.[79]

Privately officials were forced to admit that progress had been limited. Receipts for 1924–5 showed that sales were actually decreasing.[80] There was also little evidence to support the claim that the reputation of government documents had improved. During the parliamentary estimates debate in 1926, when the HMSO was criticized for not adopting a progressive sales policy, MPs characterized official papers as being too unattractive to be competitive: 'the get-up of these publications, in many cases, is deplorable. . . . No one would ever buy a Government Blue Book for what it looked like.'[81]

In response to these criticisms, the Treasury asked the publications committee to investigate HMSO advertising. After Codling informed the committee that he was endeavouring to effect improvements in the presentation of papers, it let the matter drop.[82] Yet there was growing recognition within the department that a fundamental change in approach might be necessary. In a report on publicity prepared in 1926, one official suggested that the HMSO should begin to concentrate on general background advertising, in other words, on creating a favourable image of the department and its publications, instead of marketing particular documents. Echoing Cant's suggestions, but stressing that it would be possible 'to make "copy" interesting while avoiding a commercialism which would ill accord with the public acts of a Government Department', this report advocated the use of more popular forms of advertising. The author noted that most publishers spent 6 per cent of their turnover on publicity, and argued that, while expenditure at this level would be undesirable from either an economic or a policy perspective, Stationery Office advertising was no longer in an 'experimental stage', and thus there was

[79] *The Times*, 14 July 1925.
[80] 'Report on advertising in . . . year ending 31 Oct. 1925', STAT 14/23.
[81] Hansard, 15 Feb. 1926, vol. 191, cols. 1582, 1593–5.
[82] Publications Committee (1926), *First Report* (27 July 1926), para. 2.

justification for increasing the budget back to £2,000.[83] Although others agreed that this was not an extravagant request, it was observed that, even under the higher allocation, the department would be unable to engage in the type of repetitive advertising in popular journals favoured by commercial publishers. Interestingly enough, during the discussions engendered within the HMSO, it was emphasized that this would obtain under any size budget, as the nature and content of official documents necessitated that they be advertised in specialized publications. As well, an increase in advertising expenditure was said to be justified, because even specific publicity could serve long-term objectives:

The chief difficulty in increasing the sales of Government Publications arises from the slight interest taken by the general public in administrative and policy affairs. To increase this interest is not primarily one of the duties of the Stationery Office yet it is nevertheless felt that suitably prepared advertisements may contribute to this end. In this way a sounder public interest will slowly arise upon which hopes of permanently increased sales may be more securely based.[84]

Cant's ideas were finally receiving official recognition, albeit with a twist. A public service approach to publicizing government information, that is, 'publicity', was being advocated as the best means of securing 'profits'.

Yet the Treasury was not asked to increase the budget, undoubtedly because the HMSO lacked concrete evidence that to date advertising had made any profound difference. Despite consistent discussion of the issue, the Office did not keep accurate figures,[85] but departmental records indicate that between 1919 and 1927 sales remained constant at about £115,000 a year.[86] Even if the higher figures given in parliament are assumed correct, annual sales revenue averaged under £200,000 in the mid-1920s, while the comparable figure for printing costs was £1.5 million.[87] It is also possible that Codling blocked the proposal. Asked to comment in 1929 on any potential benefits to be derived from a larger publicity budget, he informed the publications committee that

[a]s far as Press advertising is concerned the advantage would be that I could put in more advertisements.

[83] 'Report on the Advertisement of Government Publications . . . 1 Nov. 1925–31 Oct. 1926', STAT 14/23.   [84] Minutes, 24, 29 Sept. 1927; 3 Oct. 1927, STAT 14/23.
[85] Publications Committee (1917–18), *Report*, pp. 11–12. Publications Committee (1919), Proceedings, 26 Mar. 1919, mins. 83–92. Publications Committee (1920), *Third Report*, Proceedings, 10 Mar. 1920, min. 328. Publications Committee (1923), *Special Report*, Proceedings, 23 Mar. 1922, mins. 110–27; 20 June 1922, mins. 824–5. Hansard, 11 July 1922, vol. 156, cols. 1163–4.   [86] Minute, 5 Oct. 1927, STAT 14/23.
[87] Hansard, 15 Feb. 1926, vol. 191, col. 1585; 16 Apr. 1929, vol. 227, cols. 98–9.

REAR-ADMIRAL SUETER. But I mean would it be worth it financially? Would you get more sales?

MR CODLING. I very much doubt whether it would. We choose our papers very carefully, and I very much doubt if a larger sum spent in Press advertising would bring in commensurate return.[88]

Although the matter did surface again, the financial crisis of 1931 ended speculation. Indeed, the existing budget was cut to £750.[89] Ironically, because the sum was 'barely sufficient for adequately advertising the many suitable publications' available, the 'main policy' now became one of endeavouring to 'keep the name of the S.O. before as many potential customers as possible'.[90] As general press advertising could not be conducted on such a low budget, most of the funds were directed towards weekly papers. Less was spent in the specialized press, the department counting on reviews and direct mail publicity to reach targeted audiences. Only in the case of Ministry of Agriculture publications, which had a special allocation of £300, was anything of a more specific nature attempted.[91] Stationery Office advertising policy continued along these lines well into the 1930s.

Not surprisingly, these efforts met with little measurable success. Sales levels remained relatively static over the entire period, annual returns varying from £223,000 to £250,000 in the years 1930–7.[92] Addressing the publications committee in 1937, N. G. Scorgie, the deputy-controller of the HMSO, expressed the department's disappointment with results to date:

We have a limited amount which we spend on advertising but there I would anticipate an objection that it is not really economic to advertise Government Publications in the way that popular novels can be advertised, because, again, the aim of the Government has been to give the purchaser the best value that can be given for the money, so that there is not a great deal to play with for advertising and there is not an unlimited public that will buy under any conditions.[93]

The difficulty, Scorgie observed, was not with the format or presentation of documents but with their content. He believed that by their very nature official papers were unmarketable. Scorgie did not admit it, but

[88] Publications Committee (1929–30), Proceedings, 18 Dec. 1929, mins. 99–105.
[89] Minute, 11 Sept. 1931, STAT 14/23.
[90] Minute, 21 Sept. 1931, STAT 14/23.
[91] Cowell, 'Draft Scheme 1934', 26 Apr., 1934, STAT 14/23.
[92] Hansard, 15 July 1931, vol. 255, col. 462. Publications Committee (1936–7), *Second Report*, para. 4.
[93] Publications Committee (1936–7), Proceedings, 15 June 1937, min. 331.

the HMSO itself had compounded the problem. Unable to alter materials, and not obligated to awaken public consciousness, the department had to date engaged only in surface advertising, publicizing documents as though they were popular novels. The real difficulty lay in the HMSO's unwillingness to assume responsibility for educating the mass audience. Profit, not public service, still motivated departmental policy. Questioned on the subject of gratuitous distribution, Scorgie observed,

we look at free copies in the main as sprats to catch mackerels. . . . [F]ree copies is one of the things that we are constantly keeping an eye on, and one has to strike a balance between the desire of the Department to get publicity for its work and the duty of the Stationery Office to sell as many copies as possible.[94]

Although it accounted for most of the department's publicity expenditure over the period, newspaper advertising was not the only method employed. As noted above, in June 1921 Codling persuaded the Treasury to sanction the distribution of review copies to the press.[95] The department moved quickly to consolidate control over the practice, advising other ministries that in order to prevent overlapping and ensure co-ordinated publicity, it alone would issue such publications.[96] The extent to which compliance was secured is unclear,[97] for the HMSO could not enforce its dictate; as noted, the department lacked exclusive authority over the general distribution of official papers. Thus a procedure had to be devised to cover all eventualities.[98] Again, its status as a ministry of State precluded the HMSO from functioning like a regular publishing house.

The other main method of publicity employed was circularizing. Expenditure in this area was limited, ranging from £500 in 1926 to approximately £1,000 in 1929 and £4,500 by 1940.[99] Like press advertising, it was approached in a highly selective manner, with circulars being sent to individuals and groups assumed to be predisposed to have an interest in

---

[94] Ibid., mins. 336–7.

[95] Codling to Treasury, 14 June 1921; reply, 27 June 1921, STAT 14/23.

[96] Correspondence with the Scottish Education Department, 19 July, 18 Aug. 1921; Notes, 23 July, 1 Aug. 1921, STAT 14/23; and Codling to all departments, 22 Aug. 1921, HO 45/11908.

[97] e.g. MAF publications were sent out by the ministry in some cases and the HMSO in others: Minutes, 2, 3 Dec. 1929, STAT 14/23. Publications Committee (1929–30), Proceedings, 18 Dec. 1929, min. 129.

[98] Codling to the Home Secretary, 20 Mar. 1922, HO 45/11908.

[99] Hansard, 15 Nov. 1926, vol. 199, col. 1554; 16 Apr. 1929, vol. 227, cols. 598–9; 15 July 1931, vol. 255, col. 462; 20 Feb. 1940, vol. 357, col. 1149.

certain documents.[100] Only a minimal amount of general advertising was undertaken. Brochures were issued to coincide with events such as the British Empire Exhibition, for example, and specially prepared materials were submitted to the press as news articles.[101] Similarly, the BBC was persuaded to announce the publication dates of important documents as news items. However, the corporation could not guarantee that notices would be broadcast, and they were often crowded out if time pressure proved too great.[102]

A number of other important and inexpensive means of reaching the wider audience were not exploited, however, because of the department's adherence to profit motives. The HMSO was given control over the distribution of publications to public libraries in 1915. Under arrangements introduced in that year, all recognized libraries received an annual grant of £250 against the cost of official documents. Rising prices after the war, coupled with the major reclassification of parliamentary papers in 1921 (with the result that fewer documents could be secured at the subscription rate), left many institutions unable to purchase a wide selection of materials.[103] Supported by MPs, the Library Association petitioned the government for a better subsidy, arguing that every citizen ought to have easy access to public information, and that the prices charged were unfair:

the statistical and research work of Government Departments is done, at considerable cost to the nation, with the object of communicating to the public the results of their investigations. Further, as a minimum number of certain official documents must be printed and circulated for the benefit of Members of Parliament and Government Departments the initial cost of issuing them should not be chargeable to the purchasers, the purchasers should only be charged the extra cost of the additional copies printed.[104]

The HMSO agreed to alter the arrangements, inaugurating a new policy in 1924, allowing all libraries to obtain documents at half the published price.[105] Categorizing this as discriminatory against smaller institutions which needed the financial assistance, Cecil Wilson, a Labour MP,

---

[100] Publications Committee (1915), Proceedings, 13 May 1915, mins. 255–9. Publications Committee (1929–30), Proceedings, 18 Dec. 1929, min. 116. Hansard, 20 May 1920, vol. 129, cols. 1627–8.

[101] See *Advertising World*, 49/5 (1926), 500–4, 516; 53/3 (1928), 274–6.

[102] Publications Committee (1929–30), Proceedings, 18 Dec. 1929, min. 180. Publications Committee (1936–7), Proceedings, 15 June 1937, min. 331.

[103] *The Times*, 4 Mar. 1924. Hansard, 11 Dec. 1924, vol. 179, cols. 343–5; 15 Feb. 1926, vol. 191, cols. 1582–3.   [104] *The Times*, 4 Mar. 1924.

[105] Ibid. 5 Mar. 1924.

advocated that a number of free depositories be designated, as was the practice in the United States. Only by this means could the 'increasing desire on the part of the public for information upon which greater reliance can be placed than is possible with the major part of the public press' be met.[106] Claiming that sufficient concessions had already been made, the HMSO refused to reconsider the matter, despite pressure from all sides of the Commons.[107] As a result, only a small proportion of libraries subscribed regularly to an extensive variety of publications.[108] In 1937, a mere 150 stocked Hansard.[109] One MP noted in 1940 that he had felt compelled to order a copy for the library in his constituency, in order to ensure that it had one.[110]

The HMSO was also slow to adopt publicity measures designed to appeal to the general public. In the pre-war period, Wymans had used post offices to display circulars and notices advertising publications, and had not been charged for the privilege.[111] HMSO officials were apparently oblivious to these arrangements. When asked if he had ever considered trying it, Atterbury informed the publications committee in 1916 that 'the Post Office would object to any such system. I have known attempts in connection with other offices to get the Post Office to be a third wheel in the coach, but it has not been anxious to be that third wheel.'[112] When Cant recommended the idea in his 1920 report, Pearce balked, though he did include the suggestion in plans he prepared the following year. By 1921 permission had been secured to display catalogues and order forms on GPO premises, approval resting on the condition that the scheme not entail any work for postal employees. Thus, for example, notices could not be placed anywhere near counters, lest the public query the staff about them. Anticipating the imminent acceptance of a contract permitting commercial advertisements in all of its offices, the GPO also requested that the displays be as unobtrusive as possible! A small box containing catalogues was introduced into most offices by December.[113] That it was unobtrusive is evidenced by a *Manchester Guardian* article of January 1924, which suggested that it would be a 'useful advance' were post offices to

---

[106] Hansard, 11 Dec. 1924, vol. 179, cols. 343–5.

[107] Ibid. Also Hansard, 18 Dec. 1924, vol. 179, col. 1205; 31 Mar. 1925, vol. 182, cols. 1099–1100; 15 Feb. 1926, vol. 191, cols. 1582–3.

[108] Publications Committee (1923), *Report*, Proceedings, 31 May 1923, mins. 442–53.

[109] Publications Committee (1936–7), Proceedings, 15 June 1937, min. 357.

[110] Publications Committee (1939–40), *First Report* (20, 26 Feb. 1940), Proceedings, 6 Feb. 1940, min. 128.   [111] See above, p. 58.

[112] Publications Committee (1916), Proceedings, 2 Aug. 1916, mins. 1063–4.

[113] Note to Director, 23 Sept. 1921, STAT 14/23.

contain lists of publications.[114] Boxes had been placed in over 650 locations by 1933, but few sales could be traced to the circulars displayed. This is not surprising as applications from local offices for additional forms and catalogues ran to a mere twelve per year. In May 1933, Codling asked the GPO to query head postmasters regarding public interest in the scheme, only to be told to remove the display altogether. Annoyed by competition from official notices, commercial advertisers were taking the GPO to arbitration.[115] Hence the HMSO's experiment was not repeated.

This example typifies Whitehall's overall approach towards the use of public premises for official advertising. In 1926, when the Empire Marketing Board decided to erect poster frames on government land,[116] the Treasury insisted on charging rent, fearing that free access would set a dangerous precedent.[117] After the board folded in 1933, the hoardings were made available to other departments,[118] but the charges levied often precluded their use.[119] Similarly, in 1935 the GPO encountered difficulty in finally persuading the Treasury to cancel the contract for commercial advertisements in post offices, so that it could have free access to the space.[120] Treasury resistance stemmed from the fact that, once government buildings were being used for commercial advertising, space could not be reallocated to departments without a loss of revenue to the State.

The same type of logic was applied to the question of notices in official publications. Advertisements first appeared in government documents in 1886, but they did not become common until after 1923, when a general policy was adopted in the interests of economy.[121] Commercial agents handled the arrangements until 1925, when, dissatisfied with the results achieved to date, the HMSO decided to sell the space itself.[122] Accordingly,

[114] *Manchester Guardian*, 27 Jan. 1924.

[115] GPO to HMSO, 6, 29 May 1933, STAT 14/23.   [116] See below, p. 103.

[117] C. L. Stocks to Barstow; and reply, 24 Sept. 1926, T 161/479/29573/02.

[118] On this decision see Cabinet Minutes, C50(33), 5 Sept. 1933; C55(33), 25 Oct. 1933, CAB 23/77. 'The Future of the Empire Marketing Board Poster Frames', Memorandum by the Secretary of State for Dominion Affairs, C.P.211(33), Aug. 1933, CAB 24/243. Cabinet Committee on Imperial Economic Cooperation, Minutes, IEC(33), 17 Oct. 1933, CAB 27/553. 'Report on Empire Marketing Board Poster Frames and Marketing Committee', by Neville Chamberlain, C.P.239(33), 24 Oct. 1933, CAB 24/243. *The Times*, 1 Sept. 1933. Hansard, 30 Nov. 1933, vol. 283, cols. 1042–3; 1 Dec. 1933, vol. 283, cols. 1190–2; 22 Feb. 1934, vol. 286, col. 520.

[119] R. S. R. Fitter, 'An Experiment in Public Relations', *Public Administration*, 14 (1936), 464–7. Also see below, pp. 150–1.   [120] See below, pp. 104–5, 119.

[121] Publications Committee (1906), Proceedings, 25 June 1906, mins. 2243–4. Publications Committee (1915), Proceedings, 7 July 1915, min. 1058. Hansard, 16 May 1923, vol. 164, col. 464.

[122] *Advertising World*, 49/5 (1926), 500–4, 516. All arrangements, except canvassing for advertisements in Post Office stamp books, were handled by the HMSO. The exception made for the GPO invited censure; Scorgie to Phillips, 20 Mar. 1931, T 162/287/27596.

the department engaged in a limited amount of direct canvassing and endeavoured to attract clients by publishing news articles stressing what a valuable medium the documents afforded for commercial publicity. Given the department's preoccupation with sales, it is interesting to note that these articles emphasized the quality of the publications rather than the quantity sold.[123] Admittedly, it would have been difficult to advance a strong argument on the second point, but it is significant that the sales pitch centred on the idea that government papers were purchased by a selective, intelligent readership. As this implies, the HMSO had yet to make inroads with the population at large, and neither regarded nor claimed to regard the latter as its target audience.

Yet again, the HMSO could not exercise complete control over the process. Government departments were permitted to veto the types of advertisements placed in their publications.[124] However, the fact that 'unsuitable' notices could be rejected did not prevent controversy.[125] Some MPs and civil servants argued that it was unseemly for official documents to contain even dignified advertisements.[126] Codling refused to place advertisements in Hansard on these grounds.[127] This reflected both the poor reputation of advertising at the time[128] and anxiety that contributors would influence the content of the publications, thus subverting their purpose. For a number of reasons, not least among them the fact that advertising accounted for a considerable proportion of newspaper revenues,[129] the belief was widespread that advertisers used their financial leverage to manipulate the press and influence editorial content.[130] Responding to suggestions that the presentation of documents should be

---

[123] *Advertising World*, 49/5 (1926), 500–4, 516.

[124] Walter Guiness, 'Advertisements in Government Publications', 16 Nov. 1923, HO 45/17926. Hansard, 11 Mar. 1929, vol. 226, cols. 799–800.

[125] There were problems regarding alcohol advertisements: 'Liquor Advertisements in Post Office Publications', Memorandum by the Financial Secretary to the Treasury, C.P.248(25), 18 May 1925, CAB 24/173. CCHA, Minutes, HAC(13), 25 May 1925, CAB 26/7. Hansard, 10 June 1925, vol. 184, cols. 1739–41; 19 June 1925, vol. 185, cols. 794–5. 'Liquor Advertisements in Post Offices', Memorandum by the PMG, C.P.199(29), 9 July 1929, CAB 24/204. GPO to Treasury, 9 Sept. 1925, T 162/238/24816/01.

[126] See Hansard, 15 Feb. 1926, vol. 191, col. 1596.

[127] Publications Committee (1925), *Special Report*, Proceedings, 17 June 1924, mins. 1625–8.

[128] Note Codling's remarks before the Publications Committee (1921), Proceedings, 30 June 1921, mins. 590–7.

[129] Nicholas Kaldor and Rodney Silverman estimate that in 1935 the press derived 56.8 per cent of its income from advertising: *A Statistical Analysis of Advertising Expenditure and of the Revenue of the Press* (Cambridge, 1948), 7, 45.

[130] See Richard S. Lambert, *Propaganda* (1938), 48–50. Harold Lasswell, *Propaganda Technique in the World War* (1927), 192. Norman Angell, *The Press and the Organization of Society* (Cambridge, 1933), 39–40. A. S. J. Baster, *Advertising Reconsidered* (1935), 28–30.

improved, so as to make them more attractive to advertisers,[131] one member of the publications committee observed,

these journals are produced in the public interest . . . and . . . therefore it is not . . . [the] business . . . [of the editors] . . . to put in matter which, although not to great public advantage might conceivably be productive of more advertisements. . . . [Thus] it is not really an adverse criticism of . . . publications [when] . . . they show few or no advertisements . . ., seeing that the object of their existence . . . [is] not to provide a profitable property for the State, but rather to supply information of special value.[132]

Ironically, as it was incensed by the competition for revenue, the press also voiced complaints about advertisements in official publications.[133] But the policy was lucrative and thus had strong backing from the Treasury. The income derived from advertisements in publications was £32,000 in 1920–1. Between 1923 and 1925 the annual average was £115,000, rising above £130,000 by the early 1930s.[134] Not surprisingly, any blank pages in a document were viewed by the Treasury as a waste of potential revenue.[135]

That official papers were regarded more as a paying proposition than a public service is further underscored by the fact that they were not widely employed to publicize government documents. Official advertisements did appear in many publications, but the government was noted to be 'chary' of the practice.[136] Indeed, space was generally allocated only in cases where it could not otherwise have been put to commercial use. It is not clear whether a charge was exacted from departments for such fill-ups, but it is unlikely; no such moneys appear in the HMSO returns,[137] and the Treasury certainly tried to curtail the practice.[138]

G. W. Goodall, *Advertising* (1914), 15. Arland D. Weeks, *The Control of the Social Mind* (1923), 76. The National Union of Journalists convinced the government it should establish a Royal Commission in 1949 by stressing, among other things, that advertisers had long been circumventing the independence of the press: *Report of the Royal Commission on the Press 1947–1949*, Cmd. 7700 (1949), paras. 6, 23, 49, 499–528. This was also a factor impeding the introduction of advertising to radio; Hilda Matheson, *Broadcasting* (1933), 27, 236. Asa Briggs, *The History of Broadcasting in the United Kingdom*, ii. *The Golden Age of Wireless* (1965), 492–3.

[131] Publications Committee (1926), *First Report*, Proceedings, 8 June 1926, mins. 333–4. Hansard, 15 Feb. 1926, vol. 191, cols. 1595–6.
[132] Publications Committee (1926), *Second Report*, Proceedings, 7 Dec. 1926, mins. 634–5.   [133] Publications Committee (1915), Proceedings, 7 July 1915, min. 1058.
[134] Guiness, 'Advertisements', HO 45/17926. *Advertising World*, 49/5 (1926), 500–2. Hansard, 21 Feb. 1929, vol. 225, cols. 1302–3; 19 Dec. 1930, vol. 246, cols. 1620–1.
[135] Hansard, 26 Nov. 1931, vol. 260, col. 514.   [136] *The Times*, 28 July 1922.
[137] Publications Committee (1926), *Second Report*, Proceedings, 7 Dec. 1926, mins. 603–18, 653–60. Publications Committee (1929–30), Proceedings, 18 Dec. 1929, mins. 121–3.
[138] Minute, 7 Oct. 1924; Guiness, 'Advertisements', HO 45/17926.

The degree to which the profit motive impeded public service is perhaps best typified by the manner in which Hansard was handled. Of all official publications, the record of the debates of Parliament was recognized to be the most important to the democratic process.[139] Yet Hansard, too, was published on a commercial basis. The debates had been issued since the nineteenth century, only coming under official control between 1908 and 1911. Hansard received little attention from the publications committee until 1921–2, when, without the prior consent of Parliament or the committee, the HMSO increased its price from 3*d*. to 1*s*.[140] Annual expenditure on preparing and printing of the debates was in the area of £30,000–£35,000. At a charge of 3*d*. sales averaged under 1,500 copies per volume (not including the 1,750 distributed gratuitously to MPs and other officials), and the loss per copy was 7*d*. Under the new scale, sales were halved, but with a smaller loss.[141] This invited controversy; Liberals, in particular, were incensed by this 'miserable little economy', particularly when it was revealed that the higher rate was intended to compensate in part for the free copies distributed to officials. The Government was accused of suppressing information and interfering with 'grave constitutional issues': 'It is a surprising thing that when we should require, as we certainly require, an educated democracy . . . we should put what is now practically a prohibitive tax upon . . . publication[s].'[142] When the HMSO countered that costs would be lower if gratuitous distribution to MPs was curbed, several accused the department of trying to tamper with parliamentary privilege.[143] The new pricing policy was also challenged on commercial grounds.[144] Arguing that more copies would be sold under cheaper rates, the publications committee decided in 1923 to reduce the charge to its earlier level. Codling opposed this action, claiming that the demand was not determined by the cost: 'people will not take the trouble to read a verbatim report . . .; they prefer to take the newspaper report, where they get it set out according to their own fancy in the way of political

---

[139] Charles Frederick Higham, *Looking Forward* (1920), 56. Hansard, 11 July 1922, vol. 156, cols. 1166–83; 17 Feb. 1927, vol. 202, cols. 1166–90. Publications Committee (1939–40), 'Appendix: Memorandum by Commander Stephen King-Hall'. Hansard Society, *First Report*, 2nd edn. (1944), 22–4.   [140] Hansard, 11 July 1922, vol. 156, col. 1167.

[141] Ibid., cols. 1166, 1176; Publications Committee (1923), *Special Report*, Proceedings, 11 May 1922. Publications Committee (1939–40), Proceedings, 6 Feb. 1940, min. 244. Hansard, 30 Sept. 1931, vol. 257, cols. 346–7.

[142] Hansard, 11 July 1922, vol. 156, cols. 1166–73, 1183–4.

[143] Publications Committee (1923), *Report*, Proceedings, 31 May 1923, min. 366. Hansard, 17 Feb. 1927, vol. 202, cols. 1166–90.

[144] Publications Committee (1923), *Special Report*, Proceedings, 23 Mar. 1922, min. 151. Publications Committee (1923), *Report*, Proceedings, 31 May 1923, mins. 366–72. Publications Committee (1936–7), Proceedings, 15 June 1937, min. 346. Hansard, 11 July 1922, vol. 156, col. 1166; 23 Jan. 1930, vol. 234, col. 338.

ideas.'[145] As Colin Matthew has noted, this was hardly a new development; coverage of parliamentary proceedings had been on the decline since the mid-Victorian period.[146] Yet the fact that the press was devoting less attention to parliament, and was inclined to summarize its proceedings selectively, was precisely the reason why Liberal back-benchers stressed that the public had to be encouraged to purchase the actual debates; Hansard, it was claimed, served as a form of counter-propaganda.[147] Several MPs suggested that the HMSO should attempt to popularize the publication by improving its appearance and presentation. Charles Higham, who chaired the publications committee in 1923, recommended a change of title:

the bulk of the people of this country do not know that they can buy . . . a report of everything that happened in the House of Commons last night or yesterday afternoon. If they knew it, I think thousands would buy it. The point is that you have got a dull looking blue cover which looks like a blue book, and does not interest the public. If it was called: 'What happened in the House of Commons yesterday, price 6*d*.', you would have a big sale.[148]

Others believed the public would become 'Hansard-conscious', if illustrations of prominent members were added.[149] This idea was vetoed. A proposal that booksellers should be encouraged to stock the publication was also rejected, Codling claiming that it would be too expensive to print the requisite number of copies, and that shops would not handle bulky books yielding small returns.[150]

In 1940, Stephen King-Hall, a noted broadcaster, publicist, and MP,[151] set detailed proposals before the publications committee outlining plans

[145] Publications Committee (1923), *Second Report*, Proceedings, 31 May 1923, min. 440. Also see Publications Committee (1923), *Special Report*, Proceedings, 11 May 1922, min. 629. Charles Higham agreed: *Looking Forward*, 56.

[146] H. C. G. Matthew, 'Rhetoric and Politics in Great Britain, 1860–1950', in P. J. Waller (ed.), *Politics and Social Change in Modern Britain* (Brighton, 1987), 38.

[147] Arthur Balfour had raised the issue as early as 1908; Hansard Society, *First Report*, 10, 23. Also see Hansard, 11 July 1922, vol. 156, cols. 1168–9. Publications Committee (1939–40), Proceedings, 6 Feb. 1940, mins. 192–3.

[148] Publications Committee (1923), *Special Report*, Proceedings, 11 May 1922, min. 627.

[149] Hansard, 15 Feb. 1926, vol. 191, col. 1595; 20 Feb. 1940, vol. 357, cols. 1148–9. Publications Committee (1939–40), Proceedings, 6 Feb. 1940, mins. 143, 214–16.

[150] Publications Committee (1939–40), Proceedings, 6 Feb. 1940, mins. 204–8.

[151] From 1930 to 1937, King-Hall covered world affairs on the BBC's 'Children's Hour': see Stephen King-Hall, *Here and There*, 3 vols. (1932–4). In 1936 he launched the *King-Hall News-Letter*, a weekly broadsheet 'intended to represent an approach to the interpretation of current events, and the bridging of the gap between the expert and the public'. Beginning with 602 subscribers, it had a circulation of approximately 60,000 by 1939. In 1938, King-Hall assisted in planning the MOI's home publicity section. An Independent MP from 1939 to 1945, he chaired the Fuel Economy Publicity Committee in 1942 and founded the Hansard Society in 1943–4.

for a weekly abridged edition of Hansard. He believed that if 'taken in hand by a competent sales manager', Hansard would have a circulation of 100,000 copies.[152] Neither the Stationery Office nor the wartime Ministry of Information was as optimistic; they opposed the scheme because of the cost and likely problems involved in finding a fair and unbiased manner of selecting the contents.[153] It was left to private enterprise to increase public knowledge about the workings of the democratic process; King-Hall founded the Hansard Society in an attempt to arouse 'interest in and [spread] . . . knowledge throughout the world' of parliamentary proceedings.[154] Progress was slow; by 1943 only 30 per cent of libraries subscribed.[155]

Although the inter-war period saw an enormous increase in the volume of official publishing and a growing awareness of the need to make information available to the public, the principle that government, and government alone, was responsible for the widespread and gratuitous dissemination of information had yet to be accepted. Hence a publisher whose annual output could fill a catalogue of over seventy-seven pages spent under £5,000 on publicity in 1937–8, while taking in over £100,000 in revenue from commercial advertisements.[156] The HMSO may have paid lip-service to its public service responsibilities, but in practice profit motives dictated policy. The department engaged in commercial advertising rather than public relations. Indeed, when asked in 1938 to justify its publicity expenditure, the department replied that its advertising was not puffery or propaganda but 'the normal accompaniment of a publishing business. By advertising generally and circulating notices to the trade and interested parties, the sales of Government publications are increased.'[157] Because the HMSO was under the direct control of the Treasury, and was more business-orientated than most other departments, it is not surprising that the profit motive was so dominant. The irony, of course, is that concern with short-term returns impeded the development of the type of public education necessary to long-term success. Yet it was not simply a question of Treasury influence, for Stationery Office officials often shared the same prejudices. As we shall see in the next chapter, the same conflict of motives was present in the Post Office but developments there proceeded differently.

---

[152] Circulation varied between 3,000 and 3,500 copies per issue: Publications Committee (1936–7), *Second Report*, Proceedings, 15 June 1937, min. 372.
[153] Publications Committee (1939–40), Proceedings, 6 Feb. 1940, mins. 106–238, 265–7; Appendix. *Advertising World*, 70/10 (1938), 32, had made a similar suggestion in Oct.
[154] Hansard Society, *First Report*, 22–6.   [155] Ibid. 24.
[156] J. Gotts to Banham, 20 Jan. 1938, T 162/980/36055/01/2.   [157] Ibid.

4

'Bringing Alive' the Post Office

T H E public have little mind to help the Post Office, which we think unfortunate: the Post Office, on the other hand, have [*sic*] given some ground for saying that it appears to believe that the public was made for the Post Office, and not the Post Office for the public. It tends too much to a cast iron application of regulations in an improper way.... To secure ... success a more sympathetic recognition is vital by the Post Office ... that the public are human beings with human frailties, and not mere automans [*sic*] for making the telephone accounts balance.[1]

Thus concluded the House of Commons Select Committee on the Tele-phone Service in March 1922, after a year-long investigation into one aspect of Post Office administration. Despite the limited mandate of the committee, and its acknowledgement that the public was not entirely free from blame, these sentiments reflected and reinforced the widespread view of the GPO as inhumane, insensitive, and anything but orientated to public service. Within a decade the situation had been reversed. Much of the parliamentary estimates debate of June 1934, for example, focused on the department's improved image. MPs of all political opinions ob-served that a new attitude had permeated the entire GPO:

I wonder how many of us have cast our minds back, not so many years, to the time when a Post Office was a dirty building and the staff ... were renowned for their slovenliness rather than for their efficiency.... [I]t says a great deal for the present administration at the Post Office that in something like the same way as Signor Mussolini has roused Italy, so the Postmaster-General has roused the Post Office staff to feel a pride in the organization to which they belong.[2]

While the comparison with Italian fascism was somewhat far-fetched, there is little doubt that the GPO was thought to be imbued with a new and radical spirit.[3] Much of the credit went to Kingsley Wood, the Postmaster-General since 1931, and, in particular, to his 1933 decision

[1] *Report from the Select Committee on the Telephone Service, 1922* (20 Mar. 1922), paras. 2, 48.
[2] Hansard, 6 June 1934, vol. 290, col. 1019; and cols. 963–4, 993–5, 1014, 1030.
[3] *Planning*, 2/36 (23 Oct. 1934), 7. *The Times*, 10 Feb. 1936. W. H. Brown and T. L. Drury, 'Typography in the Post Office', *Public Administration*, 13 (1935), 359.

to establish a public relations division in the department under Stephen Tallents, the former secretary of the EMB.[4] Tallents's appointment was viewed as an outgrowth of the reorganization of the Post Office along business lines, following the recommendations of the 1932 Bridgeman inquiry into the service.[5] Indeed, the creation of the new division was justified on the grounds that, unlike other departments, the Post Office was a business with commodities to sell.[6]

The adoption of a permanent publicity policy was definitely related to commercial considerations, but it was also the culmination of a long process, and reflected the department's commitment to its public service responsibilities. Here lay its greatest impact for, despite the distinctions drawn between the GPO and other departments, developments within the Post Office were instrumental in fostering the growth of public relations machinery throughout Whitehall.[7] By example, the GPO showed publicity to be a necessary and legitimate adjunct to the work of every ministry of State in a democratic society.

The attention focused on Tallents's division, and the assumption that it marked a turning-point in departmental policy has obscured earlier GPO efforts in this area. The importance of maintaining good public relations was recognized in the Post Office well before 1933. As noted earlier, an annual report was introduced in 1854.[8] Certain services were also advertised; telephone slogans appeared on postmarks as early as 1904.[9] After the GPO amalgamated the telephone service in 1912, it endeavoured to forge ties with the business community by forming local area committees. Correspondingly, a *Telephone and Telegraph Journal* was created in 1914 to keep staff informed of relevant developments.[10] However,

---

[4] See *The Times*, 2 Sept., 3 Oct. 1933; 7 June 1934; 1 Aug., 12 Dec. 1935; 10 Sept. 1936. Also see M. J. Daunton, *Royal Mail* (1985), 354. Paul Swann, 'John Grierson and the G.P.O. Film Unit 1933–1939', *Historical Journal of Film, Radio and Television*, 3/1 (1983), 20. Forsyth Hardy, *John Grierson* (1979), 73.

[5] *The Times*, 2 Sept. 1933, 18 Jan. 1934. *Planning*, 1/9 (12 Sept. 1933), 15; 1/14 (21 Nov. 1933), 11. On the Bridgeman inquiry see below.

[6] *The Times*, 11 Oct. 1934; 5 Mar. 1935. *The Post Office* (1934), 11. Select Committee on Estimates (1934), Proceedings, 7 Mar. 1934, mins. 548–51, 577. Stephen Tallents, *Post Office Publicity* (1955), 5. Unsigned report on publicity, *c.*1933, MH 78/147.

[7] Contemporaries recognized this; see *Planning*, 2/45 (26 Feb. 1935), 9; 2/46 (12 Mar. 1935), 15. *Advertising World*, 67/7 (1935), 39; 69/10 (1937), 10; 70/8 (1938), 3. *The Times*, 12 Dec. 1935. Select Committee on Estimates (1938), para. 24; Proceedings, 30 Mar. 1938, min. 1535.

[8] Suspended in 1916 as an economy measure, it was revived by Tallents in 1934; see above, p. 25.   [9] *The Times*, 1 Mar. 1933.

[10] Raymond Nottage, 'The Post Office: A Pioneer of Big Business', *Public Administration*, 37 (1959), 59. *Post Office* (1934), 107.

no officers were employed specifically on publicity work, and advertising was confined mainly to publishing official announcements, with expenditure totalling a mere £1,773 in 1920.[11] Not until the economic position of the department began to change after the First World War was large-scale publicity deemed necessary, or advisable.

Noting that the profit margin of the GPO fell from nearly 40 per cent to just over 4 per cent between 1900 and 1920, M. J. Daunton has argued that after the First World War the department was forced to pay greater heed to its financial performance than it had done to date. Thus, he claims, profit motives began to dominate Post Office policy to the detriment of the public service, and it was not until the 1970s that the GPO became 'consumer oriented'.[12] Financial considerations did play a significant role in determining policy between the wars, but the consequent adoption of commercial practices, such as advertising, neither presupposed nor necessitated the abandonment of other objectives. The dual status of the GPO ensured that this could not be the case, as was manifested in its early attempts at advertising.

In 1912–13, the telephone branch showed a profit of £303,343. By 1920–1, it was losing £4,721,970.[13] The deficit was attributed to high overhead costs. As a remedy, the GPO decided to increase charges, introducing a system whereby each subscriber contributed in proportion to the services he/she required. Protests from the industry led to the formation of the aforementioned select committee in 1921.[14] Business leaders blamed low subscription levels for the losses, backing the claim with statistics indicating that under 2 per cent of the British population had telephones as compared to nearly 12 per cent in the United States. They advised the GPO to reduce rates, adopt better management techniques, and endeavour to popularize what was in effect a public service.[15] The Post Office was loath to encourage growth, claiming that an increase in customers would raise capital costs beyond the revenue generated.[16] The select committee questioned the department's logic, recommending

---

[11] GPO to Treasury, 27 Apr. 1920, T 161/3/213. 'Publicity Departments', 1920, T 162/42/2862.   [12] M. J. Daunton, *Royal Mail* (1985), 329–30, 353–4.

[13] Viscount Wolmer, *Post Office Reform* (1932), 114.

[14] Select Committee on Estimates (1922), Proceedings, 21 June 1922, min. 776.

[15] *Report from the Select Committee on the Telephone Service* (27 July 1921), Proceedings, 18 Apr. 1921, mins. 1145, 1205, 1229–39, 1471. Hansard, 16 Aug. 1921, vol. 146, col. 1220.

[16] *Report from the Committee on the Telephone Service* (1922), para. 25. Despite criticism the GPO continued to advance this argument: Sir Evelyn Murray, *The Post Office* (1927), 140. *Memorandum on Certain Proposals Relating to Unemployment*, Cmd. 3331 (May 1929), 38–9.

certain price reductions and emphasizing the need to manage the system on a more commercial basis. It also chastised the Post Office for its unbusinesslike approach towards customers.[17]

The report did not have an appreciable impact on the telephone service. An attempt was made to streamline administration by separating the telephone division from the mails branch, but charges were not reduced. On the other hand, a number of developments indicate that the department was becoming more publicity-conscious as a result of the complaints. The creation of a Post Office Advisory Council in June 1921, while the select committee was still sitting, was definitely a concession to the type of criticisms underlying the investigation. Composed of businessmen, chosen on individual merit rather than as representatives of specific interests, the council was supposed to advise the Postmaster-General on all commercial aspects of policy, and initiate proposals.[18] In practice, it met infrequently and had little opportunity to determine its own agenda.[19] Critics charged, rather ironically, that the council was merely an exercise in public relations: 'A piece of window-dressing ... [intended] to give a fictitious appearance of deference to commercial opinion without having any genuine influence on the internal conduct of the Department.'[20]

Also, in the wake of the select committee hearings, an Intelligence Officer, H. Chapman,[21] was appointed. Accorded responsibility for disseminating information on Post Office services, his functions did not extend to advertising *per se*, but rather to promoting an increasing awareness of the department and its work.[22] Given his limited mandate, the creation of this post was also termed mere window-dressing, and provoked criticism. Problems arose initially over the chosen appointee. Bypassing normal channels and acting in apparent disregard of the

---

[17] *Report from the Select Committee on the Telephone Service* (1922), paras. 24, 48.

[18] Hansard, 22 June 1921, vol. 143, col. 1389; 4 July 1921, vol. 144, col. 59; 11 Aug. 1921, vol. 146, cols. 629–30.

[19] Hansard, 27 July 1927, vol. 209, cols. 1229–30. *The Times*, 10 Jan. 1933.

[20] Wolmer, pp. 246–7. Also *The Times*, 4 Apr. 1925. Hansard, 7 Apr. 1925, vol. 182, col. 2030. G. H. Stuart-Bunning, 'The Theory of Post Office Policy', *Public Administration*, 4 (1926), 32.

[21] His qualifications are unclear: *Author's and Writer's Who's Who* (hereafter *AWWW*) (1934).

[22] Hansard, 4 Mar. 1924, vol. 170, col. 1202. Unsigned statement on publicity arrangements, 28 July 1923, T 162/42/2862. Select Committee on Estimates (1922), Proceedings, 22 May 1922, mins. 104–14, 281, 311–16. Memo for meeting 25 Oct. 1932, Post Office Archive, Post 33/3576 (9). (All future references to documents in this archive will be preceded by 'Post'. Parenthetic numbers following these entries refer to files.)

stipulations laid down by the Lytton report, the department had re-cruited a non-veteran, non-civil servant for the job. The explanation that Chapman had undertaken similar duties in the wartime Ministry of Food and had unspecified 'journalistic experience' placated no one. The issue raged until 1924, foreshadowing future conflicts within several departments over the qualifications required of publicity officers.[23]

The need for a full-time publicity officer was also questioned. Ad-dressing the Select Committee on Estimates in May 1922, Lord Curzon alluded to the government's current economy drive, and queried why a post not in existence before the war was being retained. Sir Evelyn Murray, the Permanent Secretary to the Post Office, noted the depart-ment's responsibility to disseminate information which the public was 'entitled' to know. Delegating the work to one official was said to be more economical and efficient, as it ensured that the task was conducted in a co-ordinated fashion. Not everyone was convinced by this explanation. When Murray rebutted allegations that the department was merely en-gaging in puffery, the chairman interjected, 'I think it is perfectly clear what takes place. The Post Office when they do a thing which they think will be popular inform the Press so that everybody may know. It is . . . advertising.'[24] The difficulties involved in justifying such advertising as legitimate public relations became more apparent when Chapman's activities came under closer public scrutiny.

In July 1923, Chapman issued an anonymous statement to the press, outlining the accomplishments of the Postmaster-General, Sir Laming Worthington-Evans, to coincide with the introduction of the departmental estimates in parliament. Distributing the minister's speech in advance was an established practice; Chapman added the article in an attempt to lighten the speech and attract attention to it. This was a classic example of editorial advertising, providing newsworthy information to the press in the hope of obtaining free publicity. The article itself was innocuous. Couched in popular language it exploited the human-interest angle, in-forming the public that 'Worthy' was a distinguished parliamentarian, very popular in the GPO. However, as it had emanated from a public official, the statement created a scandal. The matter was considered

[23] Hansard, 23 June 1921, vol. 143, col. 1585; 7 Mar. 1922, vol. 151, cols. 1090–1; 21 Mar. 1922, vol. 152, col. 272; 26 June 1922, vol. 155, cols. 1680–1; 28 June 1922, vol. 155, cols. 2040–1; 15 Feb. 1923, vol. 160, col. 358; 25 July 1923, vol. 167, col. 472; 31 July 1923, vol. 167, cols. 1270–2; 4 Mar. 1924, vol. 170, col. 1202.
[24] Select Committee on Estimates (1922), Proceedings, 22 May 1922, mins. 104–14, 279–83.

before the Cabinet, and Worthington-Evans publicly disassociated himself
from such 'vulgar and stupid personal puffs'.[25] Even then, a large proportion of the estimates debate centred on the incident. Broadly criticizing the GPO, MPs used the controversy to express their misgivings about
official publicity in general. Most of the participants in the debate agreed
that departments had to communicate with the press, but wanted stricter
guidelines laid down to govern the practice.[26] Linking the incident to Lloyd
George's tainted administration of 1916–22, William Pringle, an Asquith
Liberal, suggested that, in future, officials should confine their activities
to the distribution of 'facts', avoiding anything of a remotely political
nature: 'we must not have, as we had under the late Government, speeches
by the Prime Minister printed and published at the public expense.' By
inference, the distribution of ministerial policy statements was also open
to question. Labour's George Lansbury asserted that the issue involved
surpassed the mere problem of political puffery, for factual information
was not even being disseminated legitimately:

During the War, and since . . . it seems to me that every Department has used the
Press, not for personal aggrandisement, or personal puffs, as on this occasion, but
always to support the particular line of policy of the Government and to do all
it can to prove that the policy of its opponents was wrong. I think it is their right
to do that, but I do not think they have the right to use public money in paying
men in their Departments to do this sort of thing.

How departments were supposed to inform the public about politically
determined policies without advancing those policies was not taken into
consideration. Rather than addressing this issue, other MPs echoed
Lansbury's concern with preserving the neutrality and integrity of the
Civil Service. Sir Frederick Banbury, a Conservative, agreed that publicity organizations were dangerous as 'officers may be inclined, or tempted,
to use their position to put out propaganda in favour of the particular
party . . . in power at the time'. Worthington-Evans responded that the
entire matter was the concern of the Treasury, but observed that whatever decision was reached regarding government publicity divisions, his
department, a 'trading concern' with 'goods to sell', had to engage in
advertising. The Treasury concurred;[27] although most departmental
publicity bureaux were disbanded in the following months, the GPO was
allowed to retain Chapman.

[25] Cabinet Minutes, C41(23), 25 July 1923, CAB 23/46. Hansard, 25 July 1923, vol. 167,
col. 472.
[26] Subsequent references are to Hansard, 31 July 1923, vol. 167, cols. 1270–2, 1319–47.
[27] Ibid., col. 1344.

The issues raised in parliament were not pursued, nor were guidelines formulated regarding the conduct of publicity officers. Yet Chapman confined his future activities to the distribution of facts, and avoided anything controversial. Ironically this drew criticism from within the department. Frustrated by the negative public image of the GPO, the staff began to use intra-departmental machinery to lobby for a more aggressive publicity policy, denigrating the department for not defending itself against criticism. Higher officials replied that parliament was the proper forum for rebuttal, voicing anxiety lest direct contact with the press 'merely evoke further attacks'.[28]

The staff also chided the department for not publicizing its services. Criticism mounted after the United Kingdom Advertising Company was contracted in 1922 to rent wall space in post offices for the display of commercial advertisements.[29] A staff journal asserted that, were the minister 'strong',

some attention might be given to the necessity for bringing to the notice of the public the wares which the Post Office now purveys. To allow many of the services now undertaken to remain unremunerative because they are little known is the height of folly, and if the space of Post Office walls is to be used for attracting the attention of the public, the object of any displayed announcements should be to make the Post Office and all its work better known.[30]

That the department had retained the right to display announcements on official notice-boards did not appease the critics. Notices printed in black and white on foolscap paper hardly approximated to the type of advertisements desired.[31]

Services were being advertised, but in a disjointed and sporadic manner. As every branch of the department was responsible for its own publicity, campaigns were developed to meet specific requirements rather than long-term goals. Agencies were not employed and, although Chapman was sometimes consulted about the efficacy of press advertising, schemes

[28] Departmental Whitley Council, Minutes, 2 July 1926; 5 Oct. 1926; 8 Dec. 1926; 29 Apr. 1927; 12 July 1927; 27 Aug. 1929; Post 33/3576 (1). *The Post*, 25 June 1927.

[29] Minute, 2 Feb. 1925, Post 33/4308 (6). G. E. G. Forbes to W. E. Parsons, 16 Apr. 1921, Post 33/3387 (1). Hansard, 4 Apr. 1922, vol. 152, col. 2029; 10 Apr. 1922, vol. 153, col. 63; 1 May 1923, vol. 163, cols. 1220–1. 350,000 sq. ft. of space was let in 1922–3, generating a revenue of £427 per week: *The Times*, 7 Feb. 1922. Hansard, 22 July 1924, vol. 176, col. 1146. By 1928 annual revenue averaged £36,700: Hansard, 26 Feb. 1929, vol. 225, cols. 1795–6.   [30] *The Post*, 1 July 1922.

[31] Memorandum by Bayliss, Jan. 1925, Post 33/4308 (6).

were planned and administered by regular officials without outside consultations.[32] In many cases staff members designed the posters used.[33]

The 'Post Early' campaign of 1922–4 provides a good example of the type of publicity undertaken in these years. Intended to encourage staggered mailing times, and thus decrease workloads at peak hours, the scheme originated with local Whitley Councils.[34] A special subcommittee created by the Departmental Whitley Council in August 1922 suggested that the GPO display written notices on mail vans, pillar-boxes, and in post offices themselves, organize special mail collections from large firms, and provide newsworthy statements to the press.[35] Notices were prepared, but the campaign had to be suspended owing to the trade slump, and because mounting criticism of the department was thought to make advertising inopportune![36] The scheme was revived in May 1924, when a circular outlining available publicity materials (two stickers for vans and boxes, and a panel notice for counters) was sent to all post offices. Considerable emphasis was placed on local initiative in this campaign.[37] Aside from preparing and distributing materials, the central Post Office had no direct involvement.

This differed a great deal from what was being done in other countries. In mid-1924, the GPO received a report on postal advertising in Canada, which indicated that the use of lectures, broadcasts, exhibits, posters, leaflets, and bulletins had significantly reduced congestion in that country's mails division in just two years.[38] Most GPO officials believed such methods were unsuitable,[39] but L. Simon, the future head of the telephone division, argued that some were worth exploring. Advertisements of a 'boosting' kind were 'best left severely alone', but the more 'educative' type of publicity employed by the Canadians might be used to advantage. As altering public behaviour would improve the service, he claimed that more widespread advertising in support of early posting could hardly be

[32] Chapman was consulted regarding the 'Early Posting' scheme; 2nd meeting, 1 Feb. 1923, Post 33/3370 (15), but was not involved in the other campaigns discussed.

[33] Competitions were held for several campaigns: Post 33/4308 (1, 2, 5, 10, 15). Note of Deputation, 19 Dec. 1929, Post 33/3576 (2).

[34] See Post 33/3370 (3). Whitley Councils were joint consultative bodies of employers and workers. They were established after 1917 in several industries and government to discuss relevant problems. See Charles Loch Mowat, *Britain between the Wars 1918–1940* (1978), 37.   [35] Minutes, 2 Aug. 1922, Post 33/3370 (5).

[36] Minutes, 1 Feb. 1923, Post 33/3370 (15); Minutes, 9 Mar. 1923 (16).

[37] Circular, 3 May 1924, Post 33/3370 ('Bottom').

[38] Postmaster-general of Canada to GPO, 28 Aug. 1924, Post 33/4308 (4).

[39] Memorandum by Forbes, 4 Oct. 1924; Various minutes, Nov. 1924, Post 33/4308 (4).

deemed questionable, and suggested that posters be prepared for display in all offices. The mails branch was enthusiastic, but no action was taken, as yet again it was feared such an exhibit would annoy the commercial contractor.[40]

Similar problems plagued the telephone branch. In spite of the select committee findings, continued criticism, and various offers of service,[41] telephone advertising was not even considered until October 1923, when the division presented proposals to display illustrated posters in local offices. Three rudimentary designs were prepared by staff, the branch requesting permission to issue 5,000 copies. The projected cost of the campaign was £20, if 15 ft. × 10 ft. notices were used, or £60 for commercial size double crown posters (30 ft. × 20 ft.).[42] As the scheme would have placed demands on at least some of the wall space being employed by commercial advertisers, the department wavered. Under the contract the Postmaster-General could appropriate space for GPO use, but officials had no desire to antagonize the company, or to forgo revenue. Several voiced doubts about the ability of amateur designs to compete with commercial advertisements. A 'small and striking poster among the official notices' was the recommended alternative. In the end, 1,500 15 ft. × 10 ft. copies of one of the illustrations were placed in post office windows and 3,500 advertising cards were exhibited.[43] As the posters could only be viewed from the outside of buildings, the scheme was recognized to have had a limited impact.[44]

Reconciling departmental needs with the commercial contract posed obvious difficulties. Yet, despite constant references to the restraints imposed by the arrangements, the contractor was not antipathetic to the inclusion of GPO advertisements in local offices. During 1924 the firm attempted to synchronize its display with that of the department, submitting plans to the Post Office for a combined notice-board and advertisement panel. The idea was rejected by senior members of the GPO Secretariat. At 8 ft. × 6 ft., the proposed frame was said to be too big for many offices. Concern was also expressed lest close proximity lead the public to confuse GPO announcements with commercial advertisements. Several officials thought this improbable, opposing the scheme on the

[40] Memorandum, 1 Nov. 1924, Post 33/4308 (4).
[41] These run to 31 files between 1920 and 1930; Post 33/2850.
[42] Memoranda, 30 Oct., 3 Nov. 1923, Post 33/4308 (1).
[43] Minutes, 3, 6, 27 Nov. 1923, Post 33/4308 (1).
[44] Memorandum, 9 June 1925; Memorandum to Inland Telegraph, June 1925, Post 33/4308 (7).

opposite grounds that the former were likely to be dwarfed by the more 'forcible style' of the latter. Observing that government notices tended to be ignored because of their stereotyped nature, one official used the same arguments in support of the proposal, noting that if surrounded by attractive posters official notices might receive attention.[45] Only S. J. Bayliss, an executive officer, questioned the *a priori* assumption that the department should not attempt to compete with commercial advertisements.[46] He suggested that bold, artistic posters, containing 'short, pithy phrases', should be introduced into all offices, supplemented by informative pamphlets placed on counters. Bayliss argued that the time was ripe for an experiment, stressing that better advertising would improve services and thus undermine criticism of the department. Noting that wall space was limited, he proposed hanging framed roller blind calendars from post office ceilings. Impressed by the political and economic arguments behind this proposal, the Secretariat held a conference in March 1925 to consider the general question of advertising. Representatives of the stores, buildings, telephone and telegraph, and engineer-in-chief's divisions were present. As all were agreed on the need for publicity, discussion centred on how the available space in post offices was to be apportioned between the various services. Here the divergent motives underlying GPO policy came into direct conflict; in order to compensate against any losses on the contract, the Secretariat announced plans to debit departmental branches in proportion to their requirements. Adopting a policy analogous to that of the Stationery Office, the department intended to charge itself for the use of its own premises, for advertising intended to increase its own business and hence profits! Not surprisingly, other divisions opposed the plan, claiming that they had a right to make reasonable demands on the available space. As agreement could not be reached, Bayliss's scheme was held over for discussion. Yet no further meetings occurred.[47] Proposals for an automatic display device for posters did not surface again until 1928, when an unsuccessful experiment was conducted in London.[48] The suggestion that branches should be debited for their access to wall space was raised again in 1925,[49] 1927,[50] and 1930,[51] but it was not until after

[45] Various minutes, Sept.–Oct. 1924, Post 33/4308 (4).

[46] Subsequent references are to Memorandum by Bayliss, Jan. 1925; and Bayliss to James, 9 Mar. 1925, Post 33/4308 (6).

[47] Minute, 2 Feb. 1925; Bayliss to James, 9 Mar. 1925, Post 33/4308 (6).

[48] Post 33/2850 (27). Post 33/4308 (12, 13, 14).   [49] Post 33/4308 (7).

[50] Post 33/4308 (10).

[51] Forbes chaired a committee on official notices in 1930. It met four times but never reported: Post 33/5252 (Part 1) (1).

the commercial contract was terminated in December 1935 that a policy governing the use of post office premises for official advertising was laid down.[52] At this point a committee on official notices was established. It gave Post Office branches equal access to the space, but placed strict limits on its use by other government departments.[53]

Commercial considerations were not the only factor restricting the development of Post Office publicity. Simon vetoed an advertising scheme proposed by the telephone and telegraph branch in 1925,[54] not only on the grounds that it would be counter-productive to publicize competing services, as an increase in business in one would be likely to be at the expense of the other, but also because the advertising of these services might contravene the public service responsibilities of the department.[55] Again distinguishing between boosting and educating, Simon observed that advertising telegraphs connoted both persuading the public to send them and familiarizing people with available facilities. Working from the assumption that the service was already well known, he argued that it would be unethical to employ 'psychological suggestion' to induce the public to waste money on unnecessary telegrams:

a government service may be expected to have regard to other considerations than that of diverting as much money as possible into its own pockets; and it is less free than the business man to encourage the spending of money in ways which from the point of view of society as a whole was unprofitable.

Education was another matter:

The telegraph service exists for the benefit of the public; and nobody ought to be debarred from deriving advantage from it through ignorance of what it can do for him. . . . [It] is part of the duty of the Post Office to spread knowledge of these . . . facilities, whether it increases its revenue by doing so or not.

Similarly, providing information about telephones would be above reproach as there was 'no doubt' that the advantages of the system were not fully realized. Simon assessed the validity of advertising on its motives; public service objectives were accorded equal if not greater importance than business considerations. Motive was measured not by result (he recognized that financial benefits would be derived from informative

---

[52] See below, p. 119.

[53] Post 33/5252 (Part 2) (17). On other departments' use of the space, see correspondence to the Treasury from the ministries of Air, Health, and Labour, Feb. 1938 in T 162/980/36055/01/1–3.

[54] Various minutes, Feb. 1925, Post 33/4308 (7).

[55] Subsequent references are to Memorandum by Simon, 6 May 1925, Post 33/4308 (7).

campaigns), but in terms of the methods employed. His constant reference to the difference between educating and boosting suggests that Simon
believed popular publicity had little place in a government department.
Indeed, he supported Bayliss's roller blind scheme only because the posters were intended to draw attention to the leaflets provided on counters.[56]
Similarly, Simon advised the telephone and telegraph branch that, rather
than conducting a large-scale campaign, it should issue pamphlets to
supplement the telephone posters already appearing in post office windows. Although leaflets were distributed, and pronounced a success, they
did not have an appreciable effect on telephone density levels.[57]

Manufacturers were so frustrated by the department's inability to expand the system that in 1924 they formed a Telephone Development Association. Its chief aim was to encourage subscriptions. Hence, the TDA
concentrated on publicizing the service, engaging in newspaper advertising
and distributing booklets containing coupons which could be sent to the
Post Office by those desiring further information.[58] Despite the measurable success of the campaign,[59] the GPO repeatedly refused to emulate it,
claiming that further efforts were unnecessary.[60] Others observed that the
very existence of the trade organization indicated that this was untrue.[61]
When it was noted in 1925 that the GPO spent a mere £2,000 a year on
advertising, while receiving over £55,000 from the commercial contract,
the Postmaster-General was urged in parliament to reconsider whether
'having regard to the fact that every business has to advertise', he was
actually 'serving the public interest' by not spending more on publicity.[62]
This issue was a regular feature of the annual estimates debate over the
next few years, though the department consistently refused to change its
policy.[63] In an attempt to defuse criticism, the Postmaster-General informed parliament in 1927 that during the previous year the department
had spent £1,000 printing and circulating four million copies of twenty-
nine different telephone posters and brochures. When pressed, he was
unable to provide a breakdown of results, and was forced to admit that a

---

[56] Ibid.   [57] Post 33/4308 (7).
[58] On TDA activities see *The Times*, 3 Oct. 1924. TDA to GPO, 26 Apr. 1932, Post 33/
2903 (13). TDA, *The Strangle-hold on our Telephones* (1930).
[59] Hansard, 26 Feb. 1926, vol. 192, col. 913.
[60] Ibid. 15 Dec. 1925, vol. 189, col. 1200; 22 Mar. 1926, vol. 193, cols. 896–7; 17 July
1928, vol. 220, col. 217. H. E. Powell-Jones to R. A. Dalzell, 20 Apr. 1925, Post 33/4308
(8).   [61] *Hansard*, 14 July 1926, vol. 198, col. 464.
[62] Ibid. 20 July 1925, vol. 186, cols. 1888–9.
[63] Ibid. 14 July 1926, vol. 198, cols. 470–3; 31 Mar. 1927, vol. 204, col. 1470; 2 July 1928,
vol. 219, col. 963.

definite sum was not allocated to this purpose.[64] Asked why the GPO
declined offers of professional assistance and did not engage in newspaper
advertising, he replied that the distribution of pamphlets, and personal
canvassing, were more 'suitable' and 'remunerative' means of publicity.[65]
Privately, officials noted that press advertising would be a waste of money
as the TDA covered that ground.[66] Even had this not been the case, it is
unlikely that the department would have adopted this method; it was far
too committed to the use of canvassing.

After the First World War the telephone and telegraph branch had
begun to use 'contract officers' to promote its services. Over 500 were
employed by the late 1920s, at an annual cost in salaries of approximately
£180,000,[67] representing virtually all of the division's publicity expenditure. Any leaflets and posters issued were viewed as necessary supplements
to canvassing rather than vice versa.[68] Although the GPO emphasized the
general publicity value of canvassing, a 1929 report on the arrangements
casts aspersions on the oft-repeated claim that it served as an adequate
substitute for other forms of advertising:

The work may be regarded as canvassing in its narrowest sense, namely canvassing for orders for installations. Payment is by results, and the system is not
used, and is not suited, for the work of maintaining close personal contact with
subscribers. The organization at present involves an amount of attention at
Headquarters which is small in relation to the number of canvassing officers.[69]

Ironically, canvassing was being employed to more widespread purpose elsewhere in the department. In 1920, a number of officials had been
given allowances to promote the imperial cable service; by the mid-1920s,
twenty-nine staff were so employed.[70] This organization was cohesive, and
its activities were more publicity-orientated than those of the other group:

the work . . . can properly be described as canvassing only to a very limited
extent. . . . [It] consists mainly in maintaining personal and constant touch with
important firms; trying to persuade them to make increasing use of our services;

[64] Ibid. 28 June 1927, vol. 208, cols. 202–4; 29 June 1927, vol. 208, cols. 398–9; 12 July
1927, vol. 208, cols. 1944–5; 25 July 1927, vol. 209, col. 869.
[65] Ibid. 16 Nov. 1926, vol. 199, cols. 1709–10; 16 June 1927, vol. 207, cols. 1183–4; 9 July
1928, vol. 219, col. 1835.   [66] Memorandum, 30 May 1927, Post 33/2850 (6).
[67] Hansard, 9 July 1928, vol. 219, col. 1835; 17 Dec. 1930, vol. 246, col. 1275.
[68] Ibid. 9 July 1928, vol. 219, col. 1835; 24 Jan. 1930, vol. 234, cols. 492–3; 8 Apr. 1930,
vol. 237, col. 1994.
[69] Simon to Leech, 22 Apr. 1929; Simon, Grant, and Phillips to Leech, 22 May 1929,
Post 33/3557 (4).
[70] Furley Smith to Day, 25 Oct. 1929, Post 33/3576 (2); Tallents to Raven, Feb. 1934
(19). Post 33/3557 (1); Memorandum, 23 Aug. 1928 (2).

attempting to educate them to the Department's methods; and bringing their grievances or exceptional demands or suggestions to the attention of the Department.[71]

Despite the apparent success of this branch, the Treasury was wary; it questioned the need for this type of canvassing,[72] and in 1929 capitalized on the transfer of the cable service out of Post Office control and cut eleven posts.[73] But political considerations soon ensured expansion rather than contraction in the canvassing service.

In 1928, the Liberal Party outlined its plans to deal with the unemployment problem in the 'Yellow Book', *Britain's Industrial Future*, which formed the basis of its 1929 election manifesto, *We Can Conquer Unemployment*. Central to the proposed programme was a policy of national public work projects. Britain's poor record in telephone development was singled out for derision. It was noted that there were only thirty-six telephones per thousand people in Britain as compared to 160 in the United States.[74] Lloyd George pledged to broaden the service, thus providing jobs in construction and canvassing. The diverse character of labour required, and the fact that growth in the system would increase national revenue, were said to make the telephone service an ideal area for the investment of public funds.[75]

In a White Paper published in rebuttal in May, the Postmaster-General defended the level of telephone development already attained and highlighted GPO efforts to promote the service. Lloyd George's scheme was said to be fundamentally unsound; the Postmaster-General claimed that it would not provide an appreciable number of jobs, and would increase capital costs rather than revenues.[76] None the less, that same month Simon and two assistant secretaries were detailed to overhaul canvassing arrangements in order to improve the promotion of the telephone service. The first issue they considered was the advisability of amalgamating the two existing organizations. Noting the variations in method and approach employed by each group, Simon's committee reported that 'no great advantages' were to be had from common supervision. None the less, it

[71] Simon, Grant, and Phillips to Leech, 22 May 1929, Post 33/3557 (4).
[72] Minutes, 11 Nov. 1925; 28 Jan. 1927; Post 33/3557 (1).
[73] Memorandum, 11 Aug. 1928, Post 33/3557 (1); Memoranda, 23 Aug., 11 Sept. 1928 (2).
[74] Liberal Party, *We Can Conquer Unemployment* (1929), 34–7. Also, Hansard, 29 June 1927, vol. 208, cols. 398–9.
[75] Liberal Industrial Inquiry, *Britain's Industrial Future* (1928), 77. Hansard, 19 Mar. 1931, vol. 249, cols. 2170–3. Liberal Party, *We Can Conquer Unemployment*, 34–7. *Annual Register* (1930), 17–18.   [76] *Memorandum on Proposals*, 37–9.

recommended a merger, noting that the proposal had widespread support in the department.[77] The relative merits of the methods hitherto employed were not discussed, nor was a decision reached on what type of approach the new organization ought to adopt. However, when Treasury sanction for the new section was requested in July, it became clear that it was to be modelled on the example of the imperial cable services organization. Although the recent political controversies were not mentioned, the department justified its proposals by citing the general publicity value of well-co-ordinated canvassing. Referring to the need for expansion in both the telephone and telegraph systems, the department observed:

much may be done in the direction desired by the issue of pamphlets and other advertising matter, and it is intended to make full use of these methods. At the same time there is no way of ensuring that printed publicity matter distributed by post actually reaches and is read by the responsible chiefs of business firms; and it is only by means of personal canvassing that it is possible to meet the needs of the most important users of the . . . services, and to foster the fullest development.[78]

Although the GPO was hardly advocating large-scale advertising, the Treasury was concerned about the advisability of promoting competing services, and questioned the need for the type of prolonged campaign implied by the proposals. Sanction was withheld pending presentation of a stronger case.[79]

Surprisingly, given his earlier remarks, Simon observed that the competition argument was irrelevant, as no matter which service benefited financially, mutual advantage would be derived from the establishment of closer contacts between the public and the department. He advocated that the department respond by emphasizing

that the main object of canvassing . . . is to gain the confidence of the general public . . .; to lead them to appreciate our difficulties and to be more tolerant; and on the other hand to help the Department to appreciate the difficulties of the public. . . . It is hoped that such canvassing will actually have the effect of increasing traffic, but its influence in this direction will be indirect and probably slight. . . . But one thing is fairly clear: that merely by reason of answering and anticipating complaints the canvassers should certainly 'earn their keep'.[80]

Justification of canvassing on these grounds was consistent with Simon's views on the public service responsibilities of the department. The

[77] Leech to Secretary, 23 Apr. 1929; Report to Leech, 22 May 1929, Post 33/3557 (4).
[78] GPO to Treasury, 29 July 1929, Post 33/3576 (2).
[79] Trentham to Bell, 11 Sept. 1929, Post 33/3557 (5).
[80] Simon to Establishments branch, 16 Sept. 1929, Post 33/3557 (5).

Treasury withheld comment, but sanctioned the creation of a Sales and Publicity section in October. Given subsequent events, it is likely that political rather than economic or public service considerations swayed the decision.

A. G. Highet, an overseer familiar with canvassing, became head of the Sales and Publicity division on its establishment in July 1930. An acclaimed amateur publicist, who had won departmental poster design competitions, Highet was said to possess the 'special type of mind, the faculty of hitting the public taste, which did not necessarily or even probably co-exist with the qualities of a good clerk or administrator', which was required for the post.[81] Staff in the Secretariat objected to the appointment; responsible for telephone publicity to date, they resented its absorption by the canvassing organization, and interpreted the claim that Highet was better qualified as casting aspersions on their earlier efforts. The crux of the problem was that an outsider had again been brought in to do publicity work on the basis of 'special qualifications'.[82]

The new organization expanded quickly and haphazardly. Although responsible for both sales and publicity, the latter was neglected in that forms of advertising other than canvassing were not developed. Staff shortages hindered the preparation of materials. The division barely had time to co-ordinate canvassing operations, and much of the contract officers' time was occupied in administrative tasks. Participation in exhibitions and the distribution of pamphlets were sporadic.[83] A poster campaign was unveiled in December, but as it was an exact replica of the 1923–4 scheme and the usual problems arose over wall space in post offices, it hardly signified much.[84] Indeed, the bureau made little headway in its first year; telephone density levels remained relatively static, and the system was subject to increased criticism on several fronts. In May 1930, the TDA published *The Strangle-hold on our Telephones*, a pamphlet which cited comparative statistics on telephone development as supposed proof that Post Office control had hindered growth in the service. The association claimed that the system could only expand to its full potential if placed on a commercial footing.[85] Concurrently, Lord Wolmer, a former assistant Postmaster-General, was voicing similar views about the

---

[81] Memorandum, 21 Sept. 1921, Post 33/3557 (1). Post 33/4308 (1).

[82] See correspondence, 4 Oct.–29 Nov. 1929; Note of Deputation, 19 Dec. 1929; Birkett to Raven, 23 Dec. 1929, Post 33/3576 (2). Wakely to Richardson, 10 July 1930; Bell to Treasury, 29 July 1929, Post 33/3557 (5).

[83] Richardson to Secretary, 18 Mar. 1930; Clerical Committee, Minutes, 15 May 1930, Post 33/3576 (2).   [84] Post 33/4308 (15).

[85] TDA, *Strangle-hold*, 6–16, 18–26.

administration of the entire postal service in a series of influential news-paper articles which prompted the appointment of the Bridgeman inquiry of 1932.[86] Were this not enough the Liberals renewed their attack on the telephone system.

In 1930, the Labour Prime Minister Ramsay MacDonald approached the other political parties seeking assistance in addressing the worsening problem of unemployment. Several meetings were held with the Liberals, who again advocated telephone development as a partial solution. When notified that the suggestion was impracticable, because a surplus of spare plant already existed, they replied that it was thus doubly necessary that efforts should be made to increase telephone subscriptions.[87] When nothing came of the discussions, the Liberals published *How to Tackle Unemployment*, which contained a scathing attack on the telephone ser-vice. Unlike the party's earlier statements, this pamphlet focused almost entirely on the importance of publicity to the securing of further expansion in the system. The lack of a coherent advertising policy was said to be at the root of Britain's poor record in telephone development. Moreover, it exemplified the GPO's dearth of management skills:

Now no . . . company would expect to do a nation-wide business without adopt-ing intensive selling methods. The most successfully conducted telephone service in the world is that of the United States, conducted by a private company. . . . The company spends enormous sums in advertising and since it is a commercial company trading for profit, it would not do so if it did not pay. Its publicity agent is one of its chief officials, but the publicity agent in the British telephone service occupies a comparatively minor position.

If the development of the telephone service . . . is to be secured, it is essential that the question of salesmanship shall be most carefully studied under expert advice, and a sum enormously greater than at present must be devoted to ad-vertising, not just by means of circulars but in the newspapers, and possibly on the hoardings.[88]

The implication, of course, was that the State was incapable of running a business, an allegation which had to be refuted when the party in power was ideologically committed to the nationalization of essential services. Indeed, when the same issues surfaced during the parliamentary esti-mates debate in March 1931,[89] Clement Attlee, who was then Postmaster-General, began to give consideration to using publicity as a means of

---

[86] *Report of the Committee of Enquiry on the Post Office, 1932*, Cmd. 4149 (1932), para. 5. Wolmer, pp. 22–3.   [87] Attlee to Snowden, 4 June 1931, Post 33/2903 (1).
[88] D. Lloyd George *et al.*, *How to Tackle Unemployment* (1930), 75–9.
[89] Hansard, 19 Mar. 1931, vol. 249, cols. 2170–3, 2186–8.

defusing criticism. In a reversal of its policy to date, the Post Office announced plans to contribute £5,000 annually to a joint poster fund to be administered by the TDA, on the sole condition that the association match the grant.[90] Early in April, after consulting with the advertising executive William Crawford, Attlee approached the Treasury with proposals for a large-scale publicity campaign. Noting that, as a result of the economic crisis, the system was carrying 25 per cent spare plant, he maintained that 'vigorous effort' was required both to prevent any further loss in subscriptions and to create demand. Attlee claimed that advertising aimed at fostering 'telephone mind[edness]' would have a cumulative effect in attracting subscribers, while the revenue generated would offset the cost. Without referring to his source, the Postmaster-General further stated that the minimum adequate expenditure to ensure a successful campaign would be £100,000. Attlee made no attempt to hide the political motivations behind his request. Indeed, the success or failure of the campaign was irrelevant to him, provided the very existence of publicity silenced the critics:

I am not proposing at present that this expenditure should be recurrent: this must depend upon the results which it achieves. If [it] . . . do[es] not justify the cost, we shall be able to show by a practical test that the contention of the Liberals and others that all that is wanted is greater publicity is a fallacy.[91]

By June, Attlee had decided that the proposed campaign should serve as the basis of a permanent publicity policy. Again, advertising was envisioned as a form of public relations, with the very existence of a publicity policy confirming that a State-run organization could function as effectively as any business enterprise. This would serve to legitimate government control over the telephone system, while demonstrating the feasibility of nationalization. Thus Attlee wanted the department to adopt commercial methods in order to ensure that essential services became less profit-motivated and more orientated to public service. Seeking Treasury approval for his proposals, he advised the Chancellor, Philip Snowden:

it is of considerable importance that this work should be undertaken in view of the attacks made on the service . . . on the ground that it is not run as a business organisation. [I]t is . . . important that one should demonstrate that a business undertaking carried on by the State can avail itself of commercial experience, and

[90] The scheme came into effect in Mar. 1932: Murray to Treasury, 29 June 1931, Post 33/2903 (1); GPO to Treasury, 11 Feb. 1932, (2).
[91] Attlee to Pethick-Lawrence, 27 Apr. 1931. Attlee informed Snowden in June that Crawford had assisted him: Post 33/2903 (1).

adopt methods which have proved most successful in private business, in order to counteract the propaganda for the transfer of the undertaking into the hands of private enterprise.

Attlee requested a quick decision, adding quite tellingly: 'I would like to reap the fruits of this experiment while we are still in office.'[92]

Having received assurances in April that a one-year scheme at a budget of £50,000 would be approved, Attlee was already soliciting expert advice.[93] His chief adviser was William Crawford, the publicity consultant to the Ministry of Agriculture and a member of the EMB, the only official body then engaged in mass advertising. Stephen Tallents, who was responsible for the board's publicity, arranged for Attlee to meet his team and discuss methods and strategy.[94] Attlee also approached Seebohm Rowntree, head of his family's confectionery firm, requesting assistance in choosing an advertising agency. Thus he copied the EMB in treating the commercial employer of advertising as the expert in such matters.

Observing that the choice of an agent was 'almost as important as the selection of a wife or a fountain pen', Rowntree recommended the use of an American firm, claiming that they were more in touch with modern methods of publicity than English agencies. Rae Smith, the British manager of the US-based J. Walter Thompson company, readily offered assistance, noting that his agency enjoyed participating in 'any demonstration that advertising [was] . . . a force [applicable] . . . to ends of deeper significance than the distribution of merchandise'.[95] If commercial considerations alone could have determined the choice of agent, the firm might have been engaged. However, as it was a government department as well as a business, the GPO could not patronize a non-British company.

Although it was later claimed that the major catalyst for the adoption of a large-scale advertising campaign had been the failure of more personal forms of publicity,[96] Attlee continued to value canvassing. That spring, he consulted Sir Francis Goodenough, the chairman of the government's Committee on Education for Salesmanship and a controller of the Gas Light and Coke company, regarding a possible reorganization of the current operations.[97] '[G]enerally recognized as one of the most expert salesmen in the country', Goodenough had recently employed Harold

[92] Attlee to Snowden, 4 June 1931, Post 33/2903 (1).

[93] Pethick-Lawrence to Attlee, 30 Apr. 1931, Post 33/2903 (1).

[94] Tallents to Attlee, 3 June 1931, Post 33/5236 (2).

[95] Correspondence between Attlee, Rowntree, and Smith, May 1931, Post 33/5236 (1).

[96] Furley Smith to Playfair, 16 Dec. 1937, T 162/971/12190/01. Report on the Post Office, Feb. 1938, T 162/981/36055/01/2.

[97] Attlee to Snowden, 4 June 1931, Post 33/2903 (1).

Whitehead, a former professor turned business consultant, to overhaul similar arrangements in the gas industry.[98] Whitehead agreed to conduct a comprehensive study of telephone canvassing, quoting a fee of £12,860.[99] Requesting Treasury approval for this expenditure, Attlee again stressed that the costs of advertising would be quickly recouped through increased sales. The Treasury sanctioned the scheme, but refused to guarantee a permanent publicity budget.[100]

The adoption of a broadly based advertising policy did not bring about a change in approach. A publicity advisory committee, modelled on that in existence at the EMB, was assembled to supervise the £50,000 campaign. Attlee took the chair, inviting Tallents, Goodenough, and Crawford to serve, the latter as vice-chairman. Simon and Highet represented the telephone branch, and H. E. Powell-Jones, the secretary of the TDA, the industry. Ethel Wood of Management Research Groups was the final member.[101] Despite Highet's presence, canvassing operations were not included in the committee's mandate and it received little information on the work of that division. Yet, if the scheme was formulated independently of these other activities, it was intended to reinforce rather than replace them.

Although it was recognized that many factors, including social conditions and the efficiency of other means of communication, hindered the expansion of the telephone service, the committee believed that the main problem, reinforcing all the others, was prejudice. It was agreed that canvassing efforts to date had been only marginally effective because the background publicity essential to their success had been ignored:

the shortcomings of the present methods of . . . publicity are that in the main they aim at selling telephone service to the individual without first creating a sense of the need of telephone service among the public generally. In other words, there is little mass suggestion. Whilst therefore existing methods could doubtless be extended and improved upon, future publicity developments should first of all be in the direction of awakening a national 'telephone mindedness' and obtaining the good will of the public.[102]

---

[98] Stirling L. Everard, *The History of the Gas Light and Coke Company 1812–1949* (1949), 295–310, 320–1. *Advertising World*, 50/2 (1926), 164–72. *The Times*, 27 Feb. 1929.

[99] Undated proposals, Post 33/2903 (1). Harold Whitehead addressed the Institute of Public Administration on the subject; 'Salesmanship in the Public Service: Scope and Technique', *Public Administration*, 11 (1933), 267–76.

[100] Snowden to Attlee, 10 June 1931, Post 33/2903 (1).

[101] *The Times*, 3 July 1931.

[102] Telephone Publicity Advisory Committee (TPC), 1st meeting, 25 June 1931, Post 108/Minutes. (All subsequent references to the minutes of this committee are to Post 108/Minutes.)

Selling the idea of the telephone ('educating' rather than 'boosting') was thought to necessitate the use of more general methods of appeal; hence four subcommittees were appointed to consider how best to exploit press advertising, posters, exhibitions, and films.[103] Before the planning began, Crawford suggested that half of the budget should be apportioned to newspaper publicity, the remainder being divided equally between posters and other media.[104] The proposal was accepted without debate, reflecting the value attached to press advertising in commercial circles.[105] However, when Crawford endeavoured to increase the allocation at the second meeting of the committee, Goodenough objected, recommending as an alternative that the TDA be asked to contribute its £15,000 budget to this purpose. Jones rejected the suggestion, noting that as the Post Office had now assumed the responsibility for addressing the mass audience, the association intended to suspend its campaign. Quick to recognize the dangerous political implications inherent in this statement, Attlee interjected that it would be a 'calamity' were the TDA to cease advertising. After the Postmaster-General hinted that the GPO might respond by cancelling its campaign, Jones promised to advise his organization to reconsider. Goodenough's proposal was dropped. Crawford then suggested employing a journalist to prepare newspaper articles, implying that editorial publicity would be a sufficient substitute for more press advertising. As the department had by now ceased to employ an intelligence officer, this idea was approved.[106]

Budget allocations and complaints about the dearth of 'mass suggestion' aside, the committee did not intend to undertake a widespread popular campaign. Telephone advertising was framed with a select group of potential customers in mind: the small percentage of householders earning in excess of £500 a year.[107] Furthermore, the campaign was not of a popular nature as such, the committee choosing to engage in prestige advertising, for as Tallents later explained:

The Post Office . . . is a combination between a great business corporation and a government department. As such its publicity . . . must be organized to combine . . . [the needs of both]. . . . [T]here are certain limitations on the commercial aspects of Post Office publicity. It is not . . . for the Post Office . . . to go

---

[103] Ibid.　　[104] TPC, 2nd meeting, 2 July 1931.

[105] Of the estimated £53 million spent on commercial publicity in 1930, £48 million was directed into press advertising: David S. Dunbar, 'Estimates of Total Advertising Expenditures in the U.K. before 1949', *Journal of Advertising History*, 1 (1977), 9–11. Also see Charles Frederick Higham, *Looking Forward* (1920), 42–58.

[106] TPC, 2nd meeting, 2 July 1931.　　[107] TPC, 3rd meeting, 9 July 1931.

all out with methods of high-power salesmanship. . . . Mistakes in Post Office publicity are much more readily observed and traced than mistakes in purely commercial advertising; and an institution like the Post Office is permitted little cupboard space for skeletons.[108]

The committee did not openly discuss the type of approach it should adopt, but the way in which the campaign was planned and executed suggests that such assumptions guided its deliberations. The handling of poster advertising provides a case in point.

Goodenough and Powell-Jones were nominally responsible for planning the poster side of the campaign. On Crawford's recommendation, they consulted Gervas Huxley of the EMB, believed to have 'a wider range of knowledge of poster advertising than anyone else in the country', who advised the GPO to emulate the style of publicity favoured by the board.[109] The artistic educative posters employed by the EMB were already renowned, though, as noted earlier, their commercial value was often challenged.[110] Despite the public debate surrounding such designs, neither Goodenough nor Powell-Jones questioned the advisability of adopting Huxley's proposal. Indeed, they focused their attention on determining the best means of display. As ever, discussion centred on the ability of official advertisements to compete with their commercial counterparts. Huxley advised the committee not to use commercial hoardings, claiming that it would be 'impossible to *maintain dignity* and develop individuality' employing a medium in which success was dependent on being able to ' "shout" in the loudest colours [my italics]'. As an alternative, he recommended that the GPO hire the EMB's own poster frames.[111]

At Tallents's suggestion, the EMB had constructed 1,800 oak hoardings on special sites in over 400 towns throughout the country.[112] Most were located on government property, many of the rest on land owned by

---

[108] Tallents, *Post Office Publicity*, 3. Professional advertisers agreed: Higham, *Looking Forward*, 63. William Crawford and Charles Higham, *Advertising and the Man in the Street* (Leeds, 1929), 8.

[109] TPC, 2nd meeting, 2 July 1931. An assistant to Tallents at the EMB, Huxley was appointed public relations officer of the Ceylon Tea Propaganda Board in 1933. He encouraged the board to employ documentary films, winning praise for his efforts; Swann, 'Grierson', 20; Hardy, p. 77; *Advertising World*, 68/8 (1936), 55. In 1939 Huxley was appointed to serve on advisory panels which the Treasury established to aid departments in their publicity. He also assisted in the pre-war planning of the MOI, subsequently serving in the home publicity division. [110] See above, pp. 51–2.

[111] TPC, Poster Subcommittee, First Report, *c*.Aug. 1931. This was discussed at TPC, 4th meeting, 13 Aug. 1931.

[112] Elizabeth Sussex, *The Rise and Fall of British Documentary* (1975), 8–9.

railway companies or the LPTB.[113] Although praised for their beauty,[114] the frames were controversial. Some had been erected in areas where commercial advertisements were not allowed, and while the board was charged rent for most sites, including those on government property, it was receiving financial concessions which annoyed the trade.[115]

Alluding to the industry's hostility, Powell-Jones questioned the value of employing the EMB hoardings, adding that it might jeopardize the current campaign on commercial sites being conducted through the joint GPO–TDA poster fund. Citing the apparent success of that campaign, he challenged Huxley's allegation that commercial hoardings were an unsuitable medium for telephone advertising.[116] The committee seemingly endorsed his position, agreeing to contribute £3,000 of its £12,500 budget towards the joint scheme, and rejecting Huxley's proposal. However, it is worth noting that the second decision was taken only because the majority of the committee agreed that greater advantage was to be had from constructing a set of GPO poster frames on the EMB example. It was claimed that, if hoardings were erected, the department would be able to display posters rent-free throughout the country. Special sites, it was assumed, would attract attention because of their novelty, and would be 'eminently suitable for the development of prestige advertising'. Most importantly, their existence would ensure the permanency of a publicity policy; 'once . . . in position . . . it would be difficult to stop using them.'[117]

The possibility and/or desirability of employing the exterior areas of post offices for advertising purposes had already been discussed at a meeting on telephone development on 17 April 1931.[118] Attlee had voiced support for the idea, also suggesting that the commercial contract should be terminated in order to make more space available inside buildings. Permanent officials had replied that Treasury approval would be improbable in either case.[119] During concurrent negotiations with the contractor, it had become clear that more internal wall space would soon be designated

---

[113] R. S. R. Fitter, 'An Experiment in Public Relations', *Public Administration*, 14 (1936), 464–7.

[114] *First and Second Reports from the Select Committee on Estimates 1932* (21 Mar.–20 June 1932), Proceedings, 22 Feb. 1932, mins. 253, 289, 308.

[115] Ibid., min. 260. Fitter, p. 464. Judith Freeman, 'The Publicity of the Empire Marketing Board 1926–1933', *Journal of Advertising History*, 1 (1977), 13. *Advertising World*, 57/4 (1930), 317.   [116] Powell-Jones to Highet, 11 Aug. 1931, Post 108/Minutes.

[117] TPC, Poster Subcommittee, first report; and TPC, 4th meeting.

[118] Minute, 18 Apr. 1931, Post 33/3387 (1).

[119] Ibid. Forbes to Parsons, 16 Apr. 1931, Post 33/3387 (1).

for departmental use. With concessions in hand, it would be difficult to persuade the Exchequer that the existence of the contract was of strong disadvantage to the Post Office. The construction of outdoor hoardings was said to be equally untenable. Difficulties were forecast in finding a uniform shape of frame suitable for all offices, a necessity were materials to be produced centrally and economically. Problems were bound to arise once other ministries demanded right of access to the hoardings, and the department would have to contend with objections from the trade and the Office of Works. Although a decision had not been tabled at this meeting, the telephone branch, assuming that outdoor frames had been sanctioned, directed G. E. G. Forbes to investigate possible sites.[120] His report, later passed on to Goodenough, formed the basis of the poster subcommittee's favourable assessment of the idea.[121] The latter decided, Attlee concurring, to allocate £7,000 toward the construction of hoardings.

How Attlee intended to meet the obstacles involved in initiating the subcommittee's proposal is not clear, as external events intervened. After the financial crisis of August 1931 brought in a National Government intent on austerity, a £50,000 telephone publicity campaign was out of the question. As the scheme had already been announced, and the new administration could not afford to abandon a policy which seemingly gave promise of expanding employment opportunities, planning was allowed to proceed, albeit on a smaller scale and with a different focus.[122] William Ormsby-Gore, the new Postmaster-General, vetoed any proposals which he believed unlikely to achieve instant results; the emphasis shifted away from inculcating the telephone habit to obtaining immediate subscriptions. Except for the joint experiment with the TDA, the poster scheme was dropped. A journalist was not hired, and participation in exhibitions was curtailed. Press advertising in the amount of £15,000 was sanctioned, but only because an agent had already been contracted and the scheme had widespread backing.[123]

On Kingsley Wood's appointment as minister in November, the situation was again reassessed. Convinced that even in poor economic conditions advertising was sound business, Wood was concerned that an isolated campaign might be wasteful, and sought assurances that the planned scheme would achieve the immediate, measurable results needed to persuade the Treasury to approve further expenditure. With Crawford

[120] Memorandum to Secretary, 25 Apr. 1931; Telephone branch to Buildings branch, 21 Apr. 1931, Post 33/3387 (1).   [121] Various memoranda, Post 33/3387 (1, 2, 4).   [122] TPC, 5th meeting, 17 Sept. 1931.   [123] TPC, 6th meeting, 8 Oct. 1931.

reiterating the value of press advertising, the committee forecast considerable success.[124]

It is significant that, although experts were directing the scheme, claims like Crawford's were based on personal opinions and prejudices rather than market research. Nor was the content of advertisements determined in what might be considered a scientific manner. On the basis of its own investigations, the TDA had informed the advisory committee that emphasizing the pleasant aspects of telephone ownership would have greater public appeal than focusing on the value of the system in an emergency.[125] The committee did frame its press advertising campaign with these considerations in mind, but this was apparently because of a general 'feeling' among its members that the security theme would prove to be unpopular.[126] The campaign began on 12 January 1932, with advertisements appearing in the national daily newspapers. Headed by the Postmaster-General's statement, 'You are wanted on the Telephone', they endeavoured to attract residential subscribers by highlighting the varied uses of the system. A second series focusing on the additional services available to customers was introduced in March. To supplement this publicity, the department participated in a number of exhibitions and sponsored a special display for children at the Imperial Institute. As these events were not advertised, Tallents engaged the editorial officer of the EMB to distribute 'readable matter' to the press about them. Independent companies were encouraged to feature telephones in films, but the GPO itself did not commission any productions. Finally, small posters were placed on vans and on official notice-boards in post offices. When press advertising was suspended during the summer, a poster used in earlier schemes was displayed at holiday resorts and on LPTB sites provided free of charge.[127]

While emphasizing the practical aspects of the service, the campaign also served long-term objectives. It was no mere sales job; the publicity was educative and artistic. Harold Vernon, the director of the advertising agency employed, said the press advertisements were deliberately designed to counter years of 'ill-informed criticism' and make the public 'telephone minded'.[128] Finding them 'a little formal, perhaps, but dignified', Crawford

[124] TPC, 7th meeting, 8 Dec. 1931.   [125] TPC, 3rd meeting.
[126] TPC, 14th meeting, 12 July 1933.
[127] *Daily Mail*, 12 Jan. 1932. *Advertising World*, 61/3 (1932), 172; 62/5 (1932), 261, 319. GPO to Treasury, 11 Feb. 1932, Post 33/2903 (2); 'Publicity activities of the Post Office during 1932' (4); 'Publicity activities during 1933' (7). TPC, 7th meeting, 8 Dec. 1931; 8th meeting, 9 Mar. 1932; 9th meeting, 4 July 1932.
[128] *Advertising World*, 62/5 (1932), 261, 319.

agreed that a government department had to begin 'in such a way'; 'a little more of the human appeal' could be added later. In fact, the 'human appeal' was developed through more personal means of advertising, such as booths at exhibitions. Despite the emphasis placed on obtaining quick results, the latter were valued more as means of educating the public and raising the department's prestige than as business opportunities.[129]

The campaign drew mitigated praise.[130] The press advertisements seemed outdated, as they depicted candlestick-style phones rather than newer models. On responding that the former were better known and less expensive than the latter, the department was criticized for not supplying modern phones at affordable prices. The advertisements were also branded inaccurate and misleading, because they quoted the lowest possible rates. The GPO attempted to forestall further criticism through public relations; a press conference was held to address the complaints.[131] In spite of the controversy, and even before the campaign was over, the Treasury was persuaded to renew the budget for another year, undoubtedly because the request emanated from Wood.[132]

A full report on the campaign was tabled in July 1932.[133] Although publicly claiming success,[134] privately the department was forced to concede that the results had not been as favourable as expected. Telephone orders were rising, but Britain still lagged behind other countries. As well, there was little concrete evidence to link growth in the system to the campaign. Inquiry coupons had been included in all the press advertisements, but by July only 4,893 had been returned, netting 1,505 subscriptions. Crawford said the proportions were 'very high'. He had 'never known such a result'.[135] Vernon claimed the figures were encouraging and spoke of a 'new atmosphere of receptivity' emerging as a consequence of the publicity.[136] Yet the outlay had been considerable: £15,000 plus the cost of follow-up canvassing. Expenditure on exhibitions had been lower, but seemed equally unjustified. Although 450,000 people had visited the telephone stand at the Ideal Home Exhibition, only 746 orders had been obtained. Measured in commercial terms, the campaign had been 'a little disappointing'.[137] However, the advisory committee stressed its 'hidden

[129] Ibid. TPC, 8th meeting.
[130] *The Times*, 20 Jan. 1932. *Advertising World*, 61/2 (1932), 122.
[131] *The Times*, 20 Jan. 1932.
[132] Treasury to GPO, 16 Feb. 1932, Post 33/2903 (2).
[133] 'Publicity activities, 1932'; GPO to Treasury, 19 Jan. 1933, Post 33/2903 (4).
[134] Hansard, 31 Oct. 1932, vol. 269, cols. 1428–9. *The Times*, 29 Nov. 1932.
[135] TPC, 8th and 9th meetings.   [136] *Advertising World*, 62/5 (1932), 261, 319.
[137] TPC, 9th meeting.

results' (such as the number of cancellations the publicity had prevented),[138] and emphasized that 'signs were not wanting' that advertising had raised 'the prestige of the service'. The public was said to be 'talking telephones more than ever before', and the press to be publishing considerable news and less criticism about the system. Finally, it was claimed that pride in the service, the value of which could 'hardly be over estimated', had been engendered amongst the sales staff.[139]

It seems inconceivable that such claims could be made on the eve of the establishment of the Bridgeman inquiry, for controversy had hardly subsided either outside or within the department. GPO staff were pleased by the increased telephone publicity, but continued to deplore the 'attitude of dignified aloofness' assumed by the department in the face of external criticism.[140] Relations with the press were no better. In fact, the campaign had done serious damage. The Newspaper Proprietors' Association was incensed that provincial papers had received no share of the budget. During the very meeting at which the committee commented on improved press relations, the Postmaster-General revealed that the NPA had launched a protest.[141] When the committee would not reconsider its policy, provincial papers refused to print any editorial material emanating from the GPO.[142]

The Telephone Development Association also voiced dissatisfaction, suggesting in March 1932 that it should control all future campaigns in order to prevent overlapping. Comparing its own results with those of the GPO campaign (an expenditure of £96,000 from 1924 to 1931 was claimed to have accounted for 15 per cent of telephone growth over the period), the TDA queried how advertising 'guided by amateurs with no previous experience in this particular field and with nothing but a very indirect stake in the results' could be effective.[143] With Powell-Jones on the advisory committee, the association was undoubtedly aware that the scheme had been directed by professionals such as Crawford, but this was not the real issue. Informing the GPO of its plans to increase 'propaganda activities

---

[138] Tallents had forecast difficulties in assessing the campaign because of the likelihood of 'hidden results'; TPC, 7th meeting.   [139] TPC, 9th meeting.

[140] Whitley Council Minutes, 17 Aug. 1932, Post 33/3576 (8).

[141] TPC, 9th meeting.

[142] An unsuccessful experiment was conducted in 1933, see TPC, 11th meeting, 16 Feb. 1933; 12th meeting, 30 Mar. 1933. Regarding the boycott see Briant to Tickner, 11 June 1935, Post 33/3577 (21). A 1936 inquiry into publicity in the provinces upheld the policy; Paper 11, Post 33/5415 (1); 'Report of Committee of Enquiry', Oct. 1936; Memorandum by T. Daish, 19 Jan. 1937 (3).

[143] Powell-Jones to Simon, 1 Mar. 1932; Simon to Secretary, 2 Mar. 1932; Memorandum by Simon, 9 Mar. 1932; Atkinson to Wood, 26 Apr. 1932; Post 33/2903 (13).

in directions which, though perfectly legitimate and effectual in themselves, are perhaps not altogether consistent with the traditional prestige
attaching to a State Department', the TDA questioned the department's
ability to achieve maximum results, noting that its status as a ministry of
State precluded it from adopting the type of methods required:

we feel that though a certain element of prestige undoubtedly enters into the
matter, the prestige idea is in some danger at present of being overdone and of
swamping the basic consideration, which is that there is no monopoly in advertising, but very fierce competition; telephone service needs to be advertised . . . in
competition with . . . other amenities. It has to be sold, not on prestige solely or
mainly, but on the considerations that appeal to the average man . . .; i.e. value,
economy, satisfaction, comfort.[144]

In response, Simon rejected the association's claims to success, and
observed, rather ironically, that the word 'prestige' had not even been
mentioned in the Post Office campaign![145] The effectiveness of the type of
advertising employed to date was debated by the publicity committee in
July.[146] Reiterating the arguments of his association, Powell-Jones advocated the use of 'more aggressive copy'. Crawford supported the suggestion, as did Wood. Simon was adamant in his opposition, and Tallents's
contribution that a government department 'could not well adopt the
methods of some business concerns' put an end to all discussion.

Some popular forms of advertising were introduced in the second
campaign. In June 1932, for example, the Postmaster-General launched a
fleet of motorcycle vehicles designed to resemble telephone equipment.
Each machine had a microphone on its side-car, and a replica of a dialling
dish, containing the slogan 'The world at your finger tips' on the wheel.[147]
Posters were again displayed on vans and the LPTB sites, and an agent
was engaged to provide new designs.[148] However, over half of the budget
was again allocated to advertising in the national press.[149] The advertisements remained dignified, provoking criticism from Crawford, among
others, on these grounds.[150] In some cases, they were even more abstruse
than before. One series, intended to increase awareness of the complexity
of the service, attempted to depict the apparatus involved, the speed at
which it worked, and the density of calls handled. The challenge was
likened to propagating a new religion:

[144] Ibid.   [145] Report by Simon, 3 May 1932, Post 33/2903 (13).
[146] TPC, 9th meeting.   [147] *The Times*, 21 June 1932.   [148] TPC, 8th meeting.
[149] 'Publicity activities, 1932', Jan. 1933, Post 33/2903 (4).
[150] TPC, 11th and 12th meetings, and 13th meeting, 24 May 1933.

Could modern advertising 'put across' the difficult evidence of statistics and the technical intricacies of the miracle we call 'Telephone Service' in a manner that would appeal to the lay mind? It was both a fascinating and a difficult task, but not beyond accomplishment.[151]

Educational publicity prevailed. Exhibitions continued to be used mainly as channels of information, and it was decided to introduce a lecture scheme similar to one which the EMB had developed.[152] Attempts were also made to reach children through the introduction of specially prepared telephone apparatus into the schools. As the Board of Education was hostile to the dissemination of any form of propaganda, even of an informative nature, through the educational system,[153] the GPO encountered some difficulty in persuading it to accept these materials, and the policy did provoke some negative comment.[154] Personal canvassing continued to play a major role in telephone promotion. In 1931, Highet, with a staff of four, supervised 700 contract officers. Although the division was consistently overworked, the Treasury blocked expansion, citing the experimental nature of publicity;[155] only after the Whitehead report was filed was the division reorganized into a Sales and Publicity section with nine staff. G. H. Taylor, a district manager from Scotland, became controller, with Highet serving as his assistant.[156]

These changes came into effect in February 1932. By March Taylor was requesting the appointment of three additional staff, including a press officer. He intended to streamline the organization, dividing it into two branches, sales and publicity, each served by its own officials. Frustrated with change 'by instalments', the Treasury demanded a complete outline of future publicity plans. Simon responded by focusing on the importance of developing less expensive means of publicity than paid press advertising, advising the Treasury that the latter could not be abandoned until the division possessed sufficient staff to prepare materials such as leaflets and brochures. In addition, he justified the appointment of a press officer by stressing that a closer liaison with the media

[151] Advertising World, 62/5 (1932), 261, 319.

[152] TPC, 8th, 9th, and 10th meetings. 'Publicity activities, 1932', Jan. 1933, Post 33/2903 (4).   [153] See below, p. 129.

[154] The TDA had been lobbying the board on the matter since 1926; Hansard, 15 June 1926, vol. 196, cols. 2117–18; 14 July 1926, vol. 198, cols. 470–2. Also see Post 33/2275; and TPC, 1st, 2nd, 8th, 9th, and 10th meetings. For reaction to the scheme see The Times, 25 Apr. 1933; Hansard, 13 Feb. 1939, vol. 343, cols. 1386–7.

[155] GPO to Treasury, 31 July 1931, and reply, 21 Aug. 1931; H. D. Wakely to Simon, 6 Nov. 1931, Post 33/3576 (4).   [156] See Post 33/3576 (5).

would ensure that telephone news always received coverage. Treasury approval was obtained on the understanding that the arrangements would be reviewed within the year.[157] Although it had recommended the appointment of a press officer as early as 1931, the telephone publicity committee was not consulted about the post, nor the choice of officer, which shows the extent to which responsibility for publicity remained diffused.

These administrative changes did little to deflect public criticism of the system. The Bridgeman report, published in August 1932, branded the telephone service backward, expensive, and indifferent to consumer needs. Maintaining that further growth was dependent on the adoption of a more commercial outlook, the Committee of Enquiry advocated that greater attention be focused on developing salesmanship and publicity.[158] The report had an enormous influence, leading to a total reorganization of the GPO's administrative framework. Increasing attention was also given to the subject of public relations. A Post Office Advisory Council, composed mainly of businessmen, was established in January 1933 to assist the Postmaster-General in formulating policy, and serve as a 'further connecting link' between the department and the community.[159] In July, Wood announced plans to broaden the scope of GPO publicity to cover all departmental activities.[160] A public relations division was formed in October under Tallents with an advertising budget, excluding staff costs, of £95,000.[161] As noted earlier, the bureau was heralded as a new departure in GPO policy, as a foray into commercial practice. It was neither. A publicity policy was already well established, and Tallents was the least likely person to alter it. As a member of the advisory committee, he had been instrumental in determining the course of Post Office publicity to date.[162]

Other developments provide further indication that, despite the adoption of a new policy, there was never any intention of altering the orientation of GPO publicity. Broadening the mandate of the telephone publicity advisory committee in July, Wood added new lay members, namely Lord Iliffe, the newspaper proprietor, John Grierson, head of the film unit

[157] Taylor to Simon, 11 Mar. 1932; GPO to Treasury, 8 Apr. 1932; reply, 24 May 1932, Post 33/3576 (7). Treasury to Simon, 13 Apr. 1932; Memo to Secretary, 25 Apr. 1932; Simon to Thompson, 27 Apr. 1932; GPO to Treasury, 17 May 1932 (7A).

[158] *Report of the Committee of Enquiry*, 9–15. *The Times*, 22 Aug. 1932.

[159] *The Times*, 10 Jan. 1933.   [160] Hansard, 29 July 1933, vol. 280, cols. 2253–4.

[161] Hardy, p. 71; *Post Office* (1934), 107; Post 33/2903 (7, 8, 10).

[162] See above, pp. 100–1.

recently absorbed from the EMB, and A. P. Ryan[163] and Jack Beddington,[164] publicity directors of the Gas Light and Coke company and Shell-Mex respectively.[165] E. Rawdon Smith of the LPTB and J. W. Buchanan-Taylor of J. Lyons and Company were also considered for membership, only being excluded in order to keep the committee small.[166] The names of the business representatives are worth noting. All were renowned for developing prestige techniques in the sphere of commercial advertising, influencing and in turn being influenced by the EMB. Tallents planned and modelled GPO publicity on their example,[167] and all were later approached to assist other government departments in their publicity arrangements.[168]

Tallents's first concern on assuming office was staffing. The telephone committee had complained, as recently as July, about the amount of time elapsing before officials carried out its recommendations.[169] A lecture scheme had been approved in March 1932, but over a year later only one talk had been prepared. By 1936 there were fourteen complete with slides,[170] but because it relied on local initiative, the programme progressed slowly; between September 1935 and March 1936 slides were requisitioned only 494 times. The public reaction was said to be 'very favourable', though attendance at meetings was low. This was attributed to the lack of general publicity for the scheme; a policy 'adopted

---

[163] A journalist, Ryan joined the EMB under Tallents. Publicity manager of the Gas Light and Coke company 1931–6, he piloted the famous 'Mr Therm' campaigns. In 1936 Tallents appointed Ryan Assistant Controller of Public Relations at the BBC. Ryan assisted in the planning of the MOI, and during the war served as Controller of BBC news services: Everard, p. 346. A. P. Ryan, 'Intelligence and Public Relations', *Public Administration*, 14/1 (1936), 59–65. *Advertising World*, 64/5 (1933), 288.

[164] Beddington was at Shell 1927–46, introducing innovative advertising policies and creating a film unit. Also on the GPO poster advisory committee, he was a patron of the arts and film. He headed the film division of the MOI 1940–6: Swann, 'Grierson', 29–30. Paul Rotha, *Documentary Diary* (1973), 68. *Advertising World*, 59/2 (1931), 122; 64/5 (1933), 331; 70/10 (1938), 32. On his use of 'prestige' advertising see Shell-Mex and BP Limited, *Art in Advertising* (1964).

[165] The body was renamed the Publicity Advisory Committee in July 1933 (hereafter PAC). The minutes are in PRO, National Savings Committee Papers, NSC 26/19. On the choice of members see 14th meeting, 12 July 1933; and Memorandum by Taylor, 19 July 1933, Post 33/3576 (13). Wood chaired, and Crawford, Powell-Jones, and Goodenough remained on the committee. The other members were drawn from within the department and included Highet, Simon, Tallents, Taylor, and H. G. G. Welch.

[166] Post 33/5236 (7).

[167] *Advertising World*, 67/5 (1935), 13–14. Tallents believed these companies were leaders in British advertising; 'Publicity in the U.K.', 26 July 1938, INF 1/712.

[168] See pp. 232–3.

[169] TPC, 14th meeting, 12 July 1933. Memorandum by Taylor, 19 July 1933, Post 33/3576 (13).   [170] Ibid. *Post Office Magazine* (hereafter *POM*), 3/3 (1936), 93.

deliberately, as it was feared that if requests for lectures became frequent, the Post Office might be unable to meet them owing to a dearth of suitable lecturers'.[171] In other words, the publicity scheme could not be publicized lest demand exceed supply! As staff shortages were at the root of the problem, Goodenough suggested recourse to outside assistance. Tallents was convinced that publicity was a task for professionals and not average officials,[172] but also believed that a competent staff, which could get 'under the skin' of the department, had to be built up from within the Civil Service.[173] Accordingly a successful appeal for seven additional officers was directed to the Treasury.[174] The administrative structure introduced by Taylor was retained, with slight modifications. Responsible for supervising the entire division, Tallents also advised other branches on matters affecting their relations with the public. Taylor was promoted to controller of sales, overseeing canvassing and training operations. A comparable post was created for the publicity branch of the division, but was not filled until 1935, when a candidate, T. Daish, fulfilling Tallents's criteria of high Civil Service rank, considerable GPO experience, and 'special aptitude', could be found.[175] Highet continued to supervise campaigns; F. K. Tickner, a career civil servant,[176] monitored the press office and publications; J. H. Brebner,[177] a former journalist, was press officer; and Grierson controlled the film unit.

Yet as the division remained unestablished, it expanded haphazardly. Chronically understaffed, the public relations section was forced to concentrate on meeting short-term objectives; new methods and techniques of publicity could not be explored, nor any form of local organization developed.[178] Staff associations pressed the bureau to increase its numbers, while the Treasury voiced concern at the requests for expansion.[179] Between 1929 and 1934, the number of officials employed on publicity rose from five to thirty-six, and the surge showed no sign of abating.[180]

---

[171] Post 33/5415 (1) (Paper 14).

[172] Temple Willcox, 'Projection or Publicity: Rival Concepts of the Pre-War Planning of the Ministry of Information', *Journal of Contemporary History*, 18 (1983), 102.

[173] Stephen Tallents, 'Salesmanship in the Public Service: Scope and Technique', *Public Administration*, 11 (1933), 264; Tallents, *Post Office Publicity*, 8; Tallents, in *Advertising World*, 67/5 (1935), 13–14.

[174] Tallents to Raven, 28 Oct. 1933; GPO to Treasury, 3 Nov. 1933; Robinson to Raven, 22 Nov. 1933, Post 33/3576 (13).   [175] Ibid.

[176] *POM* 3/4 (1936), 110.   [177] *POM* 2/2 (1935), 54; *AWWW* (1948).

[178] Daish to Tallents, 6 June 1935, Post 33/3577 (24). 'Report of Committee of Enquiry into Post Office Publicity', July 1935, Post 33/3577 (24), and Post 108/1935/Public Relations Department.   [179] Post 33/3576 (15, 18); Post 33/3577 (24, 25, 27, 30).

[180] Robinson to Sambrook, 13 Apr. 1934, Post 33/3576 (15).

Part of the problem was the lack of a long-term guiding policy; it was difficult to restrain the growth of a bureau which created its own workload.[181] Tallents appointed an internal committee of inquiry in mid-1935 to determine priorities, but after four meetings its only concrete proposal was that the publicity budget should be frozen at its existing level of £95,000.[182] Problems of under-staffing and delineating responsibilities within the division persisted, until it was finally established along normal administrative lines in May 1936.[183]

The early activities of the publicity bureau were wide-ranging and short-term. From the outset, the emphasis was on improving relations with the public. Hence local telephone advisory committees were given a broader mandate.[184] This was largely a cosmetic change, as the committees met infrequently and by 1937 had lapsed,[185] but officials paid lip-service to their value and also attempted to forge ties with the local business community through other means, such as lectures.[186] Recognizing the psychological value of attractive premises, Tallents also initiated a 'Brighter Post Office' movement. This campaign ranged from improving furniture and fittings in offices to providing working pens on counters.[187] Schemes were also developed to train staff in customer relations.[188] Less visible, but along similar lines, was the appointment of a correspondence subcommittee to investigate how enquiries and complaints from the public were handled. Noting that unsightly forms, badly written telegrams, and brusque responses outweighed the effects of thousands of well-executed transactions, the subcommittee stressed that 'a correspondent should not be regarded as a person to be "choked off" as quickly as possible'. Prompt replies devoid of jargon were recognized to be as essential to improving the department's image as more obvious forms of

---

[181] Memorandum to Gardiner, undated, Post 33/3577 (24).

[182] Post 33/3577 (24). Post 108/1935/Public Relations Department.

[183] See Post 33/3577 (28, 31).   [184] *Post Office* (1934), 108.

[185] Daish, 'Memorandum on the Report of a Committee on Public Relations Activities in the Provinces,' 19 Jan. 1937, Post 33/5415 (3); GPO Board, Minutes, 8/36, 20 Oct. 1936, (5). PAC, Minutes, 11 Feb. 1937, NSC 26/19.

[186] E. T. Crutchley, *GPO* (Cambridge, 1938), 248. *POM* 2/3 (1935), 97; 2/4 (1935), 113, 135. *The Post Office Telephone Sales Bulletin*, 2/8 (1936), 122 (hereafter *TSB*).

[187] *Post Office* (1934), 11. Tallents, *Post Office Publicity*, 13–16. *POM* 3/3 (1936), 94. Crutchley, *GPO*, 1–2. The importance of attractive architecture was recognized elsewhere; T. S. Simey, 'A Public Relations Policy for Local Authorities', *Public Administration*, 13 (1935), 250. Tallents, 'Salesmanship', 264. Also see Frank Pick's views as noted in T. C. Barker and Michael Robbins, *A History of London Transport*, ii (1974), 250.

[188] G. C. Wickens, 'Training of the Post Office Counter Staff', *Public Administration*, 12 (1934), 58–64; and 'Staff Training in London', Post Office Green Papers, 16 (Oct. 1935).

publicity.[189] In attempting to put these proposals into practice, the department set a positive example and drew praise from within Whitehall.[190]

Experiments were also conducted into the preparation and sale of popular publications geared towards 'bringing alive' the Post Office to the public. For instance, an annual report, the first since 1916, was issued in 1934. In contrast to the formal documents of earlier years (still current elsewhere in Whitehall), it was written in simple language and contained photographs and human interest stories.[191] The publication served a double purpose; it imparted information while demonstrating that the GPO was an efficient and friendly organization concerned with pleasing its customers. *Peter in the Post Office* (1934), an animated story for children, *The Post Office in Pictures* (1935), and *Post Office Publicity* (1936), fulfilled a similar function. These booklets were praised as a new departure in official publications, but as they had a limited popular appeal the policy was discontinued in 1937.[192]

It has been argued that, under Tallents's direction, the public relations division was more concerned with creating a positive image of the department than with developing a commercial approach to publicity.[193] Admittedly, the bureau did concentrate, in its early stages, on attempting to improve the department's reputation and foster goodwill. Yet the policy did have commercial motivations. As noted earlier, the adoption of a permanent publicity policy had been justified as a business decision. Implicit in its acceptance on these grounds was the assumption that the department would engage in commercial advertising and not political puffery. The boundary distinguishing the two was apparently straightforward: the GPO could publicize its products, but not itself. Yet many business firms, including the LPTB, Shell-Mex, and the Gas Light and Coke company, had begun to employ background publicity, claiming that the creation of a positive public image—selling the company—was as

[189] Subcommittee on Correspondence with the Public, Post 108/1933, Book 258; Minutes, Post 33/4499. Brown and Drury, pp. 359–61. Tallents, 'Salesmanship', 259–60. H. F. Carlill, 'Administrative Habits of Mind', *Public Administration*, 8 (1930), 123.

[190] See articles on 'Correspondence with the Public', in *Public Administration*, 14 (1936), by Ashton Davies, 268–75; M. Kliman, 276–90; W. D. Sharp, 291–300.

[191] *Post Office* (1934). On 'humanizing' publications see Simey, pp. 246–7.

[192] Regarding their production see Post 33/4727. For praise of the policy see Simey, p. 247; *The Times*, 18 Nov. 1935. On the cessation of the experiment see 'Report of the Committee of Enquiry into Post Office Publicity', July 1935, Post 33/3577 (24), and Post 108/1935/Public Relations Department. 'Report of the Committee of Enquiry into Public Relations Activities in the Provinces', 28 Oct. 1936; Minutes of GPO Board, 20 Oct. 1936, Post 33/5415 (3).   [193] Daunton, pp. 353–4.

important to furthering sales as the advertising of goods.[194] The distinction here was superfluous, for both forms of publicity served the same
end, and neither conflicted with business standards. The case differed
when a commercial enterprise was a ministry of State. A government
department selling itself was always assumed to be attempting to enhance
its political image. Legitimate publicity could not easily be distinguished
from puffery solely on the basis of results, for publicity often fulfilled
more than one end and served purposes for which it might not have been
originally intended. Motive, too, was a difficult gauge, as the impetus
behind advertising was often blurred or unascertainable. Moreover, actual objectives were generally of little consequence, since publicity was
usually assessed primarily on its impact. The fact that more than one
legitimate motive underlay official publicity further complicated matters.
If background advertising could be justified on commercial grounds, it
was also recognized to be essential to the functioning of the modern
democratic State. Henry Bunbury, the Comptroller and Accountant-
General of the GPO, argued in 1929 that it was doubly important for a
commercially orientated government department to engage in public relations. Unlike other businesses, it could not assess the effectiveness of its
efforts solely in terms of any financial gain secured. Because it also had
public service responsibilities, a department could only measure its efficiency in terms of its reputation. Informing the public about its services,
thereby fostering goodwill, was thus of crucial importance.[195] It was also
the only means by which morale could be built up within the organization.
By creating a positive public image, a department could convince its staff
that their efforts were effective, thus increasing efficiency.[196] Conversely,
gaining public confidence was dependent on establishing good internal
morale.

Stressing the commercial benefits to be derived from better internal
public relations, Tallents's division launched a *Post Office Magazine* (*POM*)
in January 1934. Modelled on the LPTB's house journal, *Pennyfare*, it was
intended to bring the GPO 'alive' to its own staff, thus inculcating a
positive attitude and improving service.[197] Priced at 1*d*., the average issue

[194] Tallents, *Post Office Publicity*, 10–11, 14. *TSB* 2/4 (1936), 57–8.
[195] Henry N. Bunbury, 'The Management of Public Utility Undertakings', *Public Administration*, 7 (1929), 111–19. Also see J. H. Broadley, 'The Management of Public Utility
Undertakings', ibid. 125.   [196] See above, p. 49.
[197] For background see *Post Office* (1934), 112. *POM* 1/1 (1934), 5; 1/3 (1934), 110–12;
1/7 (1934), 295. PAC, 16th meeting, 23 Nov. 1933, NSC 26/19, and Post 33/3944. Tickner
to Daish, 12 June 1935, Post 33/3577 (21). Tallents, 'Salesmanship', 260; *Post Office Publicity*,
12.

contained everything from personnel news and sports pages to articles on river postmen and photographs of telephone repair shops.[198] It was an immediate success with the quarter of a million GPO employees; the first issue sold 172,000 copies, four times as many as had been expected. By 1935, there were 100,000 regular subscribers, and monthly sales averaged 160,000.[199]

Requests for articles of a more comprehensive and technical nature led to the publication of 'Green Papers'. Issued 'primarily for the information of . . . staff', they were designed to place up-to-date material relating to specific activities at the disposal of all officers. Forty-six 'Green Papers', dealing with topics as diverse as 'Room Noise and Reverberation' and 'Pneumatic Tubes and Telegram Conveyers', were issued from 1934 to 1939.[200] A *Telephone Sales Bulletin* was also published from July 1935 to keep regional staff in touch with developments in that service. It contained the usual personnel information, along with articles of particular use to canvassers. The first issue contained materials as diverse as 'Effect of the Revised Telephone Rates', 'What the Telephone Offers Farmers', and 'Sales Branch Results'. Practical issues, such as how to develop sales techniques and market research, were also addressed, and readers were invited to comment and submit articles.[201]

Since these broadsheets operated at a loss, they proved unpopular with the Treasury.[202] As with many other government publications,[203] the newspaper trade viewed them as unfair competition for advertising revenues.[204] In addition, the rationale behind the publications was far from being universally accepted, as Tallents discovered in 1934 when trying to convince the Select Committee on Estimates of the value of developing publicity inside the Post Office.[205] His plans to use the film unit to inform staff about the department encountered strong resistance; unconvinced of the need for any publicity, the committee saw little merit in his arguments concerning the value of internal public relations, and placed strict limitations on the use of films within the GPO. Similarly, Tallents's claim that EMB films on tea production in Ceylon served as excellent background material to the promotion of overseas mails and telephone services failed

---

[198] See *POM* 1/5 (1934), 205; 1/6 (1934), 254.   [199] *POM* 2/3 (1935), 87–9.

[200] The first issue, covering air mail services, was published in Aug. 1934. The majority of papers were written by GPO staff, many being based upon lectures. Their purpose was explained on the inside back cover of most issues.   [201] July 1935.

[202] Robinson to H. Sambrook, 13 Apr. 1934; reply, 30 May 1934; also see drafts regarding the funding of the magazine, Post 33/3576 (15).   [203] See above, p. 78.

[204] *The Times*, 5, 16 Oct. 1934.

[205] Select Committee on Estimates (1934), Proceedings, 7 Mar. 1934, mins. 515, 566.

to convince the committee to allow the GPO to retain control over the board's film library.[206]

Paul Swann has argued that if Tallents's main objective was to improve public relations both within and outside the department, Highet's chief concern, as head of the publicity bureau, was with increasing Post Office revenues.[207] This claim is belied by a series of articles published in the TSB from 1935 to 1936 in which Highet outlined the intentions of, and philosophy behind, the publicity campaigns conducted by his section. The value of public relations was affirmed in the opening paragraph of the first article:

Generally speaking there are two main reasons for advertising. One is to sell goods, the other is to build up goodwill. Goodwill is prestige. Prestige has a definite survival value. Many people profess a scorn for advertising; it is cheap, undignified and not at all in keeping with high reputations. . . . The Post Office advertises its services. Essentially these services are services for the community . . . and unless every member of the community knows that they are available . . . the community must suffer. . . . Surely there is nothing undignified in the State making known the services available.

Necessarily, GPO publicity would be of a high standard: 'the policy of the Post Office is to make known its services in a way which will command attention and respect. It must therefore employ . . . the greatest experts.'[208] Indeed, in the final analysis, the ultimate prestige advertisement was thought to be the publicity itself. Highet stressed the 'duty' of the department to introduce new techniques rather than following the example of others, and/or pandering to the masses. The public might prefer toying with apparatus to viewing a carefully arranged exhibition:

but playing with instruments does not necessarily mean that an instructive or prestige-building story is getting across. It is the function of the Post Office exhibition people to tell the owners of the service what it does for them and how it is done, but in so doing they must never lose sight of the fact that being a little ahead of the customer is better than lagging behind him.[209]

Similarly, he observed that, while the function of a poster was 'to shout a particular name or service', there was 'a definite field for the poster which sets up reactions in the mind of the viewer'.[210] The film unit

[206] Ibid., mins. 515–19, 524, 531, 702; Appendix 12.
[207] Swann, 'Grierson', 20.   [208] TSB 1/2 (1935), 30–1.
[209] TSB 2/2 (1936), 20–1. POM 1/6 (1934), 260–1.
[210] TSB 2/1 (1936), 5. Also see TSB, 1/3 (1935), 47; 2/3 (1936), 40.

adopted a similar philosophy. Regarding his productions as contributions to 'community knowledge', Grierson stressed the importance of developing films of high standard, adding 'the factor of appreciation to the factor of information'.[211] Like other officials, Tallents did not believe methods of 'high power salesmanship' were suitable to a government department.[212] Hence all GPO publicity campaigns were framed in principle in relation to what was assumed to be the greater public good.[213]

This ideal was manifested in the publicity materials employed by the Post Office. When a 'posters-in-schools' scheme was inaugurated in 1934, a special advisory committee was created to assist in the choice of designs. Kenneth Clark, the director of the National Gallery, Clive Bell, the art critic, and Jack Beddington, of Shell-Mex, were invited to join, in order to ensure that the posters were artistic and educational. Noted artists of the calibre of Duncan Grant and Vanessa Bell were commissioned to design the annual series.[214] The posters were praised on aesthetic grounds, and, though many questioned their value, it was recognized that posters placed in schools had to be of an educational nature.[215] This type of policy was not confined to the schools, however. After the commercial contract was terminated in 1935, the department began to exhibit similar types of posters on post office walls. A committee appointed to consider how best to exploit the available space decided to confine the display to notices of two types—'prestige' and 'selling'. The former, 'posters of artistic merit in specially constructed frames' (40 ft. × 50 ft.) were to be exhibited continuously, in order to add to the amenities of offices, and attract public interest. The latter, also artistic, but of a smaller size (30 ft. × 20 ft.), were to advertise specific services and have a limited display. The keynote of the scheme was restraint. A circular to local officials emphasized that walls were not to be 'plastered with a confusion of unrelated designs'.[216]

Campaigns in support of particular services also tended to be of a 'prestige' nature. When telephone rates were reduced in October 1934, the department launched a special 'Telephone Week'. All media available were exploited in the campaign: Wood inaugurated the scheme with a

[211] John Grierson, 'Films in the Public Service', *Public Administration*, 14 (1936), 371.
[212] See above, p. 50.   [213] See Crutchley, *GPO*, 246–8.
[214] See Post 33/4722; Post 33/3576 (17); Post 33/2903 (8, 10); and circulars to local educational authorities in Post 33/5253 (3, 4); Post 33/4722 (1). *Post Office* (1934), 110; *POM* 1/7 (1934), 295; and 3/3 (1936), 94.
[215] See *Advertising World*, 67/11 (1935), 105–6. *TSB* 3/6 (1937), 92. *The Times*, 26 May, 30 Nov. 1934, 2 May 1938, 7 Mar. 1939.
[216] Hansard, 8 Apr. 1935, vol. 300, col. 808. *TSB* 2/1 (1936), 5. Post 33/5253 (3, 27). Post 33/5252 (17, 18). Post 33/5415 (1). Post 33/3577 (28).

radio broadcast; a two-minute trailer film was produced by the film unit and distributed to all cinemas willing to screen it for free; and newsreel companies were asked to give coverage to the scheduled events. Exhibitions were held in five cities, special shops were opened, and posters were displayed. Yet, as in all earlier campaigns, dignified press advertisements containing coupons formed the basis of the appeal. None of the posters, designed by noted artists, were exhibited on commercial hoardings and, as ever, considerable emphasis was placed on local efforts. Regional offices were encouraged to sponsor exhibitions, lectures, and public meetings. Letters were sent to MPs asking them to participate in any such gatherings in their constituencies. Results were encouraging; by November, subscriptions had increased substantially, though critics linked this to the reduction in rates, and continued to question the commercial value of the type of advertising being employed.[217]

Considerable criticism of this nature actually emanated from within the GPO. A committee established in 1936 to investigate regional publicity arrangements claimed that insufficient attention was paid to the requirements of individual areas in the centrally prepared advertising materials, and recommended greater diversity in the type of posters used. Content in general was said to need review:

we desire to express the opinion that 'prestige' posters . . . should avoid the more advanced or eccentric schools of art. We are led to make this observation by the fact that some of the posters we have been shown, though doubtless highly meritorious in design or execution, seem to us quite unsuitable for general exhibition.[218]

Highet's articles in the *Telephone Sales Bulletin* (*TSB*) generated a similar response. Commenting on the advanced techniques advocated, one salesman asked, 'Are we trying to sell telephone service to the man in the suburbs, or are we running an exhibition of industrial art?'[219] Highet responded that publicity was a double-edged sword, only of value if used properly.[220] Grierson's reply was more forceful and aptly summarizes the attitude of the public relations division with regard to these issues:

If we get people to realise that the telephone will do this, that and the other thing for them, good. . . . But if the telephone has been made a symbol of all that is meant by liberty of voice, if it is represented as securing wide and intimate contacts in a world where wide and intimate contacts are necessary . . . then

---

[217] 'Telephone Week, 1934', Post 33/4856. Also see *Annual Register* (1934), 77.
[218] Post 33/5414 (3); Post 108/1936/Public Relations.
[219] See *TSB* 2/1 (1936), 11; 2/2 (1936), 28; 2/3 (1936), 44; 3/6 (1937), 92.
[220] *TSB* 2/5 (1936), 74–7.

salesmanship is beginning to graduate. Telephone officers may, on this analysis, appreciate the better why all our public relations work does not go into publicity 'blurbs' and head-stunning drives. They will appreciate why our exhibition section uses the word 'prestige' and why our film section talks not of publicising the Post Office but of bringing it alive. . . . I hope they will give practical evidence that they are conscious of this distinction. They can do it in a dozen ways. . . . They will not, for example, think we do not know what we are doing . . . because our exhibitions and posters do not appear to be selling much. They will not follow up our educational shows . . . [by advising children] to tell their mothers that they should be on the telephone.[221]

Tallents believed that the division had not gone far enough in developing prestige publicity. In a memorandum prepared on leaving the GPO in 1935, he expressed dissatisfaction with the posters supplied to date, observing that the artists employed seemed to have mistakenly assumed that a government department was 'sure to want a conventional design'. None had 'managed to get "under the skin" ' of the GPO, and really bring it alive. Lacking practical knowledge of Post Office activities, they were 'too much like boys sticking up a leaflet on a gate and running away'.[222] E. T. Crutchley, Tallents's successor as public relations director, later used the same arguments against what he regarded as the artistic excesses of GPO publicity. A career civil servant, writer, and sometime journalist, Crutchley had considerable experience in official publicity work, and was as strongly committed as Tallents to legitimating the concept of government public relations, and changing Civil Service attitudes towards publicity.[223] Under his guidance, GPO publicity continued to develop as it had done.[224] Yet Crutchley placed greater emphasis on putting control over the arrangements more fully in the hands of GPO

[221] *TSB* 2/4 (1936), 57–8.

[222] Although dated 10 Feb. 1936, internal evidence suggests it was written before Tallents left the GPO; Post 5253 (27). After joining the BBC, Tallents remained a member of the GPO publicity advisory committee, and on subsequent occasions defended the use of artistic posters when the policy was criticized; see e.g. PAC, Minutes, 11 Feb. 1937, NSC 26/19.

[223] Crutchley headed the Parliamentary and Press branch at the Ministry of Transport in 1919, and served on the Cabinet committees of 1920–1 which co-ordinated propaganda during the industrial unrest of those years. In 1921, Crutchley was assigned to Dublin Castle, a position which also entailed some involvement in publicity work. Attached to the Dominions Office in 1922, and the Overseas Settlement Board in 1925, he gained more experience in publicity work. As public relations officer of the GPO 1935–9, he was involved in the planning of the MOI. Crutchley became public relations officer at the Ministry of Home Security on its creation in 1939. Brooke Crutchley, *Ernest Tristram Crutchley* (Cambridge, 1941), 23–5; *POM* 2/10 (1936), 342.

[224] For Crutchley's philosophy, see *GPO*, 1, 246–7. Publicity activities in 1937–8 closely resembled efforts to date; see the memorandum sent to the Treasury, 4 Feb. 1938, T 162/981/36055/01/2.

officials instead of outside experts. Attending his first meeting of the poster advisory committee in February 1936, Crutchley heard complaints from Clark, Beddington, and Bell about the department's failure to exhibit many of the designs they had commissioned and approved. Crutchley believed the rejected posters were 'unsuitable' (they were too artistic for his taste), but attempted to placate the experts by explaining that present requirements were being met by the designs already displayed. Unappeased, the triumvirate continued to press for the use of all approved posters and threatened to resign over the issue. In late 1937, Crutchley urged his superiors to suspend the committee, pointing out that the enthusiasm which was shown for posters deemed unsuitable by the department was a clear indication that the committee had 'failed, like some of the artists, to grasp Post Office atmosphere and requirements'. He further observed that, in pressing the point, the committee was also overstepping its advisory functions.[225] Noting that, during the past four years, the public relations division had assembled a staff sufficiently schooled in advertising techniques and capable of understanding and interpreting the needs of the department, Crutchley questioned the necessity of further consultation with outside experts. While he agreed that the publicity advisory committee might be retained, Crutchley recommended that it should confine its future activities to providing advice about advertising agencies and other technical matters. By virtue of its internal expertise, he argued, the public relations division ought to be accorded total responsibility for the direction and execution of publicity policy.[226]

These recommendations were approved, and had important repercussions beyond the Post Office itself. The affirmation of the idea that internal expertise was of at least equal importance to advertising experience in determining publicity policy exerted an enormous influence on the department's reaction to attempts made in 1938 to centralize all government publicity in the domestic sphere under the control of one organization. Indeed, as we shall see below, the Post Office cited these arguments to block any such proposals. Interestingly enough, by 1938 even departments which lacked commercial motivations to develop publicity, such as the Ministry of Health, had reached the same conclusions.

---

[225] Crutchley to Director-General, 15 Oct. 1937, Post 33/5253 (34).
[226] Ibid. Crutchley to Director-General, 3 Apr. 1936, Post 33/5236 (11).

5

Health Publicity 1919–1939

As the Science of Medicine becomes more internal and more closely integrated, revealing more of the inner workings of the body auto-nomy, so also its application to disease becomes more personal and intimate. As the science of Government becomes more represent-ative of the aspirations of the people as a whole, so also its practice is dependent upon their education and equipment. Only an edu-cated people is an effective and healthy people.

(Sir George Newman (Chief Medical Officer, Board of Education and Ministry of Health, 1907–35), *The Place of Public Opinion in Preventive Medicine*, 1920)

At the present time the numerous agencies that try to teach the laws of health are diffused in their activities. To be effective a central directing body is necessary. The permanent officials at the Ministry of Health concur entirely in this view as to the possibilities of popular health education. For the time being this necessary function has been checked, but before long it will be necessary for the Min-ister of Health to stimulate and control national health propaganda. It would certainly be 'economy' to do so.

(Dr Christopher Addison (Minister of Health, 1919–21), 'Teaching Health Laws', *Manchester Guardian*, 3 Jan. 1923)

It is not enough for health administrators to lament the fact that only half the prospective mothers of this country seek any kind of medical advice before their confinements; part of their job is to persuade every one of these mothers that she would be wise to get ante-natal advice and to tell her where that advice can be got.

(Sir Kingsley Wood, Minister of Health, *Advertising World*, December 1937).

O N its establishment in 1919, the Ministry of Health was accorded re-sponsibility for the 'collection, preparation, publication and dissemina-tion of information and statistics' related to measures conducive to the physical well-being of the nation.[1] Neither the extent of this duty nor

---

[1] Ministry of Health Act 1919; Ministry of Health, *Annual Report of the Chief Medical Officer 1919–1920*, Cmd. 978 (1920), Appendix IX.

the manner or methods by which it was to be fulfilled was specified. None the less, that this provision was present in the legislation creating the department indicates that education was recognized as an essential means of promoting national health. This, in turn, reflected the growing emphasis being placed on prevention rather than cure in the treatment of disease. Over subsequent decades, the development of 'preventive medicine', coupled with the expansion of services, increased the importance attached to publicity. An educated public opinion came to be regarded as a necessary impetus to reform, and, once new services were in place, instruction the chief means of ensuring their use. More than an arm of policy, propaganda became an essential aspect of health administration, even to the extent of substituting for, or replacing, services when further expansion was deemed impossible. Yet if the value of education was recognized early, government was initially reluctant to undertake the task; publicity was not accepted as a legitimate and necessary responsibility of the Ministry of Health until late in the 1930s.

The creed of preventive medicine came to prominence in the years before the First World War. Noting in 1920 that current research was uncovering both the cures to serious ailments and the fundamental truths of disease causation, Sir George Newman, the Chief Medical Officer of the Board of Education (1907–35) and the Ministry of Health (1919–35), observed that 'for the first time' much illness could be prevented, provided, that is, that the public was kept informed of new discoveries and instructed in their application.[2] As better health hinged on mass education, the latter had to be developed:

An essential part of any national health policy is the instruction in the principles and practice of hygiene of the great mass of the people. In this as in other spheres of human affairs ignorance is the chief curse. We are only now, as knowledge grows, becoming more aware of the immeasurable part played by ignorance in the realm of disease. It is hardly too much to say that in proportion as knowledge spreads in a population, disease and incapacity decline, and this becomes more evident as the gross forms of pandemic diseases are overcome. As in the individual so in the community, knowledge is the sheet anchor of preventive medicine. . . . The great reforms . . . are dependent for their achievement upon an enlightened and responsive people.[3]

[2] Sir George Newman, *The Place of Public Opinion in Preventive Medicine* (1920), 4.
[3] Sir George Newman, *An Outline of the Practice of Preventive Medicine*, a Memorandum addressed to the Minister of Health, Cmd. 363 (Aug. 1919), 88. Also see MH, *Annual Report of the Chief Medical Officer 1919–1920*, 80–1; and Newman, *Public Education in Health* (1924, 1926), 1; *The Foundations of National Health* (1928), 15; *The Building of a Nation's Health* (1939), 444.

The process was cyclical; the impetus for reform in a democracy had to come from the people, but only an educated public could recognize the need for change. Once new policies were enacted, further education—indeed, persuasion—was essential to ensure their success: ' "Public Health is purchasable"—but the purchase clearly involves desire to purchase, [and] understanding of what is to be bought.'[4] Newman's position ensured that his views had a wide circulation; they were shared by many in the medical profession, including the first Minister of Health, Christopher Addison.[5]

As president of the Local Government Board in 1918, Addison championed a proposal from I. G. Gibbon, a career civil servant with wartime experience in recruiting publicity, to establish a publicity section in the board's Intelligence Division. Claiming that some form of information service was needed, Addison advised the Treasury that the task would be more efficiently conducted if handled from inside the department by an established division rather than by outsiders.[6] None the less, the Treasury was asked to sanction the employment of a non-civil servant as director as:

It is advisable that the head of the branch shall be a man familiar with the newspaper world and able to obtain the insertion of material so far as possible without payment. It will be one of the principal duties of the head of the branch to prepare articles which will be inserted as 'news'.[7]

Basil Clarke, a journalist currently directing the Special Intelligence section at the Ministry of Reconstruction, was Gibbon's candidate. He was appointed; but, holding that publicity 'need only be a temporary measure', the requirement for which was likely to 'diminish', the Treasury refused to sanction the creation of a full-fledged bureau.

On its creation in 1919, Clarke was transferred to the Ministry of Health. Responsible for stimulating public opinion, as well as the activities of local authorities, he actually had little direct contact with the general public.[8] Large-scale campaigns were not contemplated, and would have

[4] Newman, *Outline Preventive Medicine*, 45, 94. Also his *Public Opinion*, 4, 10; *Public Education*, 17; *Nation's Health*, 28.

[5] A. J. Collis, 'Diffusion of Knowledge as a Factor in the Improvement of the Public Health' (Newcastle upon Tyne, 1908), 1–13. Christopher Addison, 'The Health of the People and How it May be Improved' (1914), Bodleian Library, Oxford, MS Addison, Box 87, File 50.4. Lord Dawson of Penn, physician to King George V, was another leading exponent; see his entry in the *Dictionary of National Biography*.

[6] 'Publicity Branch', 8 Aug. 191[8]; H. L. Munro to the Treasury, 18 Feb. 1919, MH 107/23.   [7] Munro to Treasury, 18 Feb. 1919, MH 107/23.

[8] Ibid. Clarke to Director of Establishments, 22 Apr. 1920, MH 107/23.

been impossible, since the annual publicity budget was £1,000. Circulars and the insertion of news articles in the press (editorial publicity) were the chief forms of publicity employed.[9] Demands for advertising of a more popular nature did arise; during an estimates debate in parliament in June 1919, for example, the ministry was advised to adopt more aggressive tactics. Frederick Briant suggested that it should issue, 'by the million', 'striking advertisements' containing 'illustrations of large photographs of some of the germs of disease, which would be sufficiently horrifying to make the people realise what they are losing by . . . want of [health]'.[10] Addison withheld comment, but agreed to consider the possibility of conducting a mass campaign in conjunction with the implementation of the new Housing and Town Planning Act (the Addison Act).[11]

Planning for housing publicity began in July 1919 with the appointment of an advisory committee comprising mainly the representatives of Town Planning Associations. It was chaired by Sir Herbert Morgan,[12] a corporate executive and former member of the Intelligence Division of the Ministry of Munitions, who was already serving as honorary adviser to Clarke. However, neither the committee nor the propaganda section of the housing department, staffed by Gibbon and two civil servants, Bernard Townroe and Montagu Harris, maintained direct contact with Clarke.

Housing publicity was intended to serve a dual purpose, that of supplying information to 'all concerned' with the government's programme, while enlisting support for it. Although the ministry took a direct role in the scheme, preparing posters and exhibition materials, and publishing a fortnightly journal entitled *Housing*, the campaign hardly constituted a foray into the sphere of popular publicity. Statistics on the budget vary widely (from under £2,000 to over £20,000), but it is evident that most of it was directed towards staff costs and *Housing*.[13] The ministry's publicity efforts centred largely on informing local authorities of the provisions of the legislation, and encouraging county councils and voluntary

[9] Newman to Secretary, 15 June 1920, MH 55/27. In 1920, the ministry spent £800 on general press advertising: 'Summary of Returns', T 161/3/213. Publicity costs amounted to £10,600 in 1919, but the figure included the housing campaign: Hansard, 22 Dec. 1919, vol. 123, col. 1074.   [10] Hansard, 30 June 1919, vol. 117, cols. 678, 689–90, 704–5, 720.
[11] Ibid. 15 July 1919, vol. 118, cols. 232–3.
[12] MH, *First Annual Report of the Ministry of Health 1919–1920: Part II*, Cmd. 917 (1920), 9–10.
[13] Memorandum to Secretary, 15 June 1920; 'Minister's Conference on *Health Propaganda*', 10 Nov. 1920, MH 55/27. MH to Treasury, 27 Nov. 1920, T 162/42/2862. Minute by Heseltine, 3 May 1921, MH 55/27.

Health Publicity 1919–1939   127

organizations to publicize the proposals. A booklet, outlining the powers of local government under the Act, was sent directly to a wide number
of officials, accompanied by a covering letter signed by Addison, so that
'every councillor [would] feel that the Minister of Health had got his eye
on him'.[14] Similarly *Housing*, envisaged as a channel for the provision of
information and guidance to regional officers, was distributed gratuitously to all local authorities.[15] Viewed by the press as unfair competition,
it operated at a loss, never becoming a popular publication.[16] The ministry also secured the assistance of at least thirty-five voluntary organizations. By March 1920 they had sponsored over 500 meetings, providing
'expert speakers' and defraying all costs, save travel expenses.[17] Local
initiative was also exploited during a housing bond drive inaugurated in
the spring of 1920, when councils were asked to sponsor special week-
long campaigns. Some did, employing methods of a more commercial
nature than that favoured by the department itself. The London County
Council's 'Bond Week', for example, began with a meeting at the Albert
Hall at which prominent MPs gave speeches, and a special film, containing 'clever displays of "trick" cinematography with plenty of advertising
"punches" ', was screened. One segment pictured a vacant lot with a 'To
let' sign being obliterated by falling coins. These were transformed into
6 per cent Housing Bonds which in turn became the bricks of a house.
The film concluded with a 'message' from Mary Pickford and Douglas
Fairbanks, then on a well-publicized visit to England. Posters were displayed on buses, trams, and 1,000 London Underground sites provided
free of charge. Commercial firms, such as Lyons, were also persuaded
to exhibit posters in their windows.[18] Townroe and Morgan, with the
assistance of Sir John Ferguson of Lloyds Bank, and the ever-present
William Crawford, co-ordinated such local activities and supplied general advice.[19] Commercial firms were encouraged to prepare films on the
subject; Kingsley Wood, then Parliamentary Secretary to the ministry,

[14] MH, *First Annual Report*, 9–10. Advisory Committee on Housing Propaganda, Minutes, 27 June 1919, MS Addison, Box 69, File 3.
[15] Hansard, 28 Oct. 1919, vol. 120, cols. 494–5; 5 May 1920, vol. 128, col. 2102. MH,
First Annual Report, 10.
[16] Hansard, 14 Aug. 1919, vol. 119, cols. 1667–8; 28 Oct. 1919, vol. 120, cols. 494–5;
18 May 1920, vol. 129, cols. 1206–7. Publications Committee, *Second Report* (1920),
Proceedings, 6 May 1920, mins. 328–32.
[17] Advisory Committee on Housing Propaganda, Minutes, 27 June 1919, MS Addison,
Box 69, File 3.   [18] *The Times*, 1, 16, 22, 30 June, 12, 13 July 1920.
[19] *The Times*, 3, 5, 10 May 1920. Also see Housing Committee, Minutes, 27 Apr. 1920,
PRO, Housing and Local Government Board Papers, HLG 52/881.

even wrote the scenario for one, but none were produced with public money.[20] Central government was involved only at a distance.

On reviewing the housing campaign in March 1920, Addison expressed concern that under the current arrangements the intelligence services of the department were inadequate to meet its requirements.[21] Voluntary organizations, deeply rooted in the history of the British health care system, were proliferating,[22] and many were pressing the ministry for publicity grants. Thus in May 1920 the minister decided to convene a high-level departmental conference to explore the subject of health propaganda.[23] Present besides Addison were Newman and the two Permanent Secretaries, Sir Aubrey Symonds and Sir William Robinson. Gibbon, Townroe, and others attended later conferences, but conspicuous by his absence was the supposed expert, Clarke. Addison began by expressing both his unwillingness to provide sporadic funding to voluntary agencies and his uncertainty as to the position which the department ought to adopt. Both Symonds and Robinson were convinced that popular instruction was the responsibility of local authorities, and recommended that the ministry assume no more than a guiding role.[24] Newman agreed, noting that regional officers were well placed to 'provide the local percipient for the ideas which the central department might wish to inculcate'. He claimed that a 'good deal' was already being done; most county councils issued popular leaflets on health topics, and the ministry was employing a press officer, as well as funding the propaganda activities of two voluntary bodies. Since 1916 the National Council for Combating Venereal Diseases had been receiving an annual grant of several thousand pounds, and the department had recently contributed £1,000 to the National Clean Milk Society.[25] Yet seeing room for expansion, Newman advocated that the ministry engage in *ad hoc* propaganda. He suggested that the schools might serve as a good channel for the dissemination of information, but added that the Board of Education would be likely to veto any such proposal. Indeed, although health instruction was already a responsibility of local

[20] *The Times*, 16 June 1920.
[21] 'Twentyfirst [*sic*] meeting with the Housing Department', 25 Mar. 1920, MS Addison, Box 33, File 19.
[22] Newman dated their efforts from the 1870s and noted their comprehensiveness, *Nation's Health*, 446–7.
[23] 'Minister's Conference on *Health Propaganda*', 4 May 1920, MH 55/27.
[24] Ibid.
[25] Newman to Secretary, 15 June 1920; Minute by Heseltine, 3 May 1921, MH 55/27. MH, *First Annual Report, Part 1*, 57–8. Hansard, 23 Mar. 1921, vol. 139, cols. 2578–9; 8 Apr. 1925, vol. 182, cols. 2242–3. MH to Treasury, 29 Apr. 1920, T 161/3/213.

educational authorities, and hygiene and physical education were well established in the curriculum by 1920,[26] the board adopted a very narrow definition of propaganda and was reluctant to allow outsiders to distribute even informative materials to its charges. That very summer it refused to assist the Ministry of Health in promoting milk consumption by displaying posters in schools and issuing pamphlets to children, agreeing only to encourage teachers to include more information about milk in their lessons.[27] Newman averred that the Ministry of Health 'must exclude much use of the elementary schools in regard to propaganda'.[28]

The conference concluded that if the ministry did engage in propaganda, its campaigns would be of an educative nature: 'The topics would not be many in number and they would deal with the preventive side. If the cinema were used it would need to be used artistically and with great caution.'[29] However, no decision was reached on the proper role of the department with regard to publicity in general or its employment by other organizations. Yet as he believed health instruction needed to be expanded, Addison requested the preparation of reports on work in progress, which would encompass proposals for future schemes. He also recommended that experts such as Morgan be consulted for advice.

That June Newman submitted a comprehensive study on publicity to the joint permanent secretaries.[30] He summarized his views in the opening paragraph:

I am quite clear that it is part of the duty of the Ministry of Health to initiate and supervise and sometimes even to carry out, 'publicity' work. By this I mean the provision of information on Preventive Medicine. . . . Much of the success of its practice and administration is dependent upon an intelligent understanding among people at large, and this becomes all the more important as the people themselves control the activities . . . of local government.

Yet if the ministry's responsibility was clear, the phrase 'sometimes even to carry out "publicity" ' was an important qualification; Newman went on to reaffirm his conviction that the task should be under the control of local authorities and voluntary bodies. The department ought only

---

[26] Regarding health instruction in the schools see PEP, *Report on the British Health Services* (1937), 338–40, 357–8. Newman, *Nation's Health*, 267–73. Newman believed the curriculum was too limited and gave insufficient attention to preventive health care; *Public Opinion*, 28; *Outline Preventive Medicine*, 23–4; *Public Education* (1924), 10–14.

[27] Cross to Newman, 2 July 1920; Memorandum, 15 June 1920, MH 56/74. Also see below, p. 200.   [28] Newman to Secretary, 15 June 1920, MH 55/27.

[29] Conference, 4 May 1920, MH 55/27.

[30] Newman to Secretary, 15 June 1920, MH 55/27.

to encourage, and, where legally possible, finance publicity. Pointing to the success of the venereal diseases campaign and others, he proposed extending grants to all 'competent and properly authorised voluntary societies'. Of course, the ministry itself would be closely involved in health publicity of a general nature; indeed, 'its whole policy ought to be propagandist and educational in effect'. Publications, such as annual reports, could be used to disseminate important information, and from 'time to time', the department might popularize its views. Again, the qualification was significant, for, aside from special cases, such as the outbreak of an epidemic, Newman did not believe that official publications should be directed towards the mass audience:

> The idea is not primarily the popular leaflet but a reasoned statement of the particular subject which is properly considered and in good proportion for our own office use, for the use of local officers, and generally for handy reference to know how the subject stands as a matter of public health, and what it needs administratively.[31]

Impressed by Newman's assessment of what was already being done, Robinson queried the need for further expansion. Noting that recent Cabinet decisions on economy in the public sector made funding unlikely, he agreed that direct involvement in publicity would be inadvisable, as it was 'apt to be very badly done', and was 'unsuitable' to the duties of a government department. Thus, apart from distributing occasional articles to the press on special subjects, the ministry

> should . . . confine its . . . activity to the issue of the more formal reports and memoranda . . . which make their first appeal to the limited and more intellectual class and percolate down through it, while the local authority or society should undertake the issue of the more popular material aimed directly at the main mass of the population.[32]

Both these reports were considered at a second departmental conference in July. All present agreed that local authorities and voluntary organizations were an efficient and economical channel for the dissemination of propaganda. Addison commented, however, that it was incumbent on someone to supply guidance to local officials. He wanted plans formulated which would enable the ministry to act as a 'stimulating centre', and, if occasion arose, conduct *ad hoc* propaganda.[33]

---

[31] Publications Committee (27 July 1920), Proceedings, 6 May 1920, mins. 324–6.

[32] Robinson to Minister, 21 July 1920, MH 55/27.

[33] Conference, 29 July 1920, MH 55/27. For a summary see Symonds to Newman, 30 Aug. 1920, MH 55/27. On Addison's views see 'The Part of the State in the Prevention of Disease', *West London Medical Journal* (July 1921), 3–4: MS Addison, Box 87.

Both Townroe and Gibbon submitted proposals to Symonds in August. Townroe's scheme centred on the creation of a new division which would absorb Clarke's office and have four main functions: guiding regional effort through local authorities; supplying information to voluntary bodies; instructing the public through the press; and, in special cases, directing intensive campaigns on specific subjects. While suggesting that Morgan should serve as an adviser to the organization, Townroe recommended that its chief officials should be drawn from current staff rather than from outside the Civil Service, as a knowledge of the workings of the department was as essential to the prosecution of successful publicity as technical expertise.[34] The concept of internal expertise already had support within the department, as is indicated by the fact that Clarke was neither included in any of the discussions on health propaganda nor informed of the contemplated administrative changes until they were well under way. The publicity officer may have been regarded as an expert on technical matters, but clearly the framing of policy was viewed as the forte and responsibility of public servants.

Moving on to discuss techniques, Townroe advocated the adoption of a personal approach to publicity, suggesting, for example, that Ministry of Health officials forge close ties with the clerks of local authorities.[35] Contact with the public was to be secured through *Housing*, which was intended to become a popular journal. Published monthly or fortnightly, each issue was to contain a 'good "leader" ' on some specific topic, plus book reviews and up-to-date reports on public health questions.[36] As this implies, Townroe rejected the assumption that the ministry should engage merely in *ad hoc* publicity. Although he did not explain the motives behind his recommendations, it is evident that, despite his earlier praise for the efforts of voluntary bodies, Townroe doubted their effectiveness in reaching the mass audience. In 'Popular Health Literature', a study prepared independently for Addison, he characterized the publications of voluntary bodies as over-long, too detailed, often frightening, and, above all, misdirected; most of them dealt with cure rather than prevention. Moreover, little was being done to ensure their widespread distribution: 'It would seem that the Societies have often gone only half way and provided the material if people like to go for it. They seem to let the public go to them and do not go sufficiently to the public.' This contrasted sharply with American methods, which were much more aggressive: 'The

---

[34] Townroe to Symonds, 12 Aug. 1920, MH 55/27.
[35] Symonds objected, but Gibbon made similar recommendations and Addison approved: Notation on Townroe's report; Gibbon, 'Public Information'; 'Minister's Conference', 10 Nov. 1920, MH 55/27.   [36] Townroe to Symonds, 12 Aug. 1920, MH 55/27.

Public Health department of each State publishes a monthly "Journal" on "Public Health News". This it will send free to any person regularly.' He noted further that several US health authorities also published magazines and sponsored films.[37]

His recommendations with regard to *Housing* indicate that Townroe was attempting to steer the department towards the American example. Yet had the proposal been adopted, it is unlikely that the publication would have been distributed gratuitously. Those copies of *Housing* not issued to local authorities were sold, as were virtually all other government documents.[38] Indeed, the department also followed a policy of 'letting the public come to them'.

Townroe's opposition to according total control over health propaganda to voluntary organizations also reflected the problems he had recently encountered with the People's League of Health. Founded in 1917, the league had the rather vague objective of scientifically teaching the public 'the principles of life giving health'.[39] In May 1919, Clarke had noticed a press release concerning a theatrical production on housing reform being sponsored by the organization, and contacted it to offer assistance and enlist co-operation in the official campaign. After discussions with Townroe, the league had insisted on being recognized as the 'propaganda limb' of the ministry and demanded funding. Meanwhile, it was attacking the department publicly, and, so Townroe claimed, attempting to dictate government policy. A year later, when asked about the advisability of approaching the league on the subject of general health propaganda, Townroe advised extreme caution in dealing with it, and, by inference, any other unofficial body.[40]

Although Gibbon agreed that the department should act as a 'clearing house', establishing ties with leading organizations, providing speakers for meetings, and encouraging the discussion of health topics at conferences, he also opposed the suggestion that it should confine itself to a supervisory role.[41] Arguing that 'propaganda is effective in proportion as it establishes the right atmosphere', he recommended that, instead of pushing particular health topics, the department ought to concentrate on

[37] 'Popular Health Literature', *c.*1920, MS Addison, Box 33. Newman also praised the Americans: *Public Education* (1926), 17. Also see *The Times*, 3, 7 Jan. 1924.

[38] See above, p. 62, and 'Appendix C: Report by Dr Daukes', MH 55/32.

[39] *The Times*, 5 Apr. 1937.

[40] Townroe, 'Precis of Correspondence', 19 Nov. 1920; Townroe to Gibbon, 27 Nov. 1920, MH 58/153. Minute to Ward, 11 Dec. 1931, MH 58/154. The league remained a problem: Robinson to H. J. Wilson, 20 Apr. 1927, MH 58/154.

[41] Subsequent references are to 'Public Information', 25 Aug. 1920, MH 55/27.

creating a good background against which others could conduct specific campaigns. Official reports, for example, could be drafted in a more attractive and instructive form, and press attention be drawn to their release. Like Townroe, Gibbon believed that the ministry should adopt a dignified and personal approach to publicity. Thus his plans for securing better exploitation of the press included cultivating editors and persuading prominent individuals to write favourable news articles. Similarly, proposing the creation of a house journal, Gibbon noted that, though it might be written 'in a popular way', it must 'maintain a high standard of information and thought', and 'not be popular at the expense of quality'. Leaflets were also said to be a valuable means of reaching the public, provided they were not employed indiscriminately. While Gibbon recognized that direct participation in publicity activities might lay the department open to charges of puffery, he observed that, because of its expertise, the ministry was obligated both to supply information, and assist in its interpretation:

It is manifest that . . . work in connection with the Press has to be undertaken with considerable care. Any notion that the Department is trying to use the Press simply to play its own game or to cover its own faults would be disastrous. At the same time, it has to be recognized that writers in the Press often have very little notion of the real difficulties of the problem or of the issues involved, and that there is grave danger, in many instances, of harm to public good if measures are not taken to secure that each particular problem is looked at from all sides. Effective Press work depends mainly on the degree to which the Department can convince those who are responsible for the Press that it is out frankly for the enlightenment of public opinion, and that any measure which it undertakes for the dissemination of information is for the public good, and not simply for departmental glorification.

The question of how newspapers, let alone civil servants, were to distinguish legitimate publicity from puffery or partisanship, in the absence of any guidelines governing the distribution of all official information, was not addressed. This is surprising, given that the department was already experiencing difficulty in convincing critics of the justification behind some of its housing publicity.[42] Yet the entire issue was not given serious consideration within the ministry until the mid-1930s; probably because it was only then, when the department decided to adopt a more

---

[42] The department was being accused of using *Housing* as a medium for political propaganda: Hansard, 14 Aug. 1919, vol. 119, cols. 1667–8; 18 May 1920, vol. 129, cols. 1206–7. *The Times*, 30 Nov. 1920.

general and direct approach towards the public, that the subject had to be confronted.

Symonds considered both reports but, ignoring his subordinates' proposals, sent Newman a memorandum stating that all were agreed that the ministry should confine its activities to issuing formal reports aimed at the better educated, only engaging in popular appeals during crises. He contended that publicity suitable for the mass audience ought to be left to local authorities and voluntary organizations, but financial assistance should not be provided to them 'specifically and solely' for propaganda purposes. Publicity expenditure by local authorities should only be funded if it was part of larger grant-aided schemes. In exceptional cases, voluntary societies might be given support, but, where possible, this ought to emanate from local government. Citing problems experienced with the People's League of Health, Symonds advised the department to avoid arousing the hostility of unofficial bodies, while keeping them at arm's length. Embarrassing results were predicted if amateurs were in any way authorized to represent the ministry.[43] What would the department do, he queried, if an officially recognized agency disseminated information or ideas contradictory to or critical of government policy?[44]

Surprisingly, given his earlier statements, Newman endorsed these views.[45] Aside from funding venereal diseases propaganda ('rather a different case'), he argued that the ministry should do nothing more than extend a blessing to associations engaged in general health instruction. Formal connections involved too great a risk; local authorities might interpret expenditure on voluntary publicity as a criticism of their efforts, however meagre.[46] Moreover, controversy was bound to arise if the department, by chance or design, supported instruction on health matters which were not being addressed practically.[47] Newman also observed that financial resources were limited.[48] Echoing Addison, other officials countered that the ministry had to ensure that the educational material disseminated by outside bodies was guided by sound principles.[49] Michael

[43] Symonds to Newman, 30 Aug. 1920, MH 55/27.

[44] Townroe to Gibbon, 27 Nov. 1920, MH 58/153. Symonds to Newman, 30 Aug. 1920, MH 55/27. Similar questions were raised elsewhere in Whitehall when ties with voluntary organizations were considered; see 'Supply and Transport Committee: Propaganda Subcommittee', TSC(P)1, 25 Feb. 1920, CAB 27/84.

[45] Minute, 14 Oct. 1920, MH 55/27.

[46] Minute by Heseltine, 3 May 1921, MH 55/27.

[47] Newman to Heseltine, 5 Aug. 1920, MH 58/153. Conference on Propaganda, 29 July 1920, MH 55/27.

[48] Conference, 10 Nov. 1920, MH 55/27. Hansard, 24 Nov. 1920, vol. 135, cols. 465–6; 15 June 1921, vol. 143, col. 443. *The Times*, 15 Oct. 1921, 6 Apr., 29 July 1922.

[49] Note to Newman, 4 Aug. 1920, MH 58/153.

Heseltine, the assistant director of the intelligence division, believed voluntary societies could not be kept 'at a distance by sympathy without help', as this would invite hostility. He thought they should be supplied with any 'readable' literature produced by the department, including Newman's lectures, 'and *even* . . . our more popular circulars [my italics]'.[50] These views held little sway; at a final departmental conference in November, Symonds's recommendations were adopted in full.[51] A public information branch was established in the intelligence division, with Townroe as director, despite, or perhaps because of, Clarke's protests that Townroe was not a publicity expert.[52] Liaison was formalized with the medical division to ensure the free flow of technical information into the bureau, but there were few other changes. Indeed the new branch had the same functions as the organization it had replaced.[53] Requesting sanction for the new division, the department notified the Treasury that Addison was 'anxious to restrict the publicity work of the Department to the narrowest limits'.[54]

Thus, after seven months of deliberation, the ministry affirmed the importance of propaganda, decided to supervise the efforts of others, and then rendered the policy almost impossible to implement by adopting an approach which, if not restrictive, was hardly conducive to ensuring success. Voluntary organizations were expected to disseminate official information, but were not given free access to materials, let alone funds. Local authorities were not authorized to incur expenditure on publicity, and although they could provide grants to voluntary bodies in special cases, approval rested with the Ministry of Health. Hence such funding was sporadic and inconsistent. In 1920, for example, the ministry permitted 'reasonable contributions' to be made to the Royal Sanitary Institute's Health Week campaign. Sanction was withheld the following year, however, owing to the financial crisis.[55] There were obvious obstacles to extending support and recognition to voluntary bodies but, having isolated the problems, the ministry did nothing to solve them. Lacking clear-cut guidelines on the relationship to prevail between the department and outside agencies, officials could easily blunder. In 1921, for instance, the

[50] Heseltine to Symonds, 9 Aug. 1920, MH 58/153.
[51] Conference, 10 Nov. 1920, MH 55/27.
[52] Robinson to Heseltine and Woodgate, 4 Dec. 1920; Clarke to Robinson, 8 Dec. 1920, MH 107/23. Addison did not believe that technical experts should be responsible for propaganda policy: 'Twenty-fifth meeting with the Housing Department', 13 May 1920, MS Addison, Box 33, File 19.
[53] On the functions see above, pp. 125–6.
[54] Minute by Heseltine, 3 May 1921, MH 55/27.
[55] *The Times*, 3 May 1920, 10, 12 Oct. 1921.

Red Cross (hardly a controversial body) enlisted the co-operation of county medical officers, voluntary associations, and doctors in sponsoring lectures and other types of general health instruction. It did not request funding, but asked the ministry both to provide assistance in choosing districts which would benefit most from this experiment and to inform local authorities that the scheme had official approval. Yet until Addison intervened, the department hesitated, lest involvement create difficulties.[56]

A supporter of the hands-off policy throughout the 1920 discussions, Addison apparently altered his opinion soon afterwards. In 1921, he commissioned Morgan to prepare for public distribution experimental leaflets, posters, and advertisements containing simple instructions on personal hygiene.[57] The £2,000 scheme was dropped without explanation in May, though Addison later accused the Treasury of having scuppered it.[58] Pressure from that quarter seems likely; housing publicity was already under attack, and was suspended in June for financial reasons. Writing in the *Manchester Guardian* in January 1923, Addison, no longer a Government minister, cited these vetoed proposals as evidence of the neglect of general health education in Britain. Stressing the need for a central directing body, and advocating that the Ministry of Health emulate the American example, he noted that, while the Treasury might dislike the idea, his former colleagues 'concur[red] entirely' on the need to expand popular health instruction.[59] This was a questionable assessment. A week after this article was published, Robinson informed the minister that if an argument existed for maintaining a publicity bureau anywhere in Whitehall, it was in the Ministry of Health. Yet 'having no belief in a Government Department as a channel of propaganda intended to reach the mass of the people', he defended the ministry's position to date.[60] Although others were suggesting that the Ministry of Health should assume a broader role, by 1923, several higher officials had begun to question whether the department ought even to be involved in providing guidance to other bodies.

In August 1922, Dr O. K. Wright had submitted an unsolicited report to Heseltine entitled 'The Weakness of Public Health Propaganda'.[61]

---

[56] Newman to Secretary and Minister, 3 Nov. 1920; 'Extract from 210177/20', 1921; Minute by Heseltine, 3 May 1921; Robinson to Heseltine, 21 May 1921, MH 55/27.

[57] Minute by Heseltine, 3 May 1921; Robinson to Heseltine, 21 May 1921, MH 55/27. Addison, 'The Part of the State in the Prevention of Disease' (n. 33 above), 10.

[58] *Manchester Guardian*, 3 Jan. 1923.　　　[59] Ibid.

[60] Robinson to Minister, 10 Jan. 1923, MH 55/27.

[61] Subsequent references are to Wright, 'The Weakness of Public Health Propaganda', 23 Aug. 1922, MH 55/27.

Given the author's arguments and his prominence later in the ministry's dealings with the Central Council for Health Education, the document merits some consideration. The paper began with a discussion of the concept of propaganda. Noting a dearth of evidence on the subject, Wright none the less joined many of his contemporaries in assuming that the 'unthinking public' was 'intensely susceptible' to publicity. '[A]lmost' an 'exact science', propaganda could be mastered by anyone with a knowledge of the 'psychology of suggestibility'. Aware that many of his colleagues might disapprove, Wright observed that recourse to publicity need not entail a loss of dignity or decorum. Propaganda was a white knight, capable of rescuing the unsuspecting masses from commercial advertisers employing dubious means to dupe them into purchasing questionable products and/or ideas. Victory—for this was war—could only be assured by neutralizing the aggressor's effectiveness through the development of more powerful and ethically sound methods:

Why is it then that the propaganda of one side can be so much more effective than that of the other? It may be said that it is due to a policy of calumny, vituperation, and untruth which catches the popular attention, and that if we are fighting an enemy who uses poison gas we must employ the same weapon against him. But rather than *descend* to this it might be worthwhile to examine rather more deeply the nature of his weapon, to find out exactly wherein lies its efficacy, and to seek for a cleaner and more effective armament that will drive him from the invaded country. [my italics]

After outlining the psychology behind successful propaganda, Wright analysed selected pamphlets issued by various voluntary organizations, and noted that he had experienced difficulty in finding any with good points. Quoting extensively from George Newman's writings on the responsibility of the State to beget an intelligent public opinion, Wright urged the department to undertake research into propaganda methods. Only by mastering the science could the ministry hope to educate the public on the means to remain healthy. He concluded by stressing that publicity was an economical and necessary adjunct to health administration:

If we consider the amazing results that have been obtained by the application of scientific methods to commercial and other forms of propaganda we are justified in hoping that we have here a means of arousing response in the unthinking masses and so creating such a demand for the purchasable commodity, Public Health, as will sweep away all obstacles, whether due to ignorance, inertia, vested interests or prejudice.

Reviewing this memorandum, G. S. Buchanan of the establishments branch noted that it had successfully countered his impression that the subject was trivial. He agreed that the ministry might contribute to health education in many ways, for example by providing general instruction to medical officers of health, thereby encouraging them to become 'expert in the matter', yet stopped short of endorsing any type of popular appeal, noting that the department might draw attention to the leaflets of voluntary bodies, but should not distribute them, nor become a 'health-gospeller'.[62] Also asked to comment, Basil Clarke pronounced Wright's study a 'capital memo'.[63] However, claiming that valuable information was already being wasted because the department failed to disseminate it, he argued that it would be an unnecessary waste of time to conduct an investigation into publicity methods. Professional advice was readily available, and consultation with outside agencies need not impinge upon the department's control over the information imparted. Moreover, while permanent officials should by right dictate policy, they needed to recognize that publicity was not their forte:

The health texts and desiderata to be preached are very clear no doubt in the medical mind of the Ministry but the methods of the preaching—which are quite as important—are really an advertising problem and we should be wrong I think as a Ministry, if without further warranty, we posed or gave semblance of posing, as advertising experts.[64]

Thus Clarke suggested that a small group of advertising executives and literary and artistic figures, such as H. G. Wells and John Galsworthy, should be recruited to advise the department on methodology. In an apparent attempt to regain seniority he also recommended the creation of a new division to deal solely with health propaganda. Clarke noted, however, that, unless the ministry was willing to undertake a comprehensive scheme, the best results would be obtained by encouraging, funding, and grafting official policy on to existing efforts. All of these proposals were vetoed owing to financial retrenchment. Indeed, by April 1923 the publicity bureau itself had even been closed.[65] J. F. Kelly and H. S. Hunter, both regular officials, were deputed to handle press relations; portions

[62] Buchanan to Heseltine, 17 Sept. 1922, MH 55/27.
[63] Clarke to Heseltine, 4 Oct. 1922, MH 55/27.
[64] Clarke to Newman, *c*.Nov. 1922, MH 55/27.
[65] Hansard, 1 Mar. 1923, vol. 160, col. 2186.

of their salaries comprising the entire publicity budget until into the 1930s.[66]

Ironically, the department's only foray in these years into the public arena came on the heels of this development. But participation in the British Empire Exhibitions held at Wembley in 1924 and 1925 came about largely by chance and, as a discussion of the ministry's efforts will show, did not reflect any advance in terms of overall policy. When first approached in 1920 regarding a possible housing display at the 1924 event, the ministry balked.[67] Three years later, Heseltine noted that, although the department engaged in activities which might form the basis of a display at Wembley, it should restrict its contribution to aiding a voluntary committee which was planning a tropical diseases booth.[68] Uncertainty as to requirements, funding, and local assistance contributed to this decision. Citing a suggestion that the ministry publicize the National Insurance scheme by exhibiting replicas of cards and stamps, Heseltine also added that any attempt to advertise the administration of health services might prove depressing! Yet solely by chance, a ministry official was present at a meeting in May 1923 at which space and budgets were allocated for Wembley. Without consulting the department, he secured 500 ft. and £2,000 respectively, promising that this would be used for a town planning display. Informing his superiors that the Dominions would be making this a feature of their exhibits, he forecast embarrassment were the British government not to follow suit.[69] By the summer of 1923, the space and budget available had been increased, and officials began to plan a separate exhibit devoted to general health matters. With 700 ft. and £3,000 to work with, it was decided to cover several specific topics and employ a wide range of methods, including films, map illuminations, and moving toys.[70] Although it was hoped to interest experts as well as the public, the main criterion governing the choice of materials

---

[66] W. Thomas to E. Playfair, 9 Dec. 1937, T 162/971/12190/01. K. Wood, 'Press Officers Employed in Government Departments', 12 Mar. 1934; Shakespeare to Secretary and Minister, 13 Dec. 1934, MH 78/147. 'Press Officers', 1934, T 162/337/30623. The MH was criticized for maintaining even a skeleton staff: Hansard, 31 July 1923, vol. 167, cols. 1337–8.

[67] R. Unwin to Forber and Walker Smith, 10 Sept. 1920; and various minutes Oct.–Nov. 1920, HLG 52/897.

[68] Heseltine to Robinson and Newman, 18 Jan. 1923, HLG 52/898.

[69] 'British Empire Exhibition (1924)', Pepler to Gibbon, 15 May 1923; 'British Empire Exhibition', 21 June 1923, HLG 52/898.

[70] 'British Empire Exhibition', 4 July 1923; 'Ministry of Health and the British Empire Exhibition, 1924', 29 Sept. 1923, HLG 52/898.

was supposed to be their ability to appeal to the average individual: 'It is far more necessary that they should be strikingly interesting than that they should be recondite.'[71]

In fact, little of a really popular nature was done and success was limited. A list of the exhibits which excited the greatest attention—a 'brilliantly lit' 'sootfall' display in the atmospheric pollution section, which 'looked attractive amid the somewhat gloomy surroundings'; a map showing the future of Margate; estate housing photographs; and a sewage disposal exhibit, consisting only of inoperable wooden models and photographs of concrete channels—illustrates this point.[72] J. W. S. Fawcett, the chairman of the departmental committee responsible for the display and an official demonstrator at Wembley, admitted to failure, but blamed inadequate space and lighting, and the 'acrid fumes' emanating from the Admiralty's nearby theatre! Fawcett did acknowledge problems with the exhibit, agreeing that, were the ministry to participate again, the display would have to be made more attractive.[73] One official thought an improvement of 'at least 100 per cent in interest and impressiveness' was required, and recommended that, in future, the department differentiate between exhibits intended for experts and those aimed at the general public.[74]

Preparations for the 1925 exhibition were much more elaborate. Securing a larger proportion of the space and budget available, the department recruited Dr S. H. Daukes of the Wellcome Bureau of Scientific Research, who had organized a successful tropical medicine display the year before, to plan its exhibit.[75] Newman's influence was reflected in the choice of theme—the development of the science of preventive medicine. At the first meeting of the departmental committee, Daukes stressed the value of push-button exhibits, films, and broadcasting, but the display he planned was quite similar to the one used in 1924. Child welfare, for example, was publicized by fitting two 10 ft. × 12 ft. bays with cases containing infant diets and garments, feeding bottles, teeth donated by a children's centre,

[71] 'British Empire Exhibition 1924: Report of the Departmental Committee on the Ministry of Health Exhibit', 25 Nov. 1924, MH 55/32. Gibbon to Robinson, 22 Oct. 1923, HLG 52/898.

[72] 'Report of the Ministry of Health's Exhibit at the British Empire Exhibition 1924', 27 Oct. 1924, MH 55/32. *Fifth Annual Report of the Ministry of Health, 1923–1924*, Cmd. 2218 (1924), appendix IX.

[73] 'British Empire Exhibition: Report of Departmental Committee', MH 55/32.

[74] Note to Fawcett, 12 Nov. 1924, MH 55/32.

[75] 'British Empire Exhibition: Ministry of Health Participation, Meeting of Committee and others on 23 Dec. 1924', MH 55/32. *Sixth Annual Report of the Ministry of Health, 1924–1925*, Cmd. 2450 (1924–5), appendix IX. Note of meeting, 6 Jan. 1925, MH 55/32.

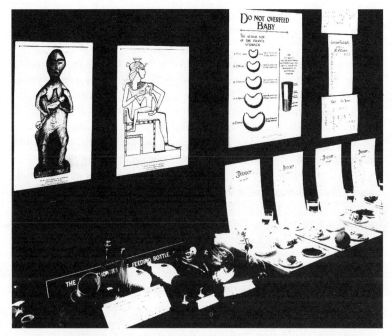

1 Ministry of Health poster: Infant Diets Display at British Empire Exhibition, Wembley 1924

and casts of feet, showing the effects of inadequate shoes. Illustrations were included, among them an illuminated infant mortality chart, photographs of tonsils and adenoid treatment, and a poster 'showing the careful preparation of an orchard thus illustrating the need for antenatal care with a picture of mother and child'. As this indicates, sections of the display were obviously directed at an intelligent audience capable of making rather complicated conceptual leaps. Many exhibits from 1924 were reused, and county councils and voluntary associations were asked to supply materials, not only in order to save money, 'but also to emphasize the extent to which public health work in this country has always been and remains a matter primarily for local administration'.[76]

Yet local councils lacked the resources and support they needed to conduct health publicity. As noted, they were not legally entitled to incur general expenditure in this area without Ministry of Health approval.

[76] Fawcett to Chamberlain, 'British Empire Exhibition, 1925: Report of the Departmental Committee', 15 Jan. 1926, MH 55/32. 'British Empire Exhibition: Meeting of the Committee and others', 20 Mar. 1925, MH 55/31.

The Society of Medical Officers of Health (SMOH) was already lobbying the department on this point.[77] Ironically, the society's interest in the matter had been aroused by O. K. Wright of the ministry. When his proposal to conduct research into publicity methods had been rejected, Wright had financed a test scheme himself, and, at the suggestion of others in the department, had endeavoured to engage the medical profession by addressing his ideas to the society, which then pressed the ministry to take action.[78] With the Geddes Axe hindering the expansion of services, the society argued that the only means available of advancing public health was publicity.[79] Acceding to the ministry's claim that regional variations had to be considered in the planning and execution of campaigns, the SMOH suggested that general health instruction should be made a legal duty of local authorities, and eligible for grant-aid. The ministry would merely have to enforce the provisions and assist local efforts by accumulating information, stocking films, assembling lists of lecturers, and issuing posters, leaflets, and periodic reports on publicity activities in general.[80]

In theory, at least, the ministry had already adopted an advisory role. Yet on considering this proposal, both Heseltine and Wright, who to date had been leading exponents of direct involvement, questioned whether it was necessary or legitimate for the department to place itself in such a position. Turning the society's arguments around, they absolved the ministry from further responsibility by arguing that commissioning a central body to direct publicity was alien to the entire concept of regional expertise. Indeed, as propaganda had to be formulated on the spot, standardization of methods or materials would be fatal. They advised that, aside from giving consideration to altering the legal powers of local government, the ministry should take no further action.[81]

George Newman disagreed; in an apparent reversal of his position to date, he deplored the dearth of 'political seers and prophets' prepared to 'foretell the new message which science has given to this generation',[82] and urged the ministry to adopt a more active role in health instruction: 'being in the vanguard of knowledge, [the department] should in the

[77] G. Elliston to MH, 24 Apr. 1923, MH 55/28.

[78] Minute by Heseltine, 8 Nov. 1922; 'Suggested programme of research in propaganda methods', 2 Jan. 1923; Minute to Wright, 7 Feb. 1923; Minute by Wright, 13 Feb. 1923; Wright to Heseltine, 6 Aug. 1923, MH 55/27.

[79] Elliston to MH, 24 Apr. 1923, MH 55/28.

[80] 'Memorandum on Health Propaganda', 21 Sept. 1923, MH 55/28.

[81] Wright and J. A. Storer to Heseltine, 25, 26 Oct. 1923; Heseltine, 'Notes for Interview', 14 Jan. 1924, MH 55/28.   [82] Newman, *Public Education* (1924), 2.

discharge of its statutory obligations, make such knowledge available
everywhere, encouraging in all ways and in every direction its spread
throughout the . . . land and indicating its practical applications to life.'[83]
On the other hand, he stressed that the ministry's propaganda activities
'must of necessity, be in large measure indirect', as this was in the best
traditions of democracy and was essential to any future progress in health
care:

Central and Local Authorities could not evolve or launch new schemes or extend
existing ones unless the mind of the people generally was in some sense prepared
for them. Official agencies cannot easily undertake such preparation; that is the
sphere of voluntary bodies and an enlightened public opinion. . . . [G]overnmental
action is the outcome of public opinion, and this in turn is formed by the more
educated section of the people and by individual exponents. They are the pio-
neers of advance as it affects the nation as a whole.[84]

Like others in the department, Newman assumed that knowledge would
be most effectively imparted to the general public if filtered down from
above through unofficial channels. While he was also wary of direct
involvement in this area, lest it provoke charges of puffery or partisanship, he concluded, none the less, that greater 'co-ordination' between
voluntary societies and government was of 'increasing importance and
necessity', and that legal changes were required so that local authorities
would be able to engage in general campaigns and fund voluntary
efforts.[85]

Ironically, by the time Newman filed this report in July 1924, the
SMOH had already given up on the ministry. In April, the society decided
to form a health education committee and requested that it be recognized
officially as the central agency responsible for assisting local authorities in
their efforts. The department balked; aside from the usual difficulties
involved in extending recognition to an external agency,[86] there was the
added impediment in this case that an organization representative of
the medical employees of local government was establishing a body to
advise its own superiors. In a classic example of situation avoidance, the
ministry informed the SMOH that, as changes in the legal position of
local authorities were now pending, it would be inopportune to discuss
centralization.[87]

[83] Ibid., p. iii.   [84] Ibid. 10–11.   [85] Ibid. 14–18.
[86] See above, p. 134, and below, p. 217.
[87] Elliston to Robinson, 23 Apr. 1924; Heseltine to Newman, 7 May 1924; Heseltine to
Newman and Robinson, 28 May 1924; Robinson to Minister, 10 July 1924; Robinson to
Elliston, 6 Aug. 1924, MH 55/28.

If the ministry believed plans for new legislation would stifle criticism, it was mistaken. Indeed, the SMOH held that, were local authorities given greater powers, a controlling body would be all the more essential. Co-ordination would be necessary to prevent overlapping and wasted effort. Furthermore, only a central agency could address the general matters not considered by voluntary bodies, which tended to focus their attention on specific issues. Local expertise aside, it would be impractical, uneconomic, and virtually impossible for councils to manufacture expensive publicity materials. No authority was likely to regard the production of films and slides as its particular responsibility, and few would be able to afford it. On the basis of these arguments, G. Elliston, the secretary of the SMOH, requested that its new committee be appointed to oversee the activities of all unofficial agencies, and assess the merits of those competing for government funds.[88]

Stressing the administrative and legal difficulties involved in allowing the new committee to stand 'half-way' between the ministry and local government and voluntary bodies, Heseltine reiterated the argument that legislation alone was required:

when the Local Authorities are clothed with proper powers for this purpose, those of them who wish to exercise the powers will, generally speaking, do so perfectly well from their own knowledge of local requirements and possibilities, and . . . our business in distributing any grant in aid of the work will be rather to see that what the Local Authority wants to do is done with reasonable efficiency than to attempt to supply a vast number of Authorities with ideas about the way in which they should educate the people in their own areas.[89]

Officials also challenged the assumption that the new committee would be qualified to act as a directing body because the society was in a 'special position to appreciate the urgency of propaganda'. On receiving a deputation in April 1925, Neville Chamberlain, then Minister of Health, questioned the need for centralization, and, echoing Basil Clarke's views on the abilities of civil servants, voiced uncertainty whether 'Medical Officers of Health, though doubtless experts on what ought to be said about public health, were necessarily experts on the best way of saying it in order to make it go down with the public'.[90] He agreed only to enact new legislation giving local authorities the power to incur grant-aided

---

[88] Elliston to Robinson, 28 Jan. 1925; 'Public Education in Health', SMOH to Heseltine, 2 Mar. 1925, MH 55/28.

[89] Heseltine to Newman and Robinson, 17 Apr. 1925, MH 55/28.

[90] Note of Deputation, 23 Apr. 1925, MH 55/28. *The Times*, 24 Apr. 1925. Also see T. Crew, *Health Propaganda (Ways and Means)* (Leicester, 1935), 19–20.

expenditure on general propaganda.[91] This did not placate the society, which went on to launch the Central Council for Health Education (CCHE) in mid-1927.

Before discussion of the activities of the CCHE, it should be noted that the role of medical officials in relation to health publicity was a subject of considerable debate in the mid-1920s. When George Newman's 1924 memorandum *Public Education in Health* was reprinted in January 1926, *The Times* drew attention to his references to the educational responsibilities of local officials, and noted the anomaly whereby the General Medical Council, to which Newman belonged, had recently issued an edict against 'indirect advertising' by doctors. The paper observed that, given the vague wording of this proclamation, even Medical Officers of Health acting at the request of their respective councils could face censure for writing press articles, as such actions might further their careers. Commenting on the absurdity of the situation, *The Times* asserted that the medical profession 'really cannot have it both ways'.[92] The issue engendered much debate.[93] After a motion was tabled at its annual conference in July 1926, the council of the British Medical Association (BMA) decided to investigate the possibility of assisting local authorities in their publicity activities.[94] In a report submitted the following year, the council recommended that the BMA should endeavour to increase public knowledge and to counteract the harmful propaganda disseminated by commercial advertisers, by providing publicity materials and encouragement to local councils. It was incumbent upon the BMA to adopt a guiding role, as only a recognized medical organization was qualified to determine what information could safely be disseminated. The council stressed that the pursuit of this policy would not entail a loss of decorum nor any impropriety. Indeed, to

avoid the difficulties and pitfalls attendant on sporadic propaganda by individual members of the profession, there should be an ordered attempt to use legitimate means to achieve the purpose. Medicine must roll out the song 'seraphically free of taint of personality'. Why should not the British Medical Association, through its network of branches, serve as chief voice?[95]

Ethically sound, a permanent publicity policy would also have more lasting value than the occasional article or lecture, 'which, like a brilliant firework, is apt to vanish in smoke'.

---

[91] Section 67 of the Public Health Act 1925.   [92] *The Times*, 18 Feb. 1926.
[93] Ibid. 10, 13, 14, 15 July, 6, 9 Aug. 1926.   [94] Ibid. 21 July 1926.
[95] Ibid. 20 July 1927.

Some members of the association demurred, arguing that, in order to be successful in reaching the mass audience, the BMA would have to over-simplify serious issues.[96] Other doctors countered that the 'unlimited gullibility' of the public made it imperative that something be done to undermine the influence of 'quacks'.[97] Although the policy was endorsed by the annual conference, little changed. The General Medical Council did not rescind its edict, and the BMA continued to be reticent in public, thus provoking criticism.[98] Not until 1937, when it appointed a public relations officer, did the association begin to engage in active publicity.[99] Ironically, its first major campaign, in support of clean milk production, provoked the type of response opponents of the policy had feared. The advertisements were criticized as they seemed to imply that all milk was unsafe. *Advertising World* commented:

For years medicine has been urged to advertise. For years medicine has resisted. And when at last it surrendered, its first advertisements aroused not mild commendation for a piece of prestige publicity nicely done, but fireworks of the fiercest kind, for the British Medical Association said things which upset all kinds of people.[100]

As noted, however, the Society of Medical Officers of Health was active much earlier, launching the CCHE in mid-1927. The latter did not get a favourable reception: Newman expressed doubts as to its potential value;[101] Ministry of Health officials voiced concern about its relationship *vis-à-vis* local government; and a number of voluntary societies, including the British Social Hygiene Council (BSHC), feared the CCHE would make them obsolete. After the CCHE affirmed its intention of assuming only a guiding role and addressing general issues, the BSHC and most major voluntary agencies and representative associations of county and urban councils did affiliate with it. True to form, the ministry refused to extend recognition to the CCHE, only maintaining a watching brief.[102] From the outset, the CCHE was engaged in direct publicity: issuing

---

[96] Ibid. 23 July 1927.   [97] Ibid. 20, 23 July 1927. Crew, p. 18.
[98] See *The Times*, 27 July 1929.
[99] Ibid. 24 Sept. 1937. *Advertising World*, 69/10 (1937), 10.
[100] 70/2 (1938), 3; 70/3 (1938), 1.
[101] Newman to Secretary, 20 June 1927, MH 55/28.
[102] Robinson to Professor Bostock Hill, 23 June 1927; BSHC to Robinson, 20 July 1927; 'Memo from Conference of Health Associations', 18 Oct. 1928; Minute by Wright, 1 Dec. 1928, MH 55/28.

pamphlets on specific topics; encouraging film production; and in 1927 establishing its own magazine, *Better Health*.[103] Yet most of its early activities were of an administrative nature, and included recruiting lecturers, negotiating with the representative organizations of teachers and the press, and seeking contributions from voluntary bodies and insurance committees.[104] Many of the latter were already active in this sphere; by 1927, seventy-five of the 128 committees in England conducted general health propaganda, with thirty-three undertaking a 'considerable' amount.[105] Some, most notably the Leicestershire committee, conducted massive campaigns along commercial lines.[106] But the total expenditure for all committees in 1926 was a mere £2,100,[107] and the council was unable to obtain much support from these bodies, as the latter were legally bound to use their funds for the benefit of their subscribers rather than the public at large. The Ministry of Health repeatedly refused to alter these stipulations, as the only additional funds to which the committees had access were non-replenishable.[108]

None the less, the ministry did maintain close ties with the council. Some officials even believed that the department had created the CCHE.[109] An article praising *Better Health* appeared in December 1927 under Chamberlain's name,[110] and Newman also contributed to the magazine.[111] With the sanction of the General Medical Council, all articles and pamphlets issued by the CCHE were submitted for Newman's perusal before distribution.[112] The ministry also allowed the council access to some resources, such as films (of which there were five in 1928) and slides, which were in turn *hired* out locally.[113] However, the CCHE was forced to rely on its members and county councils for funding. Unfortunately, only a small proportion of local authorities capitalized on their new powers

[103] On the early activities see 'Report of the Organizing Secretary (Oct. to Apr. 1928)', 23 Apr. 1928, MH 55/28.   [104] Ibid. Note, 20 Jan. 1928, MH 55/25.

[105] MH to Insurance Committees, 9 Feb. 1927; J. Teumer, 'Health Propaganda Work Undertaken by Insurance Committees', 21 Feb. 1927, MH 55/25.

[106] Activities of the Leicestershire Insurance Committee, MH 55/26. Newman, *Public Education* (1926), 15–16.   [107] Teumer, 'Health Propaganda', MH 55/25.

[108] 'Central Council for Health Education: Deputation 16 Jan. 1934'; Note of Deputation, 16 Jan. 1934; 'Report', 17 Jan. 1934, MH 55/29. Insurance Committee, Minutes, 8 May 1936, MH 82/2.

[109] Report on publicity, unsigned, undated, MH 78/147.

[110] Chamberlain to the Editor of *Better Health*, 7 Dec. 1927, MH 55/28.

[111] See e.g. *Better Health*, 1/1 (1927), 3; 3/8 (1930), 120.

[112] 'Central Council for Health Education', 2 Mar. 1928, MH 55/28.

[113] Elliston to MH, 31 Jan. 1928; 'CCHE: Ministry of Health Films', 1 Oct. 1928; CCHE, 'Report of Educational and Publicity Committee', 27 Sept. 1928, MH 55/28.

under the 1925 Act and made contributions.[114] In 1924, the SMOH had estimated the cost of running an active propaganda organization at £40,000 a year.[115] During its early years, the CCHE had an annual budget of under £500.[116] Pressure was constantly exerted on the ministry to provide a subsidy and/or encourage local councils to make contributions, but councils were not even circularized on the subject.[117] This was a matter of some importance to the CCHE, especially with the passage of the Local Government Act 1929, which drastically altered the position of county and urban councils *vis-à-vis* Whitehall and the public. According greater control over the financing and administration of social services to local authorities, the legislation replaced the system whereby councils claimed a proportion of their expenditure back from the Treasury, with a 'block grant' calculated in terms of the population, rates, etc. of each area. By virtually making health services a local responsibility, the Act also formalized the concept that propaganda was the legitimate function of local rather than central government. Newman captured the significance of these changes, observing that 'curative and preventive medicine were here joined together, as never before, in the public welfare'.[118] With the abolition of percentage grants, voluntary organizations had to rely on the councils rather than the Ministry of Health for funding. Although local authorities were given the power to subsidize publicity, no element of compulsion was included in the legislation.[119] The Minister of Health could adopt schemes and order councils to assist outside agencies included under them, but this did little to reassure voluntary bodies, many of which pressed for independent grants.[120]

One of the only forms of propaganda directly subsidized by the ministry dealt with venereal diseases. Once it was clear that this funding would be cut under the new provisions, the BSHC began lobbying to secure a supplementary clause in the legislation guaranteeing mandatory contributions to voluntary bodies engaged in venereal diseases publicity.[121] Such propaganda, it was argued, could only be conducted 'with the

---

[114] Minute, 13 Jan. 1934; Report on deputation, 17 Jan. 1934, MH 55/29.

[115] Elliston to Robinson, 23 Apr. 1924, MH 55/28.

[116] Minute, 13 Jan. 1934, MH 55/29.

[117] A circular was not sent out until 1934; Report on deputation, 17 Jan. 1934, MH 55/29.

[118] Newman, *Nation's Health*, 160. *Nineteenth Annual Report of the Ministry of Health 1937–1938*, Cmd. 5801 (1938), 28, 75.

[119] Local Government Act 1929, clause 84. *The Times*, 29 Jan. 1929.

[120] Local Government Act 1929, clauses 101, 102. Minute, 13 Jan. 1934, MH 55/29.

[121] Basil Blackett to Arthur Greenwood, 3 Oct. 1930; 'British Social Hygiene Council', undated report by Heseltine, MH 55/198.

assistance of a central body', and, unless forced, councils were likely to ignore the issue.[122] Kingsley Wood, the Parliamentary Secretary to the ministry, objected on the grounds that compulsion might foster resentment and dissuade local authorities from including coverage of venereal diseases in any general publicity schemes which they contemplated. Concessions were made privately, however; the ministry financed the BSHC through the transitional phase, providing an outright grant of £12,000 for 1929–30, double its existing allocation. The department promised to 'encourage' local authorities to make contributions, and issued a circular on the topic, the second in recent months. Finally, a clause was inserted in the Act enabling councils to direct the ministry to fund recognized voluntary bodies and deduct the appropriate block grants accordingly.[123]

Initially satisfied, the BSHC soon complained that these measures were insufficient. In October 1930, the president, Sir Basil Blackett, notified the minister that sixty of the 146 local authorities in England and Wales had not made provisions for venereal diseases propaganda in the past five years, and demanded that they be forced to act.[124] Officials retorted that £5,516 had been spent on publicity specifically about the diseases in 1929–30, and that many councils also included the subject within general schemes of health instruction. Moreover, in 1930 £7,000 had been pledged to the BSHC by 114 councils.[125] Local authorities were hardly neglecting their responsibilities, though it is worth noting that this expenditure was negligible in relation to spending on services; in 1928–9, local authorities received grants totalling £302,954 for the treatment of venereal disease.[126] It also bore little comparison to the advertising outlay of the producers of patent medicines and other health products.[127] On receiving a deputation from the BSHC, Arthur Greenwood refused to authorize yet another circular (he doubted their effectiveness!), or to exercise his power to reduce the block grants of authorities not adequately performing their duties.[128] He agreed to intervene only if surveys then being conducted

---

[122] *The Times*, 29 Jan. 1929.
[123] 'British Social Hygiene Council', 15 Apr. 1932; Circular 1023, 22 July 1929, MH 55/198.   [124] Blackett to Greenwood, 3 Oct. 1930, MH 55/198.
[125] Ibid. Robinson to Minister, 24 Oct. 1930; Maclachlan, 'British Social Hygiene Council', undated; Note of Deputation, 30 Oct. 1930; Ward, 'British Social Hygiene Council', 15 Apr. 1932, MH 55/198.   [126] Hansard, 24 Nov. 1930, vol. 245, cols. 901–2.
[127] Out of an estimated £20 million spent on press advertising in 1931–2, approximately £2.5 million was spent on patent medicines: *Statistical Review of Press Advertising*, 1/1 (1932), 11. PEP claimed in 1936 that over £5 million was spent annually on press advertising for patent medicines and health products: *Report*, 359, 391.
[128] Note of Deputation, 30 Oct. 1930; Rucker to Blackett, 19 Nov. 1930, MH 55/198.

into local administration of the health services provided conclusive evidence that venereal diseases publicity was being neglected.[129] Unsatisfied, the BSHC threatened to issue a statement to the press detailing the omissions it had uncovered.[130] Dr MacNalty, the ministry's chief expert on venereal disease, thought this would be 'most ill-judged and unfortunate'. The BSHC's report was factually incorrect and its publication would be inappropriate:

In the preparation of this memorandum and in many of their recent departures, the BSHC are far outstripping their province, which is propaganda, and are arrogating to themselves the direction and criticisms of the V.D. work of local authorities. The whole tone of the document implies that the Ministry are a supine body and that it is the BSHC alone who are competent to wake up a local authority to a sense of their responsibility for V.D. work [*sic*].

Had the council restricted its activities to the 'legitimate sphere of propaganda', he concluded, it would probably not be encountering financial difficulties.[131] Unlike Newman, MacNalty did not recognize any links between propaganda and policy. Ironically, Greenwood proceeded to advise the BSHC that mandatory contributions were impossible on these very grounds; since the council confined its activities to propaganda, its work was not broad enough to warrant the exercise of compulsion.[132] He recommended that the BSHC concentrate on establishing personal ties with local officials.

Similar arguments were used to reject requests from the CCHE, but, as ever, the ministry wanted it both ways. On occasion it made use of the council to organize health exhibits.[133] Moreover, throughout the 1930s, all local officials who approached the Ministry of Health enquiring about the practical aspects of publicity were referred to the CCHE.[134] In 1933, when the Cabinet decided to allow local authorities to use the EMB poster hoardings[135] for health propaganda, the ministry asked the council to prepare the required materials and provide advice.[136] Once the scheme was under way, the CCHE complained that it could not proceed without

[129] Note of Deputation, 30 Oct. 1930. Blackett to Greenwood, 10 Feb. 1931; reply, 18 Feb. 1931, MH 55/198. Hansard, 29 Jan. 1931, vol. 247, cols. 1140–1; 5 Feb. 1931, vol. 247, col. 2110.
[130] 'Venereal Diseases', Blackett to Greenwood, 13 Dec. 1930, MH 55/198.
[131] A. S. MacNalty to Maclachlan, 7 Jan. 1931, MH 55/198.
[132] Greenwood to Blackett, 18 Feb. 1931, MH 55/198. Minute, 13 Jan. 1934, MH 55/29. [133] Draft Annual Report 1934–5, MH 55/30. *The Times*, 12 Mar. 1935.
[134] Minute by Wright, 6 Dec. 1933, MH 55/29. [135] See above, p. 103.
[136] On the Cabinet's decision to turn the hoardings over to this purpose see above, Ch. 3 n. 118. Regarding the scheme, see PEP, *Report*, 358. Crew, pp. 23–5. *Fifteenth Annual Report of the Ministry of Health 1933–1934*, Cmd. 4664 (1934), 97. Fitter, pp. 464–7.

financial support.[137] A deputation to the ministry in January 1934 reported that in the previous year the council had received a total of £238 from local authorities. Only fifty-seven councils had made contributions. Dr James Fenton, the president of the organization, requested an annual grant of £2,000, arguing that it was unreasonable of the government to expect the CCHE to derive its income from county councils, as those most in need of assistance were the poorest. Direct funding was essential, as it was precisely those services of greatest value from the national perspective which could not be debited to individual bodies.[138] Arthur Robinson conceded the point, but replied that the 1929 Act precluded the ministry from taking action. The poster campaign was saved, but only because the ministry approached the representative bodies of local government to secure their financial assistance.[139] Even then, just over half the councils in England participated in the scheme. Fifty-six refused to be presented with frames on their own land (in some cases a small fee was requested to ensure proper upkeep), and few were willing to hire frames located on private property, because a rental of £25 was demanded. Although the rate was £10 less than what had been charged to the EMB, the cost 'was sufficient to deter nearly all local authorities'.[140]

As already noted, many factors accounted for the reluctance of government—on all levels—to be more active in its support of the publicity activities of voluntary organizations, chief among them concern over finances. But, as discussed earlier, there was also considerable concern expressed over propriety and decorum. Although there were exceptions, many officials were reluctant to see the government endorse the employment of commercial methods to advance public knowledge of health matters. As early as 1924, George Newman stressed that health propagandists should copy business practices and endeavour to assess their audience. Planning a successful campaign necessitated the adoption of near-scientific methods:

(*a*) The interest of those to be instructed must be borne in mind; their attention must be arrested, desire must be created, and self-regard must be stimulated. A commercial advertiser studies the psychology of the crowd and seeks to touch the elemental instincts of the individual. . . . We can all think of advertisements which stick in the memory because the advertiser, understanding our psychology, has impressed upon us something which we cannot forget, even if we would.

[137] Fitter, p. 465. Minutes by Wright, 6, 14 Dec. 1933, MH 55/29.
[138] Report on Deputation, 17 Jan. 1934, MH 55/29.
[139] Robinson to Fenton, 22 Jan. 1934; reply, 24 Jan. 1934; Robinson to Johnson, 25 Jan. 1934; Fenton to Robinson, 26 July 1934, MH 55/29.   [140] Fitter, pp. 466–7.

(*b*) Having thus aroused interest, the propagandist must fix or anchor it by *instruction* by providing a body of knowledge, concrete, correct and timely, attractively presented in very varied form, appealing to both eye and ear.

(*c*) Finally, also like the good advertiser, he must get *action*. The advertiser wants people to buy his ware; the propagandist wants to obtain from his clients assent to his advice, a practice and mode of life.[141]

However, viewing publications as the purview of voluntarism, Newman was of course directing this advice to unofficial bodies rather than the ministry. The rhetoric was certainly adopted outside Whitehall. Writing ten years later in a book published in 'response to many requests' to give full particulars of the objectives and methods of voluntary health organizations,[142] T. Crew, the clerk of the aforementioned Leicestershire Insurance Committee, and the former organizing secretary of the CCHE, expounded similar arguments: 'The question of Psychology has an important bearing on the methods of propaganda, which may be truly termed as "Advertising Health". The fundamental problem to-day, as in commercial matters, is to make people want things that they have not wanted before.'[143] Colour, bold wording, and a commercial approach were essential to success. A well-worded poster was as valuable to national health and as scientific as any drug:

One great advantage of slogans is that they can be administered almost like a bottle of medicine—they can be taken in a moment and act at once. 'Know Thyself' is a simple slogan that can carry a myriad of thoughts clinging to it as one advances in the knowledge it advises. . . . The introduction of health slogans has all been to the good in teaching the masses, but it is not until recently that the right appeal has been made. We have been standing by mere platitudes.

'Know Thyself' hardly seems colourful, but Crew's position was clear.

Yet not everyone agreed that commercial publicity was a viable or legitimate means of furthering health education. Posters employed in the London housing bond campaign of 1920 were condemned as a 'series of vulgar and garish advertisements'.[144] The Leicestershire Insurance Committee was praised for its 'picturesque methods' and 'personal enthusiasm' in conducting health publicity, but Ministry of Health officials observed that its methods 'may perhaps be open to the criticism that there is too much "stunt" and "slogan" about them'.[145] Prejudice ran high

[141] Newman, *Public Education* (1924), 28. Also see Wright's report on health propaganda, 23 Aug. 1922, MH 55/27.   [142] Crew, p. 3.
[143] Ibid. 17–22.   [144] *The Times*, 8 Dec. 1920.
[145] Newman, *Public Education* (1924), 15. Teumer, 'Health Propaganda', MH 55/25.

in the department, particularly among doctors. Many members of the medical profession opposed the use of slogans on the grounds that they dangerously over-simplified issues.[146] Dr Morgan, the Ministry of Health's observer on the CCHE, reported, in October 1928, that the council had recently considered a pamphlet produced for the Leicestershire Insurance Committee, by Crew. Entitled 'Health Week Message', it contained slogans, such as 'Take care of your teeth and your health will take care of itself', which Professor A. Bostock Hill, the vice-chairman of the Editorial and Publicity Subcommittee, had deemed unsuitable. Dr Morgan believed the whole enterprise, and the approach it represented, were worthy of greater censure:

Personally I regret that he did not extend his observations to the rest of these slogans. They all seem to me to be very undesirable. I am afraid Mr Crew imagines that he has a flair for slogan writing and it may be that he will unload a few more. . . . If so I hope I may be given authority strongly to protest against this sort of material. . . . I feel that we should try to stop the distribution of these half-truth slogans with the seal of the Central Council affixed. If this Council is to do any good it must eschew this sort of propaganda and try and maintain some sort of standard compatible with professional practice.[147]

The extent to which commercial methods were employed by voluntary bodies is outside the scope of this chapter. None the less, a survey of the type of materials issued indicates that, despite the prevalence of modern methods and departmental criticism of them, non-official health publicity was not always popular in the commercial sense. Crew may have abhorred platitudes, but the slogans he praised could hardly be termed catchy. Included among those he found 'searching in application' were, 'Where there's DIRT there's Danger', 'Be Full of Fresh Air', and 'Human Body—League of Organs'. 'Infant Management' and 'The Glands of Destiny' were on his list of suitable lecture titles, as was 'Psychological Health', which he believed suggested 'something mystic'.[148] Posters employed in health campaigns over the period also appear to have been unsuited to capture the attention of the mass audience. Many were aesthetically unappealing and over-crowded with information; witness those issued by the Dental Board of the United Kingdom and through the Ministry of Agriculture (Plates 2 and 3). The British Social Hygiene Council published more concise posters, but (as Plate 5 indicates), these did not

---

[146] See p. 146.
[147] Report by Morgan, 3 Oct. 1928; Editorial and Publicity Subcommittee, Report, 12 Jan. 1928; CCHE, Minutes, 26 Apr. 1928, MH 55/28.   [148] Crew, pp. 20–2.

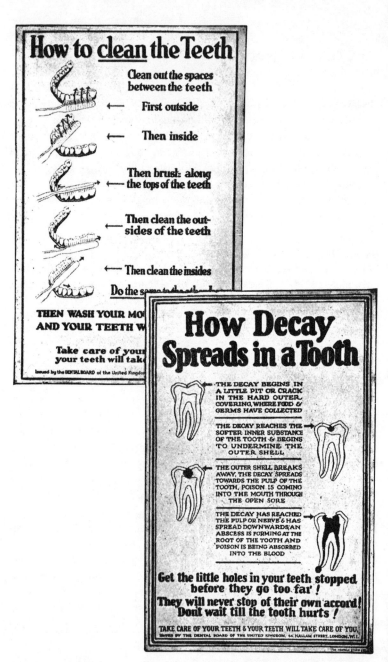

2 Dental Board of United Kingdom Posters: 'How to *clean* the Teeth', 'How Decay Spreads in a Tooth'

RAT WEEK

DISEASE FOR MAN AND ANIMALS IS SPREAD BY RATS AND MICE

£100,000,000 OF DAMAGE IS DONE BY RATS AND MICE EVERY YEAR

All persons are advised to co-operate in the destruction of Rats and Mice on or about their premises. Remember that one pair of Rats may have 800 offspring in one year

(1) Keep all food covered.

(2) Never leave 'scraps' about.

(3) Do not overfeed poultry or animals at night.

(4) Do not place garbage in dust-bins—burn it or bury it.

(5) See that all rubbish is cleared away frequently.

(6) Attention should be given to Rat-proofing premises as far as possible.

(1) *POISONING.* This can be done safely and simply by means of preparations of RED SQUILL (Liquid Extract and Biscuits are specially recommended). These products are harmless to human beings and domestic animals yet are deadly to Rats and Mice.

(2) Other poison baits containing Phosphorus or Barium Carbonate can be used, but great care must be exercised owing to their more dangerous nature.

(3) Those who can. should make organised rat-hunts with ferrets, dogs and guns.

(4) Smoke and gas apparatus can also be used to clear runs.

FULL PARTICULARS CAN BE OBTAINED FROM

3 Ministry of Agriculture Notice: 'Rat Week'

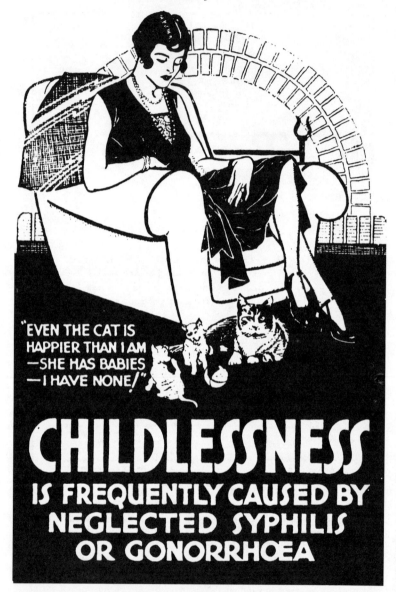

"EVEN THE CAT IS HAPPIER THAN I AM —SHE HAS BABIES —I HAVE NONE!"

CHILDLESSNESS
IS FREQUENTLY CAUSED BY NEGLECTED SYPHILIS OR GONORRHOEA

4 British Social Hygiene Council: 'Childlessness is Frequently Caused by Neglected Syphilis or Gonorrhoea'

The engine driver is responsible for *the passengers behind.* He must keep his judgment clear and cool.

The young man and woman are responsible for *the generations to follow.*

Safety lies in self-control.

Every child's right—

A clean start

All children of Parents who have ever been infected should be taken to a Clinic to make certain there is no risk of Congenital Syphilis.

THE BRITISH SOCIAL HYGIENE COUNCIL

1928 Series.

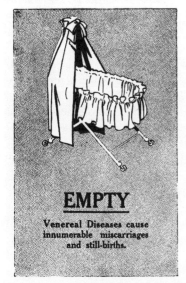

EMPTY

Venereal Diseases cause innumerable miscarriages and still-births.

Who will tell them?

A Parents Conference will be held at :–

5 British Social Hygiene Council: 'The engine driver', 'Who will tell them?'

always address the point or convey a clear message. Certainly subject-matter such as venereal diseases necessitated the exercise of tact, but it is evident that the organization was neither precluded from nor averse to mentioning the illnesses by name or in what might be termed a tasteless manner (see Plate 4).[149]

Similar remarks could be made about the films produced by voluntary bodies. They were usually of the short feature type and were often melodramatic and rather contrived. The National Baby Week Council's 'Rules for Jim' attempted to convey the idea that motherhood was a full-time job, by relating the unfortunate history of a family in which a regimented routine was not followed in rearing the child.[150] 'John Smith & Son', a silent film distributed by the BSHC, illustrated the 'disastrous results of untreated Gonorrhea' in the following manner:

The film opens with the marriage of a young couple. Present as a bridesmaid is a former friend of the bridegroom who obviously considers she still has claims on him. A few months later she seizes an opportunity of renewing their former intimacy with the result that the husband contracts Gonorrhea. He attends a clinic but for various reasons shown in the film the wife does not do so. The result is that when the baby is born she nearly loses her life and the boy is blind in one eye. The final tragedy occurs when the child is run over and killed by a lorry which he has not seen approaching.[151]

Although sometimes of a popular and dramatic nature, the unofficial health propaganda of the period was often as patronizing, unsophisticated, and didactic as the Ministry of Health's own narrow efforts.

Activities on all fronts were indeed limited. Expenditure was minimal in relation to that of other countries,[152] and was negligible in comparison to the outlay on health services or patent medicine advertising.[153] Health instruction in the schools had not been developed to a very large extent, and was not adequately pursued once children completed their formal education.[154] As school leavers were not automatically covered under the National Insurance scheme until 1937, they had virtually no point of contact with health authorities until, and if, they came into employment.[155]

The chief impediment to the development of widespread health publicity was the lack of central direction. Individual local councils could not afford to produce materials on topics which were national in scope. Even

---

[149] Crew cited these posters as examples. They are reproduced as Pls. 2–5.
[150] Crew, pp. 103–4.   [151] Ibid. 43.   [152] See above, p. 132.
[153] See e.g. above, n. 127, and below, p. 173.
[154] Note Newman's criticisms: *Outline Preventive Medicine*, 24; *Public Opinion*, 28; *Public Education* (1926), 10–14.   [155] *The Times*, 4 Jan. 1937.

after the creation of the CCHE, no single agency was willing and/or able to accept general responsibility for health education, and thus a considerable amount of information never reached the public domain.[156] By the mid-1930s, however, a number of factors had combined to induce the Ministry of Health to consider taking a more active role in health publicity, the chief being developments in the Post Office.

Throughout the inter-war years, exponents of popular health instruction often referred to the motto of the New York Public Health Department— 'Public Health is purchasable'.[157] The phrase appeared in virtually all of George Newman's writings on the subject. When not labelling health practitioners 'missionaries of hygiene', he was apt to call them 'merchants'.[158] None the less, few officials regarded the services provided by the ministry as being comparable to commodities, in the way that the Post Office spoke of the 'goods' it had to 'sell'.[159] However, commenting on Stephen Tallents's appointment as public relations director of the GPO, one civil servant argued that the Ministry of Health had as much reason, if not more, to employ publicity.[160] It had an obligation, not just to provide basic information on available services, but also to ensure that the public was properly informed about health policies:

Supposing it is desired to convince the man in the street that slum houses are coming down . . . it is arguable that the object will be furthered by telling Fleet Street all about it. In the past what has been done is to include information on such matters in annual reports or other dullish publications. Stunts then arise in the Press. . . . Then we come along with some sort of official statement that all is well—published in full in the respectable journals and perhaps getting two or three lines in the Mail or Express. In this sphere also it is obviously arguable that there should be some machine devised for the purpose of giving the press from time to time particulars of the policy of the Minister [*sic*].

Indeed, although apparently oblivious to the political and ethical problems in which it might embroil permanent officials, he asserted that it would be appropriate for the department to educate or convince the public on the efficacy of potential changes in government policy: 'Supposing it is decided, e.g. to repeal the Vaccination Acts. It is arguable that there is a case for preparing public opinion in advance for such a measure, not

---

[156] See below, p. 164.
[157] Hansard, 26 Feb. 1919, vol. 112, col. 1845. Wright, 'The Weakness of Public Health Propaganda', 23 Aug. 1922, MH 55/27.
[158] *Outline Preventive Medicine*, 45. *Public Opinion*, 4.
[159] Report on Publicity, unsigned, undated, MH 78/147.   [160] Ibid.

merely, e.g. by the procedure of enquiry by a special body, but by press inspiration specifically designed to further the object.'

He suggested that the department resurrect its intelligence division and become a 'clearing-house of general information'. Although this was the only reference made to the earlier organization, the official envisioned a publicity bureau similar in function, composition, and approach to the public information branch of 1920–3. Of necessity a civil servant, the director was to co-ordinate and disseminate all information reaching the department, on no account engaging in self-advertising, but only promoting the policies of the minister. Beneath this officer was to be an assistant 'specially appointed as a person versed in the habits of Fleet Street', who would handle press relations. As before, this outsider would not exercise control over the type of information disseminated. Indeed, it was 'vital' that 'he does not settle the policy of action which he is to popularise but takes it from those whose business it is to settle it, and "gets it across" '. The distinction drawn between expertise in publicity and policy had not altered since Basil Clarke's days in the ministry.

These suggestions were hardly new but they received a surprisingly favourable reception in the department; interestingly, little attention was directed towards the puffery issue. Commenting on recent complaints from 'friendly papers', G. H. Shakespeare, of the establishments branch, advised Robinson, and the minister, Sir E. Hilton Young, that in 'these days publicity is no less important than the higher branches of administration'. It was 'obvious' that a journalist was needed on staff to deal with the press.[161] Regarding the first remark as a 'serious overstatement of the case', Robinson none the less agreed that, 'in this Department, which touches the life and affairs of the people on so many sides, a great deal must depend, whether we like it or not, on our relations with the Press, and on an intelligent publicity'.[162] Yet as neither he nor other officials believed the task warranted full-time employment, arrangements were made to create a joint publicity branch with the Board of Education.[163] The board agreed on condition that it be allowed to retain its Office of Special Inquiries and Reports.[164]

Robinson and H. Leggett, the Director of Establishments at the ministry, planned the joint division. On approaching the Treasury in January

---

[161] Shakespeare to Secretary and Minister, 13 Dec. 1934, MH 78/147.
[162] Note by Robinson, 15 Dec. 1934; Robinson to James Rae, 11 Feb. 1935, MH 78/147.
[163] Robinson to Minister, 21 Dec. 1934, MH 78/147.
[164] M. Holmes to Secretary, 1 Feb. 1935, ED 23/589. Leggett to Robinson, undated, MH 78/147. N. D. Bosworth Smith to J. H. McC. Craig, 12 Dec. 1936, ED 23/685.

1935, they focused on the disjointed manner in which intelligence work was currently undertaken, maintaining that there was room for 'substantial improvement' in the department's relations with the media and the public. A 'central boiler' was needed, and would involve

placing the conduct of this work under the charge of an officer of high rank whose main business will be to bring together the . . . scattered threads of intelligence work; to be closely in touch with policy questions on which information either is, or is likely to be required, and to take measures . . . to ensure that Ministerial policy and action is adequately presented to the public, in addition to *preparing the ground for any future policy or action.*[165] [my italics]

The creation of a bureau along these lines was announced in March, to favourable comment.[166] S. H. Wood, the Director of Establishments at the Board of Education, was chosen to head the new Intelligence and Public Relations division under Leggett's supervision. There was general agreement that a journalist ought to be selected as press officer, but the post was not advertised. S. R. Chaloner, a former assistant editor of the *Manchester Guardian*, who had the added qualification of having written a report on wool while a marketing officer at the Ministry of Agriculture, was appointed on the recommendation of George Steward, a former journalist serving as the press officer at Downing Street.[167]

Once the bureau was in place, Leggett moved quickly to consolidate its control over all channels of information. To facilitate access to local intelligence, the ministry's general inspectorate was annexed in April.[168] Liaison officers were appointed in every division of the department, with responsibility for bringing matters of general interest to the notice of the publicity branch.[169] Yet again, faith was manifested in local expertise; it was assumed that 'better results would be got if the outposts of the Intelligence Division in the various departments and Divisions consisted of people familiar with the work, rather than outside people belonging to the

[165] Leggett, 'Intelligence and Publicity Work', 18 Jan. 1935; Draft report by Robinson; Robinson to Leggett, 28 Jan. 1935; Robinson to Rae, 11 Feb. 1935; reply, 20 Feb. 1935; Robinson to Minister, 25 Feb. 1935, MH 78/147.

[166] *The Times, Morning Post,* 5 Mar. 1935. T. S. Simey, 'A Public Relations Policy for Local Authorities, *Public Administration,* 13 (1935), 243.

[167] Robinson to Shakespeare and Minister, 15 Feb. 1935; Maclay to Secretary, 5 Mar. 1935; R. J. P. Harvey to Rucker, 25 Feb. 1938; reply, 26 Feb. 1938, MH 78/147.

[168] Establishment Minute, 1 Apr. 1935, MH 78/147.

[169] S. H. Wood, 'Intelligence and Public Relations', 2 July 1935, MH 78/147. This was published in revised form in *Public Administration,* 14/1 (1936), 41–8. Also see Robinson to Minister, 25 July 1935; Note of Conference, 24 July 1935; Leggett to Secretary, 31 July 1935; Robinson, 'Intelligence and Public Relations Division', 6 Aug. 1935, MH 78/147.

Intelligence Division itself'.[170] Of similar interest is the claim that, 'obviously', these men would have to be 'younger and more impressionable persons', who 'in due time . . . [and with guidance] might develop the press instinct, as they have to develop the instinct of administration'.[171]

General agreement on the need for publicity machinery did not prevent debate on its proper role. In June 1935, Shakespeare suggested that, rather than confining its activities to the provision of basic information to the press, the bureau should take the initiative in publicity.[172] Citing anticipated attacks from Lloyd George on unemployment policy, and the Labour Party on the general inadequacy of the health services, he noted that, because it neglected to publicize its daily activities, the ministry appeared inert. Recurrent advertising was the only solution: 'In boxing it is the knockout that counts; in publicity it is the succession of small blows.' Indeed, the 'cumulative effect of publishing items as they occur would convey the impression that there was a good deal of activity which would help to meet the charge of drift likely to be made by Mr. Lloyd George'. 'Special steps' were also needed to ensure a positive reception of important pieces of legislation. Like others before him, Shakespeare argued that, given its expertise, the department had an obligation to educate and guide public opinion. Yet was it within its rights to prepare a favourable reception for contemplated policies, or to use its publicity machinery to thwart political opponents? To date, these questions had been evaded because the ministry was not in the practice of issuing general information to the public. Popular instruction had been left to others, and the dissemination of politically sensitive material had rested in the hands of the minister's Private Secretary.[173] The creation of the new bureau brought the issue to the forefront.

S. H. Wood believed that the official propagandist had to remain non-partisan and above reproach:

The Director of Intelligence should never be selective on political grounds. . . . The assumption must be that he is providing information without fear or favour. . . . Any other system is bound . . . to undermine the work . . . by laying him open as a Civil Servant to the charge of political discrimination or caprice. . . . In this connexion it must be remembered that the Director . . . is not, like his colleagues, an anonymous Civil Servant but . . . a public identifiable Civil Servant [*sic*]. He

[170] George Chrystal to Laurence Brock, 2 Oct. 1935, MH 78/147.
[171] Robinson to Minister, 5 July 1935, MH 78/147.
[172] Shakespeare to Secretary and Minister, 26 June 1935, MH 78/147.
[173] S. Wood, 'Intelligence and Public Relations', 2 July 1935, MH 78/147.

must frequently sign documents issued to the Press and he must be prepared to be quoted by name. He is, in fact, a new type of Civil Servant.[174]

Robinson also saw serious risks in allowing public servants to disseminate information of a controversial nature. Publicity and persuasion should be confined to areas in which policy decisions had already been reached. None the less, he also agreed that a more aggressive approach was needed, advising the minister

that in modern conditions, such a department as this . . . must . . . be prepared and organized to . . . *take the initiative* [sic] in supplying information. We could, I suppose, as civil servants justify that view on the line that the public has a right to be told, *in the very way in which it is prepared to be told* [my italics], what we are doing and further that, when we want to take steps forward, it will be much easier to do so with a public which knows about us and our work. This is, of course, poles asunder from the old Civil Service traditions, but I am not too old to be unable to admit that there may be force in it.[175]

The new minister, Sir Kingsley Wood, who had presided over the establishment of the Post Office publicity bureau, agreed that publicity 'must be carefully and tactfully done', without political motivation. Although acceding to the need for a more open department, he held fast to the principle of Civil Service anonymity, even for public relations officers.[176] More importantly, Wood inferred that because it was a government department engaged in marketing a concept, public health, the ministry could not employ aggressive, that is, commercial, tactics. Rather ironically, given the publicity policy adopted by his former department, he observed that the Ministry of Health was 'not in the same position . . . as the Post Office. The latter has goods to sell and its methods of publicity must therefore be very different.'[177] This manifested more than a concern with maintaining decorum; it reflected the assumption, prevalent in some quarters, that the sale of ideas necessitated the use of a different mode of appeal than the marketing of commodities.[178] A strict policy governing the ministry's publicity activities was not laid down, but the department did not adopt an aggressive approach. During its first year, the publicity division made little attempt to address the mass audience. Financial

[174] Ibid.   [175] Robinson to Minister, 5 July 1935, MH 78/147.
[176] K. Wood to Secretary, 12 July 1935, MH 78/147.   [177] Ibid.
[178] Distinctions were often drawn between publicity 'which had in view the increase of sales and that which was concerned with advancing or defending a particular policy'; see Cairncross, 'The Report of the Select Estimates Committee on Government Publicity', 10 Oct. 1938, T 162/530/40020/1. See above, p. 51.

constraints certainly precluded large-scale campaigns.[179] None the less, a
meagre budget is not in itself an adequate explanation. One of the least
expensive means of propaganda available was editorial publicity. In July
1935, Kingsley Wood advised S. H. Wood and Chaloner to concentrate
their activities in this area; they were to establish close ties with editors
and journalists, and endeavour to insert news articles in the press, as this
would afford access to a large audience without putting pressure on the
department's budget.[180] Hindered by administrative duties and lack of
staff, S. H. Wood reported in April 1936 that it had been impossible to
make widespread contacts. Moreover, he had made no attempt to cultivate the popular newspapers, as 'rightly or wrongly, I felt it desirable to
establish good relations with the more sober press before plunging into
more flamboyant efforts'.[181] Little had changed; the emphasis was still on
influencing the educated elements in society on the assumption that
knowledge would filter downward.

Popular instruction was still regarded as the responsibility of unofficial
organizations, as was the publicizing of much important information.
Hence, when Sir John Boyd Orr's influential investigation, *Food Health
and Income*, was published in 1936, the gas industry rather than the
Ministry of Health commissioned the GPO film unit to produce *Enough
to Eat*, to ensure that the results of Boyd Orr's inquiry became widely
known. While the company hoped the production would encourage
householders to switch to gas, it also regarded its sponsorship of the film
as good public relations.[182] Yet not all important studies could or did
receive such treatment. Commenting on the valuable data and advice
present in the Medical Research Council's annual report for 1936, Political
and Economic Planning drew attention to the fact that no one had as yet
assumed responsibility for the dissemination of such materials. Hence
'information of vital importance to the future of the United Kingdom,
obtained by a large outlay of public money, . . . [was being] left pigeon-
holed . . . to the detriment of the national health and efficiency'. PEP
concluded that, if the MRC was not the proper body to inform the public
of its investigations, the duty should fall upon government.[183] It was time
for a 'large-scale attack upon the causes of ill-health. . . . The campaign

[179] The budget, exclusive of salaries and a printing appropriation, averaged £2,000 annually; *Report from the Select Committee on Estimates* (July 1938), Table II.
[180] K. Wood to Secretary, 12 July 1935, MH 78/147.
[181] S. Wood to Secretary, 3 Apr. 1936, MH 78/147.
[182] Stirling L. Everard, *The History of the Gas Light and Coke Company 1812–1949*
(1949), 347. Paul Rotha, *Documentary Diary* (1973), 142, 158.
[183] *Planning*, 3/71 (25 Mar. 1936), 15.

calls for authority and team work, and we might be tempted to suggest that what is needed is a Ministry of Health, were we not suffering under the disillusionment of having one already.'[184]

Yet behind the scenes, the department was increasing its involvement in health publicity. In 1935 the CCHE applied to become a limited company and invited the ministry to nominate two members to its council.[185] The usual objections were raised regarding financial and political difficulties, but several officials cited the unblemished record of the CCHE as justification for recognition.[186] S. H. Wood advanced stronger arguments. Noting that the very existence of the public relations bureau signified both a commitment to breaking down barriers between Whitehall and the public and an affirmation of the importance of health instruction, he asserted that if the department intended to leave the latter to others and assume only a supervisory role, it was incumbent upon it to supervise:

the Ministry ought to engage in health propaganda, but it is at least arguable that in some spheres of health it can undertake this better through accredited organizations than by direct effort, but if this is so, the Ministry must be in really close relationship with such organizations and not appear to be in a position of detached superiority, able to withdraw from all responsibility whenever a difficult or delicate situation arises.[187]

Robinson concurred; S. H. Wood and O. Kentish Wright joined both the council and its General Purposes Committee (GPC) early in 1936,[188] and became actively involved in the CCHE's plans for what was to become the Use Your Health Services Campaign of 1937, in which the ministry played a pivotal role.

Six months in length, this campaign publicized a wide variety of health care services, dealing with topics as diverse as tuberculosis and venereal diseases, and culminated in a month of publicity for a Board of Education-sponsored National Fitness campaign. As the first large-scale publicity endeavours undertaken by the Ministry of Health and the Board of Education, these complementary campaigns excited considerable attention. The Prime Minister opened them with a speech broadcast on the BBC to which major newspapers devoted extensive coverage. Several,

---

[184] Ibid. 4/72 (7 Apr. 1936), 2.
[185] Board of Trade to MH, 20 July 1935; 'Articles of Association'; Note by Brooke, 23 July 1935, MH 55/30.
[186] Dr Carnworth to A. W. Neville, 15 Aug. 1935, MH 55/30.
[187] S. Wood to Neville, 27 Aug. 1935, MH 55/30.
[188] CCHE, Minutes, 7 Feb. 1936, MH 82/1.

including *The Times* and the *Daily Telegraph*, printed supplements which outlined the schemes and contained comments by prominent individuals. *The Times* later issued its profile as a book, *The Nation's Health*.[189] Believed to be long overdue, both campaigns were on the whole favourably received.[190] As should be clear by this point they were certainly a departure from the usual policy of these two departments. The Prime Minister virtually acknowledged this fact in his speech:

Local Authorities know well the difficulty of persuading people to take full advantage of their health services. They have made great and praiseworthy efforts to spread the knowledge of what they are doing, and they have been backed up by numerous voluntary bodies with all that enthusiasm which is so characteristic of voluntary service. But we believe that something more is called for at this time; something in the nature of a national campaign with all the publicity that can only be achieved by a concerted and organised attack by Government, Local Authorities, voluntary organisations, doctors, teachers, and press, all working together for the same end.[191]

Yet if the campaigns represented a change in policy, in that both departments became directly involved in large-scale appeals to the general public, they were not that innovative. In format and approach, especially in the overwhelming reliance placed on voluntary organizations and local authorities in their execution, the schemes closely resembled the overall approach to publicity hitherto adopted. On the other hand, by their very occurrence, these campaigns signified the State's acceptance of its responsibility for addressing the mass audience, and also exerted an important influence on the development of the government's wartime publicity machinery. Thus they merit full consideration.

In reports prepared after the campaign, the CCHE claimed that it had begun to draw up proposals in March 1936, well before a government scheme was contemplated.[192] Both the GPC and the full council of the organization met in March, though the issue was not raised at either of their meetings.[193] A memorandum outlining campaigns for county councils

[189] *The Times*, 30 Sept., 1, 4 Oct. 1937. *The Times, The Nation's Health* (1937). *Daily Telegraph*, 1 Oct. 1937. *King-Hall Newsletter*, 67 (6 Oct. 1937). PEP, *Report*, 358–9. 'CCHE Report of Work, 1 Oct.–30 Sept. 1938', MH 82/1.

[190] Ibid. There was controversy over the fitness campaign, critics charging that it was militarism disguised; see below.

[191] 'The Prime Minister's Speech at the Inauguration of the Campaign', MS Addison, Box 114.

[192] 'Statement of the Chairman in introducing the Memorandum to the MH', Mar. 1938, MH 82/1.

[193] The campaign is not mentioned in the GPC Minutes of 6 Mar. or 3 June 1936; MH 82/2; or of the CCHE on 20 Mar., MH 82/1.

was prepared at about this time,[194] but the possibility of initiating a national appeal does not appear in the minutes, until a meeting on 4 September.[195] By this time some general discussion had apparently already occurred. On request, two advertising agencies, Norfolk Studios and the London Press Exchange, had prepared prospectuses for a general health campaign. The agents had been given *carte blanche* and no definite budgets on which to base their proposals. Both had prepared detailed campaign plans (one memorandum was thirty pages long), for schemes lasting six months, one costing £120,000, and the other, excluding a large press appropriation, £60,000. Two-thirds of the projected budgets under both plans was devoted to press advertising.[196] Although inexpensive by commercial standards, either proposal was beyond the means of the council. In a report prepared for county councils in March, the CCHE had suggested that a campaign of six months' length could be successfully prosecuted on a budget of £1,000.[197]

After considering the agents' reports, the GPC advised the CCHE to appoint a health campaign committee to plan a national scheme, and to appeal to the Minister of Health for assistance.[198] Dr Wright and Paul Scott Rankine, the secretary to both the committee and the council, were asked to prepare preliminary proposals incorporating the suggestions of the advertising firms. Their study was considered by the council on 18 September, and the GPC recommendations were adopted.[199] G. S. Elliston, the vice-chairman of the CCHE, was chosen to chair a National Public Health Campaign Committee (NPHCC), with Rankine as Secretary. Wright and S. H. Wood were among those invited to serve. As the latter was transferred before the committee met,[200] his successor as public relations officer, A. N. Rucker, until then the Private Secretary to the minister, took his place.[201]

The mandate of the NPHCC was to prepare a statement, justifying a campaign and outlining a programme which could be used to persuade the Ministry of Health to adopt it. Before the committee held its first

---

[194] 'General Proposals for a Health Education Campaign Suitable for Adoption by County Councils', undated; 'Memorandum', 16 Mar. 1938, MH 82/1. GPC, Minutes, 3 June 1936; MH 82/2.   [195] GPC, Minutes, MH 82/2.
[196] GPC, Minutes, 1 May 1936, ED 121/40. GPC, Minutes, 11 June 1937, MH 82/2. 'Statement of the Chairman', Mar. 1938, MH 82/1.
[197] 'General Proposals County Councils', MH 82/1. GPC, Minutes, 3 June 1936, MH 82/2.   [198] GPC, Minutes, 4 Sept. 1936, MH 82/2.
[199] GPC, Report, 18 Sept. 1936; CCHE, Minutes, 18 Sept. 1936, MH 82/1.
[200] Minute, 29 Apr. 1937, MH 78/147.
[201] NPHCC, Minutes, 30 Oct. 1936, MH 82/2. Establishment Minute, 28 Sept. 1936, MH 78/147.

meeting on 30 October, the Government announced its intention of conducting a publicity scheme in support of physical fitness.[202] Although this had been prefigured in the general election manifesto of 1935,[203] little had been said in public, until Neville Chamberlain, then Chancellor of the Exchequer, referred to the probability of a campaign in a speech on 2 October 1936, before the annual conference of the Conservative and Unionist Associations. Praising the totalitarian states for their attention to physical fitness, Chamberlain suggested that the example be emulated, albeit along different lines. Citing declining birth-rates, he stressed the importance of raising the quality of the race by encouraging exercise and games. Britain could never be 'really healthy' until the general level of fitness had been improved.[204]

There was ample evidence to suggest that physical standards were lower in Britain than in other countries. A BMA report, issued in April 1936, noted that the very appearance of the public provided sufficient proof of the poor level of national fitness. Quoting studies which indicated that 70 per cent of boys aged 14–18 received 'no proper physical training', the BMA recommended the adoption of a more organized system of sports and recreation.[205] These findings were reinforced, and seemingly confirmed, by the country's showings at the Olympic Games of 1936, both of which were held in Nazi Germany. The host nation dominated the summer competition, capturing thirty-three gold medals and the overall title with 181 points. The United States was second with twenty-four first-place finishes and 124 points. Fascist Italy was third. Great Britain won only four gold medals and was placed seventh with twenty-nine points.[206] Although it was observed that there was 'no need to lament the decadence of the race or to make sport into one of the more solemn of life's occupations', the results focused attention on the progress made by other countries and the fact that Britain lagged behind.[207]

The low standards of fitness prevailing in Britain had been recognized

---

[202] The Conservative Party Research Department had been advocating a fitness campaign since the early 1930s; John Ramsden, *The Making of Conservative Party Policy* (1980), 79–89.   [203] See below, p. 173.

[204] *The Times*, 3 Oct. 1936.

[205] Cited in PEP, *Report*, 338–9, 342–50. In 1935, 35 per cent of military applicants were rejected as unfit; Hansard, 15 June 1936, vol. 313, cols. 635–6.

[206] *The Times*, 17 Aug. 1936.

[207] Ibid. For praise of Germany's example see Hansard, 14 July 1936, vol. 314, cols. 1910–11. PEP, *Report*, 338. Newman, *Nation's Health*, 258–62. In 1937 a Board of Education delegation investigated physical training in Germany: ED 121/192. R. V. Vernon and N. Mansbergh claimed that the national fitness scheme was initiated in response to popular demand inspired by the German example: *Advisory Bodies* (1940), 208.

for some time.[208] That the issue came to the fore in 1936 reflected grow-ing concern that the success of fascism abroad was putting democracy on trial. Chamberlain's announcement received wide coverage,[209] and was applauded by many who believed it critical from a political standpoint:[210]

it would be a poor recommendation of democracy that it cultivated weediness. The cult of physical training in totalitarian states is an expansion of the self-respect, in the literal sense, which they strive to inculcate in their nationals. It must be clear, even to those who most fiercely detest the totalitarian philosophy, that if democracy can combine political freedom with an equally high physical standard this would be additional proof of the superiority of democracy and not the first step towards the imitation of political heresies.[211]

From the outset, then, the campaign had ideological undertones. Obvi-ously, this influenced the manner in which it was prosecuted. German methods were decried as unsuitable; they were said to be incompatible with British traditions.[212] A mandatory scheme was advocated in some quarters, but the majority agreed with Oliver Stanley, the President of the Board of Education, that

It is no good for us following the example of other countries where there is a tradition of a national system and an ideology of State control. Our tradition is the voluntary system, and I hope it will always remain so. People must want to go to physical training, not be forced to go.[213]

Compulsion was also ruled out lest it provoke charges of militarism or closet conscription. The fact that such allegations were made[214] ensured that the voluntary nature of the scheme and the benefits to health from

---

[208] Note the reference to the lack of available facilities in Board of Education, *Syllabus of Physical Training for Schools 1933* (1933), 7. Also see Newman, *Public Opinion*, 15–16; Charles Frederick Higham, *Looking Forward* (1920), 133. *Advertising World*, 67/7 (1935), 11, refers to a 'Fitter Britain' campaign sponsored by the King George V Jubilee Fund in 1935.

[209] *The Times* devoted four editorials to the subject in Oct. alone: 3, 8, 19, 21 Oct. 1936.

[210] *The Times*, 4, 7 Nov. 1936, 2 Oct. 1937. Hansard, 8 Feb. 1937, vol. 320, cols. 64–87, 92–108, 111–55.   [211] *The Times*, 19 Oct. 1936.

[212] Hansard, 8 Feb. 1937, vol. 320, cols. 64–87, 92–155. *The Times*, 9 Feb., 1, 6, 11, 23 Oct. 1937. 'Message from Aberdare', in NFC, *Twenty-four Ways of Keeping Fit* (1938). NFC, *The National Fitness Campaign* (1939), 5.

[213] *The Times*, 21, 22 Oct. 1936. *Physical Training and Recreation*, Cmd. 5364 (1937), 5.

[214] *The Times*, 7 Nov. 1936; Arthur Calder-Marshall, *The Changing Scene* (1937), 246–8. The churches voiced concern: M. E. Aubrey to Earl Stanhope, 1 Oct. 1937; Archbishop of Canterbury to K. Wood, 2 Nov. 1937; ED 10/263. These allegations were denied; Wood to Aubrey, 10 Nov. 1937, ED 10/263. Also Hansard, 8 Feb. 1937, vol. 320, cols. 64–82, 86–7, 92–155; *The Times*, 6, 8, 9 Feb., 8 Apr. 1937. Because the controversy persisted, grants were refused to cadet corps: see *The Times*, 29 Oct. 1936; correspondence between the Board of Education and the MH, Jan.–Nov. 1938, ED 10/263; British National Cadet Association to Board of Education, 9 May 1939; Pearson to Ellis, 24 May 1939, ED 113/24.

physical training were constantly highlighted.[215] 'Leisure for Pleasure', rather than the Nazi slogan, 'Strength through Joy', was the motto adopted.[216] Tellingly, by 1939, it had become 'Stamina for Peace'.[217]

As it seemed to imply that even greater efforts were forthcoming, the emphasis which the Government placed on health in announcing its plans proved a double-edged sword. Although official statements on the campaign made no reference to general health issues, it was widely assumed that the fitness drive would have a broad base; only healthy people, it was noted, were capable of becoming physically fit.[218] The BMA observed that organized physical education had to be 'closely related to the system of health education'.[219] Indeed, there was widespread consensus that a fitness campaign would only be successful if it rested on firm foundations, with improvements in nutrition and living conditions preceding exercise and training.[220] It was in the context of this public discussion that the CCHE laid its proposals for a general health campaign before the Government.

At the first meeting of the NPHCC on 30 October 1936, Rankine was asked to draft a report documenting the effectiveness of propaganda, and, in so doing, make the case for a general health campaign. Entitled 'A Statement . . . with Reference to the Proposals to Increase the Physical Fitness of the Nation by Encouraging a Greater Use of the Existing Health Services', it was submitted to the committee on 5 November.[221] Stressing the cost-effectiveness of advertising *vis-à-vis* expenditure on services, Rankine cited various examples, including Northcliffe's wartime exploits and recent Post Office activities, as evidence of the value of publicity. Although lacking statistics, he maintained that foreign countries spent a much higher proportion of their health budgets on advertising. Noting that available evidence suggested that services in Britain were not being exploited to their full capacity, he confirmed the need for a publicity drive. Despite its title, the report made no mention of the proposed government campaign or of physical fitness *per se*. However, on endorsing

[215] See *The Times*, 23, 28 Oct., 6 Dec. 1937. NFC, *Twenty-four Ways of Keeping Fit. The Times*, *Nation's Health*, 59–64. PEP claimed the government emphasized voluntarism in order to avoid charges of militarism: *Report*, 350.   [216] *The Times*, 16 Mar. 1937.
[217] Ibid. 4 Jan. 1939.
[218] Ibid. 8, 19 Oct., 4 Nov. 1936, 9 Jan., 5 Feb., 8 Apr. 1937. Ramsden, p. 89. *King-Hall News-letter*, 18 (27 Oct. 1936). NPHCC, Minutes, 5 Nov. 1936, MH 82/2. PEP, *Report*, 338–9.   [219] Quoted in PEP, *Report*, 338–9.
[220] *The Times*, 3 Oct. 1936, 4 Nov. 1936, 9 Jan. 1937. Also see Board of Education, *Syllabus*, 8.
[221] NPHCC, Minutes, 30 Oct. 1936; 5 Nov. 1936, MH 82/2. GPC, Report, 18 Dec. 1936; NPHCC, Report; and 'Memorandum with Reference to a National Campaign for Health and Fitness', Dec. 1936, MH 82/1.

this document, the NPHCC did make a side reference to the government announcement, minuting that the success of the physical education campaign would be dependent on the adequate employment of existing services.[222]

Rankine's report was considered and approved by the CCHE and then forwarded to the Minister of Health and the President of the Board of Education. The Ministry of Health authorized the council to formulate plans for a health services campaign and approached the Treasury for funding.[223] At the next meeting of the NPHCC, on 15 January 1937, Rucker reported that, if Treasury approval could be obtained, £10,000 of public money would be allocated to the proposed scheme.[224] Sanction was secured, and, on 26 April, Kingsley Wood announced that a general health campaign would begin in the autumn.[225]

Given the public reaction to the announcement of the fitness campaign, the ready acceptance of the CCHE proposals seems relatively straightforward. None the less, it is improbable that, in adopting a health campaign, the Government was merely bowing to external pressure to broaden the scope of the physical education drive. Nutrition, for example, never became a plank of the fitness campaign, despite the emphasis placed on it in the public debate. Moreover, it is evident that encouragement, if not assurances, had been given to the CCHE well before the fitness scheme was unveiled. In light of the council's history *vis-à-vis* the ministry, it seems unlikely that it would have initiated comprehensive proposals had it not been confident of backing. One must query the timing of the CCHE's decision to launch a campaign. As already demonstrated, the importance of publicity to 'preventive' medicine and the desirability of encouraging greater use of the health services had been recognized for years. Moreover, the CCHE had made similar campaign proposals in both 1933 and 1934. Citing a lack of public knowledge about available facilities, and the fact that economies made further expansion in the system improbable, the council had argued, then, that it would be politically expedient to persuade the public that worthwhile expenditure was being made, and had stressed that better use of existing services was an important prerequisite

---

[222] Ibid.

[223] GPC, Report, Dec. 1936; NPHCC, Report and 'Memorandum', Dec. 1936; CCHE, Minutes, 18 Dec. 1936; CCHE to MH, 16 Mar. 1938, MH 82/1.

[224] Davidson to Holmes and Secretary, 15 Jan. 1937, ED 121/41. NPHCC, Minutes, 15 Jan. 1937; draft 'Memorandum with reference to a National Campaign for Health and Fitness: Part II', Jan. 1937, MH 82/2. The final version, 'National Campaign to Encourage the Use of the Health Services', was submitted in Apr.: NPHCC, Minutes, 23 Apr. 1937, MH 82/1.   [225] *The Times*, 27 Apr. 1937.

6 Ministry of Health poster: 'Use Your Health Services'

to disease prevention.[226] Why, when these arguments had failed to win over the Government, did the CCHE advance the same case a mere two years later? Undoubtedly, because it felt more assured of success. The council later reported that it had felt encouraged to pursue its plans by the appointment of Sir Kingsley Wood as Minister of Health in June 1935, as he had 'proved the great value of propaganda', while serving as Postmaster-General.[227] The presence of government officials on the council is another factor which must be taken into consideration. Indeed, it was O. K. Wright who proposed the motion to create the health campaign committee.[228]

There were several reasons why the Ministry of Health itself may have initiated the scheme, and/or was predisposed to support it at this juncture. During the general election campaign of November 1935, the Government had promised to pursue a more positive social policy.[229] This did not result in any radical changes in the health care system when the National Government retained power, as it was assumed that sufficient basic services were in place, if only the public would make use of them.[230] Expenditure on services had grown from £35.5 million in 1900 to £201 million in 1920, and had reached £400 million by 1934. Yet evidence from a number of sources showed that the system was not being exploited to full advantage.[231] In 1936 only 49 per cent of expectant mothers attended antenatal clinics.[232] By 1936–7, the milk-in-schools scheme was functioning in over 90 per cent of educational establishments, but less than 50 per cent of school-age children participated. Studies indicated that 'indifference on the part of parents' was one of several factors accounting for the low figures.[233] Investigations conducted by and for the Ministry of Health suggested that there were extensive regional variations

[226] Elliston to Carnworth, 16 June 1933; Note of Deputation, 16 Jan. 1934, MH 55/29. Hansard, 20 June 1934, vol. 291, cols. 440–3.

[227] 'Statement of the Chairman in introducing the Memorandum to the MH', Mar. 1938, MH 82/1.   [228] GPC, Report, 18 Sept. 1936, MH 82/1.

[229] *The Times*, 25 Oct., 22 Nov. 1935, 21 Oct. 1936. Ramsden, p. 79.

[230] *King-Hall News-letter*, 55 (14 July 1937). NFC, *The National Fitness Campaign*, 4. Newman, *Nation's Health*, 278.

[231] *The Times*, 12 Mar., 17 Sept. 1935, 4 Oct. 1936, 19 Mar., 1, 30 Oct. 1937. MS Addison, Box 114. Hansard, 20 June 1934, vol. 291, cols. 442–3. MH, *Nineteenth Annual Report*, 2, 75. *The Times*, *Nation's Health*, 12. Newman, *Nation's Health*, 278. PEP, *Report*, 356.

[232] *The Times*, 30 Oct. 1937. PEP, *Report*, 356. CCHE to local authorities, 18 Mar. 1937, MH 82/1.

[233] PEP, *Report*, 330. MS Addison, Box 114. Davidson to Holmes and Secretary, 15 Jan. 1937; 'Campaign for Increased Appreciation of the Public Health Services: The Health Services for School Children', undated, ED 121/41. Davidson, 'National Health Campaign: School Medical Service', 21 Jan. 1937, MH 82/2.

in the use of services which could not be explained by differences in general conditions.[234] Special surveys of the activities of local authorities, compiled between 1930 and 1934, also indicated that health education was inadequate in most areas of the country.[235] All of these factors contributed to a growing awareness that publicity, which to date had barely been an arm of official health policy, had to become a central plank of administration. This was reflected in subtle changes in the department's attitude, best exemplified by its recognition of the CCHE and the creation of a public relations division in 1935. True, the latter had shied away from 'flamboyant efforts' during its first year, but by April 1936, 'having got a footing . . . in the more solid press', S. H. Wood believed it was ready 'to let loose the more popular appeal'.[236] Despite these remarks, the planning and administration of the health services campaign was left to the CCHE.

The fact that the ministry chose to assign control over the campaign to a voluntary organization provoked little discussion at the time and, as a result, the decision was not explained. It could be argued that, as the proposals had emanated from the CCHE, the Government had little choice. However, as the scheme may well have originated with the Ministry of Health, this is not a sufficient explanation. It is best understood in the context of the department's long tradition of relying on voluntary organizations to provide and promote services. Both Rucker, of the ministry, and D. DuB. Davidson, the director of intelligence and public relations at the Board of Education, saw 'distinct advantage' in encouraging the idea that the health campaign was 'being sponsored by a non-Governmental body'. The ministry still regarded its primary task as guidance, fearing that direct participation might provoke controversy, and/or set dangerous precedents.[237] The emphasis placed on local efforts in the health services campaign provides further indication that ministerial policy had not changed. Local councils were encouraged to conduct their own publicity schemes concurrently with the national campaign. Many did; the Surrey County Council even commissioned the CCHE to arrange its appeal.[238]

[234] MH, *Nineteenth Annual Report*, 2.
[235] MH, *Fifteenth Annual Report*. NPHCC Report; and 'Memorandum', Dec. 1936, MH 82/1. Robinson to Johnson, 25 Jan. 1934, MH 55/29. PEP, *Report*, 338. For the surveys see MH 66.
[236] Robinson to Minister, 5 July 1935; S. Wood to Secretary, 3 Apr. 1936, MH 78/147.
[237] Davidson to Secretary, 22 Jan. 1937, ED 121/41.
[238] 'General Proposals County Councils', undated; Memorandum to Surrey County Council, undated, MH 82/1. GPC, Minutes, 3 June 1936; 11 June 1937; Exhibition Committee, Minutes, 24 Sept. 1937, MH 82/2.

A draft programme was considered by the NPHCC on 15 January 1937.[239] The campaign was to begin in the autumn, so as to coincide with Empire Health Week, and run for six months. A specific topic was to be covered each month: October being devoted to general background publicity aimed at winning the support and co-operation of local authorities and voluntary organizations; November to the school medical services; December to the prevention of infectious diseases; January to maternity; February to popularizing 'the figure of the sanitary inspector', and the work of local authorities in environmental hygiene; and March to recapitulating what had gone before. It was expected that the Ministry of Health would prepare and produce any required materials, leaving the execution of the campaign to the CCHE. After 'vigorous discussion', the NPHCC agreed that, rather than focusing on abstract concepts, the council should concentrate on publicizing services which could be carried out by existing organizations, the 'efficiency of which . . . [could] be backed by statistical' evidence. Thus, and to save funds, it was decided to drop the reference to environmental hygiene and sanitary inspectors. Dr T. Drummond Shiels also wanted the committee to omit the school medical services, but D. DuB. Davidson blocked the proposal.

Davidson was only present at this conference by chance. Appointed as the board's first representative to the CCHE, effective 19 February, he had been invited to attend a meeting of the GPC and had stayed on to join the NPHCC's deliberations.[240] His success in opposing Drummond Shiels's suggestion was of crucial importance. It ensured that the board would have some input into the campaign, thus opening up the possibility of the schools being used for the distribution of publicity materials. Davidson's presence on the committee also had other long-reaching effects, for he supported Drummond Shiels's recommendation that the subject of physical education should be added to the CCHE campaign. Indeed, Davidson advised his superiors that he had 'press[ed] the point very strongly in view of the Government's promised programme, and secured the agreement of the Committee'. He also noted that, under a private agreement made with Rucker, the board was entitled to a share of any publicity moneys the Ministry of Health secured from the Treasury. The inference was that fitness publicity could be funded from this source. Both the President and the Parliamentary Secretary of the Board of Education approved, and Davidson secured permission to authorize the preparation of memoranda on the schools' medical service and physical

---

[239] MH 82/2.
[240] Rankine to Hamilton, 13 Jan. 1937; Davidson to Holmes and Secretary, 15 Jan. 1937, ED 121/41. Rankine to Secretary, 8 Dec. 1936, ED 50/175.

education to be submitted to the NPHCC.[241] As this indicates, as late as January 1937, the board does not appear to have been contemplating conducting a separate *propaganda* campaign for physical fitness.

The NPHCC met again on 22 and 28 January, and altered the format outlined above, so that November and December were devoted to maternity services, January to the schools, and February and March to services for adults and adolescents (social hygiene and physical training and recreation).[242] Drummond Shiels wanted the campaign to be broader-based, but the committee agreed that the novelty of the scheme and the need for economy necessitated that the council concentrate on publicizing existing services, and avoid controversial subjects. As this suggests, the committee was concerned less with raising public awareness of health issues than with conducting a campaign which would lead to an increased use of available services, that is, achieve immediate and measurable results.[243] In fact, Davidson had been directed by the board to raise the question of including more abstract concepts, such as nutrition, in the campaign but, faced with the committee's decision, had not broached the subject.[244] Subsequent attempts to broaden the campaign were unsuccessful, despite the public criticism engendered by the omission of topics like nutrition.[245]

Drummond Shiels also voiced misgivings about the criteria to be used in measuring the effectiveness of the campaign, cautioning against an over-reliance on statistical evidence. As he pointed out, the aim of the campaign was disease prevention, and thus the best proof of success would actually be a decrease in the use of the health services.[246] Convinced by this argument, or perhaps covering itself, the NPHCC affirmed the importance of achieving practical ends, but deleted a reference to 'obtaining results which are capable of statistical verification' from the final prospectus submitted to the CCHE on 23 April, and subsequently forwarded to Whitehall.[247]

The Treasury sanctioned a £10,000 allocation to the CCHE campaign

---

[241] Davidson to Holmes and Secretary, 15 Jan. 1937, ED 121/41.
[242] CCHE, Annual Report, 1935–6; NPHCC, Report, 9 Feb. 1937; K. Wood to CCHE, 5 Jan. 1937; CCHE to local authorities, 1 Feb. 1937, MH 82/1. Davidson to Secretary, 22 Jan. 1937, ED 121/41.
[243] 'National Campaign to Encourage the Use of the Health Services', Dec. 1936, MH 82/1.   [244] Davidson to Secretary, 22 Jan. 1937, ED 121/41.
[245] GPC, Minutes, 15 Jan. 1937; NPHCC, Minutes, 28 Jan. 1937, MH 82/2. Hamilton to Davidson, 29 Jan. 1937, ED 121/41. CCHE, Minutes, 30 Sept. 1937, MH 82/1. *The Times*, 27 Sept. 1937. *King-Hall News-letter*, 18 (27 Oct. 1936).
[246] GPC, Minutes, 15 Jan. 1937; NPHCC, Minutes, 28 Jan. 1937, MH 82/2. Hamilton to Davidson, 29 Jan. 1937, ED 121/41.
[247] NPHCC, Report, 9 Feb. 1937; CCHE, Minutes, 23 Apr. 1937; 'National Campaign', MH 82/1.

early in 1937, but there were complications. On 15 February, the Ministry of Health was informed that none of the moneys could be directed towards fitness publicity.[248] Rucker advised Davidson, on 2 March, that the board would have to make other arrangements.[249] This was already being done, and it seems inconceivable that either Davidson or Rucker was unaware of the well-publicized plans under way for a fitness campaign. A White Paper, outlining the Government's projected legislation to stimulate public interest in physical training and increase recreational facilities, had been published on 4 February.[250] Addressing Parliament four days later, Oliver Stanley had announced plans for the creation of two statutory bodies—a National Advisory Committee (NAC) and a Grants Committee (GC)—later styled the National Fitness Council (NFC), to administer the scheme.[251] Although the legislation was not passed until July 1937, the NFC was established in February. By the time he heard from Rucker, Davidson had already asked the CCHE to prepare posters for a projected NFC campaign.[252]

Lord Aberdare, a noted sportsman and member of the International Olympic Committee, was appointed to chair the NAC, with Sir Henry Pelham heading the GC.[253] The NAC was a large committee including representatives from most of the major voluntary organizations. Neither the Board of Education nor the Ministry of Health nominated members, but the former was kept fully informed of all developments by Lionel Ellis, the secretary to both committees. As the scheme was being administered by the board, neither the ministry nor the CCHE received reports on the deliberations of these two bodies. Thus, although aware of each other's existence, the CCHE and NFC had no point of contact. Only rarely did they exchange information. Not until late September 1937 was the NFC fully informed of the CCHE's plans, and when finally invited to appoint representatives to the CCHE, the NFC refused.[254]

Why did the Board of Education not follow the trend and rely on a voluntary society to undertake the fitness campaign? A suitable organization did exist; chaired by Waldorf Astor, and representative of over one hundred organizations, the Central Council for Recreative Physical

---

[248] Gilbert to Hughes, 15 Feb. 1937, ED 10/263.
[249] Rucker to Davidson, 2 Mar. 1937, ED 10/263.
[250] *Physical Training and Recreation. The Times*, 5 Feb. 1937. PEP, *Report*, 346.
[251] Hansard, 8 Feb. 1937, vol. 320, cols. 64–155.
[252] Davidson to Hamilton, 19 Feb. 1937, ED 121/41.
[253] *The Times*, 9, 13 Feb. 1937.
[254] Propaganda Subcommittee, Minutes, P(37)6, 28 Sept. 1937, ED 113/50. S. Wood to Ellis, 8 Nov. 1937; reply, 10 Nov. 1937, ED 121/41. Select Committee on Estimates (1938), Proceedings, 4 Apr. 1938, min. 1687.

Training (CCRPT) had been attempting, since 1935, to 'co-ordinate, advise on and *even direct* some of the nation's measures for promoting physical education' [my italics].[255] Yet because the scheme was being funded under parliamentary statute, it had to be administered by an official body.[256] The fact that the proposed legislation was to include grants to voluntary societies for the establishment of new facilities also made it expedient that an independent organization control the arrangements. None the less, the actual *publicity* could have been controlled by a voluntary group, as was the case in the health campaign.

Evidently the Board of Education was amenable to securing CCRPT assistance. On being informed, in January 1937, that Davidson had successfully inserted fitness into the CCHE scheme, the permanent secretary observed, 'no doubt at a later stage the Central Council for Recreative Physical Training could be consulted'.[257] The original plans for the fitness campaign actually empowered the Grants Committee to fund the CCRPT, *inter alia*, 'to promote propaganda'. However, this provision was removed without explanation from the final draft of the Government scheme. At its first meeting, in March 1937, the GC also vetoed suggestions that the CCRPT should oversee the proposed poster campaign.[258]

The NAC also opposed direct CCRPT involvement in the scheme, undoubtedly because the former regarded publicity as one of its own major functions. Indeed, Oliver Stanley had stated in February that

perhaps the most important part of the work of the Council would be more popular than scientific. It would be the work of propaganda and publicity, to bring home to the people of the country what facilities were available and how important it was that they should make use of these facilities. This was of increased importance when it was realized that there was no element of compulsion in the scheme. It had got to depend for its success entirely on persuasion and popular approval—and to that extent much of the success would depend on the work of this Council.[259]

The importance attached to publicity was reflected in the creation of a Propaganda Subcommittee at the first meeting of the NAC, on 3 March.[260]

Despite these activities, and the Treasury ruling, the NPHCC never

[255] PEP, *Report*, 343. NFC, *The National Fitness Campaign*, 19. Board of Education, *Recreation and Physical Fitness for Girls and Women* (1937).
[256] See below, p. 217.
[257] Davidson to Holmes and Secretary, 15 Jan. 1937, ED 121/41.
[258] Williams to Deputy Secretary, 4 Mar. 1937, ED 10/263.
[259] *The Times*, 9 Feb. 1937.
[260] NAC, Minutes, NAC37(1), 3 Mar. 1937, ED 113/48. *The Times*, 4 Mar. 1937. Williams to Deputy Secretary, 4 Mar. 1937, ED 10/263.

openly discussed the possibility of removing fitness from its own campaign. None the less, the final memorandum on the scheme, forwarded to local authorities on 18 March, made no reference to physical education. The outline was as follows: October would be devoted to general issues; November and December to maternity and child welfare services; January to the schools; and February–March to what were termed adult diseases, notably tuberculosis and venereal disease.[261] The same programme was sent to the CCHE on 23 April and to Whitehall on 19 May.[262] When the CCHE met on 21 May to finalize poster designs, none dealing with fitness were discussed.[263] Yet three weeks before the beginning of the health campaign, a CCHE committee approved a 'Prospectus' giving full particulars of the scheme and the publicity materials to be employed. In this booklet, the format of the campaign was altered; it was noted that a proposal 'was under consideration' to use March to publicize 'the facilities already existing for physical training and recreation and those to be provided under the [new] . . . Act'. The pamphlet stated that, were these plans approved, a supplement would be issued containing reproductions of the publicity materials to be distributed in March.[264] When the campaign opened on 30 September, fitness was a component.[265]

Available records provide no indication of when this decision was taken or by whom. The idea certainly did not emanate from the National Fitness Council. After receiving the prospectus of the CCHE scheme on 28 September, the NFC immediately planned a public meeting to emphasize the uniqueness of the fitness campaign. The council was concerned lest the public confuse the two campaigns.[266] It was too late; an editorial in *The Times* on 27 September opened with the statement that the new health campaign was intended to launch the fitness scheme.[267] In fact, the Government was active in perpetuating the illusion. In his speech

---

[261] NPHCC, Minutes, 15, 22, 28 Jan. 1937; 'Memorandum: Part II', 15 Jan. 1937; 'Memorandum with Reference to a National Campaign for Health and Fitness: Suggested Revision of Section "D" ', 22 Jan. 1937, MH 82/2. Davidson to Holmes and Secretary, 15 Jan. 1937; Hamilton to Davidson, 29 Jan. 1937, ED 121/41. 'National Campaign'; CCHE to local authorities, 18 Mar. 1937, MH 82/1. *The Times*, 19 Mar. 1937.

[262] 'National Campaign'; CCHE to local authorities, 18 Mar. 1937, MH 82/1. Rankine to Stanley, 19 May 1937, ED 121/41.

[263] CCHE, Minutes, 21 May 1937, MH 82/1.

[264] GPC, Minutes, 13 Sept. 1937, MH 82/2. Propaganda Subcommittee, Minutes, P(37)6, 28 Sept. 1937, ED 113/50. *The Times*, 27 Sept. 1937.

[265] MS Addison, Box 114. *The Times*, 1 Oct. 1936.

[266] Propaganda Subcommittee, Minutes, P(37)6, 28 Sept. 1937; P(38)1, 7 Feb. 1938, ED 113/50. NAC, Minutes, NAC(37)5, 14 Oct. 1937; NAC(38)1, 10 Feb. 1938, ED 113/48.

[267] *The Times*, 27 Sept. 1937.

inaugurating the health drive, the Prime Minister implied that the fitness campaign was part of the health scheme. Despite the fact that the NFC was already conducting publicity, he stated that the fitness campaign was due to begin in March.[268] The two schemes became one and the same in the public mind. Even Members of Parliament were ignorant of the true arrangements.[269]

Attempting to associate the two campaigns in the public mind was logical, given the widespread consensus that improvements in physical education were dependent on better health. The decision may also have been taken to further distance the NFC from allegations of militarism. Having the fitness campaign appear to be an outgrowth of the health scheme would deflect controversy. Linking the two campaigns was not difficult. Both schemes appeared to be administered by non-government bodies, and thus seemed to be unofficial in nature. However, although they were prepared independently of each other, and by different organizations, the campaigns were similar in intent and, more significantly, bore a striking resemblance in methodology and approach.

When official assent was given to the health services campaign in January 1937, all preparations were left to the CCHE. The NPHCC drew up a memorandum stressing that the main objective was to achieve specific, measurable results, rather than 'merely . . . creating in the mind of the public an impression that much is being done for them'.[270] Responsibilities were allocated between the various organizations involved; the Ministry of Health was to arrange for the production of materials and liaise with other government departments, while local authorities and voluntary societies were to display materials, organize meetings, and issue their own propaganda containing regional information. The CCHE was to act as a clearing-house: liaising with medical officers of health; obtaining the co-operation of local authorities; and co-ordinating the distribution of pamphlets and posters. The council was also expected to prepare designs for publicity materials, although the latter were to be subject to Ministry of Health approval. Since it was fielding the bulk of the administrative tasks, the CCHE requested government funding, and obtained £800.[271] Although the Ministry of Health had pledged £10,000 to the campaign, this was the only direct funding the CCHE received. The department had been allocated £20,000 for publicity purposes in 1937–8, but £18,000

[268] See above, n. 191.
[269] Select Committee on Estimates (1938), Proceedings, 4 Apr. 1938, min. 1703.
[270] 'National Campaign', MH 82/1. Rankine to Stanley, 19 May 1937, ED 121/41.
[271] 'National Campaign'; Memorandum to MH, 16 Mar. 1938, MH 82/1.

of the budget appeared on the Stationery Office Vote, covering the preparation and printing of supplies.[272]

As the CCHE had little money of its own, a commercial agency could not be hired to provide advice. Fortunately, the council was confident that professionals would only be needed to provide preliminary designs, as the members were 'of the opinion that the work usually carried out by an agency in planning such a campaign has already been completed by ourselves'.[273] Despite these claims, the preparations undertaken by the council were in no way comparable to what a professional firm would have done. The two agencies which had submitted comprehensive campaign proposals to the CCHE in 1936 had undertaken complex analyses of the media to be employed and constructed audience profiles. While drawing on these reports for ideas, the CCHE did not engage in any market research, nor attempt to target its appeal.

The financial position of the council also meant that other organizations and local authorities had to be recruited to assist in the campaign. They were expected to take the place of agents, ensuring that centrally issued publicity materials were properly utilized. There was already a predisposition to rely on these bodies; the scheme was supposed to highlight the services available in each area. Pamphlets and posters were only prepared centrally for reasons of economy and efficiency, in order to ensure that all councils had access to materials otherwise not affordable. Uniform supplies, ranging from double crown posters for indoor and outdoor display to traffic cards, folders, and bookmarks, were prepared by the CCHE each month. A rigid schedule governing their distribution was issued to each participating council, so as to secure continuity and uniformity.[274] Space was provided for the over-printing of regional information, and local authorities were encouraged to supplement the materials with their own pamphlets and posters.[275]

Similarly, while speakers and materials were provided for mass meetings, these events were generally left to local officials. Regarding lectures as the most important form of propaganda available (posters were fifth), the CCHE recommended holding large gatherings, and suggested that councils endeavour to enlist prestigious individuals to preside.[276] Christopher Addison was invited to address meetings in Plymouth on 22

[272] Thomas to Playfair, 9 Dec. 1937, T 162/971/12190/01. 'Memorandum', 16 Feb. 1938, T 162/981/36055/01/2. Select Committee on Estimates (1938), Appendix 3.
[273] 'National Campaign', MH 82/1.
[274] 'National Campaign'; CCHE to local authorities, 18 Mar. 1937, MH 82/1.
[275] Rankine to County Council Associations, 9 July 1937, ED 121/41.
[276] Note of Deputation, 31 Mar. 1938, MH 82/1.

8 Ministry of Health poster: 'In Work or Play Fitness Wins'

October 1937, Coventry on 10 December, and Preston on 15 February 1938, the CCHE providing information for his speeches. In Coventry the programme was as follows:

7:30   Organ Recital. Light music until 8 p.m.
8:00   Mayor to open meeting—explain its purpose.
8:05   Minister of Transport—Leslie Burgin—to speak.
8:35   Demonstration of physical training—Coventry Branch of The Women's League of Health and Beauty.
8:50   Rt. Hon. Lord Addison to speak.
9:30   Demonstration of physical training by men students of Coventry Technical College. Demonstration of physical training by Coventry Branch of Everywoman's Health Movement.
9:45   Captain W. F. Strickland, M.P., J. L. Giles (Captain of Coventry Rugby Football Club and English International player), Dr A. Massey (Medical Officer of Health).
         All to speak briefly.
9:55   Chairman (Councillor J. C. Lee Gordon) and Vice Chairman will propose thanks to Mayor and to two principal speakers.
10:10 God Save the King.[277]

[277] MS Addison, Box 114.

The content of the programme highlights the emphasis placed on local facilities, as well as the regional autonomy prevailing in the campaign; for example, although the meeting was held in December 1937, physical fitness was a central plank of the programme.

At many similar gatherings films and slides, borrowed by the CCHE, were shown. The council itself did not produce any films, nor could it persuade the government to commission shorts.[278] Moreover, when in June 1937 the council decided to purchase a film projector for use in the campaign it could not secure official funding, even though Local Educational Authorities were entitled to a grant of 50 per cent towards the cost of such machinery.[279] That this request was denied illustrates the ambiguous position of the council as an outside body conducting an official campaign. Whitehall was still keeping voluntary organizations at arm's length.

Noticeable by its total absence from the campaign was press advertising. The firms surveyed by the council had devoted most of their projected budgets to this, 'the most economic medium for mass propaganda'.[280] Practically speaking, however, newspaper advertising was much more expensive than other forms of publicity. The CCHE could not afford it, nor could campaign funds be used, as all publicity materials had to be procured through the Stationery Office. An independent grant for this purpose was unlikely, as the Treasury, openly hostile to display advertising in the press, was endeavouring to ban its use by government departments.[281] Still, even if funds had been forthcoming, the CCHE placed little faith in press publicity. Newspaper advertising did not even feature in its list of important media.[282] Editorial publicity was thought to be valuable, but only because it was economical and supposedly achieved practical results. Thus, rather than advocating press advertising, the campaign prospectus prepared by the NPHCC recommended the commissioning of a journalist to prepare newsworthy articles for distribution: 'We believe that given appropriate treatment, municipal developments are of sufficient news value to deserve and to obtain support in national dailies and weeklies, and we regard such notices in the news columns as of greater appropriateness and value to the campaign.'[283]

---

[278] 'National Campaign', MH 82/1. *The Times*, 27 Sept., 1 Oct. 1937.
[279] Rankine to S. Wood, 18 June 1937, ED 121/41.
[280] Memorandum from the London Press Exchange to CCHE, 1936, ED 121/40.
[281] See below, pp. 230–1.   [282] 'Notes of Conversations', 31 Mar. 1938, MH 82/1.
[283] 'National Campaign', MH 82/1.

The use of the term 'appropriateness' in this statement reflects the prestige element underlying the campaign. When preparing a memorandum to enlist local government support for the scheme, the NPHCC had consciously avoided the use of popular wording. As the document was being addressed to responsible officials, it was agreed that language suitable for an appeal to the public would be improper.[284] That such a decision was taken regarding a formal document is hardly surprising. Yet it also suggests that the council was amenable to adopting a popular approach towards the mass audience. A local campaign prospectus stated that 'a greater advertising effort and more attractive appeal is necessary to win the interest of the general public for whom *education must be presented as entertainment* [my italics]'.[285] On the other hand, the emphasis throughout the national health scheme was on meetings addressed by prominent individuals, which were unlikely to appeal to the man in the street. Little evidence is available on the extent to which meetings were attended and by whom. One MP noted that at a gathering in Oxford he observed there were more officials present than audience.[286] The meeting Addison addressed in Coventry was not 'crowded'. The Mayor sent him a letter of apology citing the poor weather on the night.[287] Interestingly, the programme for the meeting Addison attended in Preston makes reference to ticket holders, which indicates that in some cases the public may have faced admission charges.[288] This undoubtedly would have affected the nature of the audience. Similar problems of assessment arise when analysing the posters used, though the slogan 'Use Your Health Services' was hardly catchy. Few popular posters or pamphlets were issued; the emphasis was on filtering information downward, the council abhorring the type of commercial advertisements favoured by patent medicine manufacturers and the like.[289]

Though it lacked concrete proof, the CCHE claimed that the campaign had been successful.[290] But despite its earlier emphasis on measurable results, the council did not gather any statistical evidence. Although the Government supplied publicity materials free of charge, at least two hundred local authorities chose not to participate in the scheme.[291] Financially,

[284] Hamilton to Davidson, 29 Jan. 1937, ED 121/41.
[285] Memorandum to Surrey County Council, undated, MH 82/1.
[286] Select Committee on Estimates (1938), Proceedings, 4 Apr. 1938, min. 1703.
[287] MS Addison, Box 114.   [288] Ibid. *The Times*, 6, 14, 28 Oct. 1937.
[289] Annual Report, Oct. 1937–Dec. 1938, MH 82/1.   [290] Ibid.
[291] CCHE, Minutes, 23 Apr. 1937, MH 82/1. Memo, 6 Aug. 1937, ED 121/41.

it was a near disaster; overspending on a local campaign nearly bankrupted the CCHE.[292] In order to prevent the organization from folding, the Government finally agreed in 1938 to provide a steady source of income, in the form of a £5,000 annual grant, on condition that the council submit its programme in advance to the ministry for approval.[293]

The fitness campaign followed similar lines to the health appeal. Propaganda actually accounted for only a small portion of the scheme as most of the funds voted under the legislation were directed towards creating and upgrading both recreational facilities and instruction.[294] Publicity did have a central role in the overall campaign, however, as the voluntary nature of the scheme made success dependent on winning over public opinion. The primacy accorded publicity was reflected in the initial policy decisions taken by the NFC. Although it was appointed early in 1937, the council did not become a statutory body until July; hence its early activities were subject to direct Treasury approval. Accordingly, in the spring of 1937, a report was prepared outlining the council's plans and objectives. Termed the 'arrangements', this was a comprehensive policy statement, and thus provides important insight into the NFC's interpretation of its mandate.[295] The memorandum began by affirming the twofold objective of the campaign to stimulate the desire for physical fitness, while securing an increase in facilities. That both tasks were given equal weight indicates that publicity was regarded as both an arm of policy and a part of the policy itself. An annual budget of £35,000 was earmarked to cover advertising expenses. This was not deemed 'excessive', as 'the provisions specifically made in the Bill for expenditure on publicity may be regarded as a recognition that the objectives of the Council are wider than those normally aimed at by the Public Relations Branch of a Government Department'. The 'primary importance' of 'active and sustained propaganda' was said to necessitate the creation of a publicity bureau headed by a trained journalist. It was further noted that the council would have to assist the propaganda activities of selected voluntary organizations and the area committees created under the scheme.[296]

[292] 'Notes of Conversations', 31 Mar. 1938; 'Statement of the Chairman in introducing the Memorandum', Mar. 1938, MH 82/1. Finance Committee, Minutes, 10 Jan. 1938; Special Committee of Enquiry, 31 Jan. 1938, MH 82/2.

[293] Chrystal to CCHE, 16 Nov. 1938, MH 82/1.

[294] NAC and GC, *National Fitness: The First Steps* (July 1937), 11–13, 19. PEP, *Report*, 342–7.

[295] 'Grants Committee: Memorandum on "Arrangements" ', May 1937, ED 113/27.

[296] Propaganda Subcommittee, Minutes, P(37)2, 1 Apr. 1937, ED 113/50.

The memorandum excited considerable comment when it reached the Board of Education. Officials questioned the advisability of drawing rigid distinctions between the two aims of the campaign, and complained that the publicity arm was being over-emphasized.[297] The report was criticized as falsely implying that the sole purpose of the area committees was to increase public interest in the scheme. Similarly, it gave the impression that grants to voluntary agencies, devised in part to secure inspection rights on new facilities, were also mainly publicity-orientated. Placing so much emphasis on engendering a demand for fitness was said to convey a misleading picture of the Government's objectives. Indeed, from the board's perspective, the memorandum totally undermined the justification for the entire scheme. The Government White Paper on fitness had explained that new facilities were needed in order to meet an existing demand created by the schools. Any suggestion that a large proportion of the expenditure was earmarked for stimulating greater demand was likely to alarm the Treasury. After these objections were relayed to the council, the format of the memorandum was altered, but publicity still had a central role in the plans.

The propaganda committee of the NAC controlled publicity for the entire campaign, reporting to its parent committee on policy, and to the GC on expenditure. As its members were drawn entirely from the NAC, there were no publicity experts on the propaganda committee.[298] Accordingly, one of its first actions was to advocate the establishment of a publicity department in the NFC. After the 'arrangements' were approved, an experienced public relations officer, Evan Hughes, was appointed as publicity director.[299] By 1938, he had a staff of six, including a press officer, Lytton Harris, whose experience for the post is unclear.[300]

These experts actually had little impact on publicity policy. All planning was conducted by the propaganda committee on which neither Hughes nor his staff was represented. The NFC appears to have subscribed to the view that, as publicity had to be in line with overall policy,

---

[297] Davidson to Secretary, Board of Education, 2 June 1937; Williams, 'Memorandum on "Arrangements" ', 2 June 1937; Holmes to Ellis, 9 June 1937, ED 113/27.

[298] Propaganda Subcommittee, Minutes, P(37)1, 15 Mar. 1937, ED 113/50. Select Committee on Estimates (1938), Proceedings, 4 Apr. 1938, min. 1625.

[299] Select Committee on Estimates (1938), Proceedings, 4 Apr. 1938, mins. 1668–72. Propaganda Subcommittee, Minutes, P(37)4, 21 June 1937, ED 113/50. Hughes held several posts at the NSC from 1919 to 1937, and served as a regional information officer in the MOI in the Second World War.

[300] Select Committee on Estimates (1938), Proceedings, 4 Apr. 1938, min. 1592. Ellis to Accountant-General, 21 Sept. 1937; Ellis to Stanhope, 21 Sept. 1937; reply, 2 Oct. 1937, ED 113/27.

experience in advertising was of secondary importance in its formulation. That internal expertise was accorded greater weight than technical skill is evidenced by the arguments S. H. Wood advanced when the Select Committee on Estimates queried the need for an NFC publicity division:

CHAIRMAN. Who produces . . . design[s]?

S. H. WOOD. The National Fitness Council . . . have on their staff a technical assistant who is a design artist. I do not say he produces . . . the design of every poster . . . but his job is to take over the design side of the National Fitness Council work in relation to outside bodies who may be brought in to help, and to advise. . . .

CHAIRMAN. And you think it is the best policy to have one man whose sole time is given to designing, to be employed by the Department direct, rather than to ask for outside schemes, or rather asking for outside designs . . .?

WOOD. Yes, I do feel so, because I do not think a campaign of this kind trying to get over the idea of physical fitness . . . can be done on the design side without having someone on the staff who is in daily contact with the work of the National Fitness Council . . . so that there may be a day by day exposition of National Fitness in terms of design.[301]

A similar attitude governed policy-making; Wood noted that the propaganda committee, not the publicity department, was the final authority on the materials chosen.

As Wood's testimony indicates, rather than advertising specific services or forms of exercise, the NFC attempted to promote the idea of physical fitness. Local organizations were expected to focus on regional facilities, with the NFC providing background publicity and materials, such as films, articles for speeches, and posters and pamphlets, in which space was available for the inclusion of local information.[302] Thus, although it had a much larger publicity budget than the health campaign (£50,000 by 1938), the NFC also relied on local effort, employing similar media and the same type of approach as the CCHE.[303]

Since the Government's avowed policy was to expand on existing services and activities sponsored by voluntary bodies, the emphasis on local effort in the fitness campaign was not surprising.[304] The council had

---

[301] Select Committee on Estimates (1938), Proceedings, 4 Apr. 1938, mins. 1608–14.

[302] Ibid., mins. 1712–22. *The Times*, 2 Oct. 1937. *Physical Training and Recreation*, 3–5. NFC, *The National Fitness Campaign*, 3–5.

[303] Ellis to Accountant-General, 8 Mar. 1938, ED 113/27.

[304] *Physical Training and Recreation*, 2–3. NFC, *The National Fitness Campaign*, 3–5. NAC and GC, *National Fitness: The First Steps*, 12–13. *The Times*, *Nation's Health*, 59–64. The NAC and NFC issued pamphlets aimed at encouraging local efforts: NAC, *Memorandum on the powers of Local Authorities under the Physical Training and Recreation Act* (1937); NFC, *Memorandum on the Preservation of Existing Playing Field Facilities* (1938); NFC, *Flood-lighting Playgrounds and Playing Fields* (1939).

no intention of supplanting the work of others. The fact that most facilities were used at a regional level was further justification for this approach. Finally, enlisting the aid of unofficial organizations shielded the Government from charges of emulating totalitarian regimes.

With independent and more substantial funding than the CCHE, the NFC had a wider range of options available in terms of the type of publicity it could employ. Thus a more commercial approach was pursued than in the health campaign. Advertising agents were consulted regarding poster designs, a press cutting service was hired so that the council would be able to assess public reaction, a poster campaign was undertaken on the London Underground, and, as noted, a publicity staff was appointed to handle the technical arrangements.[305] The council also arranged for the production of films, entering into a contract with Gaumont-British Instructional.[306] Like the CCHE, however, the NFC could not function as a commercial enterprise. Its semi-official status and required deference to Treasury authority limited its scope of activity. Two examples should suffice to illustrate this point: the neglect of press advertising; and the problems which arose over the employment of the BBC.

In the 'arrangements' the NFC ruled out the use of display advertising in newspapers, arguing that it would be both expensive and detrimental, as it 'would tend to reduce the space given in editorial columns to announcements having a news value'.[307] Rather than purchasing advertising space, the council prepared news articles signed by members of the NFC and other notables. Like the CCHE, the NFC professed great faith in editorial advertising. After the council participated in the Lord Mayor's parade in 1937, the propaganda subcommittee reported that 'some £5,000' worth of free news publicity had been obtained from an outlay of £300.[308] No explanation was given as to how this figure was determined. Indeed, the economic value of editorial publicity was difficult to gauge. Despite its professed satisfaction with this form of publicity, the NFC did include a provision for display advertising in its second budget. The Treasury vetoed the proposal, reiterating the claim that paid press advertising was

---

[305] Ellis to Stanhope, 30 July 1937; Ellis to Accountant-General, 15 Feb. 1938, ED 113/27. Propaganda Subcommittee, Minutes, P(37)4, 21 June 1937; P(37)5, 20 July 1937; P(37)6, 28 Sept. 1937, ED 113/50. 'Fitness' was also used to market products: *Advertising World*, 69/10 (1937), 89.
[306] Propaganda Subcommittee, Minutes, P(37)5, 20 July 1937, ED 113/50. Ellis to Accountant-General, 30 July 1937; Davidson to Secretary, 4 Aug. 1937, ED 10/263. Ellis to Stanhope, 30 July 1937, ED 113/27. NAC, Minutes, NAC(37)5, 14 Oct. 1937, ED 113/48. Films were shown at several exhibitions: *Advertising World*, 70/2 (1938), 53.
[307] GC, 'Memorandum on "Arrangements"', May 1937, ED 113/27.
[308] Propaganda Subcommittee, Minutes, P(37)7, 25 Nov. 1937, ED 113/50.

extravagant, and would tend to reduce the amount of free editorial publicity secured.[309] Hence, although it could have afforded to purchase newspaper space, the NFC was precluded from employing this medium by the Treasury's intervention.

Similar difficulties, embodying many of the anomalies present in the Government's approach to publicity in these years, arose over the question of radio advertising. At its very first meeting, the propaganda committee decided to approach the BBC regarding the possibility of special fitness talks, and morning broadcasts of exercises, along similar lines to what was being done in Europe.[310] When Sir Richard Maconachie, the Director of Talks, was queried on the matter in July, he rejected the second suggestion.[311] After the corporation refused to reconsider, the NFC approached the Board of Education and asked it to intervene.[312] At this point, the BBC stated that lack of funds made regular transmissions outside the current time schedule impossible. It was willing to undertake an experiment but only if the NFC provided sponsorship. Because of a misunderstanding, the council believed that a year of broadcasts would cost £17,000.[313] Although the outlay was considerable, it was agreed that the transmissions would be of sufficient value to justify such a large expenditure. The NAC did express doubts as to the 'propriety' of paying the BBC for performing a 'national service', but allotted £3,000–£5,000 towards a three-month experiment.[314] The Board of Education was asked to approve the plan, and to approach the Treasury for an advance on the upcoming budget.

On investigation, the board discovered that a three-month programme would actually cost a maximum of £1,000. The BBC was prepared to pay for the records required and only charge the NFC for incidental expenses such as power. Davidson noted in March that the scheme seemed justified. It was only necessary to convince the Treasury.[315] Confident of the board's support, the NFC appointed a special broadcasting committee in May

[309] Ibid. Propaganda Subcommittee, Minutes, P(38)1, 7 Feb. 1938, ED 113/50. Ellis to Accountant-General, 8 Mar. 1938, ED 113/27. Evan Hughes to Cairncross, 16 Dec. 1938, T 162/530/40020/1.

[310] Propaganda Subcommittee, Minutes, P(37)1, 15 Mar. 1937; P(37)6, 28 Sept. 1937, ED 113/50.

[311] Propaganda Subcommittee, Minutes, P(37)5, 20 July 1937; P(37)6, 28 Sept. 1937, ED 113/50.   [312] NAC, Minutes, NAC(37)6, 14 Dec. 1937, ED 113/48.

[313] NAC, Minutes, NAC(37)7, 10 Feb. 1938, ED 113/48. Ellis to Davidson, 10 Mar. 1938; reply, 12 Mar. 1938, ED 113/27.

[314] GC, Minutes, 3 Mar. 1938; NAC, Minutes, NAC(38)1, 10 Feb. 1938, ED 113/48. Ellis to Accountant-General, 8 Mar. 1938, ED 113/27.

[315] Ellis to Davidson, 10 June 1938; Davidson to Secretary, 7 Mar. 1938; Ellis to Accountant-General, 8 Mar. 1938, ED 113/27.

and entered into further discussions with the BBC.[316] The Treasury soon put an end to the planning, vetoing the scheme in July 1938.[317] The decision provides interesting insight into the rather paradoxical, almost ambivalent, attitude adopted towards official advertising. On one level, the Treasury regarded government publicity as commercial in nature, and thus subject to the restrictions governing all advertisers. Because the BBC licence forbade sponsored programmes, even non-commercial transmissions could not be permitted if a charge was to be levied for them. Conversely, broadcasts emanating from an official body could not be paid for, as the Government might be compelled to fund the BBC every time non-controversial, non-political information had to be transmitted: 'We do not want to drift into the position in which they would be encouraged to expect special financial assistance in respect of any service which is for some reason or another useful to a Government Department.' Almost oblivious to the purpose of the broadcasts, but in keeping with the view that the campaign was meeting an existent demand, the Treasury claimed that if the public wanted such programmes they would already be in progress. None the less, the Board of Education persisted; the president practically begged F. W. Ogilvie, the director-general of the BBC, to fund the experiment.[318] The latter replied that, although the corporation could afford the programmes, it could only justify the expenditure if a regular service was to result. He added that the scheme was economically unfeasible. Thus not until the war were regular physical education broadcasts developed.[319]

Although there was discussion in 1938 of the need for a new approach, the NFC viewed its publicity efforts favourably, and continued to prosecute the campaign in a similar manner.[320] Assessing the actual results of the fitness drive is difficult, for, although it elicited a positive response from the public, there were fundamental problems hindering its success. One was the overwhelming reliance placed on local and voluntary effort. The available network was simply not strong enough to ensure the proper implementation of the scheme. Political and Economic Planning noted that the lack

of any effective voluntary organisations to provide facilities for physical education for men is a serious gap in the existing provision. Moreover, it is making the

[316] ED 113/49. Propaganda Subcommittee, Minutes, P(38)3, 3 May 1938, ED 113/50. NAC, Minutes, NAC(38)3, 28 June 1938, ED 113/48.
[317] Gilbert to Board of Education, 5 July 1938, ED 113/27.
[318] De La Warr to Ogilvie, 3 Nov. 1938; reply, 11 Nov. 1938, ED 113/27.
[319] Hansard, 25 Jan. 1940, vol. 356, cols. 808–9.
[320] Propaganda Subcommittee, Minutes, P(38)1, 7 Feb. 1938, ED 113/50.

Government's plan for encouraging physical education by subsidising voluntary bodies more difficult, since there are few organisations in this field to subsidise, and no nation-wide organisation.[321]

PEP also argued that the entire basis of the campaign was misdirected, asserting that no programme could be successful unless Whitehall was willing to accept greater responsibility for this and other health care tasks:

the Government have relied very largely on unofficial bodies for the execution of the scheme, and have run into serious difficulties on that account. . . . [V]oluntary social work has a great record of achievement but the attempt to force by government grants the rapid development of a flourishing organism possessing all the virtues of voluntaryism raises new dangers and difficulties. At least, if the initiative is to rest . . . with the central government, it seems essential to create a . . . vigorous headquarters personnel able to provide the stiffening, experience and staying power which large-scale and lasting development requires. Even this, however, is by no means enough. We have to face the fact that . . . adults, whatever their educational background, are at present remarkably ill-informed about the care of their bodies. The whole approach is wrong. . . . We need an educational system which will . . . evolve and teach a science of life in which physical education shall become an organic element in general education.[322]

The very fact that health and fitness campaigns were undertaken indicates that the Government had already come some way in recognizing the need for general health instruction. Yet the departments most closely involved had distanced themselves from both schemes, and although they may have signified a change in official attitudes, neither campaign was that revolutionary. On the other hand, they did have long-lasting effects. By 1938, the Ministry of Health had recognized that greater central direction was needed. As noted above, after ten years of argument the department finally agreed to fund the CCHE.[323] True, this ensured a continued reliance on an external body to conduct health publicity, but the ministry also became more active. The department's *Annual Report* for 1937–8 noted a 'new departure' in 'direct contact' with the public; for the first time since Wembley the ministry was planning to participate in large-scale public health exhibitions.[324]

The irony, of course, is that these developments occurred at the very

[321] PEP, *Report*, 344. Also Pilgrim Trust, *Men without Work* (Cambridge, 1938), 298–347.		[322] PEP, *Report*, 350.
[323] See above, p. 186.		[324] MH, *Nineteenth Annual Report*, 1–2.

time when the Government was considering the creation of a centralized publicity organization. When surveyed, the ministry, board, and NFC all opposed the suggestion that they should delegate the planning and implementation of their publicity requirements to an outside body. Each cited its internal expertise, stressing that it alone was qualified to handle its publicity arrangements.[325]

[325] See below, pp. 227–9.

6

'Drink More Milk'

By analysing developments in specific departments, the preceding chapters have illustrated how and why publicity came to be employed in the inter-war years as both a technique and a policy of a number of government ministries. At the same time, an attempt has been made to demonstrate that, while developments varied, departments adopted a similar approach towards both the public and the tool at their disposal. None the less, the lack of a central organization does make it difficult to speak of government publicity *per se*. The comparative approach is best facilitated by examining a case in which more than one department was involved. Thus this chapter will focus on the inter-war campaign to increase liquid milk consumption in Britain.

Milk publicity has been chosen for several reasons. Conducted over the entire period, it involved a number of different campaigns controlled and assisted by a variety of government departments, semi-official bodies, and private organizations. Official advertising was undertaken in 1920, 1928, and between 1935 and 1938. In the intervening period, independent schemes were initiated both with and without government aid. Hence milk publicity lends itself to a comparison of the techniques of government ministries, while at the same time providing further evidence on the relationship between Whitehall and outside organizations in the development and use of publicity. Finally, because it involved both direct commodity advertising and the publicizing of a product in order to facilitate the implementation of other policies, such as appeasing farmers and improving national health, the campaign increases our insight into the manner in which government approached both commodity advertising and the sale of ideas. In this sense, the campaign to improve milk consumption is an ideal example, for it illustrates that, in using publicity to fulfil business and/or public service aims, government departments adopted a consistent approach.

During the inter-war years, milk was often referred to as the cornerstone of British agriculture. In 1938, it accounted for one-quarter of the total agriculture output of the nation and was the major source of income for British farmers.[1] Milk production was ideally suited to British geography and climate, and, owing to transport and storage problems, the liquid product was free from foreign competition. From 1914 to 1939 100 per cent of the home market supply was domestic in origin.[2] Production expanded considerably during the First World War, as a result of the monopoly and wartime price guarantees. Censuses of production taken in 1907–8 and 1924–5 indicate that, between these dates, total output in millions of gallons rose from an estimated 1,144 to approximately 1,288. By 1930–1, the figure was 1,425.5, increasing to 1,589 in 1935–6. Throughout the entire period, approximately 70 per cent of the amount produced left the farm in liquid form, though as this figure included milk sold to factories and creameries for processing into butter, cheese, and other products, it did not represent the community's consumption of fluid milk.[3] Indeed, the consumption of liquid milk in Britain before the First World War was extremely low in both quantitative and relative terms. While annual per capita production between 1907 and 1925 averaged 150–160 pints, per capita consumption averaged 91 pints, well under half the comparable level in the USA.[4] Attempts were made to redress the balance; when the Interdepartmental Committee on Physical Deterioration, appointed after the Boer War to determine why a large proportion of recruits had been of 'C3' standard, reported that inadequate diet was a major factor restricting good health,[5] the Education (Provision of Meals) Act 1906 was enacted enabling local authorities, *inter alia*, to provide milk in schools.[6] Other schemes were introduced to aid the needy in obtaining milk at reduced rates.[7] However, no attempts were made to increase

---

[1] Viscount Astor and B. Seebohm Rowntree, *British Agriculture* (1938), 251. R. B. Forrester, *The Fluid Milk Market in England and Wales*, (1927), p. vii. Astor, 'The Production of Pure Milk', in NFU, *The Year Book of the National Farmers' Union for 1922* (1922), 255 (hereafter NFU, *Yearbook*). Keith A. H. Murray, *Agriculture*, ed. Sir Keith Hancock (1955), 21.

[2] Ministry of Agriculture and Fisheries (MAF), *The Agricultural Output and the Food Supplies of Great Britain* (1929), 35. Astor and Rowntree, p. 251. Hansard, 19 Dec. 1938, vol. 342, col. 2498. Milk Marketing Board (MMB), *An Introduction to Milk Marketing* (1937), 6; *Milk Marketing Scheme* (1939), 46.

[3] Forrester, p. 2. Astor and Rowntree, pp. 285–6. E. H. Whetham, 'The London Milk Trade, 1900–1930', in Derek Oddy and Derek Miller (eds.), *The Making of the Modern British Diet* (1976), 73.

[4] MAF, *Agricultural Output* (1929), 35; *Report of the Reorganization Commission for Milk* (1933), para. 27. Board of Agriculture and Fisheries, Committee on the Production and Distribution of Milk [hereafter Astor committee], *Final Report*, Cmd. 483 (1919).

[5] Noted in Whetham, p. 73.

[6] Board of Education Minute and Report, 15 June 1920, MH 56/74.

[7] Maternity grants were introduced in 1911 under the National Insurance Act, and expanded under the Milk (Mothers and Children) Order of 1918.

consumption amongst the population at large, undoubtedly because milk was recognized to pose serious health hazards.

Legislation designed to ensure clean production and prevent the adulteration of milk dated from the Victorian period, but before the First World War there were no regulations governing the hygiene of the actual product.[8] Thus a large proportion of the fluid milk reaching the market was unsanitary. The Royal Commission on Tuberculosis of 1911 reported that milk was a leading cause of the often fatal disease.[9] Ironically, milk was also an important component in the treatment of the illness. Given the state of the supply, this created obvious problems. In 1902, the millionaire landowner Wilfred Buckley encountered difficulty finding safe milk for his tuberculin-infected child, and as a result established his own dairy, and began to lobby for stricter production regulations, founding the National Clean Milk Society (NCMS) in 1915.[10] Reliant on voluntary support, the society endeavoured to raise hygiene standards, introduce a grading system, and educate the public on the importance of wholesome milk. It attracted noteworthy members, including Sir William Osler, Regius Professor of Medicine at Oxford, and Waldorf Astor, who had chaired a departmental committee on tuberculosis in 1912–13.[11] Improving the supply was regarded as a preliminary step to the wider objective of increasing consumption levels. Yet the society recognized that while increasing demand through publicity was dependent upon the existence of a safe product, only through advertising could a clean supply be secured: 'Coercion will never provide . . . [it]. It is only by education that such a result can be brought about—education of the producer, the distributor, and the consumer.'[12] Thus the NCMS concentrated on encouraging research, and sponsored clean milk competitions, lectures, and films.

During the First World War the Government also began to take an interest in improving the milk supply. With the market in disarray, the Board of Agriculture created a committee in 1917 to investigate the production and distribution of milk. Astor, then Parliamentary Private Secretary to the Prime Minister, was chairman. The NCMS was not officially represented, nor was it invited to give evidence, but Buckley, by then Director of Milk Supplies in the Ministry of Food, was among those

---

[8] Forrester, p. 37.

[9] Cd. 5761 (1911). *Interim Report of Departmental Committee on Tuberculosis*, Cd. 6164 (1912–13). The annual death rate, per million persons, averaged 1,250 from 1910 to 1920; *Health* (29 Oct. 1921), MS Addison, Box 12.

[10] Philip Sheail, 'Hampshire Man and the Quest for Clean Milk', *Hampshire*, Mar. 1981, 60–2.   [11] NCMS, *Campaign for Clean Milk* (1916), 1.

[12] Ibid. 37, 48.

asked to join. The committee sat until 1919 and issued five reports,[13] which centred primarily on means to safeguard the post-war market and ease the transition into peacetime. Confirming the well-known fact that liquid consumption levels were low, the committee emphasized the need to expand the market by improving quality and instilling greater public confidence in the product. It recommended the cleaning up of herds and the implementation of a grading scheme.[14]

Impressed by a grading system introduced in New York in 1912, Buckley had long been advocating the grading of milk.[15] The idea came to fruition; in August 1918, the Ministry of Food and the Local Government Board began granting licences, which enabled those who produced milk of good hygienic quality to charge higher prices than permitted under wartime regulations. Few joined the scheme; by November 1919 only thirty-four licences had been issued, a negligible figure as there were over 100,000 dairy farmers in the country.[16] Producers had little incentive to participate, as they had a monopoly in the fluid market and were receiving high returns under wartime controls. Because liquid consumption levels were low, a portion of the output was manufactured into cheese, butter, and other products.[17] Yet because the prices in both the liquid and manufactured markets were close, this did not present serious problems.[18]

After the war, the situation altered. Unlike its liquid counterpart, manufactured milk had never enjoyed a monopoly. Improvements in transport and cold storage in the 1920s increased foreign competition in the cheese and butter markets. Coupled with the cessation of controls, this drove down the price of these products, thereby reducing the rate manufacturers would pay for milk. A gulf soon emerged between the

[13] Astor committee, *Interim Report*, Cd. 8608 (8 June 1917); *Second Interim Report*, Cd. 8886 (30 Nov. 1917); *Third Interim Report*, Cmd. 315 (5 Nov. 1918); *Report*, Cd. 9095 (1918); *Final Report*, Cmd. 483 (1919).

[14] Astor committee, *Interim Report*, para. 2; *Third Interim Report*, para. 21, Appendix D; *Final Report*, paras. 19–20, 73, 81, 86.

[15] Sheail, pp. 61–2. NCMS, *Campaign*, 11–12.

[16] Two grades, 'A' and 'B', were introduced, Buckley setting the guidelines: Astor committee, *Third Interim Report*, Appendix D. Sheail, pp. 61–2. Forrester, pp. 46–7. In Mar. 1920 the designations were changed to 'A (Certified)' and 'A': Ministry of Health, 'Pamphlet in regard to the Use of Milk' (Oct. 1920); MS Addison, Box 12.

[17] The exact proportions are unclear, because statistics are lacking; MAF, *The Agricultural Output of England and Wales*, Cmd. 2815 (1927), 65; *Report of Reorganization Commission* (1933), 33.

[18] From 1906 to 1914 summertime prices, at the farm, of milk (in pence per gallon) and milk products (with 1 pound of cheese equivalent to 1 gallon) averaged: liquid milk, 5.5; cheese, 6.4; butter, 5.9 (Astor and Rowntree, p. 271).

returns secured in the fluid and manufactured markets.[19] With the onslaught of the world-wide agricultural depression, cheese and butter prices nearly halved, and manufactured milk ceased to be remunerative.[20] A joint price-fixing committee, formed by the National Farmers' Union (NFU) and the National Federation of Dairymen's Associations (NFDA), artificially stabilized prices in the liquid market.[21] However, milk producers were facing higher costs and a growing threat to their monopoly. The Milk and Dairies Order of 1915, which became effective in 1920, placed stricter regulations on the conditions of production, thereby raising overhead costs. Furthermore, fluid milk faced increasing competition from condensed, skimmed, and powdered tinned milk imported from abroad.[22] Tinned milk was safer than its liquid counterpart, as it carried no risk of tuberculosis and was easier to store. It was also cheaper; the price charged to the consumer for a pint of fresh milk averaged 3.25–3.5d. over the interwar period,[23] whereas the comparable cost of powdered milk could be as low as 2d.[24] But critics charged that tinned milk was less nutritious.[25] Producers' organizations lobbied the Government to limit imports, arguing that these products were not processed under clean conditions. In 1927, the Ministry of Health agreed to give greater prominence to the fact that tinned milk was 'unfit for babies', but imports were not curtailed.[26] Thus, increasing the demand for liquid milk became an issue of vital concern to the survival of the dairy industry. The discovery of

[19] MMB, *Introduction to Milk Marketing*, 6–7. Astor and Rowntree, pp. 271–3.

[20] Murray, pp. 17–18.

[21] Prices were stabilized in the 1920s, but fell during the 1930s. Summertime prices paid to producers (in pence per gallon) under the agreement were:

	1924	1926	1929	1931	1933
Liquid price	9.0	10.0	9.0	9.5	9.7
Manufactured price	7.5	8.6	8.2	4.6	5.0

Astor and Rowntree, pp. 272–3. MMB, *Introduction to Milk Marketing*, 6–9. Forrester, p. viii.

[22] Imports of tinned milk increased from 720,800 cwt. in 1913 to 1,250,000 by 1922. Powdered milk accounted for an estimated 12 per cent of per capita fresh milk consumption by 1924. Between 1914 and 1929, consumption of powdered and condensed milk doubled: Hansard, 18 July 1927, vol. 209, col. 17. MAF, *Agricultural Output* (1929), 35–6, 54–5.

[23] Hansard, 20 Dec. 1927, vol. 212, cols. 221–3. *Planning*, 4/96 (6 Apr. 1937), 13.

[24] *Planning*, 4/96 (6 Apr. 1937), 7–8. *Advertising World*, 70/9 (1938), 11.

[25] Hansard, 30 June 1927, vol. 208, cols. 550–1; 1 Dec. 1927, vol. 211, cols. 682, 724; 20 Dec. 1927, vol. 212, cols. 221–3. Sir George Newman, *The Foundations of National Health* (1928), 16. *The Times*, 19 Oct. 1927, 13 Feb. 1928.

[26] In 1919–20 an MH committee investigated the matter: *First Annual Report of the Ministry of Health: Part I*, Cmd. 917 (1920), 58. Regarding protests see NFU, *Yearbook* (1924), 220–2; (1925), 240; (1928), 117, 306. *The Times*, 7, 17, 19 Oct. 1927, 13 Feb. 1928. Hansard, 30 June 1927, vol. 208, cols., 550–1; 9 Feb. 1928, vol. 213, col. 251. Also see 'Report on Condition of Production of Milk (used in preparing condensed milk) in the Netherlands and Denmark', Cmd. 3004 (1927).

'vitamines', the development of the 'science' of nutrition, and research into the causes of diseases such as tuberculosis and rickets, also focused greater attention on the need to improve the national diet, and encourage milk consumption.[27]

In January 1920 the NFDA, in conjunction with the NCMS and various producers' organizations, decided to establish a committee to undertake a national milk publicity campaign. Viewed as a practical application of the recommendations of the Astor committee, the proposal was welcomed in the Ministry of Health, where Astor was serving as Parliamentary Secretary. Richard Cross, who had recently reviewed similar efforts by producers in the United States, thought the idea had potential. As the NFDA had not broached the subject of funding, he assumed it would not be requested. The department was already providing a small subsidy to the NCMS for publicity purposes,[28] but Cross believed this type of expenditure was best avoided, lest the department be exposed 'to criticism for being allied too closely with ... [a] trade organization'. Similarly, he did not think the Government should appoint representatives to the organization, only affording it limited recognition.[29]

Cross, along with officials from the Board of Education and the Ministry of Agriculture, participated in the planning of what was to become the National Milk Publicity Council (NMPC), attending its first meeting in March 1920. When the council announced its intent to seek government funding, Cross raised his aforementioned objections. Although he recognized that a grant would be in the interests of national health, J. F. Blackshaw of the Ministry of Agriculture and Fisheries (MAF), who had served on the Astor committee, agreed that the Government could not engage in what was likely to be construed as trade publicity. There would also be difficulties involved in determining which department should oversee any such arrangements.[30]

None the less, Astor, who later became President of the NMPC on its

---

[27] Post-war studies into the cause of rickets, sponsored by the MRC, confirmed the importance of milk in nutrition: J. C. Drummond and Anne Wilbraham, *The Englishman's Food* (1957), 434–45. Regarding the growing interest in nutrition, and recognition of the value of milk in improving health see MH, *Annual Report of Chief Medical Officer 1919–1920*, Cmd. 978 (1920), 36–7, 43–4, 52. *The Dairyman, Conference on the Milk Question* (1923), 7. Newman, *Foundations*, 14–17.

[28] The ministry also focused attention on the work of the NCMS in its publications and circulars: 'The Use of Milk' (20 Oct. 1920), MS Addison, Box 12. MH, *First Annual Report: Part I* (1920), 57. In 1920 the Society was awarded an annual grant of £1,000; Newman to Secretary, 15 June 1920, MH 55/27.

[29] NFDA to R. B. Cross, 19 Jan. 1920; reply, 28 Jan. 1920; Cross to Morant, 20 Jan. 1920; reply, 23 Jan. 1920, MH 56/74.

[30] Note of Meeting, 18 Mar. 1920, MH 56/74.

establishment in 1922, attempted to use his position in Whitehall to further the cause.[31] In March 1920 he wrote officially to the Board of Education advocating some form of assistance for the new committee: 'there is much to be said for the contention on which the Trade committee lay much stress, that if they put up the funds for a propaganda campaign, the Government besides being merely sympathetic ought to do their part by concerted educational action through all the channels available to them.'[32] Accordingly, Astor suggested that the three departments concerned and the Ministry of Food should meet and discuss what steps could be taken to ensure a wider distribution of information about milk. An inter-departmental conference was held in April. Cross and four others, including Basil Clarke, represented the Ministry of Health. Blackshaw and two officials from the Board of Education were also present, as was Wilfred Buckley, by then Technical Adviser on Milk to the Ministry of Food.[33] The committee assigned general responsibility for promoting milk consumption to the Ministry of Health, but agreed that it was incumbent upon other departments to use any means at their disposal to assist in publicizing the product. The Ministry of Health planned to focus on cleaning up milk supplies by circulating information on the grading system to medical officers of health and the press, and including questions on milk in examinations given to health visitors. The MAF was asked to concentrate on reaching producers, while the board was expected to arouse the interest of teachers, and to prepare, display, and distribute posters and pamphlets through the schools. Buckley ruled out participation by his department, stressing the likelihood of overlapping, but suggested that the NCMS exhibit a film on clean milk production to local health officers.

When these proposals were forwarded to the Principal Assistant Secretaries' committee, the Board of Education vetoed the suggestion that it should prepare and distribute publicity materials.[34] As noted earlier, the board strongly objected to the use of the schools for such purposes.[35] It confined its efforts to educating teachers, upgrading syllabuses, instituting refresher courses, and adding questions on milk to qualifying examinations. The Health and Agriculture ministries also adopted similar tactics. The Ministry of Health issued a 'Pamphlet in regard to the Use of Milk'

[31] The NMPC did not materialize until 1922 because distributors feared an increase in demand would jeopardize their bargaining position *vis-à-vis* producers; Minute, 21 Oct. 1920, MH 56/74.   [32] Astor to Scully Boggs, 22 Mar. 1920, MH 56/74.
[33] 'Milk Propaganda', Note of Conference, 13 Apr. 1920, MH 56/74.
[34] Minute, 15 June 1920; 'Milk Propaganda', Paper 114; Cross to Newman, 2 July 1920, MH 56/74 and ED 50/79. The proposal was removed from the 'Memorandum by the Inter-departmental Committee', Oct. 1920; MH 56/74.   [35] See above, p. 129.

to all local medical officers, district nurses, and midwives. An accompa-
nying circular stressed that it was not meant for general distribution, but
was 'intended to serve as a convenient basis for advice and oral and practical instruction to be given, *as opportunity offers*, by those engaged in local
health services'.[36] The approach was to be as subtle as possible; rather
than blatantly propagandizing about milk, officials were to introduce
the subject into ordinary conversation, informing housewives of the value
of the product, and providing helpful hints on its handling and storage.
Similarly, George Newman was asked to include references to milk in
his speeches, and was provided with a suitable text.[37] In March 1920 the
MAF advised local authorities administering schemes of agricultural
instruction to encourage county educational authorities to sponsor clean
milk campaigns. A pamphlet was issued, outlining everything from the
preliminary arrangements needed (including enlisting the co-operation
of local farmers, and sending instructors to a special course at the Dairy
Research Institute in Reading), to the lecture topics to be covered, and
the order in which they should be presented. Each campaign was to
centre around practical demonstrations designed to teach farmers how to
produce cleaner milk under ordinary conditions.[38]

That general publicity aimed directly at the mass audience was not
contemplated may have been related to the lack of safe milk on the
market, and a fear that any indiscriminate distribution of information on
the need for a cleaner supply would undermine public confidence in the
milk available. Yet it also reflected the Government's reluctance to engage in commodity advertising. By placing an almost total reliance on
local efforts, all three departments were able to distance themselves from
possible accusations of impropriety. In using intermediaries to educate
and inform the general public, they were also adhering to the principle
that influential members of the community—teachers, doctors, and
prominent farmers—were best placed to influence the mass audience.
Testimonials were common in the commercial advertisements of the
period, but this was hardly the same thing, as local officials were not
supposed to proselytize on the subject.

This was the extent of the government campaign. True, the MAF
continued to distribute pamphlets on clean milk, and the grading system
was expanded and revised after 1922;[39] by 1925 the designations were

[36] MS Addison, Box 12.   [37] Cross to Newman, 21 Apr. 1920, MH 56/74.
[38] MAF to local authorities, 29 Mar. 1920, MH 56/74.
[39] NFU, *Yearbook* (1923), 113–16; MAF, Departmental Committee on Distribution and
Prices of Agricultural Produce [Linlithgow committee], *Interim Report on Milk and Milk
Products*, Cmd. 1854 (1923), 54–5.

'Certified', 'Grade A (Tuberculin Tested)', and 'Grade A', ranked in that order. This created no end of confusion, as the public naturally assumed that 'Grade A' milk was the best.[40] Even the Red Cross was confused.[41] Yet in spite of the continuing agricultural depression, and the fact that new sanitary regulations were increasing production costs, neither the new grades nor milk itself was accorded further publicity.

Yet the industry remained under official scrutiny. In response to the worsening economic climate, the MAF appointed a committee in December 1922, chaired by Lord Linlithgow, to investigate the distribution and prices of agricultural produce. It issued an interim report on milk in 1923. After analysing probable causes for the relatively low demand for fluid milk, the committee concluded that consumers were 'influenced more by prices than by statements of dietetic values'. Thus only lower charges would lead to increased consumption.[42] Price reductions were, however, deemed impracticable under present conditions. Moreover, they were recognized to be dependent on an improvement in demand: 'the position with regard to milk is paradoxical, in the sense that the consumer can best cheapen his milk by drinking more of it.' Accordingly, the committee recommended that 'producers and distributors, with the co-operation of the Government Departments concerned, including the Board of Education, . . . should on grounds of child welfare and public health take every means of stimulating the consumption of fresh milk'.

When questioned in parliament regarding his department's probable response to this suggestion, the Minister of Health cited the existence of the pamphlet issued in 1920 as evidence that sufficient efforts were under way to promote milk consumption.[43] The trade disagreed; at a conference held a week after the report was tabled, representatives of the industry observed that there could be no 'progress as regards consuming more milk . . . unless there was something in the nature of a combined campaign of all those interested in the matter'. If the trade had obligations, so too did government:

it would be a good investment on the part of the state to put up £100,000 or £200,000 for the purposes of a great campaign to popularise and extend the consumption of milk. That sort of campaign would really get home to the public imagination and it seemed to be necessary. At present . . . [the official attitude] seemed to be 'A little "knowledge" was a dangerous thing'.[44]

[40] Forrester, pp. 46–9. *The Times*, 5 Dec. 1927. MAF, *Report of Reorganization Commission* (1933), para. 41.   [41] *The Times*, 4 June 1928.
[42] Subsequent references are to Linlithgow committee, *Interim Report on Milk*, 54–8.
[43] Hansard, 9 May 1923, vol. 163, col. 2353.   [44] *The Dairyman, Conference*, 2.

Yet only one measure was adopted as a result of the interim report. Because milk was the responsibility of several departments, the Linlithgow committee had suggested that an independent body, representative of all sides on the issue, should be appointed to provide advice on research and education. Accordingly, a joint MH/MAF Milk Advisory Committee, headed by Lord Kenyon, the chairman of the Agricultural Wages Board, was appointed in March 1924. Aside from Buckley of the NCMS, the members were drawn entirely from the NFU and dairymen's associations. Neither the NMPC nor consumer groups were represented, even though this provoked controversy.[45] Given its broad mandate and strictly consultative role, the committee served more as an exercise in public relations than as a force for change.

Trade efforts were equally limited. Conflicts between producers and distributors, coupled with funding problems, prevented the NMPC from really beginning its work until 1923–4. Despite a high profile and industry-wide representation, the organization faced constant financial difficulties.[46] The joint price-fixing committee inserted a publicity clause in its approved contract in 1924, providing for a small shared levy,[47] but only a fraction of producers and distributors assumed the obligation before it became compulsory in the 1930s.[48] Hence most of the NMPC's early activities comprised internal public relations; the committee concentrated on selling itself to the industry. For example, one of its first projects was feeding experiments, a scheme initiated in order to secure conclusive statistical evidence of the dietary value of milk. The NMPC approached the Board of Education in August 1923 offering to provide a free supply of milk and biscuits to children during school hours. The organization was also prepared to exhibit films to inspectors and teachers, and hoped

[45] Minute of Appointment, 19 Mar. 1924, MH 56/75. Relevant papers are in PRO, Ministry of Agriculture and Fisheries Papers, MAF 52/6/422, MAF 52/6/422A. The committee lapsed in 1928: Hansard, 7 June 1934, vol. 290, col. 1071.

[46] In 1922 the NFU appointed representatives and appealed to its members to contribute to the NMPC. In financial terms the response was 'disappointing': NFU, *Yearbook* (1923), 191–2. However, by 1924 most organizations involved in the milk industry had joined the council.

[47] Each party to the contract was to contribute 1*d*. per 24 gallons bought/sold; NFU, *Yearbook* (1924), 222.

[48] NFU, *Yearbook* (1925), 242. In 1930, the contract stipulated a mandatory payment of 1*d*. per 100 gallons, by both producers and distributors, but only half the moneys collected went to the NMPC; the balance was directed into a joint publicity fund established by the NFU and the NFDA: NFU, *Yearbook* (1931), 479. On the NMPC's funding problems see: Finance Committee, Minutes, 27 Nov. 1928; J. H. Maggs to Blackshaw, 31 Jan. 1929, MAF 52/7/428A. The income for 1930 totalled £7,000; MAF, *Report of Reorganization Commission* (1933), 71.

to send lecturers into the schools. While expressing support, the board refused to circularize local educational authorities on the scheme, and vetoed the lecture campaign, noting that such proposals were not usually countenanced, 'as it would be difficult to discriminate between various types of propagandist'. The council was advised to contact the National Union of Teachers and local officials if it desired to proceed.[49] Two experiments were eventually conducted in Birmingham and Blackburn, with the co-operation of school medical officers, but it was not until 1926 that a full-scale milk-in-schools scheme was initiated.[50]

The main objective of the NMPC was to advance the sale of milk through the 'publication of literature, conferences, lectures, press advertising and all such other means as the Council may think fit'.[51] It modelled its first general publicity campaign on the methods of the National Dairy Council in the United States, which A. D. Allen, the 'Organiser' of the NMPC and former General Secretary of the NFU, had investigated at first hand. Thus the NMPC concentrated on improving milk supplies through educational propaganda at the regional level. Small-scale campaigns were held in specific areas, and literature was distributed to local authorities. Advertising agencies were not employed and newspaper advertising was used only sparingly to draw attention to local efforts.[52] The council's first campaign, forming the model for the 'milk weeks' which were later to become common, took place in Bristol in the winter of 1923–4.

The Bristol 'Use More Milk' campaign centred on lectures and demonstrations at infant welfare centres, clubs, and dairymen's organizations.[53] Ninety-one meetings were held with an estimated total attendance of 7,147. Speakers were advised to emphasize the importance of sanitary production, the need for greater consumption, and the relative cost and nutritive value of milk in comparison to other foodstuffs.[54] The campaign

[49] Memorandum of Interview, 15 Aug. 1923; Bosworth Smith to Newman, 18 Aug. 1923; reply, 21 Aug. 1923, ED 50/79.

[50] 'Milk Schemes in Schools', 1929, ED 50/79.　　　[51] NFU, *Yearbook* (1925), 199.

[52] 'To Members of the NMPC', 9 Feb. 1924. The report is unsigned, but Allen referred to the trip in *Advertising World*, 50/2 (1926), 174–8. Critics of NMPC advertising policy in the 1930s claimed that in its early years the council had allotted 50 per cent of its appropriation to newspaper advertising: *Advertising World*, 60/5 (1931), 332; 65/2 (1934), 64–5. There is no evidence to support this claim, nor to suggest that press publicity was highly valued by the NMPC; see below.

[53] 'Bristol Use More Milk Campaign', 19 Feb. 1924, MH 56/74.

[54] See Astor committee, *Interim Report*, para. 2.

culminated with three larger, yet equally specific, gatherings: Buckley, Allen, and Dr R. Stenhouse Williams, of the Dairy Research Institute, addressed a group of producers; the Lord Mayor spoke to one hundred distributors; and J. H. Maggs, the head of United Dairies, chaired a forum open to the public.

Although it only reached a small audience, the campaign was believed to have been a resounding success. Lacking statistical evidence of the impact exerted on consumption levels, the NMPC based this positive assessment on the numerous requests it had received for more lectures and for the implementation of similar campaigns elsewhere. The trade had expressed 'appreciation of the work done', 'some' producers informing the council that there had been 'a marked effect as a result of the propaganda'.[55] New schemes were initiated in Eastbourne and Leeds, and a model dairy was exhibited at the British Empire Exhibitions of 1924–5.[56] But a shortage of money, coupled with the twisted logic that efforts were most needed in the district where milk consumption was highest, induced the council to confine future activities to London.[57] Lectures, demonstrations, and other personal methods of publicity continued to form the basis of its efforts.[58]

These activities had a negligible effect on consumption levels, and in 1926 the NMPC came under attack from within the trade. The NFU successfully opposed the insertion of the publicity clause in the upcoming contract and advised its members to discontinue subscriptions to the council.[59] This was the culmination of a rift over defamatory remarks about the industry which Buckley had made before the Food Council.[60] Although Ministry of Agriculture officials believed the disagreement stemmed more from personal antagonisms than business considerations,[61] it is of interest to note that the NFU justified its withdrawal from the council by questioning the value of NMPC publicity. In a statement issued in November, the NFU claimed that advertising could only be effective when controlled by those who funded it. Prominent producers, including Buckley(!), were reported to be dissatisfied with the council. Sir William Price, President of the Dairymen's Federation, was quoted as

[55] 'Bristol Use More Milk Campaign', MH 56/74.
[56] Quarterly Report, Jan.–Mar. 1924, MH 56/74. *Advertising World*, 50/2 (1926), 174–8.   [57] Quarterly Report, Jan.–Mar. 1925, MH 56/74.
[58] *Advertising World*, 50/2 (1926), 178.   [59] *The Times*, 17 Sept. 1926.
[60] *The Times*, 9, 10, 15 Nov. 1926. NFU, *Yearbook* (1927), 247–9.
[61] H. E. Dale to Tallents, 6 May 1929, CO 758/51/2.

saying that, whenever making deductions for propaganda purposes, he felt he was 'wronging the farmer concerned . . . since in his view the money was absolutely wasted'.[62] Such negative publicity did little to improve the NMPC's ability to obtain funding, particularly from the Government.[63] The rift was finally resolved in 1930, though the NMPC continued to come under attack for its educative approach to publicity and failure to employ newspaper advertising.[64]

Despite these difficulties, the council expanded its activities in the intervening period. A milk-in-schools scheme was introduced in 1927–8. Unlike earlier government forays into this area, the NMPC arrangements were not directed solely at necessitous children, but were intended to foster milk-drinking amongst the larger public. Schools were invited to form 'clubs', that is, provide facilities for children to take milk during their morning break. The NMPC supplied explanatory leaflets for teachers, and offered two pamphlets for pupils to take home, one a consent form for participation. Local dairies delivered the milk daily in one-third pint bottles, health authorities having verified the safety of the supply. A charge of 1*d*. per bottle was levied. In an effort to popularize the scheme, the council provided straws, and milk containers decorated with red enamel images of the 'Food Fairies': Minnie Mineral, Peter Protein, Susie Sugar, Violet Vitamin, and Fanny Fat. As production costs proved to be high, the latter were soon replaced by bottles bearing the caption 'Milk for Health'.[65]

Limited amounts of press advertising were conducted to promote the arrangements. Some of it was of a popular nature; after the Boat Race in 1928 a picture of one crew, superimposed on a bottle inscribed 'Cambridge won on milk', was inserted in national newspapers. When Gene Tunney became world boxing champion, his 'considered statement' on the importance of drinking milk while in training was similarly employed.[66] Yet most of the publicizing was done through advertisements placed in professional journals. Intended to reach teachers and doctors, they contained everything from details of recent nutritional studies to letters from headmistresses stressing the value of the schools scheme.

[62] Quoted in *The Times*, 10 Nov. 1926.
[63] Dale to Tallents, 3 July 1929, CO 758/51/2.   [64] See above, n. 52.
[65] NMPC, Minutes, 25 Sept., 23 Oct., 27 Nov. 1928, 1 Jan., 26 Mar., 28 May, 25 June 1929; Advertising and Publicity Committee, Minutes, 11 Feb., 8 May 1929; Quarterly Report, Jan.–Mar. 1929, MAF 52/7/428A. 'Milk Schemes in Schools', ED 50/79.
[66] NMPC, Annual Report to 31 Dec. 1928, MAF 52/7/428A.

Blatant publicity was studiously avoided. For example, rather than advertising in *Teacher's World*, the council offered the journal £25 to print a prepared 'editorial' on the reasons why milk should be supplied to children.[67]

Despite the publicity, by 1929, only 7 per cent of schoolchildren were participating in the scheme.[68] The NMPC attributed the figures to the charge levied, and the fact that the novelty value had worn off quickly.[69] There was also a problem in that local officials were apparently unaware of the arrangements, as the Board of Education had refused to inform regional authorities about the campaign. Since the impetus for forming milk clubs had to originate with the schools, ignorance impeded expansion. Not until May 1930 did the board finally issue a circular, outlining the provisions and pointing out that necessitous children qualified for subsidies.[70]

Although the NMPC encountered difficulties in securing government aid, the needs of the dairy industry were not being totally ignored. In 1927, the MAF commissioned R. B. Forrester, a lecturer at the University of London, to conduct an investigation into the market. Forrester estimated that per capita consumption of the liquid product had not altered since 1918, for, although the level now stood at one-third of a pint daily, the majority of people still averaged one-quarter of a pint. The comparable figure for the United States was one pint.[71] After analysing various factors, Forrester concluded that, although price was influential in determining quantities purchased, the elasticity of demand was by no means certain, and cost alone could not explain regional variations. He believed that lack of adequate storage facilities,[72] ignorance of the value of milk, and force of habit accounted for the consumption levels obtaining in Britain.[73] Echoing the Linlithgow report, Forrester recommended advertising as a solution, and observed that a simplified grading system would provide the perfect foundation for publicity. However, he noted that it would be counter-productive to advertise graded milk, thereby

[67] Advertising and Publicity Committee, Minutes, 19 Mar. 1929; NMPC, Minutes, 26 Mar. 1929, MAF 52/7/428A.

[68] Only eighty local education authorities were participating: Memorandum to Inspectors, 23 May 1930, ED 50/79.

[69] NMPC, Minutes, 24 June 1930, MAF 52/7/428A.

[70] 'Milk Schemes'; 'Memorandum to Inspectors', 23 May 1930, ED 50/79.

[71] Forrester, pp. 103–4, 131–2.

[72] As late as 1938, only 1 in 200 people in Britain had a refrigerator, as compared to 1 in 12 in the USA: *Planning*, 6/130 (20 Sept. 1938), 12.   [73] Forrester, pp. 34, 104, 110.

exposing the ordinary product to question, at a time when the former was still in short supply.[74] As there was little financial incentive to join the scheme, by 1927 only 537 farmers produced graded milk.[75] Hence Forrester concluded that it would be better to advertise the idea of milk rather than specific types.[76]

Forrester believed publicity was the responsibility of the trade, but contended that, because health officials were pressing the industry to clean up supplies, they had an obligation to assist in publicizing the better-quality product.[77] After all, public distrust had been engendered by the 'alarmist utterances' of medical officers.[78] The NMPC was a valuable association, but only government, free from the taint of propaganda, could successfully market the idea of milk:

A body organized by, and operating under the aegis of producers and distributors, as a whole, is likely to do the best kind of work in propaganda of the commodity type, but it will gain in strategic position if it carries with it medical and educational experience in its lecturing and teaching efforts, since the community naturally tends to place greater emphasis on disinterested statements than on trade views.[79]

Issued in December 1927, Forrester's report had little impact on any of the relevant government departments. When queried on the recommendations, they continued to stand on their records to date.[80] However, in January 1928 the Empire Marketing Board announced the launching of a campaign to promote milk consumption.[81] The EMB scheme embodied many of Forrester's recommendations, yet it did not represent government acceptance of responsibility for milk publicity. Actually, the new campaign had very little to do with the product itself. As noted in Chapter 2, the EMB had been established in 1926 to encourage the sale of Empire produce in Britain so as to place imperial producers in a better position to purchase British exports. Because its chief objective was to create a positive background against which Empire countries could

[74] Ibid. 49–50.
[75] Ibid. 52. By 1939, 1,438 producers were participating: MMB, *Milk Marketing Scheme*, 34–5.
[76] Forrester, pp. 117, 123. On the coexistence of a shortage and a surplus see Linlithgow committee, *Interim Report*, 55.　　　　　　　　　　　　　　　　[77] Forrester, p. 58.
[78] Ibid. 105. The 'counter-propaganda' of the medical profession provoked criticism throughout the period: *The Times*, 24 Oct. 1927; *Advertising World*, 70/2 (1938), 3; 70/3 (1938), 1.　　　　　　　　　　　　　　　　　　　[79] Forrester, pp. 117–18.
[80] *The Times*, 5 Dec. 1927. Hansard, 1 Dec. 1927, vol. 211, col. 724; 9 Feb. 1928, vol. 213, cols. 250–2.　　　　　　　　　　　　　　　　[81] *The Times*, 13 Jan. 1928.

publicize their wares, the board did not advertise specific commodities.[82] Although it was emphasized that 'Empire Buying Begins at Home',[83] EMB publicity was criticized as being of little value to domestic producers.[84] It was only to placate farmers and improve its image that the board decided to initiate a milk campaign.[85]

The idea of using commodity advertising as a form of public relations originated at a meeting in September 1927 between Tallents, then secretary of the EMB, William Crawford, a member of its publicity advisory committee, and Lawrence Weaver of the London Press Exchange, the board's advertising agent. Crawford and Weaver suggested that £60,000–£120,000 should be budgeted for a two-year scheme centred around a specific product.[86] Liquid milk was chosen for a number of obvious reasons. More British farmers were involved in milk production than in any other agricultural industry. Because a monopoly existed, any benefits secured from advertising would necessarily accrue to them. Consumption levels were recognized to be low and any improvement would help to decrease the growing surplus on the liquid market, and contribute to national health.[87]

The campaign was not intended to represent a departure from the EMB's current policy on commodity advertising. Fearing a precedent, one board member requested, none the less, that the publicity be conducted with a low profile![88] Frank Pick of the LPTB, a member of the board's publicity advisory committee, also expressed disapproval. His comments are worth noting:

I hope . . . that our advertising will attempt to give a general aspect to the problem of milk consumption, and that because we are embarking upon commodity advertising, we shall not adopt the practices which govern commodity advertising in general, though I am inclined to think . . . Crawford had in mind that the form of our advertising should be changed and that in this case we should certainly adopt what may be described as usual trade practices. I can only explain the large [budget proposed] . . . with reference to an ordinary commercial campaign.[89]

[82] EMB, *A Second Year's Progress* (1928), 35; *Empire Marketing Board: May 1928 to May 1929* (1929), 22. [83] *The Times*, 25 Jan. 1928.
[84] Hansard, 29 June 1927, vol. 208, cols. 8–10, 401–2, 524–5; 1 Dec. 1927, vol. 211, col. 725. NFU, *Yearbook* (1926), 242–3; (1928), 278–9.
[85] EMB, *Empire Marketing Board: 1928 to 1929*, 36.
[86] The meeting was 21 Sept. 1927; Note by Tallents; First Subcommittee of Publicity Committee, Minutes, 18 Oct. 1927, CO 758/51/1.
[87] EMB/PC/60, 25 Oct. 1927, CO 758/51/1.
[88] Minute, 5 Oct. 1927, CO 758/51/1.
[89] Pick to Tallents, 26 Oct. 1927, CO 758/51/1.

To date, the EMB had been attempting to market the concept of Empire rather than particular products. As this statement implies, it had not been so doing by engaging in what Pick termed ordinary commercial practices. As noted, the EMB had developed a novel style of advertising, similar to that adopted by the LPTB, but not regarded as commercially viable in most business circles. Pick apparently feared that, in publicizing a specific product, the organization would abandon the sale of ideas. Indeed, marketing concepts was assumed to necessitate the use of different types of techniques than selling commodities.[90] This did not occur, for, although some popular methods of advertising were employed, the board continued to use the same type of appeal. Indeed, this 'exception' to its publicity policy was intended to sell the idea that Empire marketing began at home.[91] Moreover, given the confusing grading system and dangers inherent in advertising quality milk at the expense of the total supply, the board focused on selling the idea that milk was a valuable foodstuff rather than advertising the commodity *per se*.

The campaign was to stretch from April to October 1928. £25,000 was budgeted, and the scheme was contingent on the trade maintaining its existing level of publicity expenditure (approximately £8,000 annually).[92] Tallents informed the NFU that the campaign could be extended to two years' duration, provided the industry agreed to match the EMB's expenditure over the longer period.[93] As this indicates, the Government had not abandoned the principle that the trade should pay for its own propaganda. Although reports prepared in the autumn of 1927 intimated that a campaign of only six months would achieve negligible results, the board proceeded with its plans, confidently assuming that the scheme would continue.[94] The MAF noted that, even if it was not continued, the campaign was bound to be of value, given the 'clearly inadequate' publicity being conducted by the trade.[95]

During the planning stages of the campaign, several members of the board expressed concern lest an emphasis on medical and nutritional data prove counter-productive. As in earlier schemes, it was feared that publishing evidence of the health value of milk might focus attention on the dangers still obtaining from it. On the other hand, the need to counteract

---

[90] See above, p. 51.
[91] EMB, *Empire Marketing Board: 1928 to 1929*, 36.
[92] Note of meeting, 3 Nov. 1927, CO 758/51/1.
[93] Tallents to NFU, 9 Dec. 1927, CO 758/51/1.
[94] Note of meeting, 22 Nov. 1927, CO 758/51/1.
[95] Note of meeting, 3 Nov. 1927, CO 758/51/1.

the negative public image of milk was recognized.[96] The NFU supported this type of approach, advising Tallents that optimum results were likely from a campaign which was based on medical research. It also suggested that, in framing its appeal, the board endeavour to take regional variations into consideration.[97] Despite its withdrawal from the NMPC, it is apparent that the NFU was not entirely at odds with the council's methods. It is unclear whether Tallents approached the NMPC about the campaign,[98] though the council eventually proffered advice. Even if not acknowledged, it is evident that the board modelled its appeal on the NMPC example. Indeed, the campaign centred on the distribution of small posters, cards, and pamphlets. Some press advertising was conducted.[99] Absorbing half the budget, it began on 12 April, with a full-page announcement on the front page of the *Daily Mail* (the premier advertising space of the day),[100] calling attention to the nutritional value of milk. Inserted in a wide variety of newspapers and selected agricultural journals, subsequent advertisements disclosed the results of school feeding experiments undertaken by Dr H. C. Corry Mann.[101] His findings were also published in a pamphlet, 'What Milk Can Do', for which the public was invited to *apply* free of charge. One copy was issued to each of the 18,000 schools on the EMB mailing list, as was a set of four posters accompanied by an explanatory leaflet prepared by George Newman. As well, the EMB commissioned a film illustrating different stages of milk production, which was shown on a screen erected in Victoria Station; displays were undertaken at a number of exhibitions; the Minister of Health gave a broadcast; and lecture notes were issued to all MPs and EMB employees willing to address meetings. The board even came up with a slogan, the strikingly original 'Drink More Milk', which was eventually replaced by 'Take Fresh Milk— and Plenty of it'.[102] The fact that the EMB enlisted prestigious individuals to deliver speeches and lectures indicates that it had not abandoned its dignified approach. Indeed, the posters issued were thought to be rather highbrow. An MP described one as follows: 'Another advertisement was

---

[96] Note of meeting, 6 Jan. 1928; Crawford to Tallents, 8 Dec. 1927, CO 758/51/1.

[97] Note of Meeting, 22 Nov. 1927, CO 758/51/1.

[98] The NMPC is not mentioned in a note by Tallents of 26 Sept. 1927 in which he discusses approaching the NFU and MAF; CO 758/51/1. The records of the NMPC for 1927 are missing.

[99] For details see 'Report on the Publicity Campaign in Favour of Liquid Milk Consumption', 20 July 1928, CO 758/51/2.

[100] G. H. Saxon Mills, *There is a Tide . . .* (1954), 106–8.

[101] On the experiments see Forrester, p. 105.

[102] Publicity Committee, Minutes, 8 Mar. 1928, CO 758/51/1.

one recommending people to drink more milk [*sic*]. I noticed some small capitals printed on the picture, and I crossed the road to read them. They consisted of a Latin motto. I was educated at a classical university but I could not translate those Latin words.'[103]

Before the campaign was even under way, Tallents was advised that it would be difficult to measure its effectiveness owing to a shortage of accurate data on consumption levels.[104] In December 1927, however, Crawford drew his attention to a reference in the Forrester report to the 'testing out' of the results of publicity activities in selected districts. Crawford, who subsequently became a leading exponent of market research,[105] thought the idea had considerable potential:[106] if the board 'could arrange to get such figures during the milk campaign they would afford very valuable material for publicity purposes and would help us much with the farmer on any future occasion [*sic*]'. The proposal was novel; market research was still in it infancy[107] and was far from being accepted as a recognized commercial tool.[108] Tallents did not even respond, and no action was taken to assemble statistical data, either before or after the campaign. Tallents later informed the Select Committee on Estimates that the board rarely attempted to discover if its publicity activities had resulted in a measurable increase in the purchase of Empire goods, as this would entail too much effort: 'If you cared to get a force of inspectors and put them to work methodically through a town . . . you could get quite a good report.' Yet he added, tellingly, that the EMB had 'never felt it worth while, even if we could have got Treasury sanction, to employ any substantial amount of staff on that work'.[109]

Despite a lack of concrete evidence, the EMB claimed that the milk campaign had been effective. Pointing to the 'very extensive editorial publicity', 'uniformly favourable' press comment, and considerable amount of correspondence the scheme had elicited, the board concluded a July 1928 report by stating that a 'considerable measure of success' had been achieved with regard to improving the EMB's image *vis-à-vis* the British

[103] Hansard, 12 Nov. 1928, vol. 222, col. 628.

[104] Quigley to Tallents, 16 Nov. 1927, CO 758/51/1.

[105] Sir William Crawford, *How to Succeed in Advertising* (1931), 6–9. William Crawford and Charles Higham, *Advertising and the Man in the Street* (Leeds, 1929), 8. Mills, pp. 90–4.   [106] Crawford to Tallents, 8 Dec. 1927, CO 758/51/1.

[107] See above, n. 105.

[108] *Advertising World*, 64/5 (1933), 331. T. R. Nevett, *Advertising in Britain* (1982), 150–3.

[109] Select Committee on Estimates (1932), Proceedings, 22 Feb. 1932, mins. 280–1. By the time he joined the GPO, Tallents had changed his stance: see his *Post Office Publicity* (1935), 7.

public. The EMB acknowledged that, although it could not provide proof, it was 'reasonable to suppose' that slight increases recorded in milk consumption levels were 'largely due to the Empire Marketing Board's propaganda'. Asserting that national liquid milk consumption had been increased by 1 per cent, the board stated that the campaign had benefited British producers by £119,000.[110]

These claims were ill-founded. Until it folded in 1933, the EMB was frequently berated for its failure to advance the position of the British farmer.[111] The milk campaign seems to have done little to improve its image. At a meeting of the Council of Agriculture in May 1929, George Dallas, the NMPC delegate, suggested that the EMB resume its milk publicity (the scheme had been abandoned owing to the trade's failure to meet the stipulations outlined earlier, and because of the rift between the NFU and NMPC).[112] To cries of 'hear, hear', Dallas asserted: 'the British taxpayer is providing a million pounds per year . . . and the Empire Marketing Board has scarcely wakened up to realise that the British Isles are a part of the British Empire.'[113] As for the supposed increase in consumption, press editorials published within a week of the conclusion of the campaign deprecated the low level of demand currently obtaining for milk.[114]

Why did the scheme fail? Contemporary sources provide little explanation. The industry was far too busy trying to have the campaign resumed to brand it ineffective. Inquiries such as Forrester's did indicate that income levels exerted some impact on the amount of milk purchased, so price cannot be ruled out as a factor restricting demand. Yet the limited nature and extent of the publicity campaign also hindered its success. Milk consumption was at its lowest level amongst the working classes. Posters with Latin mottoes were unlikely to appeal to this audience, nor was it probable that members of it would send away for pamphlets. It was also apparent that dietetic appeals exerted little influence on the general public.[115] Had the board engaged in market research, it might have been more successful.

Despite concerted efforts by the NMPC and MPs who had served on the Linlithgow committee to convince the Government of its obligation to

[110] 'Report on the Publicity Campaign', 20 July 1928, CO 758/51/2.
[111] Hansard, 18 Mar. 1929, vol. 226, col. 1481; 27 Mar. 1929, vol. 226, col. 2452; 12 Feb. 1930, vol. 235, cols. 386–7. NFU, *Yearbook* (1929), 348.
[112] Minute, 24 July 1928; Hildred to Huxley, 2 Aug. 1928; Minute by Tallents, 25 Oct. 1928; Publicity Committee, Minutes, 25 Sept. 1928; CO 758/51/2.
[113] Council of Agriculture for England, 30th Meeting, 9 May 1929, CO 758/51/2.
[114] *The Times*, 31 Dec. 1928.   [115] See above, n. 42.

engage in additional publicity, no further advertising occurred. When pressed, the administration reaffirmed its support for the NMPC, but refused to aid its activities.[116] Not until a Reorganization Commission appointed in 1933, in accordance with the Agricultural Marketing Act 1931, created a Milk Marketing Board (MMB)[117] was official publicity again considered.

Like earlier investigations into the subject, the report issued by the Reorganization Commission concluded that retail milk prices could not account for the unchanged levels of per capita consumption, or for variations in demand in different geographical areas and income groups. It noted that the mildness of the British climate, coupled with the popularity of tea, which required less milk than coffee, restricted the public's desire and need for milk.[118] Reaffirming Forrester's conclusions, the commission recommended that the MMB should encourage advertising by creating a mandatory publicity fund for the industry:

Commodity advertising is essentially a matter for cooperative action by the beneficiaries: such benefits as accrue from publicity cannot be confined to those who advertise, and equity demands that all should pay for a service from which all benefit. [The scheme] . . . will provide an opportunity that has never before existed . . . of launching an educational campaign financed by all engaged in the industry.[119]

The report did not address the question of government responsibilities in this area. However, speaking in parliament, the chairman of the commission, Sir Edward Grigg, observed that a marketing scheme would not in itself be sufficient to solve the problems of the industry. At least two other measures were 'essential', both of which necessitated government intervention. By far the most important was import regulations, yet, even if they were adopted, 'something should also be done . . . to encourage the demand for milk. That can be done without great cost to the Government with the cooperation of the industry and with cooperation of other Departments. . . . [T]his is also vital to the success of this scheme.'[120]

---

[116] O'Neill to EMB, 21 Mar. 1929; Tallents to Dale, 7 May 1929; Huxley to Wilkins, 2 Sept. 1929; Folkestone to Tallents, 9 Jan., 30 Dec. 1929; reply, 31 Dec. 1929, CO 758/51/ 2. Hansard, 11 Feb. 1929, vol. 225, col. 17; 18 Dec. 1929, vol. 233, cols. 1391–2; 12 May 1930, vol. 238, col. 1458; 29 Sept. 1931, vol. 257, col. 184.
[117] Two boards were created, one handling England and Wales, the other Scotland. All references are to the first body.
[118] MAF, *Report of Reorganization Commission* (1933), paras. 27–30.
[119] Ibid., para. 54.   [120] Hansard, 27 July 1933, vol. 280, cols. 2933–4.

Aside from imposing restraints on imports, the Government did not respond to this statement, nor was the issue of publicity raised during subsequent parliamentary debates. However, Grigg's words were seized upon by the NMPC. In January 1934 Sir Merrik Burrell, the president of the council, suggested that the MMB should function as a 'huge selling agency', and undertake publicity. He, too, advocated the imposition of a publicity levy. Obviously assuming that the NMPC would act as the board's agents were a mandatory levy imposed, he noted that an annual charge of a farthing per gallon on production every May would raise at least £60,000 annually, and allow the council to formulate its plans on a yearly basis.[121]

The MMB did impose a levy, and forwarded the moneys collected to the NMPC under the arrangements prevailing since 1930.[122] Hence, although it assisted milk publicity, the board did not directly participate in advertising. Officials in the MAF gave consideration to applying the 'National Mark' to milk,[123] but decided it would be impracticable, owing to the difficulties involved in explaining the complicated grading system to the public, and/or choosing a grade to advertise.[124] Thus appeals for government intervention did not subside.[125] In February 1934 the agricultural editor of *The Times*, Anthony Hurd, who had long been an advocate of milk publicity,[126] suggested that, as prospects in the industry were so poor, the Government should combine with the NMPC in supplying milk to schools at a low price, 'in order to inculcate the milk-drinking habit in the coming generation'.[127]

Hurd's article was probably a plant, for ten days later the Minister of Agriculture, Walter Elliot, informed Parliament of the Government's intention to pursue a more active milk policy. His statement, subsequently

[121] *The Times*, 24 Jan. 1934.
[122] On the MMB see MAF, *Scheme under the Agricultural Marketing Act 1931, Regulating the Marketing of Milk* (1933). The levy for 1934 was £83,308: Finance Committee, Minutes, 1 Apr. 1935, MAF 52/7/428C.
[123] Introduced in Feb. 1929, the 'Mark' was affixed to products to indicate their quality and British origin.
[124] Minute, 24 Jan. 1935; F. C. White, 'Proposed National Mark Scheme for Liquid Milk', 27 Feb. 1935; Note to Gorvin, 25 Oct. 1935; MAF 34/705. The MH, which controlled the system, refused to change the demarcations lest this further confuse the public; Minute, 24 Oct. 1936, MAF 34/705.
[125] Hansard, 27 Mar. 1934, vol. 287, col. 1807; 7 May 1934, vol. 289, col. 726; 9 July 1934, vol. 292, cols. 51–2; 17 Dec. 1934, vol. 296, col. 826. *The Times*, 24 Jan., 8 May, 9 Aug. 1934.
[126] Hurd to Ryan, 25 Oct. 1928, CO 758/51/2. His father, Percy, was a member of the Linlithgow committee.   [127] *The Times*, 12 Feb. 1934.

published as a Command paper, formed the basis of the Milk Act 1934. Observing that an increase in consumption would be beneficial from both an economic and a public health perspective, Elliot proposed to assist the industry by guaranteeing minimum prices, subsidizing manufactured milk, and earmarking £750,000 for a campaign to encourage the production of a purer supply. Provided the trade agreed to match its grant, the Government also planned to contribute, on a pound per pound basis to a maximum of £500,000 (later altered to £1 million), to a publicity fund to be administered by the MMB. This was contingent on the board submitting an approved programme to the ministry containing, *inter alia*, provision for the supply of cheap milk to schools.[128]

In initiating this scheme, the Government was endeavouring to use a publicity policy to defuse criticism. Just six days before Elliot unveiled his proposals, a group of MPs, including Grigg, had announced the formation of a 'Children's Minimum Committee', to lobby for an improvement in services for young people.[129] Objecting to the anomalies of practice between local authorities in exercising their discretionary powers to provide subsidized milk to children, in March 1934 the committee approached the Minister of Health requesting legislation extending these responsibilities. He replied that persuasion was likely to be more effective than compulsion, and, pointing to the announcement of the publicity scheme, asserted that 'a new epoch was about to open'.[130]

That publicity was intended to serve as an alternative to legislation is suggested by the fact that, in its original form, the Milk Act did not include a schools scheme. An official in the MAF, commenting on the problems involved in determining what constituted legitimate advertising expenditure, noted that the publicity clause, which had 'started from the notion of making good to Milk Marketing Boards the money spent by them in conducting a . . . publicity campaign', had 'developed into the idea of subsidizing certain classes of sales of milk at reduced prices'.[131] Officials in the Ministry of Health feared that, because the Treasury and the MMB were at loggerheads over who should incur losses on the scheme, the entire publicity budget might have to be allocated to funding the schools campaign.[132] In the end, only £30,000 a year could be directed towards conventional advertising.[133] Just as the EMB had included school

---

[128] Hansard, 22 Feb. 1934, vol. 286, cols. 503–7. *Milk Policy*, Cmd. 4519 (1934).
[129] *The Times*, 16 Feb. 1934.   [130] Note of Deputation, 26 Mar. 1934, MH 56/106.
[131] Lindsay to Stocks, 7 May 1934, MAF 52/126/5313.
[132] Minute, 9 Mar. 1934; 'Milk Publicity Scheme', 15 Mar. 1934, MH 56/106.
[133] As the trade matched the grant, annual expenditure from 1935–8 totalled £60,000.

feeding experiments under its marketing arrangements,[134] the MMB treated the supply of milk to children as a form of publicity.

While the nature of the Milk Act 1934 would seem to suggest that the Government had assumed at least partial responsibility for commodity advertising in the national interest, official acceptance of this task was belied by the efforts made to distance civil servants from the administration of the scheme. Officials in the three departments concerned with milk assumed they would be closely involved in the implementation of the legislation. Strongly opposed to the publicity arrangements, lest other industries demand similar subsidies, the Treasury forbade participation, informing administrators 'that the scheme was not a Government scheme'. In an apparent attempt to discredit the publicity policy by showing it to be unwarranted, the Treasury advised 'that the effect of the reduction in the price of milk should be allowed to operate without any direct encouragement by the departments'.[135] Indeed, the Exchequer had only grudgingly accepted the need for a campaign:

Even, therefore, on the basis that the publicity arrangements are left entirely to the Milk Boards . . . and that the publicity scheme is a Milk Board scheme . . . [the Chancellor] felt grave doubts about the publicity grant and only finally assented to it because there seemed no alternative way of securing a large increase of consumption.[136]

The new policy was greeted favourably by the industry and the NMPC.[137] The latter assumed the budget would fall under its control, and began to prepare proposals. The council soon discovered, however, that, as the Treasury could only grant funds to statutory bodies, the scheme would have to be administered by the MMB. Worse still, in order to meet the matching grant provisions of the Milk Act, the NMPC would have to relinquish £30,000 of the publicity levy it was currently receiving from the compulsory clause in milk contracts.[138] With the council up in arms, a compromise was reached whereby control over publicity arrangements was accorded to a committee representative of both the MMB and NMPC.[139] Publicly, it was stressed that this committee had been formed

[134] Select Committee on Estimates (1932), Proceedings, 17 Feb. 1932, mins. 103–7.
[135] Minutes, 8, 9 Mar. 1934, MH 56/106.
[136] Lindsay to Howarth, 1 Mar. 1934, MAF 52/126/5313.
[137] NFU, *Yearbook* (1935), 69–73, 388–9.
[138] Minute by Hildred, 6 Mar. 1935; NMPC, Minutes, 26 Feb. 1935; Publicity Committee, Minutes, 13 Mar. 1935; 'Paper 3: Notes on Suggested Appropriation of £60,000', MAF 52/7/428C.　　　　[139] NMPC, Minutes, 16 Apr. 1935, MAF 52/7/428C.

to prevent overlapping in the activities of these organizations, yet the relationship between the official and non-official campaigns conducted over the period was quite close, and it was generally assumed that no distinction existed between them.[140]

At the first suggestion of the possibility of a government-sponsored campaign, both the ministries of Health and Agriculture had advised the MMB to establish a publicity advisory committee,[141] yet again illustrating a similarity and continuity in Whitehall's approach. The choice of experts followed the pattern adopted elsewhere: the members were Ethel Wood of the Food Council (a veteran of the Telephone Publicity Advisory Committee); Sir Frederick Mander, chairman of an educational publishing company and the General Secretary of the National Union of Teachers; Arthur Jenkins, an alderman and the vice-chairman of the South Wales Miners' Federation; Burrell of the NMPC; Sir Harold Hartley, a director of the Gas Light and Coke company; and Dr John Boyd Orr of the Committee on Nutrition at the Ministry of Health.[142]

Although the board claimed to employ novel methods, MMB publicity followed closely on the type of advertising that had preceded it. The schools scheme, for example, was conducted in virtually the same manner as outlined above, except that the price charged for milk was halved, with the Government compensating the industry for the shortfall. Since milk was being supplied at half the current market rate, most of the publicity funds directed into the scheme were used to subsidize producers. Prices had been lowered because it was assumed that cost had been the chief factor restricting demand.[143] According to MMB figures, the scheme expanded rapidly under its control, but officials were forced to acknowledge a drop-off after the initial surge. By 1939, only 56 per cent of schoolchildren were purchasing milk daily.[144] A Political and Economic Planning study concluded that the arrangements had only been partially successful, 'less because of poverty than because of indifference or prejudice'.[145] Like other measures for the supply of cheap milk,[146] the

---

[140] See Hansard, 17 Dec. 1935, vol. 307, col. 1588; *The Times*, 1 Feb. 1936.

[141] Dale to Maclachlan, 10 Mar. 1934; reply, 12 Mar. 1934; Minute, 15 Mar. 1934, MH 56/106.   [142] *The Times*, 9 Aug. 1934.

[143] MAF, *Arrangements under Section II of the Milk Act 1934 for Increasing the Demand for Milk by the Supply of Milk in Schools at Reduced Rates* (1934); *Revised Arrangements* (1936; 1939). MMB, *Introduction to Milk Marketing*, 15; *Milk Marketing Scheme*, 34.

[144] MMB, *Milk Marketing Scheme*, 34–5.   [145] *Planning*, 4/96 (6 Apr. 1937), 11.

[146] MAF, *Arrangements under the Milk Acts 1934 to 1938 for Increasing the Demand for Milk . . . by the supply of Milk to Nursing and Expectant Mothers and Children under 5 Years of Age at Reduced Rates* (1939).

scheme was criticized as being counter-productive to an overall increase
in general consumption, as supplying inexpensive milk through the schools
supposedly encouraged parents to forgo providing it at home.[147]

The MMB conducted annual advertising campaigns from 1935 to
1938. Like the EMB, it engaged in educational publicity and concentrated on reaching the public through posters and press advertising.[148]
The latter accounted for two-thirds to three-quarters of the yearly
budget of £60,000, divided (in pounds) as follows:[149]

	Press	Posters	Production	Reserve
1934–5	42,000	11,000	—	7,000
1935–6	43,000	12,000	—	5,000
1936–7	36,500	11,000	2,500	10,000
1937–8	32,000	13,000	2,000	13,000

The campaign conducted in 1936 was typical of the board's efforts.[150] It
centred on press advertisements focusing on a milk-in-factories scheme
being introduced by the NMPC, and on NMPC-sponsored 'milk bars'.
Most of the advertisements consisted of articles said to have been written
by 'a Physician', or other professionals. The subject-matter ranged from
the need to encourage milk-drinking within industries employing women
to discussions of the fact that milk was a 'man's drink'. Nutritional and
other scientific data were generally cited in support of the arguments
presented. Testimonials were also given wide circulation.[151] While the
NMPC was employing more popular means of publicity, through its use
of films and the development of milk bars (an alternative to the public
house which served a new concoction called a 'milk shake'),[152] it, too,
endeavoured to educate the public by sponsoring lectures and milk weeks.[153]

None of these activities had any measurable impact on liquid milk
consumption. A second Reorganization Commission, appointed in 1936,
concluded that the marketing scheme had not as yet had an appreciable
effect on demand. Per capita consumption in Britain still averaged under

[147] Note of Deputation, 28 July 1938, MAF 52/147/6982.
[148] For a commentary on MMB publicity see *Advertising World*, 67/7 (1935), 69–70.
[149] For these figures and general information on the campaigns see MAF, *Arrangements
under Section II of the Milk Act, 1934 for Increasing the Demand for Milk . . . by Publicity and
Propaganda*, 4 schemes (1935–8).
[150] For details see MAF 52/145/6765; and *The Times*, 1 Feb. 1936.
[151] These materials are located in MAF 52/145/6765.
[152] By 1937 600 were established: 'About Milk Bars', MAF 52/145/6765. Although
praised, they did not become popular: *The Times*, 4, 7 Sept. 1936, 22, 25 Feb. 1937.
[153] *The Times*, 1 Feb. 1936.

Left : Britain's first Milk Bar. Now a well-known Fleet Street landmark, it offers a day and night service and is extensively patronised.

Right : Brisk business at a well-equipped Milk Bar in Holborn.

Left : Facing the beach at Margate, this Bar is ideally situated for attracting holiday-makers.

9 Ministry of Agriculture Photographs: Milk Bars

one-third of a pint per day;[154] this was well under four times the recommended level for children and half that suggested for adults.[155] Britain
ranked eleventh behind most other Western nations in a survey on milk
consumption conducted by PEP in 1937.[156] Correspondingly, the report
of the Advisory Committee on Nutrition of the Ministry of Health,
and John Boyd Orr's *Food Health and Income*, both published in 1936,
focused renewed attention on the almost negligible consumption of milk
by the working class. Boyd Orr's investigations indicated that finances
determined the nutritional level of each individual's diet, and he blamed
high prices for the low demand for milk.[157] PEP agreed, noting that, while
Britain ranked eleventh in terms of consumption, the price of a pint of
milk was much higher than that charged in most European countries.[158]
The Reorganization Commission, of which Boyd Orr was a member, concluded that publicity had not yet had an appreciable effect on demand
because success was dependent on lower prices. On the other hand, it
agreed that income variations alone could not account for the prevailing
levels of consumption. Working from the now accepted assumption that
the demand for milk was relatively inelastic, the commission suggested
that the MMB should increase its publicity activities and adopt a public
relations policy.[159]

In 1935, a similar commission investigating the eggs and poultry industries had devoted a section of its report to the question of co-operation
between the various marketing boards. It had recommended the creation
of a central publicity department to co-ordinate the advertising of all
products included under marketing schemes.[160] The milk commission
supported this proposal and went further in expressing

doubt [as to] whether the agricultural marketing boards have fully appreciated
the significance of their relations with the public: the success, if not the very
existence, of any marketing scheme must depend ultimately on the reactions of
consumers and public opinion. . . . The fullest publicity should be sought, and
well-informed discussion and comment should be welcomed.[161]

---

[154] MAF, *Milk: Report of the Reorganization Commission for Great Britain* (1936), 117–21.
[155] These were standards set by the Ministry of Health's Advisory Committee on Nutrition; quoted in *Planning*, 5/97 (20 Apr. 1937), 14.
[156] *Planning*, 4/96 (6 Apr. 1937), 13.
[157] Both are summarized in *Planning*, 4/96 (6 Apr. 1937), 1–15.
[158] The price of a pint (in pence), in October 1934, was 3.25 in England, as compared to
1.6 in Sweden, or 2.3 in the Netherlands: *Planning*, 4/96 (6 Apr. 1937), 13.
[159] *Milk* (1936), 268, 279–80.
[160] MAF, *Eggs and Poultry: Report of the Reorganization Commission for England and
Wales* (1935), 150–51.
[161] p. 268. *Advertising World* praised the idea; 67/8–9 (1935), 9.

In 1937, the Government published a White Paper on milk embodying the commission's recommendations, which served as the basis for a new policy adopted in 1939.[162] Despite the commission's emphasis on the need for further publicity, the subject was not discussed here. Moreover, in 1938 the Government dropped its £30,000 publicity grant to the MMB. It is difficult to ascertain why, as the decision was not publicized, nor the matter raised in parliament and the press.[163] The issue may have been ignored because the school feeding scheme was not affected. Behind the scenes, the MMB cited the withdrawal of the stipend to back its unsuccessful petitions for more funds to be directed into the school feeding project.[164] The NMPC withheld comment, hardly surprising as it was now no longer required to relinquish funds to the MMB. The timing of the decision is extremely paradoxical: in the first place, the general policy outlined in the White Paper rested on the assumption that milk consumption levels would undergo a steady increase in the next five years.[165] Secondly, in 1937 the Government was embarking on a national fitness campaign, which many claimed would only be successful if backed by a general nutrition policy. Indeed, with the publication of studies such as Boyd Orr's report, nutrition was becoming a serious political issue.[166] Finally, a number of studies published in 1937–8 indicated that milk consumption was still far too low, and was unlikely to rise. The most influential of these was K. A. H. Murray's *Milk Consumption*. Using the new technique of market research, Murray had conducted a detailed analysis of the dietary routines followed in 500 Oxford households. His conclusions resembled Forrester's:

The difficulties in the way of increasing the consumption of milk are partly lack of purchasing power and distaste, but possibly the biggest obstacles are antipathy, indifference and prejudice. The existence of wide variations in the purchases of milk between households with similar food expenditures suggests that milk consumption could be doubled without raising income levels if the consumer can be induced to do it. . . . Extensive advertisement may be a better investment than lower prices. . . . Nor can it be said to be anti-social, if it is in the national interests to increase the consumption of liquid milk.[167]

---

[162] *Milk Policy*, Cmd. 5533 (1937). MAF, *The Milk Marketing Scheme, 1933, as amended to 3rd Aug. 1937* (1938). MAF, *Scheme under the Agricultural Marketing Acts 1931 to 1933 Regulating the Marketing of Milk Products* (1939).

[163] MMB, *Milk Marketing Scheme*, 36–7, 46.

[164] Note of Deputation, 28 July 1938, MAF 52/147/6982.

[165] The MMB and the industry claimed the goals were unrealistic: Baxter to W. Morrison, 4 Oct. 1937, MAF 52/147/6982. NFU, *Yearbook* (1938), 400–1.

[166] See above, pp. 170–1.

[167] K. A. H. Murray and R. S. G. Rutherford, *Milk Consumption Habits* (Oxford, 1941), 7.

Others, notably Astor and Rowntree, who published a study in 1938 dealing with agriculture in general, continued to maintain that price was the major factor restricting demand. It was noted that milk consumption had only increased slightly in response to the publicity conducted in recent years.[168] In the absence of evidence, one can only conjecture, but it seems likely that it was this type of argument that induced the Government to suspend the MMB campaign.

There are a number of reasons why milk publicity was ineffective during the 1930s. In the first place, it is clear that, although there was an element of continuity in the publicity conducted over the period, most of the campaigns were short-lived and sporadic. Relatively speaking, they were also limited in scope. From 1935 to 1938, the MMB was spending approximately £60,000 annually in this area, and the NMPC, £40,000–£50,000. To put these figures in context, it might be noted that in 1936 the Brewers' Association allocated £1 million towards the advertising of beer and ale.[169] Milk publicity was simply not competitive in the marketplace. There is evidence to suggest that the overriding emphasis placed on the nutritional value of milk in every campaign might have been misguided. A study published by Crawford in 1938 indicated that 70 to 90 per cent of the population ignored advertisements about dietetics.[170] It appears that both the MMB and the NMPC were out of touch with their audience. PEP claimed that, as producers had made little effort to investigate 'how much . . . [consumer] demand amounts to, how it varies and why, or whether it could be increased and if so how', they were doing nothing more than 'trying to sell things in the dark'.[171] Not until 1938 did the MMB begin to engage in market testing 'on a large scale', in order to ensure that any future advertising would 'follow the right course'. Interestingly enough, it employed the institute which had sponsored Murray's investigation.[172] Finally, the role of price and income cannot be ignored. Milk consumption levels soared during the Second World War as the Government expanded its social welfare policies and made greater provision for the supply of *free* milk to children.[173]

Success or failure, the campaigns provide important insight into the way in which government approached the use of publicity in the inter-war

---

[168] Astor and Rowntree, p. 252. The MMB also believed price was the key factor limiting demand in low-income households: *Milk Marketing Scheme*, 35–6. Also, *Advertising World*, 70/9 (1938), 11–19.

[169] 'Meeting of the Astor Committee on 6 Nov. 1936', MAF 52/145/6765. Also see Publicity Committee, Minutes, 10 Nov. 1937, MAF 52/254/326A.

[170] Quoted in *Planning*, 6/130 (20 Sept. 1938), 11.

[171] *Planning*, 5/98 (4 May 1937), 5–6.   [172] MMB, *Milk Marketing Scheme*, 42.

[173] Richard M. Titmuss, *Problems of Social Policy* (1950), 509–10, 516.

years. Shying away from any suggestion that it had an obligation to undertake commodity advertising, even in the national interest, Whitehall distanced itself from direct involvement when, and if, such campaigns became unavoidable. This was largely a result of the Treasury's influence. The milk campaigns illustrate what seems to have been a characteristic feature of domestic publicity in the inter-war period; official propaganda tended to be merely semi-official. The widespread use of advisory committees and voluntary bodies to assist in publicity campaigns distanced officials from direct input or control over the arrangements. If, by 1939, the MAF, Ministry of Health, and Board of Education had considerable experience of publicity, it is questionable to what extent officials within these departments had acquired direct experience in publicity work. Yet by the late 1930s they, along with most other departments in Whitehall, were sufficiently confident in their own abilities to question the need for any form of central publicity organization.

7

Centralization Rebuffed: 1935–1946

DURING the inter-war years the subject of government publicity was given consideration in a wide variety of spheres, as the importance of information and public relations to the democratic process was increasingly recognized. Official publications, ranging from George Newman's pronouncements on national health[1] to the report of the 1928 Royal Commission on Museums and Galleries, focused on the State's responsibility to inform the public about available services and facilities.[2] Well before the onset of the Second World War pressure was being exerted from outside Whitehall for the creation of an official publicity bureau to handle domestic issues.[3] Although the Government drew criticism for its seeming reluctance to undertake concerted and consistent publicity, it is apparent that by the 1930s many departments were active in this area. The cost of staff employed wholly or partially on press, intelligence, and/or public relations work rose from £18,650 in 1930–1[4] to £137,607 by 1937–8.[5] Furthermore, the officials involved became identifiable, as most departments began to establish permanent publicity machinery.[6]

---

[1] See above, Ch. 5 n. 3.

[2] The commission was criticized for the fact that little was done to publicize the national collections; it could see no reason why 'artistic' advertisements should not be employed to this purpose: *Final Report from the Royal Commission on National Museums and Galleries: Part I*, Cmd. 3401 (1929), paras. 22, 26. Advertising was eventually permitted in isolated cases: Treasury to British Museum, 20 May 1930, T 162/155/29346/1. However, as late as 1938 general advertising was not sanctioned, and galleries relied largely on space provided free; see correspondence in T 162/980/36055/01/1.

[3] Charles Higham, 'A Ministry of Publicity', *The Times*, 25 Apr. 1933. Callisthenes, 'A Ministry of Publicity', *The Times*, 29 Apr. 1933. Frank Pick, 'Government Publicity', *The Times*, 10 Aug. 1933. *Planning*, 1/14 (21 Nov. 1933), 5–11. *Advertising World*, 66/2 (1934), 11. As noted in Ch. 2, the subject was not frequently discussed within Whitehall, but as early as 1934 Kingsley Wood recommended the creation of an inter-departmental committee of publicity officers to facilitate the exchange of ideas: 'Publicity', 12 Mar. 1934, MH 78/147.   [4] J. Simon to H. Morrison, 11 Jan. 1938, T 162/971/12190/01.

[5] *Report from the Select Committee on Estimates* (1938), appendix 3, table 1. 'Advertising and Publicity in Government Departments', c.Mar. 1938, T 162/479/36055.

[6] As noted in Ch. 2, the staff employed in 1930 is difficult to identify. A list compiled in 1934 indicates that every department, save the Home Office, HMSO, Ministry of Pensions, Scottish Office, and the Office of Works, had a press officer: 'Press Officers', Mar. 1934, T 162/337/30623. From the Civil Service lists it is possible to identify press officers in only nine of the eighteen departments so listed: *British Imperial Calendar* (1935). By 1938

Changes in publicity expenditure are not as easily measured, because it was not until 1937–8 that a serious attempt was made to secure comprehensive figures.[7] This would suggest that, to date, spending had been relatively minimal. A 1938 survey indicated that in the previous year departments had spent £381,703 on advertising and publicity, exclusive of salaries.[8] In fact, the amount was much higher, as this figure did not incorporate the printing costs of departments without a fixed budget on the HMSO Vote.[9] Moreover, in tabulating expenditure levels, departments used different criteria to define their publicity activities.[10] For example, the GPO did not include the over £4,000 cost of producing the *POM* or *TSB*, as it did not consider these publications (which served a public relations purpose within the department) to fall under the heading publicity.[11] Similarly, the Board of Trade omitted figures pertaining to exhibitions it sponsored, and the Office of the Commissioner for Special Areas excluded publicity grants made to unofficial organizations.[12] Finally, the statistics did not reflect the advertising which departments obtained free, through the display of posters in government offices, and/or on sites lent by the LPTB.[13]

Publicity arrangements in Whitehall first came under general scrutiny in 1938, when the Select Committee on Estimates decided to review the subject.[14] Given the committee's mandate, the investigation was evidently

seventeen departments employed press and/or public relations officers and identified them as such in their staff lists: *Report from the Select Committee on Estimates* (1938), appendix 3, table 1; *British Imperial Calendar* (1938).

[7] Not until 1949 was an annual statement prepared showing the cost of government information services: Committee on Home Information Services (1949), paras. 13–14.

[8] *Report from the Select Committee on Estimates* (1938), appendix 3, table I.

[9] Only seven departments had fixed limits for printing expenses. Their allowances (in pounds) for 1937–8 were: GPO, 25,000; MH, 18,500; MAF, 4,000; Department of Health, Scotland, 2,250; Department of Agriculture, Scotland, 250; Ministry of Labour, 7,500; NFC, 10,500: ibid., appendix 3, table IV.

[10] L. Bridges, Minute, 8 Mar. 1938, T 162/981/36055/02. Playfair to Barker, 20 Dec. 1937; Minute, 23 Dec. 1937, Note to Rae, 27 Dec. 1937, T 162/971/12190/01.

[11] GPO to Treasury, Feb. 1938, T 162/981/36055/01/2.

[12] BT to Treasury, 31 Jan. 1938, T 162/980/36055/01/1. Office of the Commissioner of Special Areas to A. E. Banham, T 162/981/36055/01/2.

[13] Many departments secured publicity through these means. See correspondence to the Treasury from: Wallace Collection, 17 Jan. 1938, National Portrait Gallery, 10 Feb. 1938, T 162/980/36055/01/1; Ministry of Labour, 4 Feb. 1938, T 162/981/36055/01/2; NFC, 7 Feb. 1938, Admiralty, 8 Feb. 1938, T 162/981/36055/01/3.

[14] Home information services were not the subject of a general inquiry until 1949, when the Committee on the Cost of Home Information Services was appointed by the Treasury to examine departmental expenditure in this area. The chairman was Sir Henry French, a retired civil servant and the director-general of the British Film Producers Association. The other members were A. P. Ryan, by then the literary editor of *The Times*, and three civil servants: S. Bailey, J. Crombie, and E. Nicholson.

a response to growing expenditure in this area. Timing also suggests that it was related to the rise in international tension and the Government's consequent concern with Britain's foreign image. The inquiry was carried out alongside a study chaired by Sir Robert Vansittart, the Permanent Under-Secretary to the Foreign Office, into the feasibility of co-ordinating overseas publicity arrangements.[15] Although the two investigations were not directly linked, the Government was becoming conscious of the influential role of internal publicity in influencing the manner in which Britain was perceived abroad. An inter-departmental committee of Whitehall press officers was established in 1938, for example, to co-ordinate the release of domestic news items likely to have a positive impact outside Britain.[16] Correspondingly, officials expressed concern when a new tax was placed on films, lest newsreel companies begin to portray the country unfavourably.[17]

The estimates committee was extremely critical of the publicity arrangements prevailing within Whitehall, citing the lack of co-ordination between the various departmental branches, and the fact that they were admittedly oblivious to each other's methods, procedures, and campaigns. Noting that success in advertising and public relations required long experience, not 'expected to be found already existing in Government Departments, to whose duties these activities were . . . a comparatively novel addition', the committee censured departments for failing to establish 'contact with commercial firms which advertise extensively and have already experience of results extending over many years'.[18] The GPO, alone, escaped criticism, because it employed an advisory committee composed of such experts.[19] A number of departments did maintain similar machinery,[20] but the estimates committee was ill-informed on this point, because it only took evidence from the Admiralty, War Office, Ministry of Labour, GPO, and Board of Education. Impressed by the GPO example, the committee recommended the creation of a single advisory body, 'constituted in the main of representatives of commercial or industrial firms which incur large expenditure on advertising', to which

---

[15] Philip M. Taylor, *The Projection of Britain* (Cambridge, 1981), 216–55.
[16] Ibid. 225.   [17] *Ad hoc* meeting, 3 May 1939, T 162/531/40335/1.
[18] Select Committee on Estimates (1938), para. 24.   [19] Ibid.
[20] The DOT committee was composed mainly of businessmen; see above, p. 41. The MAF had decided not to form a committee because William Crawford acted as a consultant. Yet it did seek the assistance of trade committees as to the forms of publicity best suited to national mark commodities: N. Loughnane to Robinson, 28 Mar. 1934, T 162/978/30201. Several of the marketing boards also employed special committees; see above, p. 218. The NFC had a Propaganda Committee, but it contained no 'expert[s] in the matter of publicity': Select Committee on Estimates (1938), Proceedings, 4 Apr. 1938, min. 1625.

all departments would be compelled to refer their publicity plans. Unlike the Post Office committee, its functions were to be 'explicitly critical'; rather than originating campaigns, this body was to comment on the practicality of schemes presented for consideration, and 'advise generally upon the relative magnitude of the expenditure proposed by different Departments'.[21] Although E. T. Crutchley of the GPO thought the idea of a critical committee was novel,[22] the projected organization closely resembled the defunct ACGA, in purpose if not in composition.

The Treasury responded favourably by establishing an Inter-Departmental Committee on Publicity Expenditure (ICPE), in October 1938, to consider the feasibility of placing publicity arrangements under the control of one body. This was despite the fact that all departments previously consulted had informed the Treasury of their opposition to centralization.[23] Although preparations for a wartime propaganda ministry were already under way, the new committee had no formalized contact with the planners, and was not established with the international crisis in mind; the impetus behind its deliberations was clearly financial.[24] Under the chairmanship of A. P. Waterfield, a career civil servant involved in the planning of the MOI, the ICPE drew its membership from the public relations and/or press divisions of departments which engaged in publicity on a large scale.[25]

While several ministries welcomed the concept of a central advisory body, all objected to the idea that it should have executive authority. As C. B. Coxwell of the Admiralty pointed out, his division often engaged in campaigns on relatively short notice and could not afford the risk of delay that obligatory consultation with an outside agency would entail.[26] Major-General Beith (the author 'Ian Hay'), who was public relations officer at the War Office, advanced similar arguments, noting that fluidity and the ability to seize opportunities were essential to successful publicity. He also claimed that the creation of such a powerful central committee would

[21] Select Committee on Estimates (1938), para. 24.
[22] Crutchley, 'Report of the Select Committee on Estimates, 1938', Oct. 1938, T 162/530/40020/1.
[23] *Report from the Select Committee on Estimates* (1938), appendix 3, table V.
[24] Cairncross, 'The Report of the Select Estimates Committee on Government Publicity', 10 Oct. 1938, T 162/530/40020/1.
[25] The members were Crutchley (GPO), C. Coxwell (ADM), Maj.-Gen. Beith (WO), C. Robertson (AIR), L. Reynolds (AIR), A. Manktelow (MAF), T. Chegwidden (ML), A. N. Rucker (MH), E. Hughes (NFC), T. Walker (Scottish Office), N. G. Scorgie (HMSO), R. Kingham (NSC), G. Stedman (MT), S. Harris (HO), and J. Cairncross, secretary; Minute to Rae, 15 Oct. 1938, T 162/530/40020/1.
[26] Coxwell to A. F. James, 24 Mar. 1938, T 162/479/36055.

circumvent traditions of sound administration; Beith maintained that when a directorate within a department had been created to perform specialized duties, it should be given an entirely free hand subject only to Treasury oversight.[27] Crutchley, who believed it would be valuable to create an advisory council, albeit with separate units tailored to the varying standards of experience and efficiency in different departments, also observed that ministerial responsibility might be usurped were this body accorded executive authority.[28] Ironically, as recently as 1934 the Treasury itself had used similar arguments when refusing a suggestion to centralize official publicity arrangements.[29]

Many officials also questioned the value of the current proposals. Crutchley and his colleague G. E. G. Forbes agreed that, while some departments were so inexperienced as to require external assistance, restrictions should not be imposed upon qualified divisions such as their own at the Post Office. Noting that his branch had assembled a 'very considerable knowledge' of advertising, Forbes observed: 'we can see no advantage and much duplication of work in having to explain to the Stationery Office on each occasion the type of work we want and to agree with that Department in the selection of the appropriate agents.'[30]

The GPO was not alone in claiming that it was best placed to supervise its own publicity, nor in questioning the qualifications of outsiders to provide advice. Just as they had in 1920, when blocking centralization in the ACGA, departments stressed the importance of their internal expertise. The Ministry of Labour's reply typifies Whitehall's reaction to the proposals:

Centralization of publicity of the various sub-sections of this Ministry in the hands of one Branch has proved satisfactory but in view of the specialised nature of those parts of the Department's work which require publicity it would not make for greater efficiency to hand this work over to another Department having no knowledge of the Department's special needs and peculiar relationship with its public.[31]

---

[27] Beith, 'Inter-Departmental Committee on Publicity Expenditure', 9 Jan. 1939, T 162/530/40020/2.   [28] Crutchley, 'Report', Oct. 1938, T 162/530/40020/1.

[29] In 1934, Francis Meynell, a journalist, suggested that the Treasury appoint an officer to oversee all government publicity activities. Noting that press and public relations bureaux were already in existence in many departments, the Treasury replied that new arrangements would be impractical; even were the Government starting from a 'clean slate', centralization would be problematical in view of the constitutional responsibilities of ministers: Meynell to Treasury, 27 Mar. 1934; Rae to Meynell, 9 Apr. 1934, T 162/978/30201.

[30] Forbes to James, 18 Mar. 1938, T 162/479/36055.

[31] Ministry of Labour to James, 19 Mar. 1938, T 162/479/36055. Also see Select Committee on Estimates, Proceedings, 30 Mar. 1938, min. 1535; 4 Apr. 1938, min. 1787.

As this implies, by 1938 publicity work had reached such a level of acceptance in government departments as to be regarded as no different from any other responsibility undertaken. Those directly involved saw no need to treat information and public relations activities as aberrations from the norm.

The only ministries which supported centralization were the Treasury and the HMSO, both for financial reasons. They objected to the fact, for example, that departments were allowed to place their own press advertisements, as cheaper rates were secured when this was handled through the Stationery Office. By 1937, only five departments had entered into independent arrangements with agents, yet the former spent approximately £60,000 per year on newspaper publicity, whereas annual expenditure for all other ministries averaged £74,000 under the HMSO contract.[32] However, by 1938 a number of departments planning major campaigns, including the Ministry of Transport and the armed services departments, framed schemes including large appropriations for display advertising in the press. Following the example of the GPO and DOT, they did not intend to use the government agents to supervise these arrangements.[33] Alarmed by the growing trend, the Treasury decided to ban all press advertising, except classified.[34] Antipathy to display advertising stemmed both from its cost and from the assumption that, once the press was paid to print notices, it became less willing to provide free editorial coverage to departmental news. The Treasury also opposed this method of advertising because it believed it was 'used not merely for the achievement of direct and specific objects . . . but for "background" publicity'.[35] As the introduction of a ban sparked controversy, the ICPE was asked to investigate the Treasury's claims.[36] Departments argued that it

[32] The GPO, DOT, NSC, Department of Health for Scotland, and the State Management Districts had independent contracts: Select Committee on Estimates (1938), Appendix 3. The GPO spent most of its budget on display advertising; Post 33/2903 (7, 8, 10). Regarding the HMSO contract see above, pp. 29–34.

[33] G. Stedman to Waterfield, 30 Jan. 1939, T 162/530/40020/2. Note by Bridges, 8 Mar. 1938, T 162/981/36055/02.

[34] A circular was not issued, but departments submitting new proposals were advised to drop display advertising from their plans; the NFC is an example; see above, p. 190. Display advertisements were more expensive than classified because they were costed by inch rather than by line. They were also subject to the price-fixing agreement set in 1921, whereas classified advertisements were not: Hale to Waterfield, 29 Jan. 1940, INF 1/341. Waterfield to Stedman, 1 Feb. 1939, T 162/530/40020/2.

[35] ICPE, 'Report on Display Advertising', Feb. 1939, T 162/530/40020/2.

[36] Waterfield to Stedman, 1, 3 Feb. 1939, T 162/530/40020/2.

was unfair of the Treasury to proscribe any one means of distributing information.[37] Officials denied the allegation that display advertising restricted editorial publicity, asserting that newspapers only engaged in the latter because they were already being patronized. Moreover, it was noted that the press only provided free coverage to newsworthy information.[38] There were strong grounds for this argument; provincial papers already refused to publish Post Office articles because the GPO did not accord the regional press a share of its advertising budget.[39] By 1939, the Newspaper Society was registering a general complaint that few departments advertised in provincial papers, instead expecting the latter to cover by editorial publicity a considerable amount of information which ought to have been conveyed through purchased space.[40]

Critics of the Treasury decision also argued that it would be pointless to employ a committee to advise departments on their advertising plans, if the Exchequer could intervene at will and refuse to sanction recommended expenditure.[41] Finally, departments defended their use of background publicity by claiming that it did meet specific ends. Noting the high levels of employment presently obtaining, Coxwell maintained that the Admiralty could not hope to attract recruits through classified advertisements.[42] Surprisingly, however, no one attempted to defend background publicity *per se*. The ICPE suggested a compromise, concluding that, while a total ban would be unreasonable,

display advertising should normally be used only for the furtherance of a particular object . . . which experience shows that the Press cannot be induced to print free of charge; and that it should not be used for general or background publicity save for exceptional reasons on which the Treasury would be required to be satisfied.[43]

In its final report to the Treasury, the ICPE observed that, given opposition in Whitehall, the co-ordination of all government advertising under one central body was impractical. Instead, the committee

[37] Stedman to Waterfield, 30 Jan. 1939, T 162/530/40020/2.
[38] 'Use of Display Advertising by the Admiralty', Coxwell to Cairncross, 31 Dec. 1938, T 162/530/40020/1. Stedman to Waterfield, 16 Feb. 1939, T 162/530/40020/2.
[39] See above, p. 108.
[40] 'Deputation from the Newspaper Society', 1 Dec. 1939, T 162/531/40335/3.
[41] Stedman to Waterfield, 30 Jan.; 2 Feb. 1939, T 162/530/40020/2.
[42] Coxwell to Cairncross, 31 Dec. 1938, T 162/530/40020/1.
[43] ICPE, 'Report on Display Advertising', Feb. 1939, T 162/530/40020/2.

recommended the formation of a standing Inter-Departmental Coordinating Committee on Government Publicity (ICCGP) to serve as a forum for discussion between the various information services, and suggested that panels of outside advisers be created to assist each ministry engaging in advertising.[44]

The ICCGP was established in the spring of 1939, with virtually the same membership as the ICPE.[45] At a preliminary meeting on 20 April, it was agreed, Scorgie of the HMSO protesting, that the committee should not endeavour to assess departmental estimates, but merely compare advertising methods and their application in given sets of circumstances.[46] Hence meetings were planned at six-week to two-month intervals.[47] The first task of the committee was to assemble the proposed advisory panels. Following the recommendations of the estimates committee, it was decided that these bodies would not include politicians, newspapermen, or advertising agents, but only representatives of commercial firms which engaged in publicity.[48] Originally, each department was to have been assigned its own committee, but as many requested the same individuals, and the ICCGP concluded that a limited number of 'suitable experts' was available, departments were grouped together under the headings trade and industry, social services, and service ministries, and only three were created.[49] As this indicates, all concerned had a relatively clear idea of the type of advisers required, that is, representatives of firms that had been engaging in dignified advertising in the commercial sphere. S. C. Leslie, the public relations officer of the Gas Light and Coke company, appeared on the lists submitted by the Admiralty, Air Ministry, Lord Privy Seal's department, MAF, DOT, and Ministry of Health, as did W. Buchanan-Taylor of Lyons. Gervas Huxley, formerly of the EMB, A. P.

---

[44] 'Report of the Inter-departmental Committee on Publicity Expenditure', Feb. 1939, T 162/530/40200/2.   [45] Draft Treasury Minute, 6 May 1939, T 161/531/40335/1.

[46] Meeting, 20 Apr. 1939, T 161/531/40335/1.

[47] Cairncross to Douglas, 28 Apr. 1939, T 162/531/40335/1.

[48] Cairncross to Douglas, 26 Apr. 1939, T 162/531/40335/1. Scorgie opposed the inclusion of newspapermen, arguing that they had exercised undue influence on the ACGA: Scorgie to Waterfield, 17 Feb. 1939, T 162/530/40020/2. Crutchley wanted at least one advertising agent on the panels, but the committee stressed the need for impartiality. 'Report', Oct. 1938, T 162/530/40020/1; Waterfield to Crutchley, 22 Feb. 1939; reply 23 Feb. 1939, T 162/530/40020/2. Noting that many firms used direct mail advertising, Scorgie recommended that it be represented as encouraging direct mailing would be a 'useful corrective to the great reputation of newspaper advertising': Scorgie to Cairncross, 27 Apr. 1939, T 162/531/40335/1. The proposal was rejected.

[49] *Ad hoc* meetings, 20 Apr., 3 May 1939, T 162/531/40335/1.

Ryan, by then assistant controller of public relations at the BBC, and Christian Barman, the public relations officer of the LPTB, were also popular choices.[50]

While the establishment of the committee and the advisory bodies went some way towards securing the principle of co-ordinated publicity, both developments had a relatively limited impact. The ICCGP met only four times between May and December 1939.[51] Departments were not required to submit their advertising proposals to the committee or their assigned panel for approval, nor to suspend any advisory committee already in existence, provided a member of the appropriate panel was appointed to it.[52] Since the relationship to prevail between the central advisory committees and their respective ministries was not stipulated, the consultative process could be as flexible as each department desired. In fact, the former were little more than an exercise in public relations. Informing the Treasury that the GPO no longer valued its advisory bodies,[53] Waterfield stated that the panels were 'something of a sop' to the estimates committee: 'I doubt if they will do much good; but the procedure suggested is deliberately elastic, and will allow Departments to get what may be quite useful advice.'[54] The extent to which the panels were employed is unclear. Formed in May 1939, they did not survive into the war.[55]

The sheer fact that external advisers were deemed necessary leads one to question the qualifications of those responsible for supervising departmental publicity arrangements. Until the Second World War, when a number of ministries recruited experienced publicists to their staffs,[56] public relations officers in Whitehall tended to be civil servants drawn from within their respective departments.[57] Thus control over publicity

---

[50] *Ad hoc* meeting, 20 Apr. 1939; Crutchley to Cairncross, 21 Apr. 1939; Cairncross to Douglas, 26 Apr. 1939; Manktelow to Gatliff, 11 May 1939, T 162/531/40335/1. 'Treasury Coordination Committee: Advisory Panels: Provisional List', INF 1/26.

[51] For the minutes see T 162/531/40335/3.

[52] Cairncross to Trentham, 30 Jan. 1939, T 162/530/40020/2.

[53] See above, p. 122.

[54] Waterfield to Rae, 3 Mar. 1939, T 162/530/40020/2.

[55] Hansard, 21 Mar. 1939, vol. 345, cols. 1123–5. 'Draft Press Announcement', May 1939, T 162/531/40335/1. It is unclear when they were dissolved, but early in the war the MOI considered reviving them; 'Home Publicity', 3 Dec. 1939, INF 1/26.

[56] See below.

[57] In 1939 the following departments employed civil servants in these posts: ADM, Board of Education, BT, GPO, India Office, MH, MT, NFC, NSC, Scottish Office: *British Imperial Calendar* (1939).

policy rested in the hands of permanent officials. Press officers were more likely to be recruited from outside the public service. Yet a list compiled in 1934 indicates that only seven of the eighteen ministries then employing press officers had appointed trained journalists to these posts,[58] the rest relying on ordinary officials.[59] Yet the Treasury claimed in 1938 that it was rare to assign civil servants to the task of press relations, as 'awkward culs-de-sac' were likely to arise if the former forged close ties with newspapers.[60] Wartime records indicate that by 1940 most press officers were former journalists, a policy which prevailed, for the most part, into the post-war era.[61]

There was considerable debate in the period as to whether responsibility for publicity should be entrusted to civil servants. The principle that administrative ability was the primary skill required of a government official, and that a good recruit could easily master the business of any department, came to prominence in this period. The average civil servant was expected to be expert in all fields.[62] However, it was recognized that there were many disadvantages to placing regular staff in control of information services. It was noted that most officials lacked 'specialised knowledge', and that the nature of administrative training induced them to be reticent, cautious, and distant in dealing with the public.[63] Working from the assumption that good propagandists were born not made, advertising executives such as Sidney Rogerson argued that it was useless to try to instruct civil servants in publicity.[64] By its very existence, the concept of the well-rounded administrator was also a hindrance, as

[58] C. Beckett Platt and A. Ridgway (CO/DO), C. Robertson (AIR), G. Steward (Treasury), A. Willert (FO), H. MacGregor (India), J. H. Brebner (GPO). 'Press Officers', Mar. 1934, T 162/337/30623. The posts do not appear to have been widely advertised; see above, p. 161, and 'P.O. Press Officer', May 1936, Post 33/3577 (file 28).

[59] e.g. the WO employed A. Manson, a higher clerical officer, and the MT, T. Paterson, a senior staff officer.   [60] Usher to Bosworth Smith, 26 May 1938, ED 23/685.

[61] I. Lambe to W. Vaughan, 28 Sept. 1940, INF 1/340 Part A. The Committee on the Cost of Home Information Services reported in 1949 that information officers in government departments were usually recruited from the press or advertising professions: para. 33. On the other hand, the Drogheda inquiry of 1954 praised the FO for its policy of employing all-round experts as opposed to information specialists, and thus endeavouring to make all of its staff 'information-minded'; *Summary of the Report of the Independent Committee of Enquiry into the Overseas Information Services*, Cmd. 9138 (1954), 13.

[62] Max Beloff, 'The Whitehall Factor: The Role of the Higher Civil Service 1919–1939', in Gillian Peele and Chris Cook (eds.), *The Politics of Reappraisal 1918–1939* (1975), 210.

[63] Charles Frederick Higham, *Looking Forward* (1920), 80–1, 175–6. See *Advertising World*, 70/11 (1938), 5–11, for the views of a number of experts surveyed on the subject, including Buchanan-Taylor of Lyons.

[64] Sidney Rogerson, *Propaganda in the Next War* (1938), 171.

officials who acquired the requisite knowledge could easily be transferred out of a public relations division.[65] A number of officials also stressed that publicity had to be taken seriously, and not be assigned to just anyone in a department.[66]

Yet if publicity was not a job for amateurs, every government employee was recognized to be engaging in a form of advertising through administration of policy, and in his or her day-to-day dealings with the public. Havelock Ellis stated that proper discretion necessitated the 'careful selection and training of officials' for publicity work, but also observed that a 'heavy responsibility' rested on all civil servants to devote attention to their relations with the public.[67] Tallents attempted to 'bring alive' the GPO to postal employees, in order to show them that public relations work was not confined to a particular division, but pervaded all departmental activities.[68] Moreover, a knowledge of the workings and needs of the department concerned was thought to be as important to successful publicity as advertising expertise. That a publicity officer should possess technical skill was of secondary consideration, as professional advice could be obtained when, and if, required.[69] Thus, in staffing the GPO film unit, Grierson did not recruit experts:

Problems of departmental reporting are new to art and are often complex. . . . They require a keen mind which will penetrate through the detail or routine to the organisation and the spirit within. You need directorial minds. . . . Mere cameramen are no use to you. In our unit we indicate this emphasis by making our camera-men out of promoted message boys. . . . We have taken [our filmmakers] . . . direct from . . . the universities. The first requisite is not a knowledge of film (we can give them that), but a good head and a sense of the problem involved in using film to bring alive public services.[70]

[65] Crutchley pointed this out in a 1938 memo on the Estimates Committee report, in which he also questioned the ability of civil servants to perform publicity tasks. On the other hand, he credited the success of the GPO film unit to the fact that it was staffed by permanent officials; Memorandum by Cairncross, 10 Oct. 1938, T 162/530/40020/1.

[66] See Sir Stephen G. Tallents, 'Salesmanship in the Public Service: Scope and Technique', *Public Administration*, 11 (1933), 264. A. P. Ryan, 'Intelligence and Public Relations', ibid. 14/1 (1936), 65. Sir Harold Bellman, 'The Traditions of the Public Services: Can They be Extended to Business?', ibid. 14 (1936), 126. T. S. Simey, 'A Public Relations Policy for Local Authorities', ibid. 13 (1935), 247.

[67] H. H. Ellis, 'The Relations between State Departments and the Nation', ibid. 4 (1926), 103–4.   [68] See above, pp. 116–18.

[69] Some officials, including Scorgie, found it difficult to understand why departments which maintained publicity divisions needed to employ advertising agents; Memorandum, July 1926, CO 758/101/5. Stocks to Hurst, 28 July 1926, T 161/479/29573/02.

[70] John Grierson, 'Films in the Public Service', *Public Administration*, 14 (1936), 367.

Also recognized to be important from an administrative standpoint was that those responsible for the implementation of policy should control its publicizing. As Scorgie observed in 1938,

> there was a clear distinction between a Press officer, whose essential qualification was an intimate knowledge of the working of the press and ought consequently to be chosen from the press . . . and the Public Relations Officer who was chiefly concerned with spreading a better understanding of the Civil Service among the general public, a post for which a civil servant was obviously indicated. This distinction was reflected in the degree of responsibility enjoyed by these . . . officials. The Public Relations Officer was expected to display a high degree of initiative and assume considerable responsibility, whereas the Press Officer's work was carefully controlled by his superiors.[71]

It went without saying that the former was assumed to possess the internal expertise requisite for securing successful publicity. As noted, departments emphasized the importance of internal knowledge and experience in blocking all attempts made to centralize domestic information services over the inter-war period. Not surprisingly, confidence in the ability of government departments to supervise their own publicity arrangements also hindered centralization in wartime.

Planning for a wartime propaganda bureau began secretly in October 1935, with the establishment of a subcommittee of the Committee of Imperial Defence (CID) to consider the necessary arrangements. Composed of higher civil servants, it met only six times over the next four years,[72] leaving the actual planning to a subcommittee chaired by Rex Leeper,[73] the head of the Foreign Office News Department.[74]

---

[71] *Ad hoc* meeting, 3 May 1939, T 162/531/40335/1.

[72] The chairman was J. Colville, Parliamentary Secretary of the DOT and the Minister of Information Designate. The members were W. Fisher, Secretary to the Treasury; E. Harding, Permanent Under-Secretary, DO; D. Banks, Director-General, GPO; J. Troup, Director, Naval Intelligence; R. Scott, Permanent Under-Secretary, HO; J. Reith, Director-General, BBC; J. Dill, Director of Intelligence, WO; C. Courtney, Deputy Chief, Air Staff; M. Hankey, Secretary to the Cabinet; F. Phillips, Director of Telecommunications, GPO; M. Carr, General Staff, WO; and from the FO, R. Vansittart, R. Leeper, Director, News Department, and S. Gaselee, Librarian.

[73] Involved in political intelligence work in the First World War, Leeper joined the News Department of the FO in 1929, becoming director in 1935. A founding member of the British Council, Leeper was also a member of the Vansittart committee of 1938. From 1937 to 1938 he was director-general designate of the news department of the MOI. He headed the Political Warfare Executive from 1940 to 1943.

[74] CID Subcommittee, Minutes, 25 Oct. 1935, CAB 16/127. (Hereafter the Planning Subcommittee is referred to as Leeper's subcommittee.) The members were: Carr; Dill; Gaselee; Reith; Scott; L. Hill (WO); F. Robinson (Treasury); C. Robinson (HO); and Tallents, then public relations officer at the BBC.

The relationship to prevail between a wartime ministry and established publicity and information divisions was one of the earliest subjects considered by the planners. The first issue addressed by the full subcommittee was whether extensive preparations for an independent organization were really necessary, given the existence of these bureaux. C. P. Robertson, the press officer of the Air Ministry, submitted a memorandum to the subcommittee highlighting the advantages of creating a central body which would absorb the divisions available. Leeper objected, maintaining that his news department should form the basis of any wartime propaganda machinery. However, the subcommittee concluded that the news department's lack of experience in the domestic sphere precluded its handling the dissemination of all government information.[75] Temple Willcox claims that, by rejecting Leeper's proposal, the subcommittee endorsed the principle of establishing a separate ministry, and that this carried with it 'the tacit assumption that it would assume the form proposed by Robertson of a centralized organization combining news, censorship, and propaganda under a Minister of Cabinet rank'. He argues that future plans were formulated on the basis that the MOI would be responsible for all aspects of wartime propaganda.[76]

However, Robertson's proposals did not prevail in their entirety. Alluding to the presence of publicity experts throughout Whitehall, Warren Fisher observed that 'naturally the existing staff of the various Departments concerned would be used as the ingredients to make up the Ministry of Information'. John Colville, the minister designate, agreed, adding that 'a machine existed which would be adapted'. Yet moments later Fisher seemingly contradicted his earlier statement, interjecting that 'it would be absurd to put out of action anything that was now in existence'.[77] The fact that this issue was not addressed created considerable confusion, for, although planning proceeded on the assumption that departmental organizations should serve as the foundation of the ministry, the principle of retaining them as separate entities was also affirmed. Indeed, Leeper opened the first meeting of his subcommittee, on 31 October, by 'reassuring' its members that 'there would be no suggestion of the suppression

[75] Ibid.
[76] Temple Willcox, 'Towards a Ministry of Information', *History*, 69/227 (1984), 412. Claiming that the acceptance of Robertson's ideas connoted a rejection of the decentralized 'open' society propaganda developed by the British Council and the FO, Willcox overlooks two facts: that domestic publicity bureaux, such as that in the Air Ministry, pursued a similar approach to publicity as the British Council and the FO; and that Leeper was not alone in supporting decentralization.
[77] CID Subcommittee, Minutes, 25 Oct. 1935, CAB 16/127.

or elimination of existing agencies'. Yet this neither presupposed, nor prescribed, that the new ministry would be unable to draw upon the expertise of these other organizations; while rejecting John Reith's recommendation that departmental publicity machinery should be absorbed by the MOI, the subcommittee endorsed his proposal that 'officers dealing in peace with any of the activities which come under the Ministry of Information should be taken over, they to some extent forming a nucleus of the new organization, except such as are left behind in the respective Ministries as Liaison Officers'.[78]

The subject of the staffing of the ministry *vis-à-vis* other publicity bureaux also surfaced at the next meeting a week later, the planners again failing to recognize or consider the ambiguities inherent in the policy hitherto adopted. F. P. Robinson produced a list showing the extent of publicity machinery already available within Whitehall, prompting Leeper to comment that 'it appeared that the various press agencies in Government Departments provided an adequate basis from which to draw staff'. Robinson interjected that he had not introduced the document with personnel in mind, as he assumed that the decision to form an MOI 'did not imply the elimination of existing agencies'.[79] The issue was not pursued, nor was the policy clarified. It is evident, however, that the planners intended to make as much use as possible of the available machinery, and were confident of its expertise. This is reflected in the subcommittee's decision to concentrate on preparing the administrative framework of the ministry, leaving the publicity section to be developed 'as circumstances demanded'.[80] Their concern with establishing the mechanism before considering the task it was to fulfil indicates that the planners believed little advance preparation was required in this area. Leeper assumed that the publicity division 'could be formed at once without delay', because the necessary staff was already present in Whitehall.[81]

In a preliminary report, submitted to the full subcommittee in February 1936, the planners affirmed that the ministry would be the 'centre for the distribution of all information concerning the war', but recommended that other departments be allowed to retain their own small press division to handle interviews with journalists, and to liaise with the

[78] Leeper's subcommittee, Minutes, 31 Oct. 1935, CAB 16/128. For Reith's memo see Annexe B.
[79] Leeper's subcommittee, Minutes, 7 Nov. 1935, CAB 16/128. For Robinson's report see Annexe A.   [80] Leeper's Subcommittee, Minutes, 3 Jan. 1936, CAB 16/128.
[81] See his memo in Annexe B of the Subcommittee Minutes of 7 Nov. 1935.

MOI.[82] Only the Foreign Office news department was to be absorbed fully into the ministry. These decisions were approved, though the CID subcommittee suggested that the line of demarcation between departmental press sections and the MOI needed to be more clearly defined.[83] Accordingly, Leeper's subcommittee specified that the former would act as connecting links between their respective departments and the ministry, and assist in any newspaper work of a detailed nature.[84] The full subcommittee endorsed this policy in July, but altered the reference to each department retaining a 'press section' to read a 'press officer'.[85]

When Stephen Tallents was appointed director-general designate of the MOI in July 1936, he assumed control over the planning process. Working in secret, he was assisted by a small group of civil servants, whom Ian McLaine has termed unqualified: 'Of the four top men, J. B. Beresford was recruited from the University Grants Commission [*sic*]; another, G. C. North, was an Assistant Secretary at the Ministry of Health; a third, H. E. Dannreuther, was a retired admiral; while the fourth, W. P. Hildred, was Deputy General Manager of the Export Credit Branch of the Customs Department.'[86] Beresford was unfamiliar with the field, but North had been directing public relations at the Ministry of Health since 1937; Dannreuther had experience in naval censorship; and Hildred was the former finance officer of the EMB. It is also worth noting that when the ministry was created Dannreuther served in the censorship section, while Hildred headed the finance branch. The other two did not join the MOI.

Tallents concentrated initially on studying the development of government propaganda in the First World War.[87] Home publicity arrangements were not given serious attention until August 1937 when, recognizing that the ministry would require the assistance of experts in various advertising media, Tallents suggested that a list of suitable individuals be compiled, and recommended that closer ties be forged with press divisions in other departments.[88] In pursuing the latter course, Tallents was made aware of the anomalies present in the current policy regarding the MOI's relations with other ministries,[89] an issue which he

[82] MIC 5, CAB 16/128.
[83] CID Subcommittee, Minutes, 28 Feb. 1936, CAB 16/127.
[84] Leeper's subcommittee, Minutes, 4 May 1936, CAB 16/128.
[85] CID Subcommittee, Minutes, 16 July 1936, CAB 16/127.
[86] Ian McLaine, *Ministry of Morale* (1979), 15.
[87] Tallents, 'Progress Report', 'MIC 10', 23 Feb. 1938, para. 44, INF 1/714.
[88] 'The Collecting and Publicity Divisions', INF 1/709.
[89] French to Tallents, 22 Nov. 1937, INF 1/714.

addressed in a progress report submitted to the CID subcommittee in February 1938. Noting the inconsistencies inherent in earlier decisions, Tallents observed that, although it had been agreed that the MOI would control the distribution of all wartime 'information', it was 'not clear whether it [was] . . . contemplated that the Ministry . . . should also be the centre for the preparation and distribution of other publicity material required by other Government Departments'. He requested clarification, declaring that it was of 'some importance to those who have to frame plans for this Division, and to those who will have to provide it with a staff adequate to its needs'.[90]

The CID subcommittee considered this question at its fourth meeting in March 1938. Working from the *a priori* assumption that the established publicity machinery was functioning effectively and with success, several members, including Donald Banks of the Post Office and J. A. G. Troup of the Admiralty, raised the well-worn argument that departments were best qualified to handle their own publicity requirements. Banks thought it would be 'definitely wrong' to transfer existing organizations to the MOI, and questioned the efficacy of allowing an external body to control all campaigns: 'Supposing, for example, the Post Office wished to diminish the use of the telephone, they already had an elaborate and highly efficient organization for securing publicity for such a purpose and he saw no reason for disturbing it.' The subcommittee agreed, noting that, although the work was likely to gravitate towards the central organization once it was in place, 'there should be no transfer of publicity functions unless experience proved this to be desirable'.[91] With this decision in place, Tallents asked permission to consult with outside experts about the planning of the publicity section.[92] F. P. Robinson queried this proposal, suggesting that greater account needed to be taken of existing bureaux before anyone was commissioned to design a new organization. Tallents agreed that existing bureaux should be employed to the utmost, but 'felt sure that they would be found entirely inadequate'.[93] His lack of confidence in the established publicity divisions may have stemmed from his ignorance of the extent of the machinery available.[94] Even so, given the

---

[90] MIC 10, paras. 33–4, 43, CAB 16/127.

[91] CID Subcommittee, Minutes, 18 Mar. 1938, CAB 16/127.

[92] As the ministry was being planned in secret, Tallents had to obtain sanction to consult with individuals outside Whitehall: Note of meeting, 13 July 1938, INF 1/709.

[93] Meeting of Heads of Divisions, 13 May 1938, INF 1/709.

[94] In a list of top advertisers compiled in July 1938, Tallents mentioned public relations officers in the War Office and the Ministries of Health and Labour, noting that 'no doubt . . . a few other . . . Departments have some small publicity resources': 'Publicity in the U.K.', INF 1/712.

subcommittee's directive, Tallents had little choice but to seek assistance elsewhere.

E. T. Crutchley of the GPO; Stephen King-Hall, the publicist; H. V. Rhodes, a career civil servant already assisting in the preparations; and Lady Rhys Williams, the secretary of the Pilgrim Trust, were appointed in July 1938 to plan the home publicity division.[95] Despite Banks's remarks, Crutchley confirmed, from the outset, that the Post Office public relations bureau would be at the disposal of the MOI.[96] The co-operation of other ministries was less certain. Rhodes assumed that virtually every department would continue to direct its own publicity campaigns, leaving the MOI to disseminate information on general matters of importance.[97] Since the extent to which other departments intended to distribute materials was still unclear,[98] Crutchley sent out letters asking various ministries to prepare announcements, in 'popular language', outlining instructions to be given to the public in the event of war.[99]

Although it was assumed that departments would retain at least some control over their own arrangements, by 1938 most of the press and/or publicity officers present in Whitehall had been earmarked for service in the MOI. The home affairs specialist section was to be staffed almost entirely by such officials.[100] Most of the GPO public relations division was also scheduled for transfer.[101] Yet when the MOI was established for two days during the Munich crisis of September 1938, only Crutchley, Forbes, and Brebner, of the GPO, actually served.

The temporary MOI was not a success.[102] In the aftermath, Tallents concluded that more attention had to be paid to preparing publicity materials, and criticized other departments for neglecting to address their responsibilities in this area. Attributing the problem to staff shortages, he considered linking up each ministry in Whitehall with a commercial

[95] On Crutchley and King-Hall, see above, Ch. 4 n. 223 and Ch. 3 n. 151. The subcommittee met three times between July and Sept. 1938, submitting an interim report to Tallents on 13 Sept. and a full report on 27 Sept.; INF 1/713.

[96] Home Publicity Subcommittee, Minutes, 12 July 1938, INF 1/712.

[97] 'Publicity Division: Preliminary Note on Machinery', 3 Sept. 1938, paras. 23–6; Appendix H, INF 1/709.   [98] Tallents to Rhodes, 12 Sept. 1938, INF 1/709.

[99] Correspondence, 14, 15 Sept. 1938, INF 1/714.

[100] The following were earmarked: W. R. Richardson, Principal, Board of Education; E. R. Thompson, Press Officer, Board of Education/MH; S. W. Bainbridge, Assistant Intelligence Officer, MT; N. F. McNicholl, Public Relations Officer, Scottish Office; R. S. Langford, Press Officer, MAF; A. E. Percival, Assistant Principal, Board of Trade; S. R. Chaloner, Press Officer, Ministry of Labour; F. V. Bennett, Assistant Press Officer, Board of Education/MH; Howard Marshall, Journalist/Broadcaster: 'Ministry of Information—Staff at Sept. 1938', INF 1/17.

[101] Others earmarked included publicity officers from the NFC, FO, CO, WO, and Air Ministry.   [102] McLaine, p. 16.

advertising agency.[103] Crutchley thought the idea had potential,[104] but no action appears to have been taken, although Tallents did ask the CID subcommittee to pressure departments into upgrading their efforts.[105] He also appealed for an increase in his own planning staff, and for permission to broaden contacts with outside experts. Fisher opposed both requests, objecting to the formation of a large nucleus organization, as he was 'convinced that [the MOI] . . . should not usurp in peace-time the functions of existing agencies . . . which must remain responsible for working out their own plans'. James Rae of the Treasury added that each department had to prepare its own materials as the MOI 'could not be expected to have a knowledge of the necessary subject matter'. The CID subcommittee directed the planners to concentrate on ensuring that other ministries were 'getting on with the work'.[106]

When Tallents continued to press for greater centralization, he was dismissed as director-general. By then, many of the other planners, including Leeper, had already resigned in frustration.[107] Ironically, it was at this point, with international tensions mounting, that the scope of planning was broadened. A special division was established at the Royal Institute of International Affairs (Chatham House) to deal with foreign publicity,[108] and an International Propaganda and Broadcasting Enquiry was appointed under the chairmanship of Ivison MacAdam, the director of Chatham House, to oversee domestic arrangements.[109] The latter had two publicists among its membership, W. Surrey Dane, the publicity manager of Odhams advertising agency, and Gervas Huxley.[110] Both Taylor and Willcox have argued that the departure of Tallents and Leeper signified a turning-point in the development of the wartime propaganda machinery.[111] However, the presence of Crutchley and Rhodes on MacAdam's committee ensured continuity in home-front preparations, as did the fact that the recommendations embodied in the reports filed by Crutchley's Home Publicity subcommittee, in the previous September, served as the basis for further planning.

[103] Memorandum, Oct. 1938, INF 1/711.
[104] Crutchley to Tallents, 20 Oct. 1938, INF 1/711.
[105] 'Progress Report', Oct. 1938, 'MIC 16', para. 56, CAB 16/127.
[106] CID Subcommittee, Minutes, 14 Dec. 1938, CAB 16/127.
[107] Tallents left in Jan. 1939. See Temple Willcox, 'Projection or Publicity: Rival Concepts of the Pre-War Planning of the Ministry of Information', *Journal of Contemporary History*, 18 (1983).   [108] INF 1/20, Part A.
[109] The other members were Crutchley, Rhodes, Professors R. D'O. Butler and Michael Balfour, and D. Matheson of Chatham House.
[110] On Huxley see above, Ch. 4 n. 109.   [111] See above, Ch. 1 n. 14.

Crutchley's subcommittee had concentrated on addressing three issues: the general principles to underlie domestic propaganda; the best means by which to impart the policy adopted; and the type of administrative framework required. The subcommittee drew heavily on the GPO example. The reports issued emphasized the value of educational publicity of a dignified nature. Discussing the use of posters, for example, the subcommittee suggested that the MOI should consult with the Royal School of Art. Considerable importance was attached to prestige publicity, the subcommittee assuming that the best means to reach the public was through local meetings, lectures, and the provision of 'inside track' information to prominent individuals.[112]

MacAdam's committee endorsed this policy and expanded on it: stressing the value of employing voluntary organizations and clubs as channels for information;[113] recommending that distinguished artists be commissioned to design posters and other advertisements;[114] and enlisting Herbert Morgan[115] to recruit eminent speakers.[116] The committee focused most of its attention on administrative questions, leaving the development of publicity materials to a nucleus staff appointed in May 1939. This work was supervised by an Oxford professor, R. D'O. Butler, but two advertising agents, S. Clark and W. G. V. Vaughan, were recruited to assist in the preparations, along with two journalists, K. Fairfax and J. Palmer.[117]

The fact that technical planning was left until quite late in the process is attributable to two factors. As noted, MacAdam's committee was expected to supervise the activities of other departments, on the assumption that they should be responsible for preparing any materials they required. While this relieved the committee of having to undertake work in this area, it also presented problems, because the planners had no authority to compel other departments to act. After visiting twelve ministries in March 1939, Rhodes reported that little was being done; most departments contended that their publicity staff would be able to meet demands as they arose. He believed that his visits had brought the issue to prominence, however, and that all would now begin to consider their arrangements.[118] Rhodes continued to confer with other ministries, advising them of the

---

[112] Both reports are located in INF 1/713.
[113] MacAdam committee, Minutes, 5 Apr. 1939, INF 1/300.
[114] Ibid. 13 Apr. 1939, INF 1/300.   [115] See above, p. 126.
[116] MacAdam committee, Minutes, 13 Apr. 1939, INF 1/300.
[117] Ibid. 18 May 1939, INF 1/300. 'Staff of MOI Publicity Division, Planning Section: 2 July 1939', INF 1/20 (Part B) (4).
[118] Note of Meeting, 20 Mar. 1939, INF 1/711.

type of information required by the nucleus publicity section.[119] Although the Ministry of Health sent in drafts of four emergency notices, few departments were as helpful. As late as June 1939, Rhodes could only express 'hope' that others would soon furnish similar information.[120] Advance planning was of some importance, given that the MacAdam committee assumed that domestic publicity would be completely central-ized in the MOI within one month of the outbreak of war.[121] However, as the committee resolved in May–June that its chief priority should be to assemble the MOI publicity division, it postponed reaching a decision on the exact stage at which the ministry should assume responsibility over all government publicity, and did not canvass the various departments for their views.[122]

Concern with establishing the framework of the ministry and formu-lating general policy before preparing materials also reflected the commit-tee's certainty that experts would be brought in, when necessary, to handle the technical aspects of campaigns. Believing that 'all firms would wish to be taken over' by the ministry, Crutchley suggested that the MOI could absorb a number of advertising agencies once war began.[123] Hence, instead of designing pamphlets and posters, the committee focused on administrative issues, and assembled lists of noted advertising firms, journalists, artists, and other professionals in the field.[124]

Despite mounting external pressure for the creation of an official publicity bureau,[125] the Cabinet decided that it would be inadvisable to establish an MOI before the commencement of hostilities. Wary of ant-agonizing Labour, the Prime Minister was also opposed to the idea, as it 'would mean that the existing publicity work of Departments would have to be brought within the scope of the Ministry of Information'. He thought 'the work was better done in the Departments, subject to [it] . . . being co-ordinated from a central office and extended'.[126] That this assumption prevailed into the war is manifested by the fact that depart-ments were allowed to retain control over their own arrangements; the MOI never absorbed their publicity machinery.

As noted in Chapter 1, the ministry got off to a poor start, instantly becoming everyone's whipping boy. Most of the early problems were

---

[119] MacAdam committee, Minutes, 11 May 1939, INF 1/300.

[120] Ibid. 15 June 1939, INF 1/300.

[121] Ibid. 4 May 1939, INF 1/300. Also, Memorandum by MacAdam, 18 Mar. 1939, INF 1/711.   [122] MacAdam committee, Minutes, 25 May; 8 June 1939, INF 1/300.

[123] Ibid. 27 Apr. 1939, INF 1/300.   [124] Ibid. 4 May 1939, INF 1/300.

[125] Hansard, 13 Apr. 1939, vol. 346, cols. 97–8; 21 June 1939, vol. 348, cols. 2208–9. *Advertising World*, 70/4 (1939), 5–9, 61–2; 71/6 (1939), 19.

[126] Cabinet Minutes, C32(39), 14 June 1939, CAB 23/99.

administrative in nature, and stemmed from the department's difficulties in persuading other ministries to relinquish their authority, and co-operate in co-ordinating the release of all government information. Not until Bracken's arrival was the situation rectified, through the introduction of stricter guidelines.[127] Yet the lack of centralization in the early stages of the war was not merely the product of inadequate planning, nor did it reflect a reluctance on the part of government to take propaganda seriously. Departmental opposition to relinquishing responsibility for the dissemination of information and materials to a wartime propaganda ministry was no isolated case but emanated from policies that had been pursued for almost twenty years. That centralization was blocked reflected a prevailing over-confidence in the abilities of existing publicity machinery, itself a product of the assumption that control over the dissemination of information ought to rest in the hands of those responsible for implementing the relevant policies. Indeed, ministries of State were not unwilling to take propaganda seriously; they were reluctant, however, to see it divorced from policy, the task being treated as an irregular function of a department of State. With this in mind, it is noteworthy that the issue of internal expertise even surfaced within the MOI itself. For example, the appointment of an advisory committee of experts to choose advertising agents for government campaigns was opposed on the grounds that the divisions originating the schemes were best placed to judge their own requirements.[128]

The MOI was also criticized for its clumsy and condescending publicity efforts during the early stages of the war. As noted, contemporaries and historians have attributed the department's obvious ineptitude to the dearth of qualified individuals within the organization.[129] A list of employees, presented in parliament on 9 October 1939,[130] indicates that seventy-one of the 230 senior officials in the department were civil servants, only ten of whom had experience in government publicity work.[131]

---

[127] Memorandum by Waterfield, 16 Nov. 1939; Memorandum by Bevan, 8 Apr. 1940; C. Bloxham to Vaughan, 31 Aug. 1940, INF 1/340 (Part A). Waterfield to Hale, 5 Dec. 1939, INF 1/341. Hansard, 20 Mar. 1940, vol. 358, col. 2002. Also see McLaine, pp. 34–8, 244–5. Michael Balfour, *Propaganda in War* (1979), 57–70.

[128] 'Ministry's Publicity Campaigns', 6 Dec. 1939, INF 1/341. An Advisory Committee, under the chairmanship of Lord Luke, the chairman of the *Daily Express*, was created in Feb. 1941; INF 1/341 (Part 3).   [129] See above, pp. 2–4.

[130] Hansard, vol. 353, cols. 15–22.

[131] The experienced officers were Crutchley, Forbes, Highet, and Welch of the GPO; D. H. W. Hall and W. G. Robinson of the NFC; Hughes-Roberts, the government cinematograph adviser, and his assistant J. H. Francis; W. A. B. Hamilton, formerly a press officer at the Board of Education; and N. F. McNicholl, public relations officer of the Scottish Office.

The second largest representative group comprised educationalists, of which there were twenty-nine. A mere eighteen journalists and fourteen 'publicists' were serving in the department. The former ranged from Lionel MacBride, the foreign editor of the *Daily Herald*, to the Revd Hugh Martin of the Student Movement Press, and H. V. Hodson, the editor of the *Round Table*. The publicists included copywriters, artists, and agency directors, such as R. A. P. Bevan of S. H. Bensons, who headed the general production division. As this shows, only a limited number of the staff were publicity experts *per se*. Secrecy in the pre-war period obviously precluded the planners of the ministry from actively recruiting outside the Civil Service until quite late in the process.[132] The fact that other departments retained their publicity divisions, and that new wartime ministries created similar machinery, meant that the MOI had competition in securing the services of experienced public servants as well as journalists and publicists from outside Whitehall. Many departments enlisted qualified personnel who might otherwise have joined the MOI. For example, E. T. Crutchley of the Post Office became public relations officer of the new Ministry of Home Security. The Ministry of Supply recruited S. C. Leslie and several of his colleagues from the publicity division of the Gas Light and Coke company.[133] On the other hand, it is clear that during the planning process a deliberate decision had been made not to employ many advertising professionals within the MOI. MacAdam's committee had concluded that, as the publicity division would be 'working in conjunction with large advertising concerns, . . . it was . . . unlikely that a large number of such persons would be required for the staff of the Ministry itself'.[134] Moreover, as noted earlier, it was the buyer of advertising, rather than the practitioner, who was assumed to be the right expert to advise government departments on their publicity requirements.[135] Thus, when it was decided in December 1939 to create a planning section in the publicity division to oversee the preparation of all campaigns, business leaders, such as Gordon Selfridge, who were 'to be distinguished from the advertising agents they sometimes employ', were recruited, Rhodes observing that advertising agents were 'the concern of the Production Divisions'.[136] Similarly, in employing university dons and educators, the MOI was following the example of Wellington

---

[132] Not until 15 June 1939 was the existence of the ministry made public: Hansard, vol. 348, cols. 1499–1503.

[133] For a partial list of the qualified staff secured by other departments see Lambe to Vaughan, 21 Sept. 1940 INF 1/340, (Part A).

[134] MacAdam committee, Minutes, 4 May 1939, INF 1/300.

[135] See above, p. 44.   [136] Report on Home Publicity, 3 Dec. 1939, INF 1/26.

House before it,[137] and adhering to the principle that the best means to reach the mass audience was to influence the educated minority and thereby have information filtered downward. If the MOI was not composed mainly of advertising professionals, neither was the Board of Education staffed entirely by teachers, nor the Ministry of Health by doctors. A knowledge of technical matters was not assumed to be the only, or primary, qualification required of an administrator of government policies.

It is also worth noting that staff with prior experience of publicity work were not deployed illogically within the organization. In 1940, Bevan's department, which was responsible for the preparation of publicity materials, contained only one civil servant at a senior level. W. G. V. Vaughan served as the deputy director, and the 'specialists' in the section included six advertising agents and/or publicity directors, a copywriter, an art editor, two journalists, two writers, and two businessmen. The films division was headed by Kenneth Clark, of the National Gallery, who was assisted by Forbes and Highet, of the GPO public relations division, and A. C. Bromhead of Gaumont Films.[138]

After 1941, the MOI's public image improved and the department became more effective. McLaine and Balfour link this to the fact that, under Bracken's tenure, the ministry was placed on a better footing *vis-à-vis* other government departments, grew more confident, and adopted a less condescending approach towards the British public.[139] Although the MOI experienced a relatively rapid turnover of personnel in the early stages of the war, Bracken's arrival at the department did not result in any major staffing changes,[140] a fact which suggests that undue emphasis has been placed on the staffing issue in accounting for the MOI's early difficulties.

In assessing the propaganda disseminated by the MOI during the early stages of the war, analysts have concluded that the propagandists were out of touch with both their public and the tool at their disposal.[141] Yet if the department adopted a didactic approach and shunned aggressive tactics, this also reflected the assumption prevalent in Whitehall that if and when a government department took up the task of publicity, it had to do so in a dignified manner, avoiding techniques of high-powered salesmanship. The MOI may have been unable to draw upon the resources and staff of other government publicity bureaux, but it certainly copied their example.

---

[137] See above, p. 27. [138] *British Imperial Calendar* (1940).
[139] McLaine, pp. 7, 244–5. Balfour, pp. 69–70.
[140] See the *British Imperial Calendar* (1940–3). [141] See above, pp. 1–4.

8

Conclusion

B Y the outset of the Second World War, virtually every department in Whitehall had accepted publicity and/or public relations as a legitimate part of its functions, employing staff specifically engaged on this work, and addressing the mass audience through the press and direct campaigns. As noted, government was far from assuming total responsibility for the dissemination of public information: it relied on voluntary organizations and local government in the sphere of health publicity; distanced itself from direct involvement in commodity advertising in the national interest; and restricted public access to information by limiting the gratuitous distribution of official publications. Indeed, the only department as yet pursuing an active publicity policy was the GPO.

How does one account for this state of affairs? One possible explanation, suggested by the way in which contemporary discussion conceptualized the issue, is that publicity and advertising were considered inappropriate to the functions of government. They were thought to be intimately connected with the sale of commodities, whereas government was thought to be involved in the sale of ideas. Another explanation may perhaps lie in the State's wariness of engaging in propaganda, due to the negative connotations it had acquired by the end of the First World War. Yet a third may be the reluctance of the Government in power to engage in publicity campaigns.

Although all of these factors may have played some role, the preceding chapters have demonstrated that none of them is capable of elucidating fully the lack of organization and clear-cut policy in this area. Rather, bureaucratic reasons must be accorded a central place in any explanation. The determination of the various departments to maintain control over policy and its implementation in their respective spheres of responsibility, and the Treasury's concern with keeping expenditure within limits were decisive in shaping the mechanisms of government publicity in the inter-war years.

Government departments came to pursue advertising and public relations from different motives and with divergent perspectives on the appropriate nature and role of publicity. None the less, a remarkable similarity of approach emerged in the period covered by this study. The GPO, despite being conceived of as a business, engaged in public relations, the sale of ideas, rather than mere commodity advertising. Advised by the same individuals as the Post Office, other, non-commercial departments, although precluded by Treasury rulings from employing certain commercial advertising methods, and conscious of their status and responsibilities, adopted a similar approach to their publicity work. Prestige, rather than aggressively popular, publicity was employed throughout Whitehall. Moreover, whatever the extent of their experience, ministries were confident of their own abilities and convinced that they should control their own arrangements. Assumed to be proficient in this area, departments were allowed to retain control over a large portion of domestic publicity during the war, thereby creating serious problems for the Ministry of Information.

The British government's slowness to establish a strong central wartime information agency may have reflected an abhorrence of propaganda, but it was not a result of lack of experience within Whitehall. Pre-war planning, particularly of home publicity, was neglected because of over-confidence in the abilities of existing departmental press and public relations bureaux, and reflected a long-held assumption that the dissemination of 'domestic' information ought to rest in the hands of those implementing policy decisions. After 1941, the MOI was able to secure a greater degree of authority over the distribution process,[1] but, well before the war was over, it seemed unlikely that centralization of control over the dissemination of information would last into peacetime.

The character of the post-war information services was under consideration as early as 1943. Bracken, the Minister of Information, was adamant that his department should fold with the cessation of hostilities with Germany.[2] However, officials in the ministry were convinced that, while the functions taken over from other departments should revert back to them, some form of central organization would be required to assist all departments in the technical aspects of their publicity work.[3] This view was upheld by the Official Committee on the Machinery of Government.

---

[1] This was the result of a Cabinet resolution; see WP(41)149, 'Information and Propaganda', Note by the Prime Minister, 2 July 1941, CAB 66/17. On the response to the decision see correspondence in INF 1/891.

[2] B. Bracken to B. Sendall, undated but internal evidence suggests Nov. 1943; Sendall to the Secretary of the War Cabinet, 11 Nov. 1943, INF 1/941.

[3] See J. Barlow to C. Radcliffe, 3 Feb. 1944, INF 1/941.

In a report concerning the future of the wartime ministries, tabled in August 1944, the committee recommended that existing public relations branches throughout Whitehall ought to be retained, 'as their functions, if properly conceived, are useful and indeed essential in modern government', but that the MOI should be wound up as soon as the war with Japan was over. The committee suggested, however, that certain specialist functions ought to be discharged by a single body provided it 'will be seen that this Department would have no responsibility for policy'.[4] The Prime Minister endorsed this commitment to the decentralization of publicity arrangements when he agreed that the main features of the committee's recommendations would be taken as 'assumptions for planning purposes' and that the MOI would close at the end of the Japanese war.[5]

The entire issue of the future of the information services resurfaced when the new Labour Government took office in 1945. After high-level consultations,[6] Attlee concluded that it would not be politically expedient to reverse the decision of the coalition Government to dissolve the ministry. More importantly, while accepting the need for the centralization of control over certain functions, he concurred with the importance of maintaining ministerial responsibility in this sphere.[7] Thus, when a Central Office of Information (COI) was created in April 1946 to replace the MOI, it was envisaged as a common service technical agency, charged with handling contractual questions, booking advertising space, and co-ordinating departmental campaigns. Responsibility for the initiation of publicity schemes, the formulation of policy, and the preparation of materials was assigned to each individual ministry.[8]

It has been argued that the Attlee administration did not create a strong central organization to control government publicity because of its 'inability to foresee the magnitude of the propaganda tasks' facing it.[9] This may have been the case, but it is none the less clear that the creation

[4] 'The Wartime Departments: Report by the Chairman of the Machinery of Government Committee', WP44(482), 31 Aug. 1944, CAB 66/54, paras. 24–32.

[5] MG(45)7, 'The Future of the Wartime Departments', Note by Chairman, 19 Mar. 1945, CAB 87/75.

[6] See CP(45)316, 'Government Publicity Services', Note by the Prime Minister, 30 Nov. 1945, CAB 129/5.

[7] GEN 85/1st meeting, 18 Sept. 1945, CAB 78/37. Cabinet Minutes, CAB60(45), 6 Dec. 1945, CAB 128/2.

[8] *AWWW* (1948–9), p. xxv. *Annual Report of the Central Office of Information: Part I*, Cmd. 7567 (1947–8). Hansard, 12 Feb. 1948, vol. 447, cols. 567–8.

[9] William Crofts, *Coercion or Persuasion?: Propaganda in Britain after 1945* (1989), 20.

of the COI as a technical agency rather than a policy department was a decision taken after much deliberation, and represented the culmination of a much more complex process; decentralization and departmental autonomy with regard to publicity arrangements were already well established within Whitehall before Labour took office. Moreover, even if it was unsure of the scale of future activities required, the administration was conscious of the difficulties likely to ensue in organizing publicity where more than one department was involved or for government policy in general, but hoped such problems could be ameliorated through the creation of committees at both the ministerial and official levels to coordinate such activities.[10]

On reviewing the organizational structure in 1949, the Committee on the Cost of Home Information Services concluded that, while the existence of a central agency was justified on economic grounds, it should not restrict departments from directing their own publicity. It was noted, for example, that an advertising agency could only prosecute a successful campaign if it was 'allowed to get "inside" the problem of [its] ultimate client'.[11] That public relations was now accepted as a normal administrative function of every government department was further mirrored in the fact that in 1949 the Treasury created a new permanent category in the Civil Service, the Information Officer class.[12] By the mid-1950s this class had been adopted by every ministry except the Foreign Office.[13]

It remains to be considered whether domestic publicity arrangements would have developed differently had Labour, rather than the Conservatives, dominated the governing process over the inter-war years. It has been argued that the former was more reluctant than the latter to adopt publicity as a political tool.[14] There is little doubt that the left was wary of propaganda. However, many in the Labour movement recognized the importance of publicity to the democratic process. Leading socialists, such as Sidney Webb and Fenner Brockway, believed that a Labour administration would be fully justified in employing publicity to further the social good. Advertising, in this sense, was said to be wholly compatible with the movement's principles, and a necessary adjunct to their

[10] See H. Morrison to Attlee, 2 Oct. 1945, CAB 124/985; GEN 85/2nd meeting, 3 Oct. 1945, CAB 78/37; CP(46)54, 'Government Information Services', Note by Secretary, 28 Jan. 1946, GIS(46)4, CAB 134/306; Cabinet Minutes, CAB16(46), 18 Feb. 1946, CAB 128/5. [11] Paras. 10, 19, 22, 58.
[12] See T 216/84.
[13] T. Fife Clark, 'Do We Need Government Information Services?', *Public Administration*, 35 (1957), 337. [14] Paul Rotha, *Documentary Diary* (1973), 280–1.

implementation.[15] As observed, Attlee and Snowden were willing to use publicity as a means of furthering government and party policy, when Labour was in power from 1929 to 1931. It should not be overlooked that it was Attlee who brought Tallents into the GPO as a publicity adviser. Moreover, although Labour was slow to develop mass publicity campaigns in the political sphere, it did employ educational means of reaching the public, such as pamphlets, lectures, and meetings. Indeed, during the inter-war decades, the party chose to adopt the type of prestige publicity favoured within Whitehall.[16]

John Grierson accused the post-war Labour Government of shirking its responsibility to the documentary film-makers of the 1930s, by deciding to place jurisdiction over domestic films in the hands of each individual ministry, rather than the Crown Film Unit created during the war. He dismissed claims that departmental rivalries were at the root of the policy, asserting that the 'split[ing] up' of the documentary film movement manifested the administration's reluctance to sponsor propaganda, except under strict 'ideological control', lest the success of socialism in power be questioned.[17] These allegations must be viewed with a critical eye; Grierson himself has been accorded some of the blame for the problems encountered by the Crown Film Unit.[18] This point aside, it should be noted that it was not the first majority Labour Government, but the Conservative administration of 1951–5, which closed the film unit as an economy measure.[19] As well, recent research indicates that the Attlee Government was quite willing to employ the information services at its disposal to persuade the public of the efficacy of Labour's economic policies.[20] Clearly much further investigation, into the way in which the information services were organized and functioned under successive governments of different political complexions after 1946, is necessary before a conclusive argument can be advanced on this point, but it would seem that there was a great deal of continuity in general publicity policy into the post-war period. In formulating guidelines for departments in 1949, the Committee on the Cost of Home Information Services stressed the need for

---

[15] Webb, in Goodall, *Advertising* (1914), pp. ix–xvii; Brockway, *Advertising World*, 56/6 (1929), 568–70.

[16] See Timothy John Hollins, 'The Presentation of Politics: The Place of Party Publicity, Broadcasting and Film in British Politics 1918–1939', D.Phil. dissertation, Leeds, 1981, pp. 119–211.   [17] 'Preface', Paul Rotha, *Documentary Film* (1952), 16–21.

[18] Nicholas Pronay, 'John Grierson and the Documentary—60 Years on', *Historical Journal of Film, Radio and Television*, 9/3 (1989), 240–4.

[19] Hansard, 29 Jan. 1952, vol. 495, cols. 52–3; 21 Feb. 1952, vol. 496, cols. 50–1.

[20] See Crofts.

co-ordination in the dissemination of government information, but endorsed the concept of decentralization in policy matters. It also affirmed and endeavoured to reinforce many of the stipulations imposed by the Treasury in the inter-war years, criticizing the use of background publicity, excessive press advertising, and the gratuitous distribution of publications.[21] As this suggests, the manner in which domestic publicity arrangements developed in Britain in the first half of the twentieth century owed more to the influence and attitude of the Treasury and of officials within Whitehall active in addressing the issue than of any particular party in power.

[21] Paras. 6, 30–2, 49–50.

Bibliography

All printed matter is published in London unless otherwise indicated.

I. Archival Sources and Private Papers

II. Primary Sources
- (i) Newspapers and Periodicals
- (ii) Journals
- (iii) Official Reports and Command Papers
- (iv) Other Publications
- (v) Articles

III. Secondary Sources
- (i) Books, Journals, and Government Publications
- (ii) Articles and Theses

I. ARCHIVAL SOURCES AND PRIVATE PAPERS

Addison Papers, Bodleian Library, Oxford

Post Office Archive, London:
Post 33—General Files
Post 108—Public Relations Department

Public Record Office, London (Kew):

Cabinet Papers
CAB 4—Committee of Imperial Defence—Standing Committee on Coordination of Departmental Action on the outbreak of war—Memoranda (1935)
CAB 16—Committee of Imperial Defence—Subcommittee to Prepare Plans for the Establishment of a Ministry of Information (1935–9)
CAB 23—Cabinet Minutes (1918–39)
CAB 24—Cabinet Memoranda (1918–39)
CAB 26—Committee on Home Affairs (1919–25)
CAB 27—Cabinet Committee on Imperial Economic Cooperation (1933)
Committee on Overlapping in Production and Distribution of Propaganda (1917)
Supply and Transport Committee and Subcommittees—Minutes and Memoranda (1919–34)
CAB 65—War Cabinet Minutes (1939–45)
CAB 66—War Cabinet Papers (1939–45)

CAB 78—Cabinet Committee on Post-war Organization of Government Publicity

CAB 87—Cabinet Committee on Machinery of Government

CAB 124—Lord President of the Council—Secretariat Files

CAB 128—Cabinet Minutes (1945–51)

CAB 129—Cabinet Papers (1945–51)

CAB 134—Ministerial and Official Committees on Information Services

Colonial Office

CO 758—Empire Marketing Board—Original Correspondence (1926–33)

Board of Education

ED 10—General Education (1872–1945)

ED 23—Board of Education Papers (1903–43)

ED 50—Medical Branch Files

ED 113—National Fitness Council

ED 121—Office of Special Inquiries and Reports—Department of Intelligence and Public Relations (1935–45)

Housing and Local Government Board

HLG 52—Local Government Administration and Finance; General Policy and Procedure (1919–24)

Home Office

HO 45—Correspondence and Papers; Domestic and General (1920–39)

Ministry of Information

INF 1—Files of Correspondence (1936–50)

INF 4—Work of 1914–18 Information Services

Ministry of Agriculture and Fisheries

MAF 34—Agricultural Marketing—Correspondence and Papers

MAF 39—Establishment and Finance—Correspondence and Papers

MAF 45—Information and Publicity

MAF 52—Livestock and Dairying
National Milk Publicity Council (1928–51)

Ministry of Health

MH 55—Public Health and Poor Law; Administration and Services

MH 56—Services; Food

MH 58—General Health Questions

MH 66—Local Government Act, 1929, Public Health Surveys (1930–43)

MH 78—Establishments and Organization

MH 79—10,000 Series Files (1913–61)

MH 82—Central Council for Health Education (1935–9)

MH 107—Personnel

National Savings Committee

NSC 26—Post Office Publicity Committee (1933–9)

Stationery Office
STAT 14—Stationery Office Correspondence (1917–34)

Treasury
T 161—Supply Files
T 162—Establishment Files
T 216—Civil Service: Information Officer Class

II. PRIMARY SOURCES

(i) Newspapers and Periodicals

Daily Mail
The Economist
Evening Standard
Illustrated London News
Manchester Guardian
Morning Post
Punch
Saturday Review
The Spectator
The Times
World's Press News

(ii) Journals

Advertising World (1924–39)
The Annual Register (1920–39)
Better Health: The Official Journal of the Central Council for Health Education (1927–35)
British Imperial Calendar and Civil Service Lists
British Medical Journal
Health for All
Journal of Public Administration: Index 1923–42 (1942)
The King-Hall News-Letter (1936–8)
Planning: A Broadsheet Issued by Political and Economic Planning, vols. 1–6 (1933–9)
The Post

(iii) Official Reports and Command Papers

BOARD OF AGRICULTURE AND FISHERIES, COMMITTEE ON THE PRODUCTION AND DISTRIBUTION OF MILK, *Interim Report*, Cd. 8608 (1917).

——*Second Interim Report*, Cd. 8886 (1917).

——*Report*, Cd. 9095 (1918).

——*Third Interim Report*, Cmd. 315 (1918).

——*Final Report*, Cmd. 483 (1919).

BOARD OF EDUCATION, *Handbook of Suggestions on Health Education* (1928).

——*Syllabus of Physical Training for Schools 1933* (1933).

——*Recreation and Physical Training for Girls and Women*, Physical Training Series, 16 (1937).

CENTRAL OFFICE OF INFORMATION, *Annual Report of the Central Office of Information: Part I*, Cmd. 7567 (1947–8).

EMPIRE MARKETING BOARD, *Note on the Work of the Board and Statement of Research Grants Approved by the Secretary of State from July 1926 to May 1927*, Cmd. 2898 (1927).

——*A Second Year's Progress: May 1927 to May 1928*, EMB, 9 (1928).

——*Note on the Work of the Board and Statement of Research and Other Grants Approved by the Secretary of State from July 1926 to March 31, 1928*, Cmd. 3158 (1928).

——*Empire Marketing Board: May 1928 to May 1929*, EMB, 19 (1929).

——*Note on the Work of the Board and Statement of Research and Other Grants Approved by the Secretary of State from July 1926 to March 31, 1929*, Cmd. 3372 (1929).

——*Note on the Work of the Board and Statement of Research and Other Grants Approved by the Secretary of State from July 1926 to March 31, 1930*, Cmd. 3637 (1930).

HMSO, *Government Information Services: Statement Showing Estimated Expenditure* (1949).

Interim Report from the Royal Commission on National Museums and Galleries, Cmd. 3192 (1928).

——*Final Report: Part I, General Conclusions and Recommendations*, Cmd. 3401 (1929).

Interim Report of the Departmental Committee on Tuberculosis, Cd. 6164 (1912–13).

Memorandum on Certain Proposals Relating to Unemployment, Cmd. 3331 (1929).

MINISTRY OF AGRICULTURE AND FISHERIES, Departmental Committee on Distribution and Prices of Agricultural Produce, *Interim Report on Milk and Milk Products*, Cmd. 1854 (1923).

——Departmental Committee on Distribution and Prices of Agricultural Produce, *Final Report*, Cmd. 2008 (1924).

——*The Agricultural Output of England and Wales, 1925*, Cmd. 2815 (1927).

——*The Agricultural Output and the Food Supplies of Great Britain* (1929).

——*Report of the Reorganization Commission for Milk*, Economic Series, 38 (1933).

——*Reports on the Work of Agricultural Research Institutes and Certain Other Agricultural Investigations in the United Kingdom 1931–1932* (1933).

MINISTRY OF AGRICULTURE AND FISHERIES, *Scheme under the Agricultural Marketing Act 1931, Regulating the Marketing of Milk* (1933).

—— *Arrangements under Section II of the Milk Act 1934 for Increasing the Demand for Milk by the Supply of Milk in Schools at Reduced Rates* (1934).

—— *Census of Production, 1933–1934*, Cmd. 4605 (1934).

—— *The Milk Act 1934.*

—— *Milk Policy: Statement by the Minister of Agriculture and Fisheries in the House of Commons on Thursday Feb. 22, 1934*, Cmd. 4519 (1934).

—— *Arrangements under Section II of the Milk Act 1934 for Increasing the Demand for Milk by an Enquiry into its Nutritional Value at Certain Schools and Approved Centres* (1935).

—— *Arrangements under Section II of the Milk Act 1934 for Increasing the Demand for Milk within the Area of the Milk Marketing Board for England and Wales by Publicity and Propaganda*, 4 schemes (1935–8).

—— *Eggs and Poultry: Report of the Reorganization Commission for England and Wales*, Economic Series, 42 (1935).

—— *Milk: Report of the Reorganization Commission for Great Britain*, Economic Series, 44 (1936).

—— *Revised Arrangements under the Milk Acts 1934 and 1936 for Increasing the Demand for Milk by the Supply of Milk in Schools at Reduced Rates* (1936).

—— *Milk Policy*, Cmd. 5533 (1937).

—— *The Milk Marketing Scheme, 1933, as amended to 3rd Aug. 1937* (1938).

—— *Arrangements under the Milk Acts 1934 to 1938 for Increasing the Demand for Milk within the Area of the Milk Marketing Board for England and Wales by the supply of Milk to Nursing and Expectant Mothers and Children under 5 Years of Age at Reduced Rates* (1939).

—— *Revised Arrangements under the Milk Acts 1934 to 1938 for Increasing the Demand for Milk by the Supply of Milk in Schools at Reduced Rates* (1939).

—— *Scheme under the Agricultural Marketing Acts 1931 to 1933 Regulating the Marketing of Milk Products* (1939).

MINISTRY OF HEALTH, *Annual Reports* (1920–39).

—— *Annual Report of the Chief Medical Officer 1919–1920*, Cmd. 978 (1920).

MINISTRY OF RECONSTRUCTION, *Report of the Machinery of Government Committee*, Cd. 9230 (1918).

PARLIAMENTARY DEBATES: Hansard (1906–48).

Physical Training and Recreation: Memorandum Explaining the Government's Proposals for the Development and Extension of the Facilities Available, Cmd. 5364 (1937).

Post Office Commercial Accounts (1920–39).

Report of the Committee of Enquiry on the Post Office, 1932, Cmd. 4149 (1932).

Report of the Committee on the Cost of Home Information Services, Cmd. 7836 (1949).

Report of the Royal Commission on the Press 1947–1949, Cmd. 7700 (1949).

Report of the Royal Commission on Tuberculosis, Cmd. 5761 (1911).

Report on the Condition of Production of Milk (Used in Preparing Condensed Milk) in the Netherlands and Denmark, Cmd. 3004 (1927).

Reports from the Select Committee on Estimates (1922–39).

Reports from the Select Committee on Publications and Debates (1906–45).

Reports from the Select Committee on the Telephone Service (27 July 1921 and 20 Mar. 1922).

Reports of the Comptroller-General of Patents, Designs and Trade Marks (1919–39).

Summary of the Report of the Independent Committee of Enquiry into the Overseas Information Services, Cmd. 9138 (1954).

Third Report of the Committee on National Expenditure, Cmd. 1589 (1922).

(iv) Other Publications

A Better Way to Better Times: Reprint of Statement Issued by His Majesty's Government on Mr. Lloyd George's Proposals (July 1935).

The Advertising Register: A Directory of Advertisers Keyed by Trades and Classified Territorially (1928).

ALBIG, WILLIAM, *Public Opinion* (1939).

ANGELL, NORMAN, *The Public Mind: Its Disorders; Its Exploitation* (1926).

—— *The Press and the Organization of Society* (Cambridge, 1933).

ASTOR, VISCOUNT, and SEEBOHM ROWNTREE, B., *British Agriculture: The Principles of Future Policy: A Report of an Enquiry Organized by Viscount Astor and B. Seebohm Rowntree* (1938).

Author's and Writer's Who's Who (1934–9).

BALDWIN, STANLEY, *On England and Other Addresses* (1926).

—— *Service of our Lives: Last Speeches as Prime Minister* (1937).

BASTER, A. S. J., *Advertising Reconsidered: A Confession of Misgiving* (1935).

BAXTER, BEVERLEY, *Men, Martyrs and Mountebanks: Beverley Baxter's Inner Story of Personalities and Events behind the War* (1940).

BELGRAVE, A. C., *Telephone Service*, Post Office Green Papers, 37 (Jan. 1938).

BERNAYS, EDWARD L., *Propaganda* (1928).

BERNSTEIN, HILLEL, *Choose a Bright Morning* (1936).

BEVERIDGE, SIR WILLIAM, *Some Experiences of Economic Control in War-Time*, Sidney Ball Lecture (1940).

BRUNTZ, GEORGE G., *Allied Propaganda and the Collapse of the German Empire in 1918* (Stanford, Calif., 1938).

BRYANT, ARTHUR, *The National Character* (1934).

—— *Stanley Baldwin: A Tribute* (1937).

CALDER-MARSHALL, ARTHUR, *The Changing Scene* (1937).

CAPLES, JOHN, *Tested Advertising Methods* (1932).

CARR-SAUNDERS, A. M., and CARDOG-JONES, D., *A Survey of the Social Structure of England and Wales as Illustrated by Statistics* (1927).

CHAKOTIN, SERGE, *The Rape of the Masses: The Psychology of Totalitarian Political Propaganda*, trans. E. W. Dickes (1940).

CHILDS, HARWOOD LAWRENCE (ed.), *Propaganda and Dictatorship: A Collection of Papers* (Princeton, NJ, 1936).

CRAWFORD, SIR WILLIAM, *How to Succeed in Advertising* (1931).

——and HIGHAM, SIR CHARLES, *Advertising and the Man in the Street* (Leeds, 1929).

CREW, T., *Health Propaganda (Ways and Means): Covering the Propaganda Services of the National Health Associations and Others, Organisation of Health Exhibitions and Health Week Campaigns* (Leicester, 1935).

CRUTCHLEY, E. T., *GPO*, English Institutions Series, ed. Lord Stamp (Cambridge, 1938).

The Dairyman, Conference on the Milk Question Reprinted from The Dairyman (1923).

The Encyclopedia of Advertising and Selling: A Complete Manual in Three Parts on the Latest Plans and Methods for Selling Goods through Advertising Postal Publicity and through Salesmen (1923).

FLOUD, FRANCIS L. C., *The Ministry of Agriculture and Fisheries*, Whitehall Series, ed. Sir James Marchant (1927).

FORRESTER, R. B., *The Fluid Milk Market in England and Wales*, Ministry of Agriculture and Fisheries, Economic Series, 16 (1927).

GALLUP, GEORGE, *Public Opinion in a Democracy* (Princeton, NJ, 1939).

GIBBS, PHILIP, *Now It Can Be Told* (Garden City, NY, 1920).

GOODALL, G. W., *Advertising: A Study of a Modern Business Power* (1914).

GRAVES, ROBERT, *Goodbye to All That: An Autobiography* (1929).

——and HODGE, ALAN, *The Long Weekend: A Social History of Great Britain 1918–1939* (New York, 1940).

GRIERSON, JOHN, *Grierson on Documentary*, ed. Forsyth Hardy (1946).

HANSARD SOCIETY, *First Report*, 2nd edn. (1944).

HARGRAVE, JOHN, *Propaganda: The Mightiest Weapon of All: Words Win Wars* (1940).

HENDERSON, H., *et al.*, *Books and the Public: By the Editor of The Nation* (1927).

HIGHAM, CHARLES FREDERICK, *Looking Forward: Mass Education through Publicity* (1920).

——*Advertising: Its Use and Abuse* (1925).

——*Tittle Tattle: Being Old Saws Resharpened with One or Two New Ones* [1925].

HITLER, ADOLF, *Mein Kampf*, trans. Ralph Manheim (1969).

HOBHOUSE, L. T., *Liberalism* (1911).

KAUFFER, E. MCKNIGHT (ed.), *The Art of the Poster: Its Origin, Evolution and Purpose* (1924).

KEYNES, J. M., and HENDERSON, H. D., *Can Lloyd George Do It? An Examination of the Liberal Pledge* (1929).

KING-HALL, COMMANDER STEPHEN, *Here and There: Broadcast Talks for Children*, 3 vols. (1932–4).

——*Chatham House: A Brief Account of the Origins, Purposes, and Methods of the Royal Institute of International Affairs* (1937).

——*King-Hall Survey 1936* (1937).

LAMBERT, RICHARD S., *Propaganda* (1938).

LASSWELL, HAROLD, *Propaganda Technique in the World War* (1927).

——CASEY, RALPH D., and LANNES SMITH, BRUCE, *Propaganda and Promotional Activities: An Annotated Bibliography* (Minneapolis, 1935).

LAWRENCE, T. B. (ed.), *What I Know about Advertising: Being a Series of Lectures Given at the International Advertising Exhibition (1920) (Promoted by the Thirty Club of London Ltd) in the White City London and Made into a Book for the Benefit of Students of Business by Fourteen Leading Experts* (1921).

LEAGUE OF NATIONS, *The League of Nations and the School: A Memorandum of Suggestions for Teachers* (Glasgow, 1929).

LE BON, GUSTAVE, *The Crowd: A Study of the Popular Mind* (1896).

LEWIS, C. DAY (ed.), *The Mind in Chains: Socialism and the Cultural Revolution* (1937).

LIBERAL INDUSTRIAL INQUIRY, *Britain's Industrial Future* (1928).

LIBERAL PARTY, *We Can Conquer Unemployment: Mr. Lloyd George's Pledge* (1929).

LIPPMANN, WALTER, *Public Opinion* (New York, 1922).

LLOYD GEORGE, DAVID, *Organizing Prosperity: A Scheme of National Reconstruction* (1935).

——*et al.*, *How to Tackle Unemployment: The Liberal Plans as Laid before the Government and the Nation* (1930).

LOWELL, ABBOTT LAWRENCE, *Public Opinion in War and Peace* (1923).

LUMLEY, FREDERICK E., *The Propaganda Menace* (1933).

MCDOUGALL, WILLIAM, *The Group Mind: A Sketch of the Principles of Collective Psychology with Some Attempt to Apply them to the Interpretation of National Life and Character* (Cambridge, 1920).

MACPHERSON, WILLIAM, *The Psychology of Persuasion* (1920).

MADGE, CHARLES, and HARRISSON, TOM, *Britain by Mass-Observation* (1939).

MARTIN, EVERETT DEAN, *The Behavior of Crowds: A Psychological Study* (New York, 1920).

——*The Conflict of the Individual and the Mass in the Modern World* (New York, 1932).

MASS-OBSERVATION, *Us: Mass-Observation's Weekly Intelligence Service* (1940).

——*War Begins at Home*, ed. Tom Harrisson and Charles Madge (1940).

——*Home Propaganda, Change: Bulletin of The Advertising Service Guide no. 2* (1941).

——*The Pub and the People: A Worktown Study* (1943).

MATHESON, HILDA, *Broadcasting* (1933).

MILK MARKETING BOARD, *An Introduction to Milk Marketing*, Series PB 9 (1937).

——*Milk Marketing Scheme: Five Years' Review 1933–1938* (1939).

MUGGERIDGE, MALCOLM, *The Thirties: 1930–1940 in Great Britain* (1940).

MURRAY SIR EVELYN, *The Post Office*, Whitehall Series, ed. Sir James Marchant (1927).

MURRAY K. A. H., and RUTHERFORD, R. S. G., *Milk Consumption Habits: Preliminary Report* (Oxford, 1941).

THE NATIONAL ADVISORY COUNCIL and the GRANTS COMMITTEE FOR PHYSICAL TRAINING AND RECREATION, *National Fitness: The First Steps* (July 1937).

NATIONAL ADVISORY COUNCIL FOR PHYSICAL TRAINING AND RECREATION, *Memorandum on the Powers of Local Authorities under the Physical Training and Recreation Act 1937* (1937).

NATIONAL CLEAN MILK SOCIETY, *Campaign for Clean Milk: A Series of Articles that have Appeared in the 'Observer'* (1916).

NATIONAL FARMERS' UNION, *The National Farmers' Union Yearbook* (1922–39).

NATIONAL FITNESS COUNCIL, *Twenty-four Ways of Keeping Fit* (1938).

NATIONAL FITNESS COUNCIL FOR ENGLAND AND WALES, *Memorandum on the Preservation of Existing Playing Field Facilities* (1938).

—— *Floodlighting Playgrounds and Playing Fields* (1939).

—— *The National Fitness Campaign* (1939).

NEWMAN, SIR GEORGE, *An Outline of the Practice of Preventive Medicine*, Memorandum addressed to the Minister of Health, Cmd. 363 (1919).

—— *The Place of Public Opinion in Preventive Medicine*, The Lady Priestly Memorial Lecture, delivered before the National Health Society, 22 Apr. 1920 (1920).

—— *Public Education in Health*, Memorandum addressed to the Minister of Health (1924).

—— *Public Education in Health*, Memorandum addressed to the Minister of Health, revised 1925 (1926).

—— *The Foundations of National Health* (1928).

—— *The Building of a Nation's Health* (1939).

NICHOLS, BEVERLEY, *The Star-Spangled Manner* (1928).

ORR, JOHN BOYD, *Food Health and Income: Report on a Survey of Adequacy of Diet in Relation to Income* (1936).

ORTEGA Y GASSET, JOSÉ, *The Revolt of the Masses* (New York, 1930).

Oxford English Dictionary, 12 vols. and *Supplement* (Oxford, 1933).

PETERSON, H. C., *Propaganda for War: The Campaign against American Neutrality 1914–1917* (Norman, Okla., 1939).

PILGRIM TRUST, *Men without Work: A Report Made to the Pilgrim Trust* (Cambridge, 1938).

POLITICAL AND ECONOMIC PLANNING, *Report on the British Health Services: A Survey of the Existing Health Services in Great Britain with Proposals for Future Development* (1937).

PONSONBY, ARTHUR, *Falsehood in War-Time: Containing an Assortment of Lies Circulated throughout the Nations during the Great War* (New York, 1928).

THE POST OFFICE, *Peter in the Post Office* (1934).

—— *The Post Office: A Review of the Activities of the Post Office 1934* (1934).

——Post Office Green Papers, 1–46 (Aug. 1934–May 1939).

——*The Post Office Magazine* (1934–9).

——*The Post Office in Pictures* (1935).

——*The Post Office Telephone Sales Bulletin* (1935–9).

PRAIGG, NOBLE T. (ed.), *Advertising and Selling: By 150 Advertising and Sales Executives* (1924).

PRESBREY, FRANK, *The History and Development of Advertising* (New York, 1929).

READ, JAMES MORGAN, *Atrocity Propaganda 1914–1919* (New Haven, Conn., 1941).

RIDDELL, LORD, *Lord Riddell's War Diary 1914–1918* (1933).

RILEY, NORMAN, *999 and All That* (1940).

ROGERSON, SIDNEY, *Propaganda in the Next War*, Next War Series, ed. Captain Liddell Hart (1938).

ROTHA, PAUL, *The Film Till Now: A Survey of the Cinema* (1930).

——*Documentary Film* (1936).

RUSSELL, HON. BERTRAND, *Free Thought and Official Propaganda*, Conway Memorial Lecture, delivered at South Place Institute on 24 Mar. 1922 (1922).

SAYERS, DOROTHY L., *Murder Must Advertise* (1933).

SIMON, ERNEST, and HUBBACK, EVA M., *Training for Citizenship* (1935).

SQUIRES, JAMES DUANE, *British Propaganda at Home and in the United States from 1914 to 1917* (Cambridge, Mass., 1935).

Statistical Abstract for the United Kingdom (1919–36).

The Statistical Review of Press Advertising (1932–9).

STEED, HENRY WICKHAM, *Through Thirty Years 1892–1922: A Personal Narrative*, 2 vols. (1924).

STUART, SIR CAMPBELL, *Secrets of Crewe House: The Story of a Famous Campaign* (1920).

TALLENTS, SIR STEPHEN, *The Projection of England* (1932).

——*Post Office Publicity*, Post Office Green Papers, 8 (1935).

THE TELEPHONE DEVELOPMENT ASSOCIATION, *The Strangle-hold on our Telephones: A Practical Remedy* (1930).

THOMAS, IVOR, *Warfare by Words* (1942).

THOMSON, SIR BASIL, *The Scene Changes* (1939).

THOULESS, ROBERT H., *The Control of the Mind: A Handbook of Applied Psychology for the Ordinary Man* (1927).

——*Straight and Crooked Thinking* (1930).

——*Social Psychology* (1935).

THE TIMES, *The Times History and Encyclopedia of the War: British Propaganda in Enemy Countries*, xxi (1919), pt. 270, ch. 314.

——*The Nation's Health* (1937).

——*The Readership of the Times: Its Nature and Privileges* (1937).

TROTTER, W., *Instincts of the Herd in Peace and War* (1916, 1920).

VERNON, R. V., and MANSBERGH, N. (eds.), *Advisory Bodies: A Study of their Uses in Relation to Central Government 1919–1939* (1940).

VIERECK, GEORGE SYLVESTER, *Spreading Germs of Hate* (1931).

WAUGH, EVELYN, *Put Out More Flags* (1942).

WEEKS, ARLAND D., *The Control of the Social Mind: Psychology of Economic and Political Relations* (1923).

WHITE, AMBER BLANCO, *The New Propaganda* (1939).

WICKENS, G. C., *Staff Training in London*, Post Office Green Papers, 16 (Oct. 1935).

WOLMER, VISCOUNT, *Post Office Reform: Its Importance and Practicability* (1932).

(v) Articles

ADAMS, W. G. S., 'University Education in Public Administration', *Public Administration*, 4 (1926), 431–3.

BELLMAN, SIR HAROLD, 'The Traditions of the Public Services: Can They be Extended to Business?', *Public Administration*, 14 (1936), 119–33.

BEVIN, ERNEST, 'The Management of Public Utility Undertakings', *Public Administration*, 7 (1929), 130–2.

BIGELOW, BURTON, 'Should Business Decentralize its Counter-Propaganda?', *Public Opinion Quarterly*, 2/2 (1938), 321–4.

BROADLEY, J. H., 'The Management of Public Utility Undertakings', *Public Administration*, 7 (1929), 120–9.

BROWN, W. H., and DRURY, T. L., 'Typography in the Post Office', *Public Administration*, 13 (1935), 359–61.

BUNBURY, SIR HENRY N., 'The Management of Public Utility Undertakings', *Public Administration*, 7 (1929), 111–19.

CARLILL, H. F., 'Administrative Habits of Mind', *Public Administration*, 8 (1930), 119–30.

CASEY, RALPH D., 'The National Publicity Bureau and British Party Propaganda', *Public Opinion Quarterly* (New York), 3 (1939), 623–34.

CATLIN, GEORGE E. GORDON, 'Propaganda as a Function of Democratic Government', in Harwood Lawrence Childs (ed.), *Propaganda and Dictatorship: A Collection of Papers* (Princeton, NJ, 1936), 125–45.

CLAN, KAMMERHERRE J., 'Officials and Policy', *Public Administration*, 5 (1927), 478–81.

CLARKE, SIR GEOFFREY, 'Business Management of the Public Services', *Public Administration*, 8 (1930), 10–15.

COLE, G. D. H., 'The Method of Social Legislation', *Public Administration*, 9 (1931), 4–14.

COLLIS, A. J., 'Diffusion of Knowledge as a Factor in the Improvement of the Public Health', Presidential Address to the Newcastle Clinical Society, 1 Oct. 1908 (Newcastle upon Tyne, 1908), 3–15.

CORNER, H. G., 'The Aims of the Institute of Public Administration', *Public Administration*, 1 (1923), 49–55.

COWELL, F. R., 'The Uses and Dangers of Publicity in the Work of Government', *Public Administration*, 13 (1935), 290–3.

CROMWELL, PETER, 'The Propaganda Problem', *Horizon*, ed. Cyril Connolly, 3/13 (1941), 17–32.

DAKYNS, ARTHUR L., 'Democracy and the Public Service', *Public Administration*, 13 (1935), 338–43.

DAVIES, ASHTON, 'Correspondence with the Public', *Public Administration*, 14 (1936), 268–75.

ELLIS, H. H., 'The Relations between State Departments and the Nation', *Public Administration*, 4 (1926), 95–106.

ENGELBRIGHT, H. C., 'How War Propaganda Won', *The World Tomorrow* (Apr. 1927), 159.

FARNSWORTH, PAUL R., and BEHNER, ALICE, 'A Note on the Attitude of Social Conformity', *Journal of Social Psychology: Political, Racial and Differential Psychology*, ed. John Dewey and Carl Murchison, 2 (1931), 126–8.

FINER, HERMAN, 'Officials and the Public', *Public Administration*, 9 (1931), 23–36.

FITTER, R. S. R., 'An Experiment in Public Relations', *Public Administration*, 14 (1936), 464–7.

FOLEY, E. J., 'Officials and the Public', *Public Administration*, 9 (1931), 15–22.

FOSTER, H. SCHUYLER, JUN., 'The Official Propaganda of Great Britain', *Public Opinion Quarterly* (Princeton, NJ), 3 (1939), 263–71.

GIBBON, I. G., 'The Appellate Jurisdiction of Government Departments', *Public Administration*, 7 (1929), 269–77.

GRIERSON, JOHN, 'Films in the Public Service', *Public Administration*, 14 (1936), 366–72.

HALDANE, VISCOUNT, 'An Organized Civil Service', *Public Administration*, 1 (1923), 6–16.

HALL, SIR DANIEL A., 'The Economic Position of Agriculture', *Contemporary Review*, 133/746 (1928), 137–49.

HART, SIR WILLIAM E., 'Officials and Policy', *Public Administration*, 5 (1927), 471–7.

HENDERSON, EDGAR H., 'Toward a Definition of Propaganda', *Journal of Social Psychology: Political, Racial and Differential Psychology*, ed. Carl Murchison, 18 (1943), 71–87.

HILL, L., 'Advertising Local Government in England', *Public Opinion Quarterly*, 1/2 (1937), 62–72.

HINCKLEY, E. D., 'The Influence of Individual Opinion on Construction of an Attitude Scale', *Journal of Social Psychology: Political, Racial and Differential Psychology*, ed. Carl Murchison, 3 (1932), 283–96.

HORE, SIR ADAIR, 'Officials and Policy', *Public Administration*, 5 (1927), 461–70.

'In the Propaganda Arena', *Public Opinion Quarterly*, 2/3 (1938), 491–7.

J.J.T., 'The Message of the Institute of Public Administration', *Public Administration*, 8 (1930), 236–9.

KLIMAN, M., 'Correspondence with the Public', *Public Administration*, 14 (1936), 276–90.

LARSON, CEDRIC, 'How Much Federal Publicity is There?', *Public Opinion Quarterly*, 2/4 (1938), 636–44.

LASKI, HAROLD J., 'The Growth of Administrative Discretion', *Public Administration*, 1 (1923), 92–100.

LEE, JOHN, 'The Parallels between Industrial Administration and Public Administration', *Public Administration*, 4 (1926), 216–22.

LICHTENBERG, BERNARD, 'Business Backs New York World Fair to Meet the New Deal Propaganda', *Public Opinion Quarterly*, 2/2 (1938), 314–20.

LOWES-DICKINSON, SIR ARTHUR, 'Publicity in Industrial Accounts with a Comparison of English and American Methods', *Journal of the Royal Statistical Society*, 87/3 (1924), 391–433.

LUNDHOLM, HELGE, 'Mark Antony's Speech and the Psychology of Persuasion', *Character and Personality: An International Quarterly of Psychodiagnostics and Allied Studies*, (Durham, NC), 6 (1937–8), 293–305.

LYEL, P. C., 'Some Psychological Factors in Public Administration', *Public Administration*, 8 (1930), 131–47.

LYON, LEVERETT S., 'Advertising', in *Encyclopedia of the Social Sciences*, ed. Edwin R. A. Seligman, i (1930), 469–75.

McCORD, FLETCHER, 'A Blueprint for Total Morale', *Character and Personality: An International Psychological Quarterly* (Durham, NC), 11 (1942–3), 89–107.

MACKIE, T. J., 'The Relationship of the Universities to Public Affairs,' *Public Administration*, 8 (1930), 180–91.

MARTIN, KINGSLEY, 'The Ministry of Information', *Political Quarterly*, 10/4 (1939), 502–16.

MERCEY, ARCH A., 'School for Federal Publicity Men at American University', *Public Opinion Quarterly*, 2/2 (1938), 324–9.

MILNER, VISCOUNT, 'The Aims of the Institute of Public Administration', *Public Administration*, 1 (1923), 85–91.

MILWARD, G. E., 'The Collection and Distribution of Information', *Public Administration*, 15 (1937), 226–9.

NICOLSON, HAROLD, 'British Public Opinion and Foreign Policy', *Public Opinion Quarterly*, 1/1 (1937), 53–63.

ODEGARD, PETER H., 'Review of Books', *Public Opinion Quarterly*, 1/4 (1937), 144–6.

POTTER, PITMAN B., 'League Publicity: Cause or Effect of League Failure?', *Public Opinion Quarterly*, 2/3 (1938), 399–412.

POWERS, FRANCIS F., 'The Influence of Intelligence and Personality Traits upon False Beliefs', *Journal of Social Psychology: Political, Racial and Differential Psychology*, ed. John Dewey and Carl Murchison, 2 (1931), 490–3.

READ, JAMES MORGAN, 'Atrocity Propaganda and the Irish Rebellion', *Public Opinion Quarterly*, 2/2 (1938), 229–44.

REMMERS, H. H., 'Propaganda in the Schools: Do the Effects Last?', *Public Opinion Quarterly*, 2/2 (1938), 197–210.

REYMERT, MARTIN L., and KOHN, HAROLD A., 'An Objective Investigation of Suggestibility', *Character and Personality: An International Quarterly of Psychodiagnostics and Allied Studies* (Durham, NC), 9 (1940–1), 44–8.

ROBERTSON, C. GRANT, 'University Education in Public Administration: The Universities and Administrative Science', *Public Administration*, 4 (1926), 438–42.

ROGERS, CHARLES E., 'Book Review', *Public Opinion Quarterly*, 2/2 (1938), 348–9.

RYAN, A. P., 'Intelligence and Public Relations', *Public Administration*, 14/1 (1936), 59–65.

SHARP, W. D., 'Correspondence with the Public', *Public Administration*, 14 (1936), 291–300.

SIMEY, T. S., 'A Public Relations Policy for Local Authorities', *Public Administration*, 13 (1935), 242–50.

SLY, JOHN F., and ROBBINS, JAMES J., 'Popularizing the Results of Government Research', *Public Opinion Quarterly*, 2/1 (1938), 7–23.

STAMP, SIR JOSIAH C., 'The Contrast between the Administration of Business and Public Affairs', *Public Administration*, 1 (1923), 158–71.

STARR, JOSEPH R., 'Research Activities of British Political Parties', *Public Opinion Quarterly*, 1/4 (1937), 99–107.

STEWART, A. C., 'Reviews: Post Office Publicity and the Green Papers', *Public Administration*, 14 (1936), 66–71.

STUART-BUNNING, G. H., 'The Theory of Post Office Policy', *Public Administration*, 4 (1926), 24–40.

—— 'The Personal Relations of Officials with the Public', *Public Administration*, 9 (1931), 36–40.

TALLENTS, SIR STEPHEN G., 'Salesmanship in the Public Service: Scope and Technique', *Public Administration*, 11 (1933), 259–66.

TOWNSHEND, H., ' "Practical Psychology" in Departmental Organisation', *Public Administration*, 12 (1934), 65–9.

VIVIAN, S. P., 'Statistics in Administration', *Public Administration*, 1 (1923), 108–16.

WHITEHEAD, HAROLD, 'Salesmanship in the Public Service: Scope and Technique', *Public Administration*, 11 (1933), 267–76.

WICKENS, G. C., 'Training of the Post Office Counter Staff', *Public Administration*, 12 (1934), 58–64.

WOOD, S. H., 'Intelligence and Public Relations: Intelligence and Public Relations in a Government Department', *Public Administration*, 14/1 (1936), 41–8.

WRIGHT, C. KENT, 'Intelligence and Public Relations: Local Authorities', *Public Administration*, 14/1 (1936), 49–58.

YOUNG, KIMBALL, 'Book Reviews', *Public Opinion Quarterly*, 1/1 (1937), 160–1.

268   *Bibliography*

III. SECONDARY SOURCES

(i) Books, Journals, and Government Publications

A Supplement to the Oxford English Dictionary, iii (Oxford, 1982).

ABBEY, CHARLES J., and OVERTON, JOHN H., *The English Church in the Eighteenth Century*, ii (1878).

ABRAMOVITZ, MOSES, and ELIASBERG, VERA F., *The Growth of Public Employment in Great Britain* (Princeton, NJ, 1957).

ADDISON, PAUL, *The Road to 1945: British Politics and the Second World War* (1975).

THE ADVERTISING ASSOCIATION, *The Advertising Quarterly: A Critical and Professional Review*, 1/6 (1964–5).

ANDREWS, ALEXANDER, *The History of British Journalism*, i (1968).

ANGLO, SYDNEY, *Spectacle, Pageantry, and Early Tudor Policy* (Oxford, 1969).

ASPINALL, A., *Politics and the Press c.1780–1850* (1949).

BALFOUR, MICHAEL, *Propaganda in War, 1939–1945: Organisations, Policies and Publics in Britain and Germany* (1979).

BARKER, T. C., and ROBBINS, MICHAEL, *A History of London Transport: Passenger Travel and the Development of the Metropolis*, ii. *The Twentieth Century to 1970* (1974).

BARMAN, CHRISTIAN, *The Man Who Built London Transport: A Biography of Frank Pick* (1979).

BEER, SAMUEL H., *Modern British Politics: Parties and Pressure Groups in the Collectivist Age* (1965).

BEGLEY, GEORGE, *Keep Mum! Advertising Goes to War* (1975).

BENTLEY, MICHAEL, *The Liberal Mind 1914–1929* (Cambridge, 1977).

BERGER, PETER L., and LUCKMANN, THOMAS, *The Social Construction of Reality: A Treatise in the Sociology of Knowledge* (1967).

BIDDISS, MICHAEL D., *The Age of the Masses: Ideas and Society in Europe since 1870* (Hassocks, Sussex, 1977).

BIRKENHEAD, LORD, *Walter Monckton: The Life of Viscount Monckton of Brenchley* (1969).

BLACK, JOHN B., *Organising the Propaganda Instrument: The British Experience* (The Hague, 1975).

BOGDANOR, VERNON, *The People and the Party System: The Referendum and Electoral Reform in British Politics* (Cambridge, 1981).

BOYLE, ANDREW, *Only the Wind Will Listen: Reith of the B.B.C.* (1972).

——*Poor, Dear Brendan: The Quest for Brendan Bracken* (1974).

BRADLEY, JAMES E., *Popular Politics and the American Revolution in England: Petitions, the Crown, and Public Opinion* (Macon, Ga., 1986).

BRAMSTED, E. K., *Goebbels and National Socialist Propaganda 1925–1945* (Detroit, 1965).

BRENDON, PIERS, *Eminent Edwardians* (New York, 1981).

BRIDGES, LORD, *The Treasury* (1962).

BRIGGS, ASA, *The History of Broadcasting in the United Kingdom*, ii. *The Golden Age of Wireless* (1965).

—— *The History of Broadcasting in the United Kingdom*, iii. *The War of Words* (1970).

BRIGGS, SUSAN, *Keep Smiling Through* (1975).

CALDER, ANGUS, *The People's War: Britain 1939–1945* (1969).

—— and SHERIDAN, DOROTHY (eds.), *Speak for Yourself: A Mass-Observation Anthology 1937–49* (1984).

CANTRIL, HADLEY (ed.), *Public Opinion 1935–1946* (Princeton, NJ, 1951).

CARPENTER, S. C., *Eighteenth-Century Church and People* (1959).

CEADEL, MARTIN, *Pacifism in Britain 1914–1945: The Defining of a Faith* (Oxford, 1980).

CLARK, SIR FIFE, *The Central Office of Information*, New Whitehall Series, 15 (1970).

CLARK, SIR KENNETH, *The Other Half: A Self-Portrait* (1977).

CLAY HENRY (ed.), *The Inter-War Years and Other Papers: A Selection From the Writings of Hubert Douglas Henderson* (Oxford, 1955).

COHEN, EMMELINE W., *The Growth of the British Civil Service 1780–1939* (Hamden, Conn., 1965).

COOPER, ALFRED DUFF, *Old Men Forget: The Autobiography of Duff Cooper* (1953).

CRICK, BERNARD, *George Orwell: A Life* (1980).

CRITCHLEY, R. A., *U.K. Advertising Statistics: A Review of the Principal Sources and Figures* (1974).

CROFTS, WILLIAM, *Coercion or Persuasion? Propaganda in Britain after 1945* (1989).

CRUICKSHANK, CHARLES, *The Fourth Arm: Psychological Warfare 1938–1945* (Oxford, 1981).

CRUTCHLEY, BROOKE, *Ernest Tristram Crutchley: A Memoir* (Cambridge, 1941).

DAUNTON, M. J., *Royal Mail: The Post Office since 1840* (1985).

DAVENPORT-HINES, R. P. T., *Dudley Docker: The Life and Times of a Trade Warrior* (Cambridge, 1984).

DICKINSON, H. T., *British Radicalism and the French Revolution 1789–1815* (Oxford, 1985).

DICKINSON, MARGARET, and STREET, SARAH, *Cinema and the State: The Film Industry and the Government 1927–1984* (1985).

Dictionary of Business Biography.

Dictionary of National Biography.

DOZIER, ROBERT R., *For King, Constitution, and Country: The English Loyalists and the French Revolution* (Lexington, Ky., 1983).

DRUMMOND, J. C., and WILBRAHAM, ANNE, *The Englishman's Food: A History of Five Centuries of English Diet* (1957).

ELLIOT, BLANCHE B., *A History of English Advertising* (1962).

ELLIS, JACK C., *A History of Film* (Englewood Cliffs, NJ, 1979).

ELLIS, KENNETH, *The Post Office in the Eighteenth Century: A Study in Administrative History* (1958).

EVERARD, STIRLING L., *The History of the Gas Light and Coke Company 1812–1949* (1949).

EWEN, STUART, *Captains of Consciousness: Advertising and the Social Roots of the Consumer Culture* (New York, 1976).

FRASER, LINDLEY, *Propaganda* (1957).

FUSSELL, PAUL, *The Great War and Modern Memory* (1975).

GALLUP, GEORGE H. (ed.), *The Gallup International Public Opinion Polls Great Britain 1937–1975*, i. *1937–64* (New York, 1976).

GILBERT, BENTLEY B., *British Social Policy, 1914–1939* (1970).

GREENWOOD, JEREMY, *Newspapers and the Post Office 1635–1834* (1971).

HARDY, FORSYTH, *John Grierson: A Documentary Biography* (1979).

HARRISSON, TOM, *Living through the Blitz* (1976).

HASTE, CATE, *Keep the Home Fires Burning: Propaganda in the First World War* (1977).

JENKINS, SIR GILMOUR, *The Ministry of Transport and Civil Aviation* (1958).

JONES, THOMAS, *Whitehall Diary, 1916–1930*, ed. Keith Middlemas, 2 vols. (1969).

KALDOR, NICHOLAS, and SILVERMAN, RODNEY, *A Statistical Analysis of Advertising Expenditure and of the Revenue of the Press* (Cambridge, 1948).

KELSALL, R. K., *Higher Civil Servants in Britain: From 1870 to the Present Day* (1955).

KNIGHTLEY, PHILIP, *The First Casualty: From the Crimea to Vietnam: The War Correspondent as Hero, Propagandist and Myth Maker* (1975).

LAKE, BRIAN, *British Newspapers: A History and Guide for Collectors* (1984).

LANDBRIDGE, R. H., *Advertising in the Times Literary Supplement 1902–1972* (1972).

LEE, ALAN J., *The Origins of the Popular Press in England 1855–1914* (1976).

LEMAHIEU, D. L., *A Culture for Democracy: Mass Communications and the Cultivated Mind in Britain between the Wars* (Oxford, 1988).

LOW, RACHAEL, *The History of British Film*, iv. *1918–1929* (1971).

MACKENZIE, JOHN M., *Propaganda and Empire: The Manipulation of British Public Opinion 1880–1960* (Manchester, 1984).

MCLAINE, IAN, *Ministry of Morale: Home Front Morale and the Ministry of Information in World War II* (1979).

MACMILLAN, LORD, *A Man of Law's Tale: The Reminiscences of the Rt. Hon. Lord Macmillan* (1952).

MARETT, SIR ROBERT, *Through the Back Door: An Inside View of Britain's Overseas Information Services* (1968).

MARWICK, ARTHUR, *The Deluge: British Society and the First World War* (Harmondsworth, Middlesex, 1965).

—— *Britain in the Century of Total War: War, Peace and Social Change 1900–1967* (Boston, 1968).

—— *The Home Front: The British and the Second World War* (1976).

MIDDLEMAS, KEITH, *Politics in Industrial Society: The Experience of the British System since 1911* (1979).

——and BARNES, JOHN, *Baldwin: A Biography* (1969).

MILL, J. S., *'On Liberty' and 'Considerations on Representative Government'*, ed. R. B. McCallum (Oxford, 1946).

MILLS, G. H. SAXON, *There is a Tide . . . : The Life and Work of Sir William Crawford, K.B.E., Embodying an Historical Study of Modern British Advertising* (1954).

MOGGRIDGE, D. E., *Keynes* (1976).

MORGAN, KENNETH O., *Lloyd George* (1974).

——*The Oxford History of Britain* (Oxford, 1988).

MOSLEY, LEONARD, *Backs to the Wall: London under Fire 1939–1945* (1971).

MOWAT, CHARLES LOCH, *Britain between the Wars 1918–1940* (1978).

MURRAY, KEITH A. H., *Agriculture: History of the Second World War*, United Kingdom Civil Series, ed. Sir Keith Hancock (1955).

NATIONAL BOARD FOR PRICES AND INCOMES, *Costs and Revenue of National Newspapers*, Report 141, Cmd. 4277 (1970).

NEVETT, T. R., *Advertising in Britain: A History* (1982).

NEWSAM, SIR FRANK, *The Home Office*, New Whitehall Series (1954).

NICOLSON, HAROLD, *Diaries and Letters 1930–1939*, ed. Nigel Nicolson (1966).

——*Diaries and Letters 1939–1945*, ed. Nigel Nicolson (1967).

NORMAN, E. R., *Church and Society in England 1770–1970: A Historical Study* (Oxford, 1976).

NOWELL-SMITH, SIMON (ed.), *Edwardian England 1901–1914* (1964).

OGILVY-WEBB, MARJORIE, *The Government Explains: A Study of the Information Services* (1965).

ORWELL, GEORGE, *The Collected Essays, Journalism, and Letters of George Orwell*, ii. *An Age Like This 1920–1940*, ed. Sonia Orwell and Ian Angus (New York, 1979).

PANTER-DOWNES, MOLLIE, *London War Notes 1939–1945*, ed. William Shawn (New York, 1971).

PEACOCK, ALAN T., and WISEMAN, JACK, *The Growth of Public Expenditure in the United Kingdom* (Princeton, NJ, 1961).

PERKIN, HAROLD, *Origins of Modern English Society* (1969).

——*The Rise of Professional Society: England since 1880* (1990).

PHILLIPS, G. A., *The General Strike: The Politics of Industrial Conflict* (1976).

POLLAY, RICHARD W. (ed.), *Information Sources in Advertising History* (1979).

POUND, REGINALD, and HARMSWORTH, GEOFFREY, *Northcliffe* (1959).

PRONAY, NICHOLAS, and SPRING, D. W. (eds.), *Propaganda, Politics and Film, 1918–1945* (1982).

PUGH, MARTIN, *The Making of Modern British Politics 1867–1939* (1982).

RAMSDEN, JOHN, *The Making of Conservative Party Policy: The Conservative Research Department since 1929* (1980).

RAYMOND, JOHN (ed.), *The Baldwin Age* (1960).

RENSHAW, PATRICK, *The General Strike* (1975).

ROETTER, CHARLES, *Psychological Warfare* (1974).

ROSE, KENNETH, *King George V* (1984).

ROTHA, PAUL, *Documentary Diary: An Informal History of the British Documentary Film, 1928–1939* (1973).

—— et al., *Documentary Film: The Use of the Film Medium to Interpret Creatively and in Social Terms the Life of the People as it Exists in Reality* (1952).

SANDERS, M. L., and TAYLOR, PHILIP M., *British Propaganda during the First World War, 1914–1918* (1982).

SHELL-MEX AND BP LIMITED, *Art in Advertising* (1964).

SMITH, LACEY BALDWIN, *This Realm of England 1399–1688* (Toronto, 1988).

STEWART, J. D., *British Pressure Groups: Their Role in Relation to the House of Commons* (Oxford, 1958).

STUART, CHARLES (ed.), *The Reith Diaries* (1975).

SUSSEX, ELIZABETH, *The Rise and Fall of British Documentary: The Story of the Film Movement Founded by John Grierson* (1975).

SWANN, PAUL, *The British Documentary Film Movement, 1926–1946* (Cambridge, 1989).

SYMONS, JULIAN, *The General Strike* (1957).

—— *The Thirties: A Dream Revolved* (1975).

TAYLOR, A. J. P., *Beaverbrook* (1972).

TAYLOR, PHILIP M., *The Projection of Britain: British Overseas Publicity and Propaganda 1919–1939* (Cambridge, 1981).

THOMSON, OLIVER, *Mass Persuasion in History: An Historical Analysis of the Development of Propaganda Techniques* (Edinburgh, 1977).

THURTLE, ERNEST, *Time's Winged Chariot: Memories and Comments* (1945).

TITMUSS, RICHARD M., *Problems of Social Policy: History of the Second World War*, United Kingdom Civil Series, ed. W. K. Hancock (1950).

TURNER, E. S., *The Shocking History of Advertising* (1952).

—— *The Phoney War on the Home Front* (1961).

Who Was Who.

WIENER, MARTIN J., *English Culture and the Decline of the Industrial Spirit 1850–1980* (Cambridge, 1981).

WILLIAMS, GLYN, and RAMSDEN, JOHN, *Ruling Britannia: A Political History of Britain 1688–1988* (1990).

WILLIAMS, RAYMOND, *Keywords: A Vocabulary of Culture and Society* (1977).

WILSON, TREVOR, *The Downfall of the Liberal Party 1914–1935* (1966).

WOOD, JAMES PLAYSTEAD, *The Story of Advertising* (New York, 1958).

WRIGHT, GORDON, *The Ordeal of Total War 1939–1945* (1968).

YASS, MARION, *The Home Front: Britain 1939–1945* (1973).

YOUNG, G. M., *Stanley Baldwin* (1952).

(ii) Articles and Theses

AITKEN, IAN, 'John Grierson, Idealism and the Inter-War Period', *Historical Journal of Film, Radio and Television*, 9/3 (1989), 247–58.

BELOFF, MAX, 'The Whitehall Factor: The Role of the Higher Civil Service 1919–1939', in Gillian Peele and Chris Cook (eds.), *The Politics of Reappraisal 1918–1939* (1975), 209–32.

BRIGGS, ASA, 'The Language of "Class" in Early Nineteenth-Century England', in Asa Briggs and John Saville (eds.), *Essays in Labour History: In Memory of G. D. H. Cole* (1967), 43–73.

—— 'The Language of "Mass" and "Masses" in Nineteenth-Century England', in David E. Martin and David Rubinstein (eds.), *Ideology and the Labour Movement: Essays Presented to John Saville* (1979), 62–83.

CLARK, T. FIFE, 'Do We Need Government Information Services?', *Public Administration*, 35 (1957), 335–47.

CUNNINGHAM, JOHN, 'National Daily Newspapers and their Circulations in the U.K., 1908–1978', *Journal of Advertising History*, 4 (Feb. 1981), 16.

DUNBAR, DAVID S., 'Estimates of Total Advertising Expenditures in the U.K. before 1949', *Journal of Advertising History*, 1 (1977), 9–11.

EMSLEY, CLIVE, 'The Home Office and its Sources of Information and Investigation 1791–1801', *English Historical Review*, 94 (1979), 532–61.

FREEMAN, JUDITH, 'The Publicity of the Empire Marketing Board 1926–1933', *Journal of Advertising History*, 1 (1977), 12–14.

HOLLINS, TIMOTHY JOHN, 'The Presentation of Politics: The Place of Party Publicity, Broadcasting and Film in British Politics 1918–1939', D.Phil. dissertation, Leeds, 1981.

HOWARD, MICHAEL, 'Total War in the Twentieth Century: Participation and Consensus', in B. Bond (ed.), *War and Society* (1975), 216–27.

LERNER, DANIEL, 'Introduction: Some Problems of Policy and Propaganda', in Daniel Lerner (ed.), *Propaganda in War and Crisis: Materials for American Policy* (New York, 1951), pp. xi–xvi.

MARQUIS, ALICE GOLDFARB, 'Words as Weapons: Propaganda in Britain and Germany during the First World War', *Journal of Contemporary History*, 13 (1978), 467–99.

MARWICK, ARTHUR, 'Middle Opinion in the Thirties: Planning, Progress, and "Political Agreement" ', *English Historical Review*, 79 (Jan. 1964), 285–98.

—— 'The Impact of the First World War on British Society', *Journal of Contemporary History*, 3/1 (1968), 51–65.

MATTHEW, H. C. G., 'Rhetoric and Politics in Great Britain, 1860–1950', in P. J. Waller (ed.), *Politics and Social Change in Modern Britain* (Brighton, 1987), 34–58.

NORTHEDGE, F. S., '1917–1919: The Implications for Britain', *Journal of Contemporary History*, 3/4 (1968), 191–209.

NOTTAGE, RAYMOND, 'The Post Office: A Pioneer of Big Business', *Public Administration*, 37 (1959), 55–65.

PRONAY, NICHOLAS, 'John Grierson and the Documentary—60 Years on', *Historical Journal of Film, Radio and Television*, 9/3 (1989), 227–46.

QUALTER, TERENCE HALL, 'The Nature of Propaganda and its Function in Democratic Government: An Examination of Principal Theories of Propaganda since 1880', Ph.D. dissertation, London, 1956.

SANDERS, M. L., 'Wellington House and British Propaganda during the First World War', *Historical Journal*, 18/1 (1975), 119–46.

SHEAIL, PHILIP, 'Hampshire Man and the Quest for Clean Milk', *Hampshire* (Mar. 1981), 60–2.

SOFFER, R. N., 'New Elitism: Social Psychology in Prewar England', *Journal of British Studies*, 8/2 (1969), 111–40.

SPEIER, HANS, 'Morale and Propaganda', in Daniel Lerner (ed.), *Propaganda in War and Crisis: Materials for American Policy* (New York, 1951), 3–25.

SWANN, PAUL, 'John Grierson and the G.P.O. Film Unit 1933–1939', *Historical Journal of Film, Radio and Television*, 3/1 (1983), 19–34.

TAYLOR, PHILIP M., 'Techniques of Persuasion: Basic Ground Rules of British Propaganda during the Second World War', *Historical Journal of Film, Radio and Television*, 1/1 (1980), 57–67.

TITMUSS, R. M., 'War and Social Policy', in *Essays on 'The Welfare State'* (1963), 75–87.

WADSWORTH, A. P., 'Newspaper Circulations, 1800–1954', *Transactions of the Manchester Statistical Society* (1954–5), 1–30.

WAITES, B. A., 'The Effect of the First World War on Class and Status in England 1910–1920', *Journal of Contemporary History*, 11/1 (1976), 27–48.

WHETHAM, E. H., 'The London Milk Trade, 1900–1930', in Derek Oddy and Derek Miller (eds.), *The Making of the Modern British Diet* (1976), 65–76.

WILLCOX, TEMPLE, 'Projection or Publicity: Rival Concepts of the Pre-War Planning of the Ministry of Information', *Journal of Contemporary History*, 18 (1983), 97–116.

—— 'Towards a Ministry of Information', *History: The Journal of the Historical Association*, 69/227 (1984), 398–414.

WILSON, TREVOR, 'Lord Bryce's Investigations into Alleged German Atrocities in Belgium, 1914–1915', *Journal of Contemporary History*, 14/3 (1979), 369–85.

Index